T0326973

"Gregg Allison, in *40 Questions About Roman Ca[...]* guide in tracing the development of Roman Cath[...] the centuries. Offering careful responses to 40 imp[...] and drawing on the insights of both Protestant theologians and Roman Catholic thinkers, readers are introduced to the foundational beliefs and practices of Roman Catholics, especially since Vatican II. Particularly helpful for readers are the sections that provide insightful comparisons and contrasts between Protestant and Roman Catholic understandings of key doctrines. Though written from the perspective of an evangelical Protestant, Allison—drawing upon his exemplary skills as both church historian and theologian—has given us an excellent introduction to Roman Catholicism. I am delighted to recommend this thoughtful, convictional, accessible, and irenic book to both Protestant and Roman Catholic readers."

—David S. Dockery,
President, International Alliance for Christian Education,
Distinguished Professor of Theology, Southwestern Seminary

"This book is long overdue. Deftly providing perspective from Scripture and the history of Christian thought, Gregg Allison answers 40 critical questions about Roman Catholic teaching and practice. This outstanding volume will equip you to lovingly and accurately engage with your Catholic friends and loved ones over issues that we all hold so dear."

—Chris Castaldo,
Lead Pastor of New Covenant Church, Naperville, IL,
Author of *Talking with Catholics About the Gospel: A Guide for Evangelicals*

"There is a pressing need right now to understand more clearly the Roman Catholic Church and all she entails—who she is, what she does, what matters to her, what are her differences and distinctives, what issues she is facing. Confusion on these crucial issues has huge ramifications for Protestants and Catholics alike. But how does one get started? This book is an essential tool in the hands of anyone seeking to understand the Roman Catholic Church today. It does exactly what it promises— with clarity, sensitivity, and expertise. It is born out of years and depth of experience, research, teaching, and ministry in this field, and it shows. It is up-to-date, crystal clear, and expertly written, being wonderfully concise yet thorough. Quite simply, this book knows what it is talking about, and says it brilliantly.

"Whilst written from a self-confessed Protestant perspective, it is always warm and respectful, and yet does not dodge the questions that need to be answered. Dr. Allison does justice to Roman Catholicism, presenting a fair and accurate portrait, continually using the Roman Catholic Church's own words to do this, while also offering thoughtful, biblical, theological, and historical assessment along the way. It is thoroughly accessible, and just a skim through of the questions it answers makes you want to read this book. Whether you are a specialist in this field, or have fleetingly wondered about these questions, this book will have gems to offer you."

—Rachel Ciano,
Lecturer in Christianity in History at Sydney Missionary and Bible College,
Co-author of *10 Dead Guys You Should Know*

# 40 QUESTIONS ABOUT
# Roman Catholicism

## Gregg R. Allison

Benjamin L. Merkle, Series Editor

KREGEL
ACADEMIC

*40 Questions About Roman Catholicism*
© 2021 Gregg. R. Allison

Published by Kregel Academic, an imprint of Kregel Publications, 2450 Oak Industrial Dr. NE, Grand Rapids, MI 49505-6020.

This book is a title in the 40 Questions Series edited by Benjamin L. Merkle.

The Greek font, GraecaU, is available from www.linguistsoftware.com/lgku.htm, +1-425-775-1130.

ISBN 978-0-8254-4716-7

*This book is lovingly dedicated to my three children-in-law: Troy Schneringer, married to Lauren; Michael Schuetz, married to Hanell; and Chelsi Allison, married to Luke.*

*I have the best two sons-in-law and the best daughter-in-law any father could ask for!*

# Contents

# Part 3: Contemporary and Personal Questions

# Introduction

With more than one billion members, the Roman Catholic Church is present almost everywhere in the world today. You may have family, friends, neighbors, or work colleagues who are part of the Church.[1] Some of them may be committed Catholics, while others may attend Mass infrequently or may be completely inactive. Perhaps you yourself are Catholic, or used to be Catholic, or want to become Catholic. Alternatively, you may belong to one of the other two main branches of Christianity, either Protestant or Orthodox. Or you may belong to another religion, or to no religion at all. No matter who you are, if you have questions about Roman Catholicism, this book is designed to answer your questions.

But what is Roman Catholicism? It is quite different from the early church, which experienced significant unity as it was rapidly expanding during its initial centuries. It is far removed from the medieval church, which was characterized by renewal through monastic movements and scholastic theology, even as the papacy was cementing its position among the powerful monarchs of the age. It is not the Roman Catholicism that split from Protestantism during the Reformation, a division that expressed itself in damning opponents to hell and sending them there through wars of religion. And it is very different from what it was throughout most of the modern period, thanks in no small part to Vatican Council II and the papacies of John Paul II, Benedict XVI, and Francis.

This book answers questions about Roman Catholic theology and practice, doctrine and liturgy, sacraments and Mariology, contributions and scandals, and other things Catholic. The answers, however, are not given from a Roman Catholic viewpoint. On the contrary, I answer these questions as a Protestant, specifically an evangelical, more precisely a Reformed Baptist, and even more particularly a systematic theologian and local church pastor. I regularly teach courses about Catholic theology and have even written a couple of books about Roman Catholicism from an evangelical

---

1. When referring to the Roman Catholic Church, the last word (even when it stands alone in a sentence) will be capitalized. When referring to the church in general (e.g., the evangelical church) or to the universal church (e.g., the church is the body of Christ), the word will not be capitalized.

perspective.[2] If you are a Catholic reading this book, you will hear how a Protestant views your Church. If you are a Protestant reading this book, you will listen in as I answer forty common questions that we as Protestants have about Roman Catholicism.

These forty questions fall into three categories. The first part covers historical and foundational matters, like how Vatican Council II influenced contemporary Roman Catholicism and which doctrines Catholics and Protestants share and which doctrines divide them. The second part covers specific theological questions about revelation and authority, sacraments, salvation, and Mary and the saints. The third part covers contemporary and personal questions, like the contributions of the last three popes and why Protestants leave their churches and join the Roman Catholic Church.

I hope you will find me to be a helpful and reliable guide as we explore *40 Questions About Roman Catholicism*!

---

2. Gregg R. Allison, *Roman Catholic Theology and Practice: An Evangelical Assessment* (Wheaton, IL: Crossway, 2014); Gregg Allison and Chris Castaldo, *The Unfinished Reformation: What Unites and Divides Catholics and Protestants after 500 Years* (Grand Rapids: Zondervan, 2016).

# Abbreviations

| | |
|---|---|
| CCC | Catechism of the Catholic Church. United States Catholic Conference (Cittá del Vaticano: Libreria Editrice Vaticana, 1994), https://www.vatican.va/archive/ENG0015/_INDEX.HTM |
| LCC | Library of Christian Classics, eds. John Baillie, John T. McNeill, and Henry P. Van Dusen, 26 vols. (Philadelphia: Westminster, 1953–1969) |
| LW | Luther's Works, eds. Jaroslav Pelikan, Hilton C. Oswald, and Helmut T. Lehmann, 55 vols. (St. Louis: Concordia, 1955–1986) |
| *NPNF1* | *Nicene- and Post-Nicene Fathers*, first series, eds. Alexander Roberts, James Donaldson, Philip Schaff, and Henry Wace, 14 vols. (Peabody, MA: Hendrickson, 1994) |
| *NPNF2* | *Nicene- and Post-Nicene Fathers*, second series, eds. Alexander Roberts, James Donaldson, Philip Schaff, and Henry Wace, 14 vols. (Peabody, MA: Hendrickson, 1994) |
| *RCTP* | *Roman Catholic Theology and Practice: An Evangelical Assessment*, by Gregg R. Allison (Wheaton, IL: Crossway, 2014) |

# PART 1

# Historical and Foundational Questions

# Historical Questions

In this first section, I explore questions about the origin of the name *Roman Catholic*, trace the history of the Church up to the Reformation, highlight the key events and doctrines that led to the division of Roman Catholicism and Protestantism, and conclude with a look at the impact of Vatican Council II.

# Why Is It Called the Roman Catholic Church?

The story behind the title "the Roman Catholic Church" goes back to the early church and its self-identification. But one specific word in that title did not appear until the beginning of the thirteenth century.

## The Four Traditional Attributes of the Church

Early in its history, the church defined itself as "one, holy, catholic, and apostolic."[1] As for *oneness*, the true church is characterized by unity, with special reference to sound doctrine: "The church, though dispersed throughout the whole world, even to the ends of the earth, has received from the apostles and their disciples this [one] faith."[2] This attribute of oneness is well supported biblically. Jesus prays that we, his followers, would be united (John 17:11, 21–23). The Holy Spirit grants unity to the church, which is one body with one Spirit, one hope, one Lord, one faith, one baptism, and one Father (Eph. 4:1–6; cf. 4:13). The church is one, identified by unity.

The church's *holiness* stands in stark contrast to the world and its sinfulness. The holy church is set apart for God and for his purposes. At the same time, the church often falls short of this mark, living as already-but-not-yet pure. This disappointing reality demands that church leaders, like Justin Martyr, call the church to cease from sin and to pursue holiness: "Let it be understood that those who are not found living as Christ taught are not Christians, even though they profess with the lips the teachings of Christ."[3] This attribute of holiness is well supported biblically as seen in the description of the church as a sanctified, saintly assembly (1 Peter 2:9), a

---

1. Nicene-Constantinopolitan Creed (381).
2. Irenaeus, *Against Heresies* 1.10.1–2 (*ANF* 1:330–31). The text has been rendered clearer.
3. Justin Martyr, *First Apology* 16 (*ANF* 1:168). The text has been rendered clearer.

depiction that is true even of the worldly church of Corinth (1 Cor. 1:2). Given this status of holiness, church leaders exhort their members to live as holy people (1 Peter 1:14–16).

The term *catholicity* needs clarification. Rather than referring to the particular Roman *Catholic* Church, this descriptor refers to the church's universality.[4] The church is catholic for two reasons. The first reason is the presence of Christ in it, as Ignatius explained: "Where there is Christ Jesus, there is the Catholic Church."[5] The second reason is Christ's commission for the church: "Go therefore and make disciples of all nations" (Matt. 28:19). This Great Commission is universal in scope.[6] Because the true church is catholic, Ignatius warned others: "Whoever does not meet with the congregation/church[7] thereby demonstrates his arrogance and has separated [or judged] himself."[8] The church's universality is well supported biblically, as seen above.[9]

*Apostolicity* means that the church follows the teachings of the apostles. Such apostolicity stands in contrast with counterfeit churches that invent and promote false doctrine. From the beginning, Christ taught his apostles, they planted apostolic churches, and these apostolic churches planted other churches, which in turn planted still other churches.[10] Groups that could not trace their origins to the apostles or to these apostolic churches were false churches. More critically still, apostolicity applies to those churches that obey the written teachings of the apostles—Scripture itself. Apostolicity finds biblical support in the foundational role of the apostles (Eph. 2:20) and their

---

4. Greek καθολικός (*katholicos*), or universal.
5. Ignatius, *Letter to the Smyrneans* 8 (shorter version; *ANF* 1:90). Later, Irenaeus would add, "Where the church is, there is the Spirit of God; where the Spirit of God is, there is the church." Irenaeus, *Against Heresies* 3.24.1 (*ANF* 1:458).
6. As explained by Cyril of Jerusalem, the church is catholic because "it extends over all the world . . . and because it teaches universally and completely one and all the doctrines which ought to come to men's knowledge . . . and because it brings into subjection to godliness the whole race of mankind . . . and because it universally treats and heals the whole class of sins . . . and possesses in itself every form of virtue which is named, both in deeds and words, and in every kind of spiritual gifts." Cyril of Jerusalem, *Catechetical Lectures* 18.23 (*NPNF2* 7:139–40).
7. Greek ἐκκλησία (*ekklēsia*), or church.
8. Ignatius, *Letter to the Ephesians* 5 (*ANF* 1:51).
9. With growing concern about inclusivism at work within the Roman Catholic Church, Leonardo De Chirico issues an appropriate warning: "Catholicity is not a stand-alone ecclesiological parameter but one organically linked to the other three. In this way, it is protected from becoming an omnivore capable of integrating all. If catholicity takes precedence over apostolicity (i.e., biblical teaching), it becomes universalism. If holiness is left out, catholicity becomes a box void of spiritual content. If catholicity loses its connection to unity, it explodes into a myriad of self-referential units." Leonardo De Chirico, "Contested Catholicity: In What Sense Is the Church Catholic?," *Vatican Files* 168, October 1, 2019, http://vaticanfiles.org/en/2019/10/vf168/.
10. Tertullian, *Prescription against Heretics* 21, 32 (*ANF* 3:252, 258).

authoritative instructions (e.g., 1 Cor. 14:37; 2 Thess. 2:15; 3:4, 6, 10, 12; Titus 1:3; 2 Peter 2:3).

In summary, the early church acknowledged four identity markers: the church is one, holy, catholic, and apostolic.

## The Additional Attribute of *Roman*

Up to the beginning of the thirteenth century, these four attributes were sufficient to identify the church of Jesus Christ. The adjective *Roman* was added to this list of descriptors in 1208. The occasion was sparked by an incident involving a pastor named Durand of Osca. He had left the Catholic Church and become a preacher for the Waldensians, a splinter movement condemned as heretical.[11] In returning to the Catholic Church, he made this confession: "We believe with our heart and confess with our mouth one church only, not that of the heretics, but the holy church—Roman, catholic, apostolic—outside of which we believe that no one is saved."[12] To abbreviate, it is the *Roman* Catholic Church.

As we will soon see, the descriptor *Roman* came to be emphasized at this point because the church in Rome was beginning to flex its religious and political muscles and to make exaggerated claims for itself.

## *Roman* and *Catholic*: Particularity and Universality

Today, these two words—*Roman* and *Catholic*—express two distinct but related aspects of the Roman Catholic Church. The first describes its particularity; the second, its universality. According to Leonardo De Chirico:

> There's the *Roman* side, with its emphasis on centralized authority, pyramid leadership structure, binding teaching, and the rigidity of canon law. And there's the *Catholic* side, which emphasizes a universal outlook, an absorption of ideas and cultures, and the inclusive embrace of cultural practices into the Catholic whole. The human genius of Roman Catholicism and one of the reasons for its survival across the centuries has been its ability to be both, even amid disruptions and tensions.[13]

---

11. Jean Gonnet and Amedeo Molnar, *Les Vaudois au Moyen Âge* (Torino: Claudiana, 1974), 5.
12. "Nous croyons de notre cœur et confessons de notre bouche une seule Église, non celle des hérétiques, mais la sainte Église romaine, catholique, apostolique, en dehors de laquelle nous croyons que personne n'est sauvé." Heinrich Denzinger, *Enchiridion Symbolorum: A Compendium of Creeds, Definitions and Declarations of the Catholic Church* (San Francisco: Ignatius, 2012), my translation.
13. De Chirico, "Contested Catholicity."

As the *Roman* Catholic Church, it expresses its particularity in terms of its claim to be the only true church of Jesus Christ, the possessor of the fullness of salvation, and the ongoing incarnation of Christ with the pope as his vicar, or representative. Its distinctiveness is further seen in its locatedness in Rome, its political and financial organization centered in the Vatican, its spectacle as a medieval monarchical institution, its claim to possess the only true Eucharist, and its grandeur of religious pageantry. As the Roman *Catholic* Church, it expresses its universality as it embraces all ecclesial communities (Protestants and Orthodox), pluralistically respects other religions to which God communicates his grace (e.g., Hinduism, Buddhism, Islam, Sikhism), and is itself oriented to the salvation of the world. Its comprehensiveness is further seen in its ecclesiology of *totus Christus* (the Church is the *whole Christ*—divinity, humanity, and body), its common liturgy (with its former common liturgical language of Latin), its common confession of faith, and its incorporation of many diverse elements into its theology and practice.[14]

This dual identity helps explain why the Church is such a broad-tent movement. Again, De Chirico underscores a key principle of Catholic theology and practice. In Latin, it is "*et—et.*" In English, it is "and—and" or "both—and." Because it operates on this basis, the Church is able to keep together what appears to many people to be mutually exclusive alternatives—*both* X *and* Y, even though X and Y are like oil and water. To give several examples, in terms of divine revelation, the Church looks to *both* Scripture *and* Tradition. It views the accomplishment of salvation as synergistic:[15] *both* God *and* the Catholic faithful work together. As for its doctrine of justification, the Church believes it embraces *both* the forgiveness of sins *and* moral transformation. And justification comes about by *both* faith *and* baptism. Whereas it once fervently maintained that there is no salvation outside the Catholic Church, it now holds that *both* Roman Catholics *and* _____ (fill in the blank: Protestants, Muslims, agnostics) can be saved.[16]

---

14. For further discussion, see De Chirico, "Contested Catholicity." He notes the important book by Kenneth J. Collins and Jerry L. Walls, *Roman but Not Catholic: What Remains at Stake 500 Years after the Reformation* (Grand Rapids: Baker Academic, 2017).
15. Gr. *sun* = with; *ergon* = work; thus, two parties (in this case, God and people) work together.
16. As a recent example of "both—and," at the Vatican's Synod of Bishops for the Pan-Amazon region (October 6–27, 2019), several events featured pagan elements from Amazonian culture. These included statues of Pachamama, a pagan fertility goddess. At one point, Pope Francis blessed one of these statues and even prayed in front of one that had been brought into St. Peter's Cathedral. His critics voiced outrage at this blending of *both* orthodoxy *and* idolatry. Paul Smeaton, "Did Pope Francis Defend Pachamama Idolatry at Vatican in New Amazon Synod Exhortation?," *LifeSiteNews*, February 12, 2020, https://www.lifesitenews.com/news/did-pope-francis-defend-pachamama-idolatry-at-vatican-in-new-amazon-synod-exhortation. The pope's response to his critics is *Querida Amazonia*, February 12, 2020, Vatican.va.

The Catholic principle of *"et—et"*/"and—and"/"both—and" is the opposite of the Protestant principle of *sola*, that is, *alone*. *Sola Scriptura*: Scripture alone. *Solus Christus*: Christ alone. *Sola fidei*: faith alone. *Sola gratia*: grace alone. *Soli Deo Gloria*: the glory of God alone. Additionally, a Protestant criticism of the Church during the Reformation was that it had become overly Roman and lost its true catholicity.[17] Indeed, the Reformers claimed that the Protestant movement was a return to Christianity's true foundation—the Bible and the early church (for example, the theology of Augustine). Moreover, they saw the Reformation as a protest against the many accretions that the Church had introduced over the course of many centuries. Their complaint was that these additions had unmoored the Church from its anchor and caused it to lose its historical, traditional catholicity.[18]

## Summary

For well over a thousand years, the church of Jesus Christ identified itself as *one, holy, catholic, and apostolic*. It was not until the thirteenth century that the descriptor *Roman* was added. Today, the adjective *Roman* describes the Church's particularity and the adjective *Catholic* expresses its universality. Still, the Roman Catholic system, based on the principle of *"et—et"*/"and—and"/"both—and," seeks to hold together very diverse elements. Indeed, the Protestant principle of *sola*—"alone"—dissents from "both—and," maintaining that many opposing positions embraced by the Church are mutually exclusive. They can't be held together because they are contradictory.

---

17. For a contemporary expression of this complaint, see Collins and Walls, *Roman but Not Catholic*.
18. As Carl Braaten expressed, "The Reformers made their protest against Rome on behalf of the whole church, out of love and loyalty to the truly catholic church. . . . The Reformation was not intended to bring about a Protestant Church, much less a collection of Protestant churches. The Reformation was a movement of protest for the sake of the one church." Carl A. Braaten, *Mother Church: Ecclesiology and Ecumenism* (Minneapolis: Fortress, 1998), 12. Interestingly, within contemporary evangelicalism a movement is developing that seeks to underscore its rootedness in the great catholic tradition. D. H. Williams, *Evangelicals and Tradition: The Formative Influence of the Early Church* (Grand Rapids: Baker, 2005); Michael Allen and Scott R. Swain, *Reformed Catholicity: The Promise of Retrieval for Theology and Biblical Interpretation* (Grand Rapids: Baker Academic, 2015); Gavin Ortlund, *Theological Retrieval for Evangelicals* (Wheaton, IL: Crossway, 2019); and the books in the Zondervan series New Studies in Dogmatics, with Michael Allen and Scott R. Swain as general editors: Christopher R. J. Holmes, *The Holy Spirit* (2015); Fred Sanders, *The Triune God* (2016); Michael Allen, *Sanctification* (2017); and Michael Horton, *Justification* (2 vols., 2018).

## REFLECTION QUESTIONS

1. As you think about the four traditional adjectives, how do you assess your own local church in terms of its expression of unity, holiness, catholicity, and apostolicity?

2. How did the Church's addition of the descriptor *Roman* alter its history?

3. In what areas (other than the above examples) do you see the Roman Catholic Church attempting to be a broad-tent movement?

4. Do you find helpful the idea that the Protestant principle of *sola*, that is, *alone*, stands over against the Catholic principle of "*et—et*" / "and—and" / "both—and"?

5. What is your assessment of Scripture alone, Christ alone, faith alone, grace alone, and the glory of God alone?

# What Are Some Significant Events Prior to the Reformation?

### The Early Church

Outside the New Testament, the earliest information that we possess about the Christian faith is from the writings of a group of men known as the "apostolic fathers."[1] One important contribution was six letters from Ignatius, an early Christian leader, to various churches. Facing the twin dangers of heresy and church divisions, Ignatius proposed a practical solution to ward off these threats: each church should be led by one bishop, who would be the rallying point for all church meetings. He would ensure sound doctrine and would prevent factions among members. Eventually, this monepiscopacy (Gr. *mono* = one; *episkopos* = bishop) developed so that one bishop ruled over numerous churches in his geographical area.[2] The early church became bishop-led.

### The Development of the Papacy

In the mid-third century, a disagreement erupted between two church leaders: Stephen, bishop of Rome, and Cyprian, bishop of Carthage (North Africa).[3] Both disputants appealed to Jesus's promise to Peter: "I tell you, you

---

1. In 1672 a Frenchman—Cortelier—wrote a book in Latin, the English translation of which is *The Fathers Who Flourished in Apostolic Times*; hence, the phrase "apostolic fathers."
2. In time, five bishops became the leading authorities for Christianity: the bishops of Jerusalem, Antioch, Alexandria (Egypt), Constantinople (the capital city of the eastern Roman Empire), and Rome (the capital city of the western Roman Empire).
3. Stephen and Cyprian were at odds over the validity of baptism administered by the Novatian schismatics, a movement that had split off from the church. What was the status of a Christian who had been baptized by a Novatian pastor? Stephen affirmed the validity of that baptism while Cyprian denied its legitimacy.

are Peter, and on this rock I will build my church, and the gates of hell shall not prevail against it. I will give you the keys of the kingdom of heaven, and whatever you bind on earth shall be bound in heaven, and whatever you loose on earth shall be loosed in heaven" (Matt. 16:18–19). According to Stephen, Jesus conferred on Peter and his successors, the bishops of Rome, the "keys," or supreme authority in the church. According to Cyprian, Jesus conferred on Peter and all the apostles the "keys," or equal authority in the church. Eventually, Stephen's view won the day. The bishop of Rome, as the successor of Peter, became the ultimate authority in the church. By the seventh century, he was called the pope.

There were several other important reasons for the elevation of the papacy in Rome. Rome was the capital and chief city of the western Roman Empire and thus enjoyed political and commercial importance. When Rome was sacked by barbarians in 410, a power vacuum emerged in the western empire. This void paved the way for the emergence of the bishop of Rome as the key leader. Additionally, the orthodoxy of the church of Rome was widely acknowledged; rarely had a bishop of Rome held to false doctrine.[4] Indeed, he played an increasingly important role in the controversies about Christology in the fourth and fifth centuries.[5] Moreover, the tradition of Peter's burial in Rome became an important reason for the elevation of that church and its bishop. Though the Roman church had not been founded by an apostle, it was blessed by the presence of Peter's bones (as well as those of the apostle Paul) and thus promoted in stature. Finally, several Roman bishops made increasingly exaggerated claims for the importance of the bishop of Rome.[6]

A singular development helped cement the Roman bishop's claim to authority and dominance. In 754 the city of Rome was under attack by the Lombards, a barbarian tribe. Pope Stephen II appealed to Pepin the Short, king of the Franks—a tribe in what is now France—to repulse the Lombardian invasion. Successful in coming to the aid of Stephen, Pepin recovered much of northern and central Italy from the barbarians and donated them to the pope. Why did he commit such a generous act? Stephen presented to Pepin a document written by Emperor Constantine (306–337) in which the Roman ruler described his miraculous healing from leprosy and his conversion to Christianity through the ministry of the Roman bishop Sylvester I. Out of

---

4. Two exceptions are Vigilius, bishop of Rome from 537–55, and Honorius I, bishop from 625–38. See Question 14.
5. For example, the Roman bishop Leo I's *Tome* paved the way for the Chalcedonian Creed—the classical statement of the person of Christ—and its denouncement of the heresy of Eutychianism. At the same time, it should be noted that other bishops of Rome played a minor role in other early general councils such as the Council of Nicaea (325).
6. Damasus I (366–384), Leo I (440–461), Gelasius (492–496), and Gregory the Great (590–604) are examples. For further discussion, see Gregg R. Allison, *Historical Theology: An Introduction to Christian Doctrine* (Grand Rapids: Zondervan, 2011), 596–98.

gratitude to this man, Constantine had bequeathed "the city of Rome and all the provinces, districts, and cities of Italy," as well as the western part of the empire, to the bishop of Rome. Thus, by handing over the conquered lands to Pope Stephen, Pepin was fulfilling the terms of (what came to be called) the "Donation of Constantine." Amassing this huge amount of land enabled the bishop of Rome to become a powerful and extensive landowner—these lands became the Papal States—and the single most important leader in the West. Additionally, the donation stipulated that the pope should exercise authority over all the churches in the world in honor of Peter and Paul who had been martyred in Rome. For centuries to come, all the West would look to Rome for leadership.

It was not until the fifteenth century that the "Donation of Constantine" was exposed as a fraud.[7] It was probably forged by someone (perhaps Stephen himself) as the pope traveled to enlist Pepin's intervention. It would serve the purpose of demonstrating to Pepin the authority of the pope. Thus, one of the foundational elements in the emergence of the papacy turned out to be a forgery. Regardless, it expanded papal authority and political control for centuries.

Persecution in the early church had a way of sifting between true Christians and people who only professed the faith. After all, why would anyone risk confiscation of their property, exile, and possible martyrdom unless they were genuine believers? When persecution of the church gave way to the legalization of Christianity with Constantine in the fourth century, an important question arose: How could true Christians live godly lives to the fullest extent possible if "the world" hindered them from such an ideal? The answer was the monastic movement, which focused on different models of Christian piety. Individual monasticism called for people to live as hermits, completely separated from the world and its allurements.[8] Community monasticism offered groups of Christians the opportunity to pursue purity through ascetic practices.[9] By the fifth century, monasticism became a notable characteristic of the church.

Monks and monasteries developed different rules that helped to shape monasticism in the church. Augustine, for example, introduced the aspect of a community of monastic clergy living together and serving a local church. Many monastic movements became missionary centers from which the

---

7. This exposé was the work of the textual critic Lorenzo Valla, who uncovered linguistic and historical errors in the document.
8. An example was Antony (ca. 250–356), who lived an isolated life outside a village. His ascetic—rigorous, self-disciplined—practices consisted of eating and drinking sparingly, fasting regularly, and sleeping little on the bare ground.
9. An example was Pachomius (ca. 290–346) and his monastic community that featured daily prayer and Scripture meditation, compulsory manual labor, regular community fasts, obedience to one's superiors, chastity, and poverty.

evangelization of Europe took place. Monasteries cared for the needs of the poor, orphans, and widows while providing literacy training and education for boys and young men.

## The Middle Ages

In the early Middle Ages, monastic movements played a crucial role in the expansion of Christianity. Examples include Patrick (389–461) and the evangelization of Ireland; Columba of Iona (521–597) and the conversion of the Scots and Picts; Aidan of Lindisfarne (d. 651) and the Christianization of the Anglo-Saxons; and Boniface (680–754), the evangelization of Germany, and the renewal of the church in Gaul (part of the Frankish kingdom, now France). The Carolingian Dynasty of the Frankish Empire produced both Pepin the Short (who we've already seen) and his son Charlemagne, who ruled it for nearly fifty years (768–814) and expanded the kingdom to include much of Europe. On Christmas Day, 800, Charlemagne was crowned Holy Roman Emperor by Pope Leo III. The dream was for a revival of the old Roman Empire, but now with both its emperor and its people transformed by the Christian faith.

Following the death of Charlemagne, the dream was shattered by weak and divided Carolingian kings, chronic European wars, and foreign invasions that devastated civilization. Scandinavian sea raiders—the Vikings—laid waste to the churches and monasteries. Muslim invaders wreaked havoc as well. The papacy became overwhelmed, and the quality of its leadership was eroded by incompetency, fornication, and more. Political struggles and theological disagreements between the pope in Rome and the leader of the Eastern church in Constantinople eventually led to a (still unhealed) split between the (Western) Catholic Church and the (Eastern) Orthodox Church in 1054.[10]

Into this darkness stepped new monastic movements that brought renewal to the church and its institutions. Examples include the Cluny monastic movement (founded ca. 900) and the Cistercian monastic movement (founded ca. 1100), with Bernard of Clairvaux as a leading figure. A key factor in this renewal was the appearance of mendicant (= begging) orders: the Carmelites (founded ca. twelfth century), the Franciscans (founded 1209/1210), the Dominicans (founded 1216/1217), and the Augustinians (founded 1244). All four orders combined a monastic lifestyle with the ideals of poverty, chastity, obedience, and community living with preaching to those outside of the

---

10. The theological division was over the *filioque* ("and the Son") clause in the Nicene-Constantinopolitan Creed. Written in 381 with the affirmation that the Holy Spirit "proceeds from the Father," the creed was modified in 589 by the inclusion of the word *filioque*. The result was the affirmation that the Holy Spirit "proceeds from the Father and the Son." The (Western) Catholic Church made the change and the (Eastern) Orthodox Church refused to accept the addition. Other factors that contributed to the split were the iconoclastic controversy of the eighth and ninth centuries and the issue of papal authority.

movements. Also, they all engaged in the practice of begging money for the support of their order and for the poor. Their zeal and unflagging activity sparked significant renewal of the church. At the same time, these orders attacked popular religious movements outside the church. Examples were the heretical Cathari (or Albigenses) and the Waldensians, a pre-Reformation type of protest movement.

In addition to spiritual renewal, the church of the second half of the Middle Ages experienced significant theological development. Indeed, theology arose as the "queen of the sciences." Of particular importance was scholasticism, a movement that joined theology and philosophy—faith and reason—to better understand God and his ways.

One example of scholasticism is Anselm (1033/1034–1109), who is known primarily for two discussions. The first is the ontological proof for God's existence. That is, reasoning from the concept that "God is that being than which nothing greater can be conceived," and assuming that existence is an attribute, the existence of God is proved.[11] The second is the satisfaction theory of the atonement. It reasons from the idea that sin is robbing God of his honor, and that sinners must render satisfaction to God so as to restore his honor. Accordingly, the work of Christ in redeeming sinners becomes this: as the sinless God-man who had no obligation to die, Christ's death on behalf of sinners is passed on to them as a satisfaction for their sins.

A second example of scholastic theology is the work of Thomas Aquinas (1225–1274). Among his many contributions are his proofs for God's existence and his support for the doctrine of transubstantiation. As for the first, Aquinas offered the "Five Ways" to prove the existence of God by reason alone. Four of the ways are cosmological proofs: from the existence of the cosmos (Gr. *kosmos* = world), we must conclude that God exists. The fifth way is a teleological proof: from the fact of order and design (Gr. *telos* = purpose, aim) in the world, we must conclude that God exists.

As for transubstantiation, the Fourth Lateran Council (1215) had already proclaimed this doctrine to be the church's official position on the presence of Christ in the celebration of the sacrament of the Eucharist (or the Lord's Supper): "His body and blood are truly contained in the sacrament of the altar under the forms of bread and wine, the bread and wine having been changed in substance, by God's power, into his body and blood."[12] To demonstrate the appropriateness of transubstantiation, Aquinas modified two key concepts—substance and accidents—from the philosophy of Aristotle. A substance is that which exists in itself and makes something what it is. For example, think

---

11. Immanuel Kant later demonstrated that Anselm's ontological proof is faulty.
12. Fourth Lateran Council, canon 1. For further discussion, see Question 21. The Fourth Lateran Council was the twelfth ecumenical (or general) council convened by the Catholic Church in 1215. The Lateran is a prominent Roman Catholic Church in Rome.

of human nature, or substance, as including both body and soul. Accidents are attributes like color and texture that adhere in a substance and that can be detected by the senses. For example, think of human characteristics, or accidents, such as brown hair and a lean body type. As applied to the sacrament of the Eucharist, at the consecration of the elements, the substance of the bread transubstantiates, or changes, into the substance of the body of Christ. Similarly, the substance of the wine transubstantiates, or changes, into the substance of the blood of Christ. Yet, the bread still smells like, looks like, feels like, and tastes like bread. And the wine still smells like, looks like, feels like, and tastes like wine. By the power of God, the substance of the bread and wine changes but the accidents remain the same. Thus, Aquinas provided an explanation for the doctrine of transubstantiation.

Scholasticism was a powerful movement that continues to shape Catholic doctrine and practice today.

## Papal and Church Disasters

At the height of the Middle Ages, the papacy rose to unprecedented status. The peak of papal power came with Pope Innocent III (1198–1216). He declared that as pope he is the vicar (Latin *vicarius* = deputy), that is, "the representative of Christ, the successor of Peter, the anointed of the Lord, the God of Pharaoh set midway between God and man, below God but above man, less than God but more than man, judging all other men, but himself judged by none." He further claimed that papal authority was preeminent "not only over the universal church, but the whole world."[13]

Eventually, such exaggerated claims led to the humiliation of the papacy. When Pope Boniface VIII (1294–1303) excommunicated King Philip IV of France and died suddenly thereafter, Clement V, a Frenchman, was elected pope as a result of French pressure. Although he intended to go to Rome, he never left France. And in 1309 he moved the papacy to Avignon (southern France). Thus began what is called "the Babylonian captivity of the Church" (1309–1378).[14] It was not until 1378 that Pope Gregory XI succeeded in bringing the papacy back to Rome. But even this return of the papacy to its original home did not put an end to the papacy's troubles.

---

13. Innocent III, "Empire and Papacy," in Henry Bettenson, ed., *Documents of the Christian Church*, 2nd ed. (New York: Oxford University Press, 1963), 111. One example of papal power was the Albigensian Crusade against the heretical Cathari (1209–1229). Another was the Fourth Crusade (1202–1204) that, instead of carrying out its intended purpose of recapturing Jerusalem from its Muslim occupiers, was rerouted to seize Constantinople in an attempt to bring it back under Roman Church control.

14. As the Avignon papacy lasted nearly seventy years, it was similar to the Babylonian captivity of the people of Israel (597–538 B.C.). The Avignon popes lived an extravagant, luxurious lifestyle, and sexual immorality among the clergy was not uncommon. Some of these popes were nothing more than puppets of the French kings.

When an Italian, Pope Urban VI, was elected in Rome, the displeased French cardinals voted to depose the Italian pope and elected a French pope, Clement VIII, in his place. Clement took "his" papacy back to Avignon, resulting in what is known as "the Great Schism": two popes, two administrative headquarters, and the various countries of Europe lined up on one side or the other. The attempt at a solution was worse than the original problem, resulting in three popes instead of two.[15] The Great Schism was eventually healed by the Council of Constance (1414–1418) through its election of Pope Martin V, who ruled in Rome.

In the midst of these struggles, "the notion of church tradition—the unwritten teaching of Christ that was communicated orally from him to his disciples, and from them to their successors, the bishops—gained ascendancy in the Roman Catholic Church."[16] For example, one leader proposed that divine revelation comes "from the tradition of the Apostles outside of the Scriptures."[17] Another leader opined, "Many things that are not in the canon of the Bible were communicated to the church by the apostles and have come down to us through episcopal succession."[18] To be noted is the appeal to "episcopal succession," or apostolic succession, the doctrine that Jesus delegated his authority to Peter and to his successors. The pope along with the bishops—the Magisterium—of the Roman Catholic Church have the authority to determine the canon of Scripture, that is, the list of writings that belong in the Bible. Additionally, they possess the authority to proclaim official doctrines that are outside of Scripture and are yet divine revelation, that is, Church Tradition. Furthermore, the Magisterium exercises rightful authority in offering the official interpretation of both Scripture and Tradition. These developments in the latter part of the Middle Ages were decisive for the Roman Catholic Church on the verge of the Reformation.

## Summary

From a Catholic perspective, from its inauguration on the day of Pentecost to the time of the Reformation, the church made steady progress. According to the plan of God and guided by the Holy Spirit, it developed from simple beginnings to the massive, papal-led, socio-economic-political-military powerhouse that rescued and then dominated European society

---

15. Cardinals from both Rome and Avignon convened a general council of the church (in Pisa, 1409) to decide who was the true pope. When the council deposed both the Avignon pope and the Roman pope and elected Pope Alexander V in their place, neither pope complied with the council's decision.
16. Allison, *Historical Theology*, 150.
17. Gerald of Bologna, *Commentary on the Sentences*, 457, as cited in Allison, *Historical Theology*, 150.
18. Gabriel Biel, *Collectorium super 4 Libros Sententiarum*, bk. 4, chap. 7, q. unica, as cited in Allison, *Historical Theology*, 86.

for many centuries. From a Protestant viewpoint, this fifteen hundred years of history is a story with both highlights—the expansion of the church, its constant battles against heresies, its withstanding of fierce persecutions, and important theological developments—and lowlights—the rise of the papacy, the Babylonian Captivity, the Great Schism, and a morally compromised and spiritually bankrupt clergy.

## REFLECTION QUESTIONS

1. Do you see the history of the church in its first fifteen hundred years as more of a positive development or a negative decline?

2. How was the development of the papacy decisive for the future of the Catholic Church?

3. In what ways were heresies beneficial to or dangerous for the church? In what ways were persecutions beneficial to or dangerous for the church?

4. Why was the development of the idea of Tradition so important for the Church?

5. What conditions can you identify that prepared the church toward the end of the Middle Ages for the Reformations of the sixteenth century?

# What Led to the Division between Catholicism and Protestantism?

Though historians offer various interpretations of the Reformation—for example, the Reformation was a reaction to the sociological, political, and economic disruptions in European society; or Protestantism was an anticlerical movement—our view focuses on doctrinal and ecclesial matters that led to the split between these two traditions.

## Precursors to Reform

Several developments set the stage for the Reformation. In the fourteenth century, the pre-Reformers John Wycliffe and John Hus openly criticized the worldliness of the papacy, the spiritual bankruptcy of the Church, the sale of indulgences, and transubstantiation. Rumblings within the Church itself led to renewal movements such as the Devotio Moderna that emphasized practical piety and community life. The cultural and educational movement called humanism promoted a return to the sources of antiquity, leading to a rediscovery of the Hebrew Bible, Greek New Testament, and the writings of the early church (for example, Augustine). Mysticism—for example, St. Francis's stigmata, Thomas Aquinas's beatific vision, and Thomas à Kempis's *Imitation of Christ*—fostered an intense craving for a direct experience of God. The modern invention of moveable type provided the Reformers with a way to mass-produce their writings and their translations of the Bible for the common people.

## Martin Luther

Generally speaking, the Reformation began on October 31, 1517, when Martin Luther nailed his *Ninety-Five Theses* on the door of the Castle Church in Wittenberg. He called for a debate on the sale of indulgences, the remission of the temporal punishment suffered by souls in purgatory. For Luther, Jesus's command to repent (Matt. 4:17) "cannot be understood as referring to the sacrament of penance, that is, confession and satisfaction, as administered by the clergy."[1] His action caused an intense and widespread reaction indicative of an underlying restlessness with the pope and discontentment with the Church. Declared a heretic by the Church, Luther lived in constant threat of danger.[2]

In 1520 Luther authored four writings that expressed his distinctive convictions. His *Sermon on Good Works* (May) protested the Church's limitation of good works to spiritual activities like praying in church, fasting, and giving alms. By contrast, Luther insisted that good works, when done joyfully according to God's will and without concern for a reward, could include working well in one's profession, eating, and drinking. Yet, the greatest of all good works is to believe in Jesus Christ. Luther's radical perspective attacked the Church's emphasis on human cooperation in salvation.

*To the Christian Nobility of the German Nation* (August) lamented the fact that the Church, in self-defense, had erected three walls that led instead to Christendom's suffering. Luther attacked the first wall, the alleged superiority of the clergy over the laity: "It is pure invention that pope, bishops, priests, and monks are to be called the 'spiritual estate'; princes, lords, artisans, and farmers the 'temporal estate.' . . . [On the contrary,] all Christians are truly of the 'spiritual estate,' and there is among them no difference at all but that of office."[3] Thus, Luther proposed the doctrine of the priesthood of all believers, that "all who have faith in Christ and are baptized are designated priests and share in Christ's royal priesthood. This meant that every believer has equal access to the Father through Jesus. The corollary was that every believer has the responsibility to act as a priest to other believers, to minister to them, particularly through proclaiming Scripture to them."[4]

Luther attacked the second wall, the Church's claim that the pope possesses the exclusive authority to interpret Scripture. Luther complained that many popes, as unbelievers, had been incapable of understanding the Bible. But every genuine Christian, as part of the priesthood of believers, is competent to grasp the message of the gospel. Thus, "it is the duty of every Christian to espouse the cause of the faith, to understand and defend it, and to denounce every error. . . . When the pope acts contrary to the Scriptures, it is our duty to stand by

---

1. Martin Luther, *Ninety-Five Theses*, https://www.luther.de/en/95thesen.html.
2. From the humble start of the Reformation, the Catholic Church misunderstood this movement. Pope Leo X (papacy from 1513–1521) brushed off Martin Luther's protest as the ravings of a drunken monk. Moreover, Luther was accused of breaking away from the Church so that he could justify having sexual intercourse and getting married.
3. Martin Luther, *To the Christian Nobility of the German Nation* (LW 44:129).
4. Gregg R. Allison and Rachel Ciano, "Roman Catholic Theology and Practice of the Priesthood Contrasted with Protestant Theology and Practice of Priesthood," *Southern Baptist Journal of Theology* 23, no. 1 (2019): 139–40.

the Scriptures."[5] In these sentences we hear the development of Protestantism's formal principle of *sola Scriptura* (Scripture alone as ultimate authority).[6]

Luther attacked the third wall, the Church's claim that only the pope could convene a general council of the Church. By contrast, Luther insisted that when the pope contradicts Scripture, the secular authorities have the right to call a council to deal with him. In these three ways, Luther struck at important doctrines and practices of the Church, including the mediatorial function of priests to forgive sins, the Church's limitation of reading and interpreting the Bible to the clergy, and the supreme authority of the papacy.

In his *Babylonian Captivity of the Church* (September), Luther paralleled the seventy-year captivity of Israel in Babylon with the seventy-year hiatus of the papacy in Avignon, France. He especially criticized the Church's sacraments. He complained that the denial of the communion cup to the laity was wrong. Rather, they should partake in both elements—the bread and the cup, as Jesus had instructed (Matt. 26:26–29). Luther protested that transubstantiation is grounded on philosophy and not the Bible; thus, lay people are not bound to believe it. He repudiated the Mass as a good work and sacrifice, complaining that it had become little more than a money-making project. Luther lamented the sorry state of baptism, which hardly anyone took seriously. Finally, he dismissed four other rites—confirmation, anointing of the sick, holy orders, and matrimony—as being sacraments. By the end of this writing, he added penance to the list of non-sacraments. They had not been ordained by Christ himself as a word of promise with an accompanying sign. Only two rites—baptism and the Lord's Supper—qualified to be considered sacraments.

*The Freedom of the Christian Man* (November)[7] proposed an apparent contradiction: "A Christian is a perfectly free lord of all, subject to none. A Christian is a perfectly dutiful servant of all, subject to all."[8] By his first affirmation, Luther referred to the doctrine of justification: through God's grace alone, received by faith alone in Christ alone, sinful people may be declared not guilty but righteous instead. Thus, they are free from trying to cooperate with divine grace by engaging in good works in an effort to merit eternal life. Justification became

5. Luther, *To the Christian Nobility* (LW 44:136).
6. The term "formal principle" refers to the key framework or structure according to which the Reformation was shaped: biblical authority only rather than the threefold authority of Scripture, Tradition, and the Magisterium as held by the Roman Catholic Church.
7. Prior to the treatise itself, Luther penned an open letter to Pope Leo X. While he expressed his support for the pope himself, Luther denounced the Curia—the administrative office (the See)—for its corruption of the papal office: "I have truly despised your see, the Roman Curia, which, however, neither you nor anyone else can deny is more corrupt than any Babylon or Sodom ever was, and which, as far as I can see, is characterized by a completely depraved, hopeless, and notorious godlessness." *Martin Luther,* "An Open Letter to Pope Leo X," *in Three Treatises* (Philadelphia: Fortress, 1970), 277.
8. *Luther,* "Open Letter," 277.

the material principle of Protestantism.[9] By his second affirmation, Luther insisted that the justified are bound by faith working through love (Gal. 5:6) to work for the good of their neighbors. Thus, good works follow and flow from justification and do not contribute to God's salvation of his people.[10]

In his earliest writings, Luther initiated the themes that would characterize much of his career as a Reformer and set in motion the movement that would lead to Protestantism: Indulgences and purgatory. The nature of good works, with the greatest being faith in Christ. The priesthood of all believers. The interpretation of Scripture. *Sola scriptura.* The authority of the papacy. The Eucharist and transubstantiation. Two sacraments instead of seven. Justification through God's grace alone embraced by faith alone in Christ alone. To these topics Luther added a fresh approach to biblical interpretation (a "literal" or "grammatical-historical" hermeneutic[11] that is Christocentric[12]), an insistence on the clarity of Scripture,[13] and a rejection of the apocryphal writings.[14] His decisive break from the Catholic Church is seen in his two marks of a true church: "The church is the congregation of the saints in which the gospel is rightly taught and the sacraments rightly administered. And unto the true unity of the church, it is sufficient to agree concerning the doctrine of the gospel and the administration of the sacraments."[15]

## John Calvin

As a second-generation Protestant, John Calvin (1509–1564) authored the theological masterpiece of the Reformation, *The Institutes of the Christian Religion* (final edition, 1559).[16] By contrast with Thomas Aquinas's proofs for the existence of God—the Catholic starting point for religious knowledge—Calvin addressed the knowledge of God the Creator and the knowledge of God the Redeemer. While some knowledge of God may be obtained from

---

9. The term "material principle" refers to the key doctrine on which the Reformation was centered: justification as God's declaration of forgiveness and righteous standing rather than the life process consisting of forgiveness, regeneration, and sanctification through the sacraments as held by the Roman Catholic Church.

10. In this writing, Luther again underscored his full submission to Scripture. Speaking directly to Pope Leo X, Luther insisted: "I have no dispute with any man concerning morals, but only concerning the word of truth. In all other things I will yield to anyone, but I neither can nor will forsake and deny the Word." Luther, "Open Letter," paragraph 4.

11. Martin Luther, *Answers to the Hyperchristian, Hyperspiritual, Hyperlearned Book by Goat Emser in Leipzig* (LW 39:181).

12. Martin Luther, *Prefaces to the New Testament* (LW 35:396).

13. Martin Luther, *On the Bondage of the Will* (LCC 17:101–334).

14. Martin Luther, *Prefaces to the Apocrypha* (LW 35:337–54).

15. Augsburg Confession, 7, in Philip Schaff, *Creeds of Christendom*, 3 vols. (New York: Harper, 1877–1905), 3:11–12.

16. John Calvin, *Institutes of the Christian Religion*, ed. John T. McNeill, trans. Ford Lewis Battles (Philadelphia: Westminster, 1960) (LCC vols. 20 and 21).

general revelation in the created order and through an innate sense of God, such knowledge is ultimately not beneficial due to human sinfulness. The only corrector for this weakened vision is Scripture, which, "gathering up the otherwise confused knowledge of God in our minds, having dispersed our dullness, clearly shows us the true God."[17] The Bible, pointing sinful people to God the Redeemer in Jesus Christ, resonates in their hearts as the inspired, authoritative Word of God through the secret testimony of the Holy Spirit.[18]

The doctrine for which Calvin is most known is predestination. It is absolute, not conditioned on God's foreknowledge of human faith and salvation, but solely on God's good pleasure and will. It is particular, applying to individual people, not to groups. It is double in the sense that God ordains some to eternal life—election—and others to eternal damnation—reprobation. More specifically, the planning of predestination is double but its application is different, because God causes the salvation of the elect but does not cause the sin and condemnation of the non-elect. A matter that is far beyond theoretical, predestination leads to intense evangelization and provides comfort and assurance to believers.

Calvin reinforced many of Luther's important themes: *Sola scriptura* as the formal principle of Protestantism. Justification through God's grace alone embraced by faith alone in Christ alone as the material principle of Protestantism. The priesthood of all believers. The interpretation of Scripture and its clarity. The rejection of the apocryphal writings. The rejection of the authority of the papacy. The Eucharist and transubstantiation. Two sacraments instead of seven. Like Luther, his contrast with the Catholic Church is evident in his two marks of the true church: "Wherever we see the Word of God purely preached and heard, and the sacraments administered according to Christ's institution, there, it is not to be doubted, a church of God exists."[19]

## The Reformation's Impact

The combined impact of Luther and Calvin—together with other Reformers like Huldrych Zwingli, Philip Melanchthon, Heinrich Bullinger, and Theodore Beza—was widespread. The Lutheran Reformation initially spread into part of Germany and throughout the Scandinavian countries. The Calvinist Reformation initially expanded into Switzerland, Scotland, and the Netherlands. For theological and other reasons, the Reformation transformed England through the development of the Anglican Church. These so-called Magisterial Reformations[20] were joined by the so-called Radical Reformation

---

17. Calvin, *Institutes*, 1.6.1 (LCC 20:70).
18. Calvin, *Institutes*, 1.7.4–5 (LCC 20:78–81).
19. Calvin, *Institutes*, 4.1.9 (LCC 21:1023).
20. The term "Magisterial" is used because these movements incorporated an important role for the magistrates, or civic authorities, in church matters. This centuries-old state-church

of the Anabaptists and, later in the seventeenth century, the Baptists. Featuring distinctives such as regenerate church membership, baptism by immersion for believers (not infants), and the repudiation of the state-church relationship, baptistic churches continued the legacy of the early Reformers while making significant alterations to worship, church government, pastoral offices, and more.

As might be expected, the Catholic Church did not approve of this upstart Reformation movement. In 1542 Pope Paul III created the Roman Inquisition to stamp it out. Through its Sacred Congregation of the Roman Inquisition, one of the Church's measures was to list books written by Protestants or favorable to Protestant doctrines on the Index of Forbidden Books. These writings were banned from public reading. In its four sessions from 1546 to 1563, the Council of Trent denounced many Protestant doctrines and practices. As the movement spread, Protestants were fiercely persecuted in various countries. As one example, the Saint Bartholomew's Day massacre (1572) resulted in the deaths of thousands (tens of thousands?) of Protestants in France.

## Summary

Though various individuals and movements had sought to bring reform to the Church prior to the sixteenth century, the Reformation was decisive in a unique way. Martin Luther and John Calvin, among other Reformers, articulated and defended the key Protestant issues that contrasted with the Roman Catholic Church of their day. For example, the formal principle of *sola Scriptura* and the material principle of justification established Protestantism on axioms that were far removed from foundational Catholic theology. Other examples include a new vision of the nature and role of the laity, a fresh approach to the interpretation of Scripture (which did not include the Apocrypha), a renumbering of the sacraments (two instead of seven), a rejection of papal authority, and the establishment of true churches characterized by two marks.

## REFLECTION QUESTIONS

1. Do you think that the Reformation was a mistake?[21] If yes, why? If not, why not?

2. How did each of Martin Luther's 1520 writings—*Sermon on Good Works, To the Christian Nobility of the German Nation, Babylonian Captivity of*

---

relationship, embraced by Lutheranism, Calvinism, and Anglicanism, was denounced by the Radical Reformers.

21. This phrase is borrowed from the title of Matthew Levering's book *Was the Reformation a Mistake? Why Catholic Doctrine Is Not Unbiblical* (Grand Rapids: Zondervan, 2017).

*the Church*, and *The Freedom of a Christian Man*—contradict key Catholic Church doctrines and practices and spark the Reformation?

3. Why were the two principles of Protestantism—*sola Scriptura* and justification—so revolutionary in the religious situation of the sixteenth century?

4. Why were the two marks of the true church—the right preaching of the Word of God and the proper administration of the sacraments—so revolutionary in the religious situation of the sixteenth century?

5. As a Catholic, how do you assess the Roman Catholic Church's reaction to the Reformation? As a Protestant, how do you assess the Church's reaction to the Reformation?

# How Did Vatican Council II Influence Roman Catholicism?

During my theological studies, I was privileged to take a course titled "The Documents of Vatican II" at St. Mary of the Lake Seminary near Chicago. At that time, twenty-five years after Vatican II, the flood of changes that the council unleashed was in its initial phase. Today, more than fifty years after the council, the Church continues to implement significant changes set in motion by the council. Many Protestants, though they have heard of Vatican II, wonder what influence it has had on the contemporary Roman Catholic Church. Additionally, many of the Catholic faithful themselves wonder about the soundness of the council's decisions and, in their aftermath, the notable transformation of their beloved Church.

### Important Facts about the Council

Vatican Council II took place in four sessions between 1962 and 1965, initially during the papacy of John XXIII, who convened it, and extending into the papacy of Paul VI, who concluded it. By the reckoning of the Roman Catholic Church, it is its twenty-first general, or ecumenical, council.[1] These

---

1. 1. First Council of Nicaea (321). 2. First Council of Constantinople (381). 3. Council of Ephesus (431). 4. Council of Chalcedon (451). 5. Second Council of Constantinople (553). 6. Third Council of Constantinople (680–81). 7. Second Council of Nicaea (787). 8. Fourth Council of Constantinople (869–70). 9. First Lateran Council (1123). 10. Second Lateran Council (1139). 11. Third Lateran Council (1179). 12. Fourth Lateran Council (1215). 13. First Council of Lyon (1245). 14. Second Council of Lyon (1274). 15. Council of Vienne (1311–12). 16. Council of Constance (1414–18). 17. Council of Ferrara-Florence (1438–45). 18. Fifth Lateran Council (1512–17). 19. Council of Trent (1545–63). 20. First Vatican Council (1869–70). 21. Second Vatican Council (1962–65). Eastern Orthodox churches affirm the first seven ecumenical councils. In a different sense, many Protestant churches agree doctrinally with the first four councils, and some Protestants would extend this agreement to include the doctrines affirmed by the fifth, sixth, and seventh councils.

councils constitute part of the Tradition of the Roman Catholic Church and thus are authoritative in a way that is not accepted by Protestant churches.[2]

To describe Vatican Council II in one word, it is *aggiornamento*, or updating. The Council sought to move the Church out of its traditional, conservative mindset into full engagement with the modern world. It did so by means of sixteen documents (four constitutions, nine decrees, and three declarations), which constituted a new overarching framework for the Church going forward. From the conclusion of the council and continuing today, these documents have generated an impressive amount of new positions, new practices, new openings, and new approaches to everything from revised Masses to ecumenical dialogues, and from new methods of priestly formation to inclusivist views of salvation.

## The Constitutions, Decrees, and Declarations of Vatican Council II

The four main issues that Vatican II addressed in the form of constitutions (major documents) were the liturgy, the nature and mission of the Catholic Church, divine revelation, and the relationship of the Church to the world. Other issues that the council addressed in the form of decrees were social communication, Catholic Eastern churches, ecumenism, the office of bishop, the religious life, priestly training, the laity, missionary activity, and the ministry and life of priests. Finally, three issues were treated in the form of declarations on Christian education, non-Christian religions, and religious liberty.

*The Constitution on the Sacred Liturgy* (Sacrosanctum Concilium)

The purpose of *The Constitution on the Sacred Liturgy* was to undertake "the reform and promotion of the liturgy."[3] It set forth the nature and importance of the liturgy for the life of the Catholic Church. According to the constitution, in order for Jesus's disciples to fulfill their mission (Matt. 28:18–20), Christ purposed that "they might accomplish the work of salvation which they had proclaimed, by means of sacrifice and sacraments, around which the entire liturgical life revolves."[4] It continues,

---

2. This statement does not mean that Protestant churches dismiss out of hand the biblically warranted theological consensus of the church throughout its history. See Question 39. For the idea of the presumptive authority of such traditions, see Gregg. R. Allison, "The *Corpus Theologicum* of the Church and Presumptive Authority," in *Revisioning, Renewing, and Rediscovering the Triune Center: Essays in Honor of Stanley J. Grenz*, eds. Derek Tidball, Brian Harris, and Jason S. Sexton (Eugene, OR: Wipf & Stock, 2014).
3. Vatican Council II, *Sacrosanctum Concilium*, December 4, 1963, 1. https://www.vatican.va/archive/hist_councils/ii_vatican_council/documents/vat-ii_const_19631204_sacrosanctum-concilium_en.html.
4. Vatican Council II, *Sacrosanctum Concilium*, 6.

> To accomplish so great a work, Christ is always present in his
> Church, especially her liturgical celebrations. He is present
> in the sacrifice of the Mass not only in the person of the min-
> ister, "the same now offering, through the ministry of priests,
> who formerly offered himself on the cross," but especially
> in the Eucharistic species. By his power he is present in the
> sacraments so that when anybody baptizes, it is really Christ
> himself who baptizes.[5]

Christ, his Church, divine grace, the sacraments, and the liturgy are all
tied together in the sacramental economy of the Roman Catholic Church for
the salvation of the world.

This constitution also outlined principles for the reform of the liturgy.
These included promoting the reading of Scripture at Masses, highlighting
the sermon, and insisting on the contextualization of the liturgy among different people groups. Immediate changes evoked by this constitution included structuring the Mass with two necessary movements, the Liturgy of
the Word and the Liturgy of the Eucharist, and administering communion in
two kinds, that is, serving both the bread and the wine to the lay participants
in in the liturgy.

### *The Dogmatic Constitution on the Church* (Lumen Gentium)

*The Dogmatic Constitution on the Church* addressed the nature and universal mission of the Catholic Church. As a Trinitarian reality, the Church is
represented biblically in terms of various symbols and images: a sheepfold
or flock, a cultivated field, a building/house/temple of which Christ is the
cornerstone and the apostles are the foundation, the mother of the faithful,
and more. There is only one church of Christ as described by the creed—one
holy, catholic, and apostolic—and "this Church . . . subsists in the Catholic
Church, which is governed by the successor of Peter and by the Bishops in
communion with him."[6]

To the question "Who belongs to the Catholic Church?" this constitution
gives an answer that is startling to those familiar with the millennia-old adage
"there is no salvation outside of the Church." Long gone is the view that only
Catholics can be saved. This exclusivist perspective has been replaced with
an inclusivist hope that everyone can be saved. Picture concentric circles. In
the innermost circle are Catholics; they experience the fullness of salvation.
Moving outward one circle, we find the Orthodox and Protestants who, while
not enjoying the fullness of salvation, possess many elements of it. Further

---

5. Vatican Council II, *Sacrosanctum Concilium*, 7, citing the Council of Trent, Session 22,
   *Doctrine on the Holy Sacrifice of the Mass*, September 17, 1562, chap. 2.
6. Vatican Council II, *Lumen Gentium*, November 21, 1964, 8.

out from the center are other monotheists, the Jews and Muslims. By following the tenets of their religion, they can be saved. Still further out are adherents of non-Christian faiths; their religions contain elements of truth and grace for salvation. Even more removed are the circles containing polytheists and animists, theists who live according to the dictates of their conscience, and agnostics and atheists (in the outermost circle) who strive to live a good life. Even these people fall within the reach of grace and thus can possibly be saved.[7] These sections emphasize the catholic—universal—element of the Roman Catholic Church.

The next section on the Church's hierarchy emphasizes the Roman—particular—element of the Roman Catholic Church. It affirms apostolic succession; the three-tiered hierarchy of bishops, priests, and deacons; the pope as the vicar of Christ to whom is joined the college of bishops; and episcopal government. The constitution closes with a lengthy section on the role of the Virgin Mary in the divine plan of salvation.

Accordingly, this constitution reaffirmed some traditional Church teachings—it is Roman, Catholic, Petrine (papal), and Marian. At the same time, it departed from its long-held position of the Church's exclusivist role in the salvation of the world. The reforms it set in place include the opening of many ecumenical discussions (for example, the Lutheran World Federation and the Roman Catholic Church) and inter-religious dialogues (for example, the National Catholic/Muslim dialogue).

### The Dogmatic Constitution on Divine Revelation (Dei Verbum)

The purpose of *The Dogmatic Constitution on Divine Revelation* was "to set forth authentic doctrine on divine revelation and how it is handed on."[8] As for divine revelation itself, it consists of both deeds—the mighty works of God, such as the exodus—and words that "proclaim the works."[9]

This divine revelation is transmitted by both Scripture and Tradition. The first aspect is the Word of God written under the inspiration of the Holy Spirit. The second aspect is the teaching of Christ that he orally communicated to his apostles, who in turn communicated that instruction to their successors, the bishops of the Catholic Church. An example of Tradition is the canon of Scripture, which, according to the Church, includes the apocryphal writings. "Hence there exists a close connection and communication between sacred Tradition and Sacred Scripture. For both of them, flowing from the same divine wellspring, in a certain way merge into a unity and tend toward the same

---

7.  Vatican Council II, *Lumen Gentium*, 14–16.
8.  Vatican Council II, *Dei Verbum*, November 18, 1965, 1. https://www.vatican.va/archive/hist_councils/ii_vatican_council/documents/vat-ii_const_19651118_dei-verbum_en.html.
9.  Vatican Council II, *Dei Verbum*, 2.

end."[10] Clearly, Vatican II did not alter the Church's view of divine revelation as consisting of Scripture plus Tradition, a position that was challenged by the Reformers and the Protestant principle of *sola Scriptura*. Indeed, as *The Dogmatic Constitution on Divine Revelation* reiterated, "it is not from sacred Scripture alone that the Church draws her certainty about everything which has been revealed. Therefore, both sacred Tradition and sacred Scripture are to be accepted and venerated with the same sense of loyalty and reverence."[11]

Additionally, Vatican II echoed the Church's historical insistence on its Magisterium, or teaching office, as possessing the authority to provide an authentic interpretation of both Scripture and Tradition. Accordingly, authority in the Catholic Church is like a three-legged stool: "sacred tradition, Sacred Scripture and the teaching authority of the Church . . . are so linked and joined together that one cannot stand without the others."[12]

After addressing the inspiration and interpretation of Scripture, this constitution paralleled Scripture and the Eucharist, both of which "the Church has always venerated."[13] Application of this parallel is seen in the revision of the Church's liturgy (noted above) to include two movements, the Liturgy of the Word and the Liturgy of the Eucharist. Other changes called for by Vatican II included greater emphasis on Scripture in the sermon during the Mass, provision of wider access to Scripture through good translations, and encouragement to the laity to frequently read Scripture.

### *The Pastoral Constitution on the Church in the Modern World* (Gaudium et Spes)

Following its lengthy focus on the Church, Vatican II turned lastly to address itself "not only to the sons of the Church and to all who invoke the name of Christ, but to the whole of humanity. For the Council yearns to explain to everyone how it conceives of the presence and activity of the Church in the world of today."[14] Following an analysis of contemporary human problems, *The Pastoral Constitution on the Church in the Modern World* spoke to the dignity of human beings, the importance of human society, and the value of human activity in the universe. It then turned to a discussion of the relationship between the Church and the world:

> Pursuing the saving purpose which is proper to her, the Church does not only communicate divine life to men but in

---

10. Vatican Council II, *Dei Verbum*, 9.
11. Vatican Council II, *Dei Verbum*, 9.
12. Vatican Council II, *Dei Verbum*, 10.
13. Vatican Council II, *Dei Verbum*, 21.
14. Vatican Council II, *Gaudium et Spes*, December 7, 1965, 2. https://www.vatican.va/archive/hist_councils/ii_vatican_council/documents/vat-ii_const_19651207_gaudium-et-spes_en.html.

some way casts the reflected light of that life over the entire earth, most of all by its healing and elevating impact on the dignity of the person, by the way in which it strengthens the seams of human society and imbues the everyday activity of men with a deeper meaning and importance. Thus, through her individual matters and her whole community, the Church believes she can contribute greatly toward making the family of man and its history more human.[15]

*The Pastoral Constitution on the Church in the Modern World* made specific contributions addressing the urgent problems of marriage and the family, the proper development of culture, economic and social life, the political community, and the fostering of peace and the establishment of a community of nations. This constitution generated many subsequent and amplified Church pronouncements concerning its role in the world.

### *The Decree on Ecumenism* (Unitatis Redintegratio)

I highlight one other issue of the council that is of particular interest. *The Decree on Ecumenism* called for "the restoration of unity among all Christians," bemoaning the fact that the division that exists "openly contradicts the will of Christ, scandalizes the world, and damages that most holy cause, the preaching of the gospel to every creature."[16] Specifically, it affirmed that Protestants are "separated brothers" in the sense that their communities are "separated from full communion with the Catholic Church" and their differences "create many obstacles, sometimes serious ones, to full ecclesiastical communion."[17] At the same time, this decree noted that "some and even very many of the significant elements and endowments which together go to build up and give life to the Church itself, can exist outside the visible boundaries of the Catholic Church: the written word of God; the life of grace; faith, hope and charity, with the other interior gifts of the Holy Spirit, and visible elements too."[18]

Accordingly, this decree explained that Protestant communities "have been by no means deprived of significance and importance in the mystery of salvation" even to the point that the Holy Spirit "has not refrained from using them as means of salvation which derive their efficacy from the very fullness of grace and truth entrusted to the Catholic Church."[19] Still, the message for

---

15. Vatican Council II, *Gaudium et Spes*, 40.
16. Vatican Council II, *Unitatis Redintegratio*, November 21, 1964, 1. https://www.vatican.va/archive/hist_councils/ii_vatican_council/documents/vat-ii_decree_19641121_unitatis-redintegratio_en.html.
17. Vatican Council II, *Unitatis Redintegratio*, 3.
18. Vatican Council II, *Unitatis Redintegratio*, 3.
19. Vatican Council II, *Unitatis Redintegratio*, 3.

Protestants is clear: "It is through Christ's Catholic Church alone, which is the universal help towards salvation, that the fullness of the means of salvation can be obtained."[20] Until Protestant communities become reunited to the Catholic Church, "the fullness of catholicity" proper to the Church cannot be realized and indeed is made "more difficult."[21]

Like *The Dogmatic Constitution on the Church*, this decree resulted in an increased ecumenical engagement of the Roman Catholic Church with Eastern Orthodox and Protestant churches.

## Summary

Vatican Council II took place between 1962 and 1965. As an *aggiornamento* of the Roman Catholic Church, it updated its doctrines, practices, liturgy, structures, and relationships. This impetus toward change continues today and influences nearly every aspect of the Church.

Vatican II is known especially for its four major documents. *The Constitution on the Sacred Liturgy* set in motion a major reform of the liturgy. *The Dogmatic Constitution on the Church* articulated the nature and mission of the Church and pushed it in the direction of inclusivism in salvation. *The Dogmatic Constitution on Divine Revelation* reiterated the threefold authority structure of the Church: Scripture, Tradition, and the Magisterium. *The Pastoral Constitution on the Church in the Modern World* championed a significant role for the Church in contributing toward human dignity, the flourishing of human society, and the value of human activity. Though not a major constitution, *The Decree on Ecumenism* reframed the relationship of the Catholic Church to Eastern Orthodox and Protestant churches.

## REFLECTION QUESTIONS

1. Why is it right, even necessary, for churches—whether the Catholic Church through Vatican II, or Protestant churches through other means—to engage occasionally in *aggiornamento*? What are some possible dangers of such an updating?

2. If you are an older Catholic, what has been your experience of the many significant changes that have resulted from Vatican II? If you are a younger Catholic, do you feel that your parish is well-connected with you, your friends, your neighborhood, and contemporary issues and events?

---

20. Vatican Council II, *Unitatis Redintegratio*, 3.
21. Vatican Council II, *Unitatis Redintegratio*, 4.

3. What does it mean for the Church to be Roman, Catholic, Petrine (papal), and Marian?

4. What do you think of the answer in *The Dogmatic Constitution on the Church* to the question, "Who belongs to the Catholic Church?" (Remember the concentric circles of salvation.)

5. If you are Protestant, how do you assess *The Decree on Ecumenism*? How do you react to being referred to as a "separated brother (or sister)?" That your church does not possess the "fullness of salvation"? That the Catholic Church is the only church that does possess such fullness? That your church derives whatever grace and gifts it has from the Catholic Church? That your church is an obstacle to full catholicity, which can only become reality if your church reunites with the Catholic Church?

SECTION B

# Foundational Questions

In this second section, I treat questions about the two axioms, or key principles, of Roman Catholicism and provide a Protestant assessment of both axioms. I then outline the beliefs that Protestants and Catholics share in common and those on which they differ.

# How Do Catholics Understand the Interdependence between Nature and Grace?

Think about three sacraments as administered by the Catholic Church. The first is baptism. A priest pours a handful of consecrated water three times on the head of an infant girl as he baptizes her "in the name of the Father, and of the Son, and of the Holy Spirit." The second is confirmation. When this girl is ten years old, she participates in this sacrament. A bishop anoints her forehead with consecrated oil as he lays hands on her and says, "Be sealed with the Gift of the Holy Spirit." The third is the Eucharist. As is her weekly practice, the twentysomething woman goes forward in her parish church during the Mass and eats the consecrated bread and drinks the consecrated wine as the priest announces "the body of Christ" and "the blood of Christ." Three rites, each of which has a sacramental sign: water for baptism, oil for confirmation, and bread and wine for the Eucharist.

In Catholic thought, these three sacraments effect what they symbolize. Baptism cleanses the infant of her original sin, regenerates her so that she is saved from condemnation and corruption, and incorporates her into Christ and his Church. Confirmation binds the ten-year-old girl more perfectly to the Church and strengthens her with an outpouring of the Holy Spirit. The Eucharist transmits the body and blood of Jesus Christ to the woman. This infusion of Christ's presence enables her to act in love and engage in good deeds throughout the week so she can merit eternal life.

Three rites, each of which has a sacramental sign, effect what they symbolize: Cleansing and new birth by the water of baptism. Anointing with the Holy Spirit by the oil of confirmation. The body and blood of the crucified Christ by the bread and wine of the Eucharist. In one word, *grace* is transmitted through water, oil, bread and wine. How can this be? The nature-grace interdependence explains it.

## Nature and Grace Together

To begin, a few definitions will be helpful. *Nature* is what God has created. It encompasses the Milky Way galaxy, our sun and moon, planet earth, Mt. Everest and the Pacific Ocean, red-bellied woodpeckers, whale sharks, lions and tigers and bears, angels, Congolese men and Italian women, Mary and the saints, and—as we've just discussed—water, oil, bread, and wine. This is the realm of nature.

*Grace* is God's unmerited favor.[1] It is expressed in the world that he created. As self-sufficient and independent, God has never lacked for anything. So he did not create the world and all it contains to make up for some deficit in himself. Rather, out of the overflow of his superabundant goodness, he graciously created that all exists. Additionally, divine grace is expressed in salvation. The triune God who created human beings in his image and permitted them to fall graciously rescues the sinful people whom he loves. This is the realm of grace.

According to Roman Catholicism, God has designed nature and grace to be interdependent. Nature is capable of receiving and transmitting grace, and grace must be concretely communicated by nature. Elements in the realm of nature—water, oil, bread, and wine—when consecrated by the Church, receive and convey God's grace. Moreover, by divine design, this grace must be conferred through these elements of nature.

Water that is consecrated by the Church becomes a conduit for divine grace that, through the sacrament of baptism, cleanses an infant from her original sin, recreates her, and joins her to Christ and his Church. Consecrated oil becomes a channel for divine grace that, through the sacrament of confirmation, pours out the fullness of the Holy Spirit on a ten-year-old girl. Bread and wine that are consecrated by the Church become a medium for divine grace that, through the sacrament of the Eucharist, nourishes a twentysomething woman with Christ's body and blood so she can earn eternal life through her grace-aided good works. As George Weigel explains, "It is through the ordinary materials of life—the materials of the seven sacraments, such as bread, wine, oil, and water—that the extraordinary grace of God enters history, nourishes the friends of Jesus, and empowers them in their missionary discipleship."[2]

*Grace* is transmitted through water, oil, bread, and wine—elements of *nature.*

---

1. Grace is defined as "favor, the free and undeserved help that God gives us to respond to his call to become children of God, partakers of the divine nature and of eternal life." CCC, 1996. This section appeals for biblical support to John 1:12–18; 17:3; Rom. 8:14–17; 2 Peter 1:3–4.
2. George Weigel, *Evangelical Catholicism: Deep Reform in the 21ˢᵗ-Century Church* (New York: Basic, 2013), 44.

## The Impact of Sin

What about the disturbance of nature that Adam and Eve's fall into sin introduced? How did that tragic event affect this nature-grace interdependence? For the Church, the fall marred or tainted nature, rendering it spoiled. Nonetheless, nature retains the capacity to receive and convey divine grace. Sin has a serious effect, but not a devastating effect, on nature.

As for grace, "an overall positive posture toward nature, coupled with a mild concept of sin, leads to a corresponding vision of grace."[3] For example, the reception of grace through the sacraments transforms the Catholic faithful such that, cooperating with grace, they may engage in good deeds and thus merit eternal life. Sin has seriously affected the Catholic faithful, but its effect is not total. They are not devastatingly depraved and completely incapable of collaborating with God's grace. Rather, helped by grace, they are able to do their part in the process of obtaining salvation by their meritorious good works.

Throughout the course of this book, I will point out this nature-grace interdependence. You will probably be surprised by how often it appears. This prevalence is due to the fact that it is one of two key axioms, or principles, on which the entire Roman Catholic system—the Church, its theology and practice, its sacraments, its view of salvation, and much more—rests. It is a foundational element at the heart of the Catholic Church.

## Summary

One of two key elements on which the Roman Catholic Church is grounded is the nature-grace interdependence. Nature is whatever God has created. Grace is his unmerited favor. According to the Church, nature and grace are divinely designed to be interconnected. When consecrated by the Church, elements of nature—water, oil, bread, and wine—are capable of receiving and transmitting the grace of God. Additionally, divine grace must be communicated concretely through elements of nature. While the fall tainted nature and marred its interdependence with grace, sin's effect is serious but not devastating. An example is that while human beings have been corrupted by sin, they are not so fallen to be incapable of cooperating with God's grace infused through the sacraments so as to do their part to merit eternal life.[4]

## REFLECTION QUESTIONS

1. What is nature? What is grace? How does the Catholic Church relate these two realms?

---

3. Leonardo De Chirico, *Evangelical Theological Perspectives on Post-Vatican II Roman Catholicism*, Religions and Discourse 19 (Bern: Peter Lang, 2003), 240.
4. For further discussion, see chapters 18 and 25.

2. If you are Catholic, have you ever viewed the Church's sacraments as expressing the nature-grace interdependence? Does looking at baptism, confirmation, and the Eucharist with this principle in mind help you make sense of what is transpiring when the Church celebrates these sacraments?

3. If you are Protestant and yet somewhat familiar with the Catholic Church, does using this lens of the nature-grace interdependence help you make more sense of the Church and its sacraments?

4. If you are Protestant, what is your assessment of this principle of the nature-grace interdependence?

5. What is your evaluation of the Catholic process of salvation? Do you think that salvation is a cooperative effort between God's grace and human good works by which people may merit eternal life?

# How Does Protestantism Assess This Nature-Grace Interdependence?

Think about two different traditions within Protestantism. The first tradition—the Reformed or Calvinist tradition—is represented by Trinity Presbyterian Church. It baptizes the infants of believing parents. The elders and members do not consider paedobaptism to cleanse children from original sin, regenerate them, and incorporate them into Christ. While Trinity views baptism as a means of grace, it does not believe that the sacrament is salvific. The grace of forgiveness, regeneration, and so forth comes through the gospel, through which those baptized infants will hear about the saving work of Christ and put their trust in him in their adolescent or adult years. While the sacrament promises certain blessings—for example, it joins them into a covenant community in which the gospel of grace is preached—those benefits are very unlike the effects envisioned by the Catholic Church for its sacrament of baptism.

When Trinity Presbyterian Church celebrates the Lord's Supper, its elders and members do not consider this rite to be an offering and a sacrifice and thus to infuse grace into those who participate. While Trinity views the Lord's Supper as a means of grace, it does not believe that the sacrament, through transubstantiation of bread and wine, represents the body and blood of the crucified Savior. While the sacrament promises certain blessing—for example, Christ is spiritually present to sanctify those who participate in it—those benefits are very unlike the effects envisioned by the Catholic Church for its sacrament of the Eucharist.

The second tradition—the Baptist or free church tradition—is represented by Crossroads Community Church. It baptizes people who have heard the gospel, repented of their sins, and believed in Christ for salvation. The pastors and members do not consider credobaptism to cleanse people (infants or adults) from original sin, regenerate them, and incorporate them into

Christ. To distinguish itself from that sacramental notion, Crossroads does not view baptism as a means of grace. Rather, it considers baptism to be an ordinance rather than a sacrament that is salvific. While the ordinance offers certain blessings—for example, it attests to the saving faith of those who are baptized and symbolizes their identification with Christ's death and resurrection—those benefits are very unlike the effects envisioned by the Catholic Church for its sacrament of baptism.

When Crossroads Community Church celebrates the Lord's Supper, its pastors and members do not consider this rite to be an offering and a sacrifice and thus to infuse grace into those who participate. Crossroads does not believe that the rite, through transubstantiation of bread and wine, represents the body and blood of the crucified Savior. To distinguish itself from that sacramental notion, Crossroads does not view the Lord's Supper as a means of grace. Rather, it considers the Lord's Supper to be an ordinance rather than a sacrament that is salvific. While the ordinance offers certain blessings—for example, it proclaims the death of Christ and thereby prompts those who participate to remember his atoning sacrifice—those benefits are very unlike the effects envisioned by the Catholic Church for its sacrament of the Eucharist.

What can account for the divergence between the Protestant views of these two rites and that of the Roman Catholic Church? Why is there such a chasm between the two Protestant traditions—Reformed/Calvinist and Baptist/free church—and the Catholic tradition? One key factor is that Protestantism is not grounded on the principle of the nature-grace interdependence.

## Lack of Biblical Support

What Protestantism finds lacking or amiss with this principle can be summarized in three points. The first point is the lack of a scriptural basis for the Catholic notion of nature. The principle is philosophical rather than biblical. To demonstrate the absence of a biblical basis, ask yourself (assuming you are a Protestant) when was the last time you heard a sermon, done a Bible study, or read a book on *nature*. My guess is that the subject has never come up. The Bible does not present nature as consisting of elements that are capable of receiving and transmitting divine grace; it does not present divine grace as something that must be concretely transmitted by nature. This lack of biblical basis leads to the observation that nature is "perhaps the only theological topic in which Catholic and Protestant thought have gone their own ways, passing like ships in the night, with no sense of common problems and standards of judgement."[1]

---

1. Eugene TeSelle, "Nature and Grace in the Forum of Ecumenical Discussion," *Journal of Ecumenical Studies* 8 (1971): 540.

## Contradiction of Scripture

The second point goes beyond the principle's lack of biblical support to its contradiction of Scripture. Put simply, the Bible does not view *nature* as hospitable to grace. Certainly, in the original creation, nature expressed God's design for it. To take one example, the tree of life in the middle of the garden of Eden was God's gracious provision of eternal life for Adam and Eve in their upright state (Gen. 2:9, 22). But when they rebelled against God, not only did their fall result in spiritual, relational, and personal disaster for Adam and Eve. It plunged the realm of nature into ruin as well. Indeed, God cursed nature because of their fall:

> Cursed is the ground because of you;
>> in pain you shall eat of it all the days of your life;
> thorns and thistles it shall bring forth for you;
>> and you shall eat the plants of the field.
> By the sweat of your face
>> you shall eat bread,
> till you return to the ground,
>> for out of it you were taken;
> for you are dust,
>> and to dust you shall return. (Gen. 3:17–19)

God cursed nature because of the sin of Adam and Eve.

Furthermore, in an act of both judgment and mercy, God expelled the disobedient couple from the garden of Eden (Gen. 3:24). He cast them away from his gracious presence. The cursed realm of nature became inhospitable to human beings who, by God's grace, had been created in his image and yet, by their disobedience, rebelled against him. To use more Protestant language, "if the garden of Eden represents the nature-grace interdependence, post-fall human beings are violently and decisively cut off from it, living instead in exile, the wilderness, a wasteland of their own undoing."[2]

Thus, Scripture does not present nature in a positive light, as a realm that is open to grace and that can serve as a conduit between God and human beings.

## An Errant Concept of Grace

A third point for Protestant concern about the Catholic concept of *nature* ties into its concern about the Catholic concept of *grace*. Catholics and Protestants alike may underscore the fact that both traditions employ elements of nature as either means of grace (the Catholic Church, Trinity Presbyterian Church) or as symbols of faith and obedience (Crossroads Community Church). The two traditions share the rites of baptism and the

---

2. *RCTP*, 54.

Lord's Supper, so we will focus on them. Water, bread, and wine are the elements of nature in both celebrations. So what are we to make of this similarity in the use of nature?

Despite this family resemblance, the two traditions separate over the idea of the grace that is conferred or symbolized by these elements of nature. Within the Catholic framework, the elements infuse a grace that transforms its recipients' character, thereby rendering them able to cooperate with divine grace to do good works to merit eternal life. From the Protestant perspective, the elements of nature promise or portray the mighty acts of God and the human response to them. But these elements do not infuse grace for character renewal. At Trinity Presbyterian Church, infant baptism is a sacrament by which God pledges to draw the baptized girl to himself later in life as she grasps the gospel and believes in Christ for salvation. Furthermore, the Lord's Supper is a sacrament by which God promises this presence, sustaining nourishment, and sanctifying action. At Crossroads Community Church, believer's baptism is an ordinance by which the baptized express their faith in what God has done to mightily save them. It also vividly portrays their identification with the death and resurrection of Christ on their behalf. Furthermore, the Lord's Supper is an ordinance by which the gospel is proclaimed such that participants are prompted to remember Christ's saving death for them.

The Catholic Church and Protestant churches employ similar elements of nature, but the two traditions divide significantly over their understanding of God's gracious action and the human response associated with those elements.

A lack of biblical basis. An idea of nature that contradicts Scripture. A concept of infused grace that effects character transformation. For these three reasons, Protestantism rejects the nature-grace interdependence.

## Summary

One of two key elements on which the Roman Catholic Church is grounded is the nature-grace interdependence. Nature is whatever God has created. Grace is his unmerited favor. According to the Church, nature and grace are divinely designed to be interconnected. Protestantism does not operate according to this principle because of the absence of a biblical basis for it. Indeed, Scripture contradicts the idea that nature is hospitable to grace. Additionally, the idea of grace and how it functions for the Catholic faithful—it is transmitted through nature and transforms their character—is far removed from how Protestant churches understand divine action through nature.

## REFLECTION QUESTIONS

1. If you are Protestant, is your tradition represented more by Trinity Presbyterian Church or Crossroads Community Church? How has this discussion helped you understand better your tradition's view of the sacraments or ordinances?

2. Can you think of places (other than the garden of Eden story) in which Scripture presents the hostility between nature and grace? Does the world's rejection of the incarnate Word of God (John 1:9–13) provide another example of this enmity? How does Jesus Christ resolve this enmity?

3. What implications does opposition between nature and grace in Scripture have for the Catholic principle of the nature-grace interdependence?

4. If you are Catholic, do you view the Church's sacraments as infusing grace so that your essence is transformed, thereby enabling you to do good deeds by which you can merit eternal life? Do you understand how this view is connected to the principle of the nature-grace interdependence?

5. To anticipate our next question and discussion, what go-between is going to bring together these two different realms of nature and grace? What intermediary is going to consecrate elements of nature so that they are capable of receiving and transmitting God's grace? What agent or agency is going to offer divine grace through concrete means such as water, oil, bread, and wine?

# How Do Catholics Understand the Interconnection of Christ and the Church?

According to the foundational principle of the nature-grace interdependence, God has designed the two disparate realms to be connected. This principle raises an important question: How do nature and grace connect?

If you answer that Jesus Christ is the go-between for these two different realms, you are correct! Through the incarnation of the Son of God as the mediator Jesus Christ, these two realms are related.

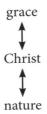

While the Catholic Church agrees with this response, it considers the answer to be incomplete. The Catholic Church relates the two realms through both Christ and the Church. Indeed, the two are so intimately connected that it is not possible to think of one without thinking about the other.

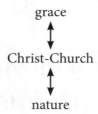

grace

Christ-Church

nature

What is the reason for this intimate Christ-Church interconnection?

## The Law of Incarnation

The Catholic Church addresses the concept of incarnation in a unique way. It proposes that God has designed his creation with a law of incarnation. There are two important manifestations of this law. The first manifestation is the one with which we are all familiar: the incarnation of the Son of God about two thousand years ago as Jesus Christ. The second manifestation is the Roman Catholic Church. It too is an incarnation, but not on its own. Rather, its incarnation is closely connected to the first incarnation. Indeed, the Church considers itself to be the continuation of the incarnation of the Son of God. The Catholic Church is the prolongation of the incarnation that took place about two thousand years ago in Jesus Christ. Specifically, the Church is the *totus Christus*—the whole Christ: deity, humanity, and body.

This notion of the Church as continuing the incarnation of Christ is so important that it is the second fundamental principle of Roman Catholicism: the Christ-Church interconnection. Along with the principle of the nature-grace interdependence, the principle of the Christ-Church interconnection is the ground of Roman Catholic theology, practice, liturgy, sacraments, mission, and more. In terms of their relationship, there is this important parallel. The first manifestation of the law of incarnation is the incarnation of the God-man, Jesus Christ. He mediated grace to nature. He connected nature to grace. The second manifestation of the law of incarnation is the Church as the continuation of Christ's incarnation. The Church mediates grace to nature. It connects nature to grace. The Christ-Church interconnection is the go-between for the two realms of nature and grace.

## The Church Mediates between Nature and Grace

The Roman Catholic Church acts as another (or second) person of Christ, mediating between the two realms. By God's design, nature is open to grace; it receives the grace mediated to it by the Church. Grace, which must be tangible and concrete, is communicated through elements of nature that are consecrated by the Church. Two examples follow. First, a priest administers consecrated water (in the realm of nature) for the sacrament of baptism, which cleanses an infant from her original sin, regenerates her, and unites her to Christ and the Church (all in the realm of grace). The priest acts in the person of Christ such that it is really Christ who baptizes. Second, a bishop administers consecrated oil (in the realm of nature) for the sacrament of confirmation, which strengthens that ten-year-old girl through the outpouring of the Holy Spirit (in the realm of grace). The bishop acts in the person of Christ such that it is really Christ who confirms by pouring out his Spirit. The Roman Catholic Church, by virtue of its ministers, acts as another person of Christ and mediates between the realms of nature and grace.

This Christ-Church interconnection is the second foundation of Catholic theology.

## Support for the Christ-Church Interconnection

In support of this principle, the Church points to the biblical affirmation of the church as the mystical body of Christ. As Paul explains, God the Father "raised him [the crucified Christ] from the dead and seated him at his right hand in the heavenly places, far above all rule and authority and power and dominion, and above every name that is named, not only in this age but also in the one to come. And he put all things under his feet and gave him as head over all things to the church, which is his body, the fullness of him who fills all in all" (Eph. 1:20–23). Christ is the head of the church, which is his body. In this same letter, Paul addresses the intimate connection between husband and wife, concluding with, "This mystery is profound, and I am saying that it refers to Christ and the church" (Eph. 5:32). Accordingly, the Catholic Church underscores the Christ-Church interconnection, identifying itself as the continuation of Christ's incarnation.

Additionally, the Church relies on Augustine's concept of *totus Christus*: "The whole Christ consists of Head and body. The Head is he who is the savior of his body, he who has already ascended into heaven; but the body is the Church, toiling on earth."[1] Certainly, Christ has ascended to heaven, but he remains closely united to his church. After all, when he confronted Saul along the road to Tarsus, Jesus didn't say, "Saul, Saul, why are you persecuting *the*

---

1. Augustine, *Exposition of the Psalms*, in *The Works of Saint Augustine: A Translation for the 21st Century*, ed. John E. Rotelle, trans. Maria Boulding, 6 vols. (New York: New City, 2000–2004), 4:149.

*church?*" Rather, he asked, "why are you persecuting *me?*" (Acts 9:4). Though it is not quite right to use the equation "Christ is the church," he is identified as closely as possible with the church. To reverse the concept, the Church is the *totus Christus*—the whole Christ: deity, humanity, and body.

Finally, the Catholic Church describes itself in sacramental terms: "The Church, in Christ, is in the nature of a sacrament."[2] As we know, a sacrament is a visible and tangible sign of an invisible yet real grace. So, in sacramental terms, the Church considers itself to be "a sign and instrument . . . of communion with God and the unity of all men."[3] The Church does not claim to be an actual sacrament; rather, it is "in the nature of a sacrament." Thus, the Church represents the union between God and his people as well as their unity among themselves through him. More than that, the Church is the means to establish and develop that divine-human communion and that human-human community. And the Church, in its likeness to a sacrament, achieves that goal as the ongoing incarnation of Christ. As the incarnate Christ was the go-between with nature and grace, so is the Catholic Church, as the prolongation of his incarnation, the intermediary between the two realms. The Church mediates grace to nature as it connects nature to grace.

## Summary

In addition to the nature-grace interdependence, the Christ-Church interconnection is the second key foundation of the Roman Catholic Church. It considers itself to be the continuation of the incarnation of the Son of God as Jesus Christ. While this latter incarnation took place about two thousand years ago, the Church is the ongoing manifestation of a law of incarnation. Like the Son incarnate mediated grace to nature and connected nature to grace, similarly the Catholic Church mediates grace to nature and connects nature to grace.

Accordingly, when priests and bishops celebrate the sacraments, they act in the person of Christ. Though a priest administers baptism, it is Christ who actually baptizes. Though a bishop administers confirmation, it is Christ who actually confirms.

The Church supports this principle of the Christ-Church interconnection in three ways. Scripture presents the church as the mystical body of Christ. Augustine developed the concept of the church as the *totus Christus*: the whole Christ, deity, humanity, and body. And the Church identifies itself in sacramental terms.

---

2.    Vatican Council II, *Lumen Gentium*, November 21, 1964, 1. http://www.vatican.va/archive/ hist_councils/ii_vatican_council/documents/vat-ii_const_19641121_lumen-gentium_en.html.

3.    Vatican Council II, *Lumen Gentium*, 1.

## REFLECTION QUESTIONS

1. How do the disparate realms of nature and grace connect? If you are a Protestant, how do you answer? If you are a Catholic, how do you answer?

2. Do you agree with the Catholic Church's idea that God created the world with a law of incarnation? What are the strengths and weaknesses of this idea?

3. How does the Catholic Church view its priests and bishops as they administer the seven sacraments? How do Protestant churches view their leaders as they administer the two sacraments or ordinances? What are the strengths and weaknesses of both views?

4. What is your assessment of Augustine's concept of the church as the *totus Christus*? What are its strengths and weaknesses?

5. Why are the two principles—the nature-grace interdependence and the Christ-Church interconnection—so foundational to Roman Catholic theology, practice, liturgy, sacraments, mission, and more?

# How Does Protestantism Assess This Christ-Church Interconnection?

Protestants raise three concerns about this principle. The first concern is about the law of incarnation; the second is about Augustine's *totus Christus*; and the third is about Christ's ascension and outpouring of the Holy Spirit.

### Concerns with the Law of Incarnation

Both Catholics and Protestants affirm the incarnation of the Son of God about two thousand years ago. This world-altering event was prophesied in the Old Testament in terms of a future Messiah, who would be a Suffering Servant, Second Adam, Davidic King, Mosaic Prophet, and Faithful High Priest. According to God's sovereign plan, the incarnation became a necessity to rectify the dismal state of guilt and corruption into which human beings have fallen.

> Since therefore the children share in flesh and blood, he himself likewise partook of the same things, that through death he might destroy the one who has the power of death, that is, the devil, and deliver all those who through fear of death were subject to lifelong slavery. For surely it is not angels that he helps, but he helps the offspring of Abraham. Therefore he had to be made like his brothers in every respect, so that he might become a merciful and faithful high priest in the service of God, to make propitiation for the sins of the people. For because he himself has suffered when tempted, he is able to help those who are being tempted. (Heb. 2:14–18)

Following Scripture, both Protestants and Catholics alike affirm the incarnation and its divinely planned necessity for the salvation of sinful people.

At the same time, Protestants find no biblical support for a law of incarnation. Without such a law, there is one and only one incarnation: the manifestation of the incarnate Son of God as Jesus Christ. Without such a law, the Catholic Church does not have grounds for associating itself with another manifestation: the Church as the prolongation of the incarnation of the Son.

## Concerns with Augustine's *Totus Christus*

A second concern focuses on Augustine's idea of the church as the *totus Christus*—deity, humanity, and body. Certainly, Protestants embrace Paul's imagery of Christ as the head of his body (Eph. 1:20–23), which is indeed a mystery (Eph. 5:32). But there are two interpretations of this metaphor that explain the difference between Catholic and Protestant views of the *totus Christus*.

The Catholic perspective is based on Augustine's realistic interpretation of Paul's head-body metaphor:

> The core of the metaphor refers to the indissoluble, organic bond between head (i.e., Christ) and members (i.e., the Church) within the unity of a single body so that what can be ascribed to the head can also be ascribed in some measure to its members. . . . While the members are dependent on the head in the sense that they receive from it direction and serve its cause, they are also so inextricably united to it as to form a single body so that the head cannot operate apart from its members and cannot be separated from them.[1]

This realistic interpretation is at the heart of Augustine's emphasis on Jesus's words to Saul: "Why are you persecuting *me*?" In some realistic way, Christ is his church and the church is Christ, such that to persecute Christ's body is to persecute Christ the head. Accordingly, the Catholic Church combines both divine and human elements within itself. In essence, the Catholic Church is the *totus Christus*.[2]

The Protestant perspective holds that Paul's metaphor is to be understood as an analogy: *like* or *similar to* the relationship between a human head and its body, so is the relationship between Christ and his church. It is not a realistic, organic unity that Paul has in mind. The church's essence is not the whole Christ, with divine and human elements. Rather, due to the fact that one part

---

1. Leonardo De Chirico, *Evangelical Theological Perspectives on Post-Vatican II Roman Catholicism*, Religions and Discourse 19 (Bern: Peter Lang, 2003), 261.
2. The Catholic Church acknowledges the potential difficulties with this understanding and thus seeks to clarify the relationship between Christ and the Church: "While the Son of God owns divine nature in a proper, ontological, and substantial way, the Church derives her divine elements by participating in the life of Christ which makes him present in the Church and through it." De Chirico, *Evangelical Theological Perspectives*, 259.

of the analogy is about a divine being (Christ) and the other part is about a human entity (the church), it is an analogous relationship that features far more discontinuity than continuity between the two parts.

Indeed, Paul himself emphasizes the element of analogy in his discussion of the husband-wife and Christ-church relationship: "the husband is the head of the wife *even as* Christ is the head of the church, his body" (Eph. 5:23). "Even as" indicates a parallel relationship:

| husband | ‖ | head | ‖ | Christ |
|---------|---|------|---|--------|
| wife | | body | | church |

If Paul were addressing an essential relationship, problems would ensue: "to apply the *totus Christus* concept in interpreting this analogy results in the near identification of the two marriage partners, with the primacy of the existence of the husband and the contingency of the existence of the wife being reinforced; this is neither a Pauline nor a biblical idea."[3] Thus, Paul's metaphor is more properly understood as an analogy and not as affirming an essential, organic unity between Christ and the church.

But what of Jesus's confrontation of Saul? "Why are you persecuting *me*?" highlights the reality of suffering to which Jesus's followers are called. He himself promised: "'A servant is not greater than his master.' If they persecuted me, they will also persecute you" (John 15:20). Paul adds, "For it has been granted to you that for the sake of Christ you should not only believe in him but also suffer for his sake" (Phil. 1:29). As it was for Jesus, so also for his disciples—humiliation precedes exaltation: "if children, then heirs—heirs of God and fellow heirs with Christ, provided we suffer with him in order that we may also be glorified with him" (Rom. 8:17). Suffering is part and parcel of living for Christ: "all who desire to live a godly life in Christ Jesus will be persecuted" (2 Tim. 3:12). Christ's church suffers not because it is "in *essence* Christ," but because it is "in Christ." These Scriptures "underscore that the church, which is 'in Christ,' stands in intimate relationship to Christ but is not a prolongation of his ascended being—the ontological interpretation."[4]

Thus, the *totus Christus* is not grounded biblically.

## Concerns Raised by Christ's Ascension and the Outpouring of the Holy Spirit

The mention of the ascension of Christ raises another concern about the foundational principle of the Christ-Church interconnection. Following his

---

3. *RCTP*, 64.
4. *RCTP*, 64.

accomplishment of salvation through his death and resurrection, the incarnate Son ascended into heaven (Acts 1:11; Eph. 1:20–21). With his own mission accomplished, the Son (together with the Father) poured out the Holy Spirit. He engages in the ongoing application of the saving work of the Son to sinful people. Christ's ascension and the outpouring of the Holy Spirit emphasize five important points.

First, the ascended Jesus is *not* here. This is not a denial of the fullness of Christ filling his body (Eph. 1:23) in the sense of his divine omnipresence. But it does underscore the error of the *totus Christus* because King Jesus, the ascended God-man, is not in his church in terms of its essential nature. Second, this reigning King will one day return from heaven to earth. If he is already here as the Christ-Church interconnection maintains, then in what sense can he come back again? Third, if he is not here now but will return later, how is he present in the Lord's Supper? The ascension presents problems for the Catholic sacrament of the Eucharist, specifically its belief in the presence of Christ through transubstantiation. If he is *not* here, how can he be here in his body and blood?[5]

Fourth, between the first and second comings of Christ, the Holy Spirit is characteristic of the new covenant church. He gives birth to it, empowers its mission, guides it, endows it with gifts, grants it unity, and establishes its leaders. The Christ-Church interconnection seems to have little room for this ongoing work of the Holy Spirit. Together with the Father, the Son sent the Spirit not for the continuation of the incarnation, but for the continuation of his mission of saving fallen people. Certainly, the Catholic Church appeals to, even focuses on, the work of the Holy Spirit throughout its hierarchy, liturgy, ministries, and mission. But this emphasis has a certain hollow ring to it, appearing as almost an afterthought or add on to the Christ-Church prominence.

Fifth, the ascension of Christ and the subsequent outpouring of the Holy Spirit upon all the people of God raises serious questions for the Catholic Church's insistence that it, and it alone, is the one true church of Jesus Christ. This point goes beyond the matter of salvation, for ever since Vatican Council II the Catholic Church affirms that salvation is possible for those outside of the Church. Rather, the point is that according to the Catholic Church, the universal church is identical with the visible Catholic Church. One application of this belief is the Catholic view that Protestant Christians do not assemble in and belong to churches. Rather, they are members of ecclesial communities, lacking apostolic succession, a proper hierarchy, and a true Eucharist. Of course, Protestants reject this Catholic perspective, which flows from its foundational principle of the Christ-Church interconnection.

---

5.  As we will see, the Catholic Church has a ready answer to this question. But its answer—transubstantiation accounts for the sacramental presence of Christ—is one that no Protestant historically or presently accepts.

### The Nature-Grace Interdependence and the Christ-Church Interconnection

We bring our discussion of the two key principles of Roman Catholicism to a conclusion. We have highlighted several concerns about both. Given that these principles are not unrelated but intimately connected, the weaknesses of both present problems for the two combined as the foundation of Catholic doctrine, practice, liturgy, mission, and more. If there is no nature-grace interdependence as conceived by Catholicism, then the reason for the Christ-Church interconnection evaporates. If nature is not capable of receiving and transmitting divine grace, which is thought to be communicated concretely through elements of nature, then the Christ-Church interconnection is not needed as the go-between that links the two realms. Moreover, if there is no Christ-Church interconnection as conceived by Catholicism, and if a need for a mediator still exists (even if the mediation is different from how the principle of the nature-grace interdependence imagines it), then the possibility of identifying a different mediator is opened up. Protestants identify that Mediator with Jesus Christ, but Christ shorn of his interconnection with the Catholic Church according to its second key principle.

### Summary

One of two key principles on which the Roman Catholic Church is grounded is the Christ-Church interconnection. In order to link the realms of nature and grace (according to the other key principle of the nature-grace interdependence), an intermediary is necessary. While both Protestants and Catholics agree that Christ is the mediator, the Catholic Church goes one step further. It maintains that the go-between of these two realms is the Church as the *totus Christus*: the whole Christ—deity, humanity, and body. Accordingly, it is not possible to think of Christ and his mediatorial role apart from the Catholic Church.

Protestants raise several concerns about this foundational principle. They find no biblical basis for the Catholic notion of a law of incarnation. They consider Augustine's concept of the *totus Christus* to be based on a weak interpretation of several key biblical texts. Finally, Protestants maintain that Christ's ascension and the outpouring of the Holy Spirit create unresolvable problems for the principle.

## REFLECTION QUESTIONS

1. How are the two key principles of Catholicism—the nature-grace interdependence and the Christ-Church interconnection—related?

2. Do you agree with the Catholic Church's idea that God created the world with a law of incarnation? Why or why not?

3. What is your assessment of Augustine's concept of the Church as the *totus Christus*? Is Jesus's confrontation of Saul—"Why are you persecuting me?" rather than "Why are you persecuting the church?"—support for his realistic interpretation?

4. When Paul uses the head-body analogy to describe Christ and the church, why is a metaphorical interpretation better than a realistic one?

5. What is your assessment of the various concerns that Christ's ascension and the outpouring of the Holy Spirit raise for the principle of the Christ-Church interconnection?

# What Beliefs Do Catholicism and Protestantism Share in Common?

Even though Roman Catholic and Protestant theology differs significantly, the two great traditions share important areas of doctrinal agreements. Broadly speaking, there are ten areas of common beliefs.[1]

## Trinity

The first commonality is *the doctrine of the Trinity*. Catholics and Protestants alike agree that God eternally exists as Father, Son, and Holy Spirit. There is only one God and he is triune, that is, three persons. Each of the three is fully God. The Father is fully God. The Son is fully God. The Holy Spirit is fully God. Yet, there are not three gods but one, because the Father, the Son, and the Holy Spirit share in the one divine nature.

Though equal in nature, the three are distinct divine Persons. The Father is not the Son and he is not the Holy Spirit. The Son is not the Father and he is not the Holy Spirit. The Holy Spirit is not the Father and he is not the Son. How are they distinct, divine persons? In two ways. First, they are distinct in terms of their eternal relations. That is, even before God created the universe and everything in it, he existed as the Father, the Son, and the Holy Spirit. Second, they are distinct in terms of their roles in terms of creation, salvation, and sanctification.

As for their distinction in eternal relations, both Catholics and Protestants alike agree with the following: (1) The eternal characteristic that is unique to the Father is *paternity*. He is eternally the Father of the Son. (2) The eternal characteristic that is unique to the Son is *generation*. He is eternally the Son

---

1. For further discussion, see Gregg Allison and Chris Castaldo, *The Unfinished Reformation: What Unites and Divides Catholics and Protestants after 500 Years* (Grand Rapids: Zondervan, 2016), chap. 2.

of the Father. (3) The eternal characteristic that is unique to the Holy Spirit is *procession*. The Holy Spirit eternally proceeds from the Father and the Son.

As for their distinction in roles, both Catholics and Protestants agree with the following: (1) All three persons always operate together in all divine works. This doctrine of inseparable operations means that the Father, the Son, and the Holy Spirit work together in creation, salvation, and sanctification. (2) At the same time, the three persons engage in the divine works in particular ways. This is the doctrine of appropriation, meaning that their inseparable works bear distinguishing marks of their participation. As an example, the Father speaks the creation into existence through his Word, the Son, who is the agent of creation, together with the Holy Spirit, who is the preparer and perfecter of the creation. In every case, there is one divine work in which all three persons operate in ways appropriate to them being the Father, the Son, and the Holy Spirit.

## God

The second area of agreement is *the nature of God*. Both Protestants and Catholics alike agree that God is self-existent, unchangeable, eternal, spiritual or immaterial, sovereign, everywhere present, all-powerful, all-knowing, wise, truthful, faithful, loving, good, gracious, merciful, patient, holy, just, righteous, jealous, wrathful, glorious, simple (not composed of parts), and blessed. Furthermore, these divine attributes characterize all three persons equally. There is no difference whatsoever between the three persons in terms of their divine attributes because the three share in the one divine nature.

## Revelation

The third commonality concerns *the revelation of God*. Both Catholics and Protestants alike agree that God reveals himself through general revelation. The four aspects of this revelation, which is divinely given to all peoples at all times and in all places, are the following: the *creation*, which manifests God's existence and some of his divine attributes; the *human conscience*, by which people know that God is a divine law-giver, along with some basic principles of right and wrong; God's *providential care*, which testifies to God's goodness and kindness in supplying what his image bearers need to live; and an *innate sense* of God, that is, an inner awareness of his existence and his worthiness to be worshiped. Additionally, Catholics and some Protestants agree in proposing *proofs for God's existence*.

Furthermore, Catholics and Protestants concur about *special* or *divine revelation*, which is divinely given to particular peoples at particular times and in particular places. Special revelation is of various kinds: *The mighty acts of God* are historical displays of God's existence and power. Examples include the crossing of the Red Sea and Jesus's resurrection. *Dreams and visions* are internal manifestations of God's glory, purposes, and will. Isaiah received a vision of the holiness of God. Nebuchadnezzar had dreams that

Daniel interpreted as God's plan for the future. *Direct divine speech* occurs when God announces his will, gives direction, rebukes, warns, and more. God called the pagan Abram to leave his homeland and family and to follow him. Upon Abram's faith, God pronounced him justified. *The incarnation* is the event by which the Son took on human nature and became the God-man. His works, words, and very nature reveal who God is. *Inspired communication* is a form of direct divine speech. While there is significant disagreement on this mode of divine revelation, Protestants and Catholics do agree that Scripture is the God-breathed, or inspired, written revelation of God and thus of great importance. And many affirm its complete truthfulness, or inerrancy.

### Person of Christ

The fourth area of agreement is *the person of Jesus Christ*. Both Protestants and Catholics alike agree that the Son, who is eternally generated by the Father, became incarnate as Jesus Christ. Specifically, he was "conceived by the Holy Spirit and born of the Virgin Mary" (Apostles' Creed). He is the God-man through the hypostatic union; that is, in becoming incarnate, he is one person with two natures—one divine, one human. As a consequence, both traditions condemn historical and contemporary heresies about the person of Jesus Christ.[2]

### Work of Christ

The fifth commonality is *the saving work of Jesus Christ*. Both Catholics and Protestants alike affirm that God the Son incarnate, even though facing the trials and temptations common to all human beings, never failed a test nor yielded to a temptation. On the contrary, and as was necessary for him to be the perfect Mediator between God and us, he lived a sinless life. At the end of his life, Jesus faced intense pressure and persecution, part of his sufferings on our behalf. In the garden of Gethsemane, when faced with the ultimate choice of life or death, he fully obeyed the Father on whose mission the Son had been sent.

Jesus Christ was crucified for our sins, died, and was buried. His atoning sacrifice is multifaceted. It is a *propitiation*, assuaging the divine wrath against sin. It is an *expiation*, removing our liability to suffer eternal punishment for

---

2. These heresies are the following: *Docetism*: Jesus only appeared to be a human being but was not. *Arianism*: the Son is a created being, not eternal, and not of the same nature as God the Father. *Nestorianism*: the divine Second Person did not become united with a human nature but cooperated with the human person of Jesus of Nazareth—he is two persons collaborating, not one person with two natures. *Eutychianism*, with two errors: (1) the divine nature dominated the human nature, so was DIVINEhuman; (2) the two natures fused so that Christ's one nature was d$^h$i$^u$v$^m$i$^a$n$^n$e. *Apollinarianism*: the only aspect of human nature that the Son took on in the incarnation is a body. Thus, Jesus Christ is fully divine but only partially human. *Kenoticism*: in becoming incarnate, the Son emptied himself of certain nonessential attributes. Divesting himself of, for example, his omnipresence and omniscience, the Son was able to become fully human, that is, become located in his body and emplaced in Palestine, and not know the time of his own return.

our sin and guilt. It is *redemption*, the price paid to liberate us from enslavement to sin and death. It is *reconciliation*, the removal of enmity that once existed between God and us and thus restoring us to friendship with God. It is *Christ's victory*, his conquest of Satan, sin, and death so that we overcome these enemies through him.

## Holy Spirit

The sixth area of agreement is *the person and work of the Holy Spirit*. Protestants and Catholics alike believe "in the Holy Spirit, the Lord and Giver of life, who proceeds from the Father and the Son, who together with the Father and the Son is worshiped and glorified, who spoke by the prophets" (Nicene-Constantinopolitan Creed). As the Third Person of the Trinity, he is fully God, of the same nature as the Father and the Son, with whom he operates inseparably in all divine works. At the same time, he engages in particular aspects of the common works. Specifically, the Spirit speaks, creates/re-creates/perfects, and fills Christians and the church with the presence of the triune God.[3]

## Human Beings

The seventh commonality is *the glory and depravity of human beings*. Catholics and Protestants alike affirm that God created human beings as the pinnacle of his creation. We are divine image-bearers, and as such, full of significance and dignity. Moreover, human beings are complex persons, consisting of both a material aspect (body) and immaterial aspect (soul or spirit). God created his original bearers, Adam and Eve, upright, as people of integrity who rightly obeyed and trusted him.

Sadly, Adam and Eve fell into sin, losing their original righteousness and becoming liable to death because of sin. The consequences of their fall were not confined to them. Rather, because of human solidarity with Adam and Eve, the entire human race was plunged into sin. Original sin is the state of corruption (and guilt, according to some) into which all human beings are born. Thus, from their first moment, all people are in dire straits. Unless God intervenes—by prevenient grace to remove original guilt, or sanctifying grace to overcome the corrupting influence of fallen nature, or saving grace to bring salvation—their demise is sealed.

## Salvation

The eighth area of consensus is *the divine initiative in salvation*. Both Protestants and Catholics affirm the divine initiative in both the accomplishment of salvation and the application of salvation. God's initiative in accomplishing salvation focuses on Jesus Christ's death by crucifixion as an atoning sacrifice for

---

3. Gregg R. Allison and Andreas J. Köstenberger, *The Holy Spirit: Theology for the People of God* (Nashville: B&H Academic, 2020), 282–94.

human sin. Both traditions agree that his sacrifice is a once-and-for-all offering to pay the penalty for sin.[4] Having accomplished salvation, he rose from the dead on the third day, demonstrating that his death is a sufficient sacrifice for sin. He later ascended into heaven, from which he sent the Holy Spirit.

The divine initiative in applying salvation focuses on God's mighty acts by which the salvation accomplished by Jesus Christ becomes activated in individuals. These mighty divine acts include election, calling, union with Christ, regeneration, adoption, and more. Even in regard to justification, Catholics agree with Protestants that no role for human initiative and merit at the outset of salvation is allowed.

## Church

The ninth commonality is *the community of faith*. From the early centuries of its existence, the church has identified itself by four attributes: oneness (unity), holiness (purity), catholicity (universality), and apostolicity (association with the apostles). Though united in terminology, the two traditions divide over the meaning of these terms. Similarly, because Scripture uses three prominent metaphors for the church—it is the people of God, the body of Christ, and the temple of the Holy Spirit—both Protestants and Catholics use these images to shape their doctrine of the church. At the same time, there is a good deal of disagreement over the significance of these metaphors.

Accordingly, the commonalities between the two traditions when it comes to the church mask a substantial amount of disagreement. This point highlights the fact that the doctrine of the church, according to the opinion of many Protestants and Catholics alike, is the single most divisive area between the two.

## Future

The tenth and final area of agreement is *the living hope*, or *eschatology* (Gr. *eschatos* = last things). Catholics and Protestants alike affirm many points with regard to both personal eschatology and cosmic eschatology.

The personal hope of Christians, based on Christ's atoning sacrifice to pay the penalty for sin, is to escape eternal punishment and enjoy eternal life. The cosmic hope features several aspects. The second coming of Jesus Christ is the next great eschatological event that awaits actualization. He will return bodily to earth. Accompanying this event will be the resurrection of the good and the wicked alike. Both the resurrected righteous and the resurrected unrighteous will appear before Christ at the last judgment. In a public display of salvation and judgment, Christ will reward the righteous with eternal life and

---

4. Importantly, Catholics do not believe that at every Mass, Jesus Christ is re-sacrificed for the sacrament of the Eucharist. (We will have much more to say about this later.) Rather, there is agreement that God the Son, by virtue of his human nature, died by crucifixion, and that his death was rendered on behalf of sinful people.

punish the wicked with eternal death. At long last, and as anticipated from the moment that God initiated the salvation of sinful people, believers will live with the triune God in the new heaven and new earth.

## Summary

Ten commonalities unite Catholics and Protestants. The doctrine of the Trinity. The nature of God. The revelation of God. The person of Christ. The saving work of Christ. The person and work of the Holy Spirit. The glory and depravity of human beings. The divine initiative in salvation. The community of faith. And the living hope.

One major caution needs to be heeded. Roman Catholic theology and practice and Protestant theology and practice are very different systems operating on different principles. This diversity should caution us that, even when the two traditions use similar words, they may mean significantly different things by those similar terms. Grace, mercy, justification, evangelization, the gospel, sacraments—just to take a few examples—are words that are beloved by both Catholics and Protestants alike. At the same time, the two different systems of theology and practice often have different concepts at work when they use those terms. Thus, both traditions need to be cautious about embracing commonalities that have only a thin veneer of agreement.

## REFLECTION QUESTIONS

1. Which of the areas of commonality surprised you the most? Why?

2. Which of the areas was the least surprising? Why?

3. If you are more apt to emphasize the divergences between Roman Catholics and Protestants, what should you take away from these ten areas of commonality?

4. If you are more apt to emphasize the commonalities between Roman Catholics and Protestants, what should you take away from the concluding warning about similar words masking very different concepts?

5. In respectful discussions with your friends who are of the other tradition than you, how can you appreciate the commonalities (the point of this question) without overlooking the divergences (the point of the next question)? That is, how can dialogue between Catholics and Protestants best take place?

# Where Do Catholic and Protestant Beliefs Differ?

Even though the Roman Catholic theological system and that of Protestant theology share many commonalities, the two great traditions have many doctrinal disagreements. Broadly speaking, there are six areas of doctrinal differences.[1]

## Divine Revelation

The first area of disagreement concerns *divine, or special, revelation*. Though Catholics and Protestants alike agree that God reveals himself through general revelation and special revelation, the two traditions differ as to what constitutes that second type of revelation. According to Catholics, divine revelation (this is their preferred term for it) consists of both Scripture and Tradition. For Protestants, special revelation (this is their preferred term for it) is Scripture only.

According to the Catholic perspective, "Sacred Scripture is the speech of God as it is put down in writing under the breath of the Holy Spirit."[2] Tradition is the oral teaching that Jesus communicated to his disciples who, in turn, communicated it to their successors, the bishops of the church. Examples of Tradition are the two dogmas about Mary: her immaculate conception and bodily assumption. Importantly, the Catholic Church "does not derive her certainty about all revealed truths from the holy Scriptures alone. Both Scripture and Tradition must be accepted and honored with equal sentiments of devotion and reverence."[3]

---

1. For further discussion, see Gregg Allison and Chris Castaldo, *The Unfinished Reformation: What Unites and Divides Catholics and Protestants after 500 Years* (Grand Rapids: Zondervan, 2016), chaps. 3 and 4. Because I will address these differences in detail in subsequent questions, this question will describe them in broad terms.
2. CCC, 81.
3. Vatican Council II, *Dei Verbum*, 9.

By contrast, the formal principle of Protestantism is *sola Scriptura*: Scripture alone. This principle does not mean that the Bible is the only authority for Christians, but it is their ultimate authority for doctrine and practice. The principle includes an explicit rejection of the Roman Catholic view of Scripture plus Tradition.

## The Canon of Scripture

Second, Protestants and Catholics diverge over which books rightly belong in the Bible. The canon (not cannon) of Scripture refers to the list of the inspired, authoritative writings in the Old and New Testaments. Both traditions agree on the twenty-seven books of the New Testament. The difference appears, however, in the canon of the Old Testament. Protestants have thirty-nine writings:

- *The Law*: Genesis, Exodus, Leviticus, Numbers, and Deuteronomy
- *The Prophets*: Joshua, Judges, Ruth, 1 Samuel, 2 Samuel, 1 Kings, 2 Kings, Jeremiah, Lamentations, Ezekiel, Isaiah, Hosea, Joel, Amos, Obadiah, Jonah, Micah, Nahum, Habakkuk, Zephaniah, Haggai, Zechariah, Malachi, Job, Daniel, Ezra, Nehemiah, 1 Chronicles, 2 Chronicles, Esther
- *The Writings*: Psalms, Proverbs, Ecclesiastes, Song of Songs

In addition to these books, the Catholic Bible includes the apocryphal writings, or Apocrypha for short:

- *The Apocrypha*: Tobit, Judith, 1 Maccabees, 2 Maccabees, Wisdom of Solomon, Ecclesiasticus, Baruch, additional sections of Esther, and additional sections of Daniel

For various reasons (see Question 11), Protestants rejected the Apocrypha. Thus, since the Reformation, Protestant Bibles contain only thirty-nine writings in their Old Testament. Their rejection of the Apocrypha was condemned by the Council of Trent, which also declared the official version of the Bible to be the Latin Vulgate. Protestants do not have an official version but depend on the Hebrew Bible and the Greek New Testament as foundational for the Bible.

## The Nature of Scripture

The third divergence focuses on the question, What is the Bible? Whereas both Catholics and Protestants place great emphasis on Scripture, the two traditions disagree on some of its characteristics or attributes. This disagreement is not about the inspiration, truthfulness, and importance of Scripture, all of which Catholics and Protestants alike affirm. Rather, specific attributes of Scripture that are embraced by Protestants and not Catholics are authority, sufficiency, necessity, and clarity.

Certainly, the Catholic Church affirms the *authority* of the Word of God. But divine revelation for Catholics is not just Scripture, but Scripture plus Tradition. So, the written Word is *an* authority but it's not *the* authority (*sola Scriptura*) as held by Protestants. Because of this Scripture-plus-Tradition formula, the Catholic Church denies the sufficiency of Scripture.

According to Protestants, the *sufficiency* of Scripture means that it provides everything that nonbelievers need to be saved and everything believers need to please God fully. For Catholics, this sufficiency comes from Scripture and Tradition together. The Bible in and of itself is not sufficient for Catholic doctrine and practice.

The *necessity* of Scripture, as affirmed by Protestants, means that the church could not exist without the Word of God. If Scripture, being essential, were to vanish, the church would lose its way. By contrast, for Catholics, who do not affirm the necessity of Scripture, the Catholic Church could continue to exist even if Scripture were to disappear. This is the case because divine revelation consists not only of Scripture but Tradition as well. Thus, if Scripture were lost, the Church could not flourish but, being nourished by Tradition, could still exist.

Finally, the *clarity* of Scripture as affirmed by Protestants means that the Bible is understandable to all Christians. Because of this attribute, Protestant churches teach and encourage their members to read and study the Bible personally and in small groups. By contrast, the Catholic Church, denying the clarity of Scripture, specifies that the Magisterium possesses the right and duty to provide its proper interpretation. Certainly, the Church encourages its members to read and study the Bible, but their involvement in such reading and studying is significantly less than such activity in Protestant churches.

## Mary

The fourth area of disagreement between Catholics and Protestants is the doctrine of Mary. Before presenting the differences, it's good to note the commonalities. Both Catholics and Protestants affirm the virginal conception of Jesus. Both traditions bless her because Mary believed the angel's announcement that she would give birth to Jesus, who would save his people from their sins (Luke 1:46–55). And both Catholics and Protestants rightly look to her as a stellar model of the obedience of faith. She trusted that God would fulfill his promise to her, and all Christians desire to do similarly.

As for disagreements, there are several major areas that divide the two traditions. Catholics believe that Mary was immaculately conceived; that is, she was preserved from the stain of original sin from the moment of her conception.[4] Protestants deny this doctrine. Flowing from the immaculate conception is

---

4. The immaculate conception maintains that Mary was "preserved immune from all stain of original sin." Pope Pius IX, *Ineffabilis Deus*, December 8, 1854, https://www.papalencyclicals.net/pius09/p9ineff.htm.

the Catholic belief that Mary was sinless throughout her entire life. Protestants maintain that she, like all other human beings after the fall, was infected with original sin and actually sinned in common human ways. Because of their belief in Mary's immaculate conception and sinless life, Catholics maintain that she was full of grace and thus well prepared to cooperate with the divine plan for the incarnation of God the Son in her womb. Protestants object to this tendency to elevate her obedience of faith to a level of decisiveness, even to the point of making the divine plan dependent on her cooperation. Instead, Protestants underscore that her participation in the incarnation was the result of God's unmerited favor toward her and not grace plus her consent.

Catholics further hold that Mary enjoyed a particular understanding of Jesus's person and work during his earthly ministry. An example is Mary's intervention at the wedding at Cana, which Catholics interpret to be a type of intercession by Mary on behalf of humanity (John 2:1–11). Protestants counter that certain Gospel texts contradict this idealized portrait of Mary. Indeed, those texts present her like they present the apostles and others acquainted with Jesus—as largely misunderstanding and doubting him and his ministry. This misunderstanding is particularly acute when it comes to the Catholic view of her motherly suffering and sacrifice. While Catholics assign a central role to Mary in Jesus's saving death, Protestants fear that her (alleged) comediatorial role seriously detracts from his redemptive work. When Catholics translate this cooperative action into the belief that Mary is Mother of the Church, Protestants object that it attributes to Mary an undeserved role in the work and application of salvation.

Flowing from this overall theology of Mary is the Catholic doctrine of the bodily assumption of Mary, that "when the course of her earthly life was finished, [she] was taken up body and soul into heavenly glory."[5] Protestants point to the lack of any biblical evidence for this belief and object that Mary, like all other Christ-followers, died and now exists in the intermediate state as a disembodied believer. Finally, Mary's titles—Advocate, Helper, Benefactress, Mediatrix, and Queen—sum up well Catholic Mariology but are problematic for Protestants.

## The Church and Its Sacraments

The fifth and sixth areas of disagreement—the church and salvation—are perhaps those where the divergence between Protestants and Catholics is most evident. According to Catholicism, "there exists a single Church of Christ, which subsists in the Catholic Church, governed by the Successor of Peter and by the Bishops in communion with him."[6] Without denying that

---

5. Pope Pius XII, *Munificentissimus Deus*, November 1, 1950, 44. http://www.vatican.va/content/pius-xii/en/apost_constitutions/documents/hf_p-xii_apc_19501101_munificentis-simus-deus.html.
6. Cardinal Joseph Ratzinger, *Dominus Iesus*, August 6, 2000, 17, Vatican.va; Pope Benedict XVI, "Responses to Some Questions regarding Certain Aspects of the Doctrine of the

Protestants are Christians saved by Christ, Catholic theology does not consider them to gather in churches (there is only one true assembly, which is the Roman Catholic Church) but in ecclesial communities. Obviously, Protestants decry this demeaning view of their churches.

At the heart of the Catholic Church is the sacramental economy; that is, the Church transmits Christ's saving benefits by means of seven sacraments. By contrast, Protestants administer only two ordinances: baptism and the Lord's Supper. No Protestants believe that these sacraments are valid and effective *ex opere operato*, simply by the administration of the rites, as Catholics hold. Rather, Protestant theology closely aligns baptism and the Lord's Supper with the Word of God, the power of the Holy Spirit, and faith on the part of those who participate in them.

There is another major point of difference in regard to the sacraments/ordinances: their role in salvation. That divergence takes us to our sixth and last area of disagreement.

## Salvation

The ultimate goal of the Catholic Church and its sacramental economy is the salvation of the entire world. While Protestant churches also operate under a universal mission—Jesus's Great Commission for making disciples of all nations (Matt. 28:18–20)—they part company with the Catholic Church in their understanding of salvation.

Catholics maintain that salvation is a lifelong process. The journey begins with the sacrament of baptism and continues with the other sacraments. These rites provide an infusion of grace that transforms the nature of the Catholic faithful, thereby enabling them to engage in good works and merit eternal life.

For Catholics, justification is "not only the remission of sins, but also the sanctification and renewal of the interior man."[7] Salvation, then, combines forgiveness, regeneration, progress in holiness, and the loving performance of good deeds—it is a lifelong process. Because most Catholics will fall short of the purity they should have achieved in this earthly life, when they die, their soul goes to purgatory. By contrast, Protestants understand justification to be a divine declaration that sinful people are "not guilty" but "righteous instead." Grace, then, is not infused into people to transform their character so they can merit eternal life. Rather, the righteousness of Jesus Christ is imputed to them—credited to their account—such that they stand completely holy before God. Thus, according to the Protestant system, purgatory is completely unnecessary, because no further purification after death is needed—or possible.

Church," July 10, 2007, Vatican.va. The reference and citation are from John Paul II, *Ut Unum Sint*, 11.3, and Vatican Council II, *Lumen Gentium*, 8.

7. Council of Trent, Session 6, *Decree on Justification*, January 13, 1547, chap. 7. See the discussion in CCC, 1989.

## Summary

In Question 9 we rehearsed ten areas of commonalities between Catholics and Protestants. In this question we presented six areas of divergences. The two traditions have significant disagreements over the following: (1) divine or special revelation: Scripture plus Tradition, or Scripture only; (2) the canon of Scripture: thirty-nine Old Testament books plus the apocryphal writings, or the Old Testament without the Apocrypha; (3) the nature of Scripture: authority, sufficiency, necessity, and clarity as embraced by Protestants or denied by Catholics; (4) Mary: an exalted status associated with her immaculate conception, sinlessness, cooperative role in the Son's incarnation, intervention and solicitude on behalf of humanity, comediatorial work alongside the crucified Jesus, help as Mother of the Church, bodily assumption, and noble titles; or a measured respect for her; (5) the Church and its sacraments: the Roman Catholic Church as the only true church headed by the Magisterium and centered on the sacramental economy, or Protestant churches that are very far removed from such an ecclesiology; (6) salvation: a lifelong process (that could be extended after death to purgatory) featuring a collaborative effort between God and his grace and the Catholic faithful who engage in good works to merit eternal life; or a focus on justification as God's declaration of forgiveness and perfect standing before him, with no need for purgatory.

## REFLECTION QUESTIONS

1. Which of the areas of differences surprised you the most? Why?

2. Which of the areas was the least surprising? Why?

3. If you are more apt to emphasize the commonalities between Roman Catholics and Protestants, what should you take away from these six areas of divergence?

4. How are these areas of disagreement grounded on the foundations of the two churches, that is, the Catholic axioms of the nature-grace interdependence and the Christ-Church interconnection, and the Protestant principles of *sola Scriptura* and justification by grace alone in Christ alone through faith alone?

5. In respectful discussions with your friends who are of the other tradition than you, how can you appreciate the commonalities (the point of the last question) without overlooking the divergences (the point of this question)? That is, how can dialogue between Catholics and Protestants best take place?

# PART 2

# Theological Questions

# Questions about Revelation and Authority

Roman Catholics and Protestants alike affirm two forms of revelation, that is, God's self-disclosure so that people may know him and his ways. The first type is general revelation; the second is special, or divine, revelation. The focus of the next few questions is on the second form.

Two modes of divine revelation are divine acts and divine speech. As for the first, think of God's rescue of his people from enslavement in Egypt. He intervened mightily to save his chosen people. As for the second, and related to the first, is God's communication of the Ten Commandments to Moses. He spoke authoritatively to direct his people toward holy worship. While the stories of this mighty divine act and of the giving of the law originally circulated orally among the people, they were eventually recounted in the Pentateuch as written divine speech. Rightly so, then, Roman Catholic theology insists that divine revelation "is realized simultaneously 'by deeds and words which are intrinsically bound up with each other' and shed light on each other."[1]

## Transmission of Divine Revelation

Catholic theology further affirms that this divine revelation is transmitted through two modes: Tradition and Scripture.

This twofold pattern of communication is grounded in the two ways of preaching the gospel by the apostles, as commanded by Christ himself:

- "orally 'by the apostles who handed on, by the spoken word of their preaching, by the example they gave, by the institutions they established, what they themselves had received—whether from the lips of

---

1. CCC, 53; the citation is from Vatican Council II, *Dei Verbum*, 2.

Christ, from his way of life and his works, or whether they had learned it at the prompting of the Holy Spirit';

- in writing 'by those apostles and other men associated with the apostles who, under the inspiration of the same Holy Spirit, committed the message of salvation to writing.'"[2]

Thus, the first means of transmission is Tradition; the second is Scripture. To these modes of transmission, the Church adds its preservation: the Magisterium, or teaching office of the Church, ensures that this divine revelation in Tradition and Scripture is properly preserved and authoritatively taught through the pope and the bishops.

Roman Catholicism further explains that Tradition and Scripture "are bound closely together and communicate one with the other. For both of them, flowing out from the same divine well-spring, come together in some fashion to form one thing and move toward the same goal."[3] Thus, they are not two distinct sources of revelation but one fountain of two intimately joined modes of revelation. However, they should not be confused: "Tradition transmits in its entirety the Word of God which has been entrusted to the apostles by Christ the Lord and the Holy Spirit."[4] In a sense, this mode, Tradition, is the broader of the two and encompasses within itself the other mode, Scripture: "Sacred Scripture is the speech of God as it is put down in writing under the breath of the Holy Spirit."[5] In terms of the first, think of the immaculate conception of Mary. As for the second, think of Paul's letter to the Romans. Both means of divine revelation are essential and binding for the Catholic faithful. Indeed, the Church "does not derive her certainty about all revealed truths from the holy Scriptures alone. Both Scripture and Tradition must be accepted and honored with equal sentiments of devotion and reverence."[6] Accordingly, as the Catholic faithful are bound to affirm that "all have sinned and fall short of the glory of God" (Rom. 3:23), they are also bound to affirm that Mary was conceived without sin (and lived her entire life without sin).[7]

---

2. CCC, 76; both citations are from Vatican Council II, *Dei Verbum*, 7.
3. CCC, 80; the citation is from Vatican Council II, *Dei Verbum*, 9.
4. CCC, 81.
5. CCC, 81.
6. Vatican Council II, *Dei Verbum*, 9.
7. While Catholic theology has an explanation for this seeming contradiction, it grates against Protestant sentiments and is a key reason why Protestantism rejects Tradition as a means of divine revelation. At the same time, Protestantism does not reject tradition (small t) in the sense of wisdom from the past. Many Protestant churches embrace the rich legacy of valid biblical interpretation and sound theological formulation handed down from the early church and the medieval church. Examples include the Nicene-Constantinopolitan Creed and the Chalcedonian Creed, Protestant churches consider that tradition to enjoy presumptive authority as I sketch out in Gregg R. Allison, "The *Corpus Theologicum* of

## Magisterium

As for the role of the Magisterium, "the task of giving an authentic interpretation of the Word of God, whether in its written form or in the form of Tradition, has been entrusted to the living teaching office of the Church alone."[8] To expand a bit on its responsibilities, the Magisterium determines the canon—the list of authoritative writings—of Scripture and its official interpretation. Similarly, the Magisterium determines the content of Tradition and its official interpretation. For the Church, this tripartite structure of authority is divinely designed: "It is clear therefore that, in the supremely wise arrangement of God, sacred Tradition, Sacred Scripture and the Magisterium of the Church are so connected and associated that one of them cannot stand without the others. Working together, each in its own way, under the action of the one Holy Spirit, they all contribute effectively to the salvation of souls."[9] In other words, "just as the three poles of a three-legged stool provide support for whatever sits on it, these three elements provide divine revelation and its authoritative interpretation for the Church."[10]

We now turn to three specific questions about Scripture, Tradition, and the Magisterium.

the Church and Presumptive Authority," in *Revisioning, Renewing, and Rediscovering the Triune Center: Essays in Honor of Stanley J. Grenz*, eds. Derek Tidball, Brian Harris, and Jason S. Sexton (Eugene, OR: Wipf & Stock, 2014).

8. Vatican Council II, *Dei Verbum*, 10.
9. Vatican Council II, *Dei Verbum*, 10.
10. *RCTP*, 80.

# How Does the Catholic Church View Biblical Authority?

As just outlined, authority in the Roman Catholic Church resides in Scripture, Tradition, and the Magisterium. This question focuses on the first of these three matters, Scripture. We begin with the Church's view of the inspiration, the truthfulness (inerrancy), and the importance of Scripture because of broad agreement with Protestants concerning these characteristics of the Bible.

## Points of Agreement

*Inspiration*

In accordance with biblical teaching itself, Roman Catholic theology affirms that Scripture is inspired, or God-breathed (2 Tim. 3:16; 2 Peter 1:19–21; 3:15–17): "The divinely revealed realities, which are contained and presented in the text of Sacred Scripture, have been written down under the inspiration of the Holy Spirit."[1] At the same time, it affirms that Scripture was written by human authors, who were fully engaged in the process: "To compose the sacred books, God chose certain men who, all the while he employed them in this task, made full use of their own faculties and powers so that, though he acted in them and by them, it was as true authors that they consigned to writing whatever he wanted written, and no more."[2] Thus, the Catholic view of inspired Scripture avoids Docetism (Gr. *dokeō* = appears), the heresy— originally applied to the doctrine of Christ but appropriately extended to the doctrine of Scripture—that the Bible only *appears* to be written by human

---

1. Vatican Council II, *Dei Verbum*, November 18, 1965, 11.
2. Vatican Council II, *Dei Verbum*, 11.

authors. On the contrary, Scripture is dually authored, by God and by Moses, Isaiah, John, Paul, and the other authors.

Scripture is the inspired Word of God written in human words.

*Truthfulness (Inerrancy)*

Because it has the Holy Spirit for its author, inspired Scripture is also true: "Since therefore all that the inspired authors or sacred writers affirm should be regarded as affirmed by the Holy Spirit, we must acknowledge that the books of Scripture firmly, faithfully, and without error teach that truth which God, *for the sake of our salvation*, wished to see confided to the Sacred Scriptures."[3] The italicized section in this affirmation of Scripture's truthfulness is the cause of significant debate among Catholics.

One interpretation is that the phrase allows for the existence of errors in Scripture. On the one hand, the parts of Scripture that address matters of salvation are without error. Prophecies of the coming of Messiah, Gospel narratives of the life and ministry of Jesus, accounts of Jesus's death and resurrection, Paul's instructions about sin and redemption, and similar examples are truth-telling parts of the Bible. On the other hand, the parts that deal with, for example, the creation of the natural world, historical details, and genealogical lists may—or, do indeed—contain errors.

Two illustrations suffice: Mark's gospel (2:26) is wrong when it locates the event of David's eating of the sacred bread "in the time of Abiathar the high priest." In the Old Testament narrative of the event (1 Sam. 21:1–6), Ahimelech is identified as the priest. Thus, there is a contradiction in Scripture, but it is not in a part of the Bible that addresses salvation and thus is not worrisome. Additionally, the gospel of Matthew (27:9) incorrectly attributes a citation to the prophet Jeremiah. Scour as one may in that prophetic writing, no such statement can be found. Rather, the citation should have indicated the prophet Zechariah (11:12–13), though even that passage does not fit exactly either.[4] This is a concrete example of an error in Scripture, but again it is not in a section about salvation and thus is of no concern.

A second interpretation of the disputed phrase is that the statement as a whole rules out the presence of any error in Scripture. This view draws attention to the phrase "all that the inspired authors or sacred writers affirm should be regarded as affirmed by the Holy Spirit." Because everything the human authors wrote is affirmed by the divine author—who, because he is God, cannot lie—everything written in Scripture must be true. Nothing the biblical authors wrote can

---

3. Vatican Council II, *Dei Verbum*, 11 (italics added).
4. During the procedures at Vatican Council II (October 2, 1964), Cardinal Franz König of Austria pointed to these two examples as reasons why the Council could not affirm the inerrancy of all Scripture.

contain error.[5] This debate parallels the dispute among many Protestants, with some lining up in the noninerrantist camp and others in the inerrantist camp.

*Importance*

Additionally, the Catholic Church underscores the importance of Scripture. It appeals to the famous expression of Jerome (347–420)—"Ignorance of Scripture is ignorance of Christ"—to exhort the faithful to read the Bible frequently.[6] It insists that "the Church has always venerated the Scriptures as she venerates the Lord's Body. She never ceases to present to the faithful the bread of life, taken from the one table of God's Word and Christ's Body."[7] This reference is to the two parts of the Mass: the Liturgy of the Word and the Liturgy of the Eucharist. Together, they compose the "one table" of "the bread of life" on which the faithful feed for eternal life.[8] As Vatican Council II expressed, "Just as the life of the Church is strengthened through more frequent celebration of the Eucharistic mystery, similar[ly] we may hope for a new stimulus for the life of the Spirit from a growing reverence for the word of God, which 'lasts forever' (Is. 40:8; see 1 Peter 1:23–25)."[9]

Accordingly, there is broad agreement between Catholics and Protestants about the inspiration, truthfulness (inerrancy), and importance of Scripture.

As for the other aspects of the doctrine of Scripture, there is sharp disagreement. These are the canon, the sufficiency, the necessity, and the authority of the Bible.[10]

---

5. Other support for this position is a series of footnotes in *Dei Verbum*, 11. Cited in support of this section are Augustine, Thomas Aquinas, the Council of Trent, Pope Leo XIII's encyclical *Providentissimus Deus* (November 18, 1893), and Pope Pius XII's encyclical *Divino Afflante Spiritu* (September 30, 1943). The point is that all these sources held to the inerrancy of the whole of Scripture. For further discussion, see Cardinal Alois Grillmeier, "The Divine Inspiration and the Interpretation of Sacred Scripture," in *Commentary on the Documents of Vatican II*, vol. 3, ed. Herbert Vorgrimler (New York: Crossroad, 1989), 199–246.

6. CCC, 133; the citation is from Jerome, prologue to *Commentary on the Book of Isaiah* (*Patrologia Latina* 24, 17B). While this intimate connection between the incarnate Word of God, Jesus Christ, and the inspired Word of God, Scripture, is commonly emphasized, at times Catholic theology seems to drive a wedge between the two. An example is from the International Theological Commission: "The Church greatly venerates the Scriptures, but it is important to recognize that 'the Christian faith is not a "religion of the book"; Christianity is the "religion of the word of God," not of "a written and mute word, but of the incarnate and living Word."'" International Theological Commission, *Theology Today: Perspectives, Principles, and Criteria*, November 29, 2011, 7, Vatican.va; the citation is from *Verbum Domini*, 7.

7. Vatican Council II, *Dei Verbum*, 21.

8. As we will see later, this claim is more theoretical than actual.

9. Vatican Council II, *Dei Verbum*, 26.

10. I present the disagreement over the clarity of Scripture in Question 13 on the Magisterium.

## Points of Disagreement

*Canon*

By the *canon* of Scripture, we mean the list of divinely inspired writings that compose the Bible. The Roman Catholic canon differs from the Protestant canon. The divergence does not occur in the New Testament. Both traditions affirm the twenty-seven writings that have been considered canonical from early in the church's history. Rather, the difference appears in the Old Testament. While both canons include the thirty-nine writings that are found in the Protestant Old Testament, the Catholic canon includes additional materials. These are seven extra writings, called the Apocrypha: Tobit, Judith, 1 and 2 Maccabees, Wisdom of Solomon, Ecclesiasticus (Sirach), and Baruch. And the books of Esther and Daniel have additional sections.

How did this disparity between the two canons of Scripture develop? Since the close of its writing (about 435 B.C.), the Hebrew Bible has always contained the thirty-nine writings as found in the Protestant Bible.[11] However, the apocryphal writings were included in the Septuagint, a Greek translation of the Hebrew Bible that was used by Greek-speaking Jews who lived away from Palestine.

The early church did not consider the Apocrypha to be inspired, authoritative revelation. Indeed, key church leaders—for example, Melito of Sardis, Origen, Athanasius, and Jerome—explicitly denied that it belongs in the canon of the Old Testament. At the end of the fourth century, however, Augustine insisted that a new Latin version of the Bible include translations of the apocryphal writings. He maintained that the Septuagint (again, the translation of the Hebrew Bible) was inspired by God, as seen in the fact that the New Testament authors quoted from it; therefore, Augustine reasoned, the apocryphal writings, being contained in the Septuagint, must be divinely inspired and thus included in the canon of the church's Old Testament.[12] Against his better judgment, Jerome included those extra writings in his Latin Vulgate. Regional church councils approved the Old Testament with the Apocrypha.[13] Even then, key church leaders—John of Damascus, Hugh of St. Victor, John of Salisbury, and Venerable Bede—insisted that the Old Testament canon should not include the apocryphal writings.

At the time of the Reformation, Protestants such as Martin Luther and John Calvin argued against retaining the Apocrypha. They reasoned that if the Bible of Jesus and the apostles had been the (shorter) Hebrew Bible,

---

11. The numbering and arrangement of these writings is different in the Hebrew Bible, but it is made up of those books, and only those books.
12. Of note is the fact that the New Testament authors never quoted the Apocrypha.
13. The Council of Hippo (393), the Third Council of Carthage (397), and the Fourth Council of Carthage (419) approved the longer Old Testament canon.

then the church's Old Testament should not include the apocryphal writings. Moreover, they argued that key leaders in the early church had rejected the Apocrypha's inclusion in the Bible. Additionally, they exposed wrong doctrine and practice that was found in those writings. For example, the Catholic Church pointed to 2 Maccabees 12:38–45 to ground its doctrine of purgatory and its accompanying practices of indulgences, praying for the dead, and saying Masses for the dead. And the Church supported its theology of earning merits before God by appealing to the practice of almsgiving as set forth in Ecclesiasticus (29:12–13) and Tobit (4:7). Thus, since the Reformation, Protestant Bibles contain only thirty-nine writings in their Old Testament.

The Catholic Church responded aggressively to this Protestant challenge. The Council of Trent warned, "If anyone does not receive, as sacred and canonical, these books, with all their parts, as they have been read in the Catholic Church and as they are contained in the old Latin Vulgate edition, and knowingly and deliberately rejects the above mentioned traditions, let him be anathema."[14] Accordingly, a major divide between Roman Catholics and Protestants is the canon of Scripture. A further difference, again underscored at the Council of Trent, is the Catholic Church's insistence that the official version of the Bible is the Latin Vulgate.[15]

*Sufficiency*

Another point of divergence concerns the sufficiency of Scripture,

> an attribute of Scripture (in written form or orally transmitted) whereby it provides everything that non-Christians need to be saved, and everything Christians need to please God fully. However, Scripture is not absolutely sufficient; indeed, there is much about God that he chose not to reveal (Deut. 29:29). Rather, the sufficiency of Scripture is restricted to its purpose, which is instructing non-believers about salvation and training believers to be "equipped for every good work" (2 Tim. 3:16–17).[16]

Importantly, the sufficiency of Scripture and *sola Scriptura*—the Protestant formal principle of "Scripture alone"—are closely connected. Specifically, this principle of sufficiency stands against the Roman Catholic insistence that the Church "does not derive her certainty about all revealed truths from the holy

---

14. Council of Trent, Session 4, *Decree Concerning the Canonical Scriptures*, April 8, 1546, Papalencyclicals.net. The text has been rendered clearer.
15. Council of Trent, Session 4, *Decree Concerning the Edition, and the Use, of the Sacred Books*, April 8, 1546, Papalencyclicals.net.
16. Gregg R. Allison, *The Baker Compact Dictionary of Theological Terms* (Grand Rapids: Baker, 2016), s.v. "sufficiency of Scripture."

Scriptures alone. Both Scripture and Tradition must be accepted and honored with equal sentiments of devotion and reverence."[17] Thus, the Catholic view is Scripture plus Tradition, with the corollary that Scripture is not sufficient in terms of providing all divine revelation. The Protestant view is Scripture alone, with the corollary that it is sufficient to provide all divine revelation.

*Necessity*

Yet another point that distinguishes the two traditions is the necessity of Scripture,

> an attribute of Scripture (in written form or orally trans-
> mitted) whereby it is essential for knowing the way of salva-
> tion, for progressing in godliness, and for discerning God's
> will. Negatively, without Scripture, there can be no salvation,
> growth in holiness, and knowledge of God's will. However,
> Scripture is not absolutely necessary; indeed, before the Old
> Testament was written, people were saved, pleased God,
> and knew his will. Rather, there is a necessity conditioned
> on God's good pleasure to reveal his truth through a written
> Word. Without Scripture, people cannot have what God
> willed to reveal through Scripture.[18]

What is true of individuals is also true of the church: it "shall not live by bread alone, but by every word that comes from the mouth of God" (Matt. 4:4).

Contrast this Protestant perspective with the Catholic view. Because of its inclusion of Tradition as a means of divine revelation, the Catholic Church maintains that Scripture is not necessary for the *being*, or *existence*, of the Church. It would continue to exist without Scripture because it would still possess Tradition. Rather, the Church affirms that Scripture is necessary for the *wellbeing*, or *fullness of existence*, of the Church. Certainly, if Scripture would disappear, the Church would be hampered and not thrive as it should. So Scripture is necessary for its flourishing, but not for its existence. Protestants, however, insist that the Church would lose its way without Scripture.

*Authority*

A final matter over which the two traditions separate is the authority of Scripture,

---

17. Vatican Council II, *Dei Verbum*, 9.
18. Allison, *Baker Compact Dictionary of Theological Terms*, s.v. "necessity of Scripture." This definition makes a clear distinction between absolute necessity and contingent necessity. As all Protestants would affirm, the doctrine of the necessity of Scripture is of the latter, rather than the former, type.

a property of Scripture whereby it possesses the right to command what believers are to do and prohibit what they are not to do. Such authority is a corollary of inspiration: because God is its author, Scripture possesses divine authority. Evidences of biblical authority include the prophets' messages ("Thus says the Lord"), Jesus's attitude toward the Bible ("Scripture cannot be broken"; John 10:35), and Paul's consciousness of writing from divine imperative (1 Thess. 4:1–2).[19]

It is certainly true that Catholic theology agrees with this attribute, so the discord does not come with regard to the authority of *Scripture*. Rather, it is found in the Church's insistence on multiple authorities in relationship to divine revelation and its interpretation. In addition to the authority *of Scripture*, the Church relies on the authority of *Tradition* and the authority of *the Magisterium*. A good image for this structure is a three-legged stool. Remove one of the poles, and the structure collapses. Authority is not found in Scripture alone, as it is in Protestantism.

Two issues deserve our attention. One is the fact that multiple authorities are present almost everywhere. For example, citizens of the United States are under the authority of their federal, state, and local governments. Businesspeople are under the authority of their boss or, if they are the chief officer of a company, they are responsible to their board of directors. Children are under the authority of their parents. Church members are under the authority of their confessional statement, their constitution, and their leaders. In some denominations, there are authoritative structures above the local church authorities (for example, a presbytery, general assembly, or a national conference).

The point is that even Protestant churches have multiple authorities. Indeed, they do. And the principle of *sola Scriptura* does not contradict this point. Scripture alone does not mean there is *only* one authority. Rather, it means that Scripture is the *ultimate* authority. It is the supreme authority when it comes to matters of faith and practice. Thus, creeds, confessions, and statements of faith must yield to the authority of Scripture. Should it be demonstrated that a certain belief is contradicted by Scripture, the church must give up that belief. Moreover, Scripture is the final authority when it comes to human leaders. As a matter of course, Christians are expected to obey secular authorities. But if those authorities demand that Christians violate the will of God as revealed in Scripture, Christians must disobey. Church leaders are to be in submission to Scripture. Thus, their personal agendas and corporate preferences must give way to God's design for their church as revealed in Scripture. Accordingly, Scripture is not the *only* authority but the *ultimate* authority. This contrasts with the Catholic view that "the word of God is given

---

19. Allison, *Baker Compact Dictionary of Theological Terms*, s.v. "authority of Scripture."

to us in *sacred Scripture* as an inspired testimony to revelation; *together with the Church's living Tradition*, it constitutes the *supreme* rule of faith."[20]

Another issue is the inherent instability of any multiple-source authority. While the theoretical structure of the Catholic Church is a harmony between Scripture, Tradition, and the Magisterium, what happens practically when one or more disagrees with the other(s)? I've used the example of Scripture's teaching that "all have sinned and fall short of the glory of God" (Rom. 3:23) and the contrasting Roman Catholic belief that Mary was conceived without sin (and lived her entire life without sin). In the latter case, the Magisterium proclaimed a dogma, in accordance with Tradition, that is an exception—the only exception—to biblical teaching. Something had to give, and Scripture gave way. Indeed, any multiple-source authority structure like that of the Catholic Church is inherently unstable. Thus, the issue of authority is problematic for the multiple-source structure of the Catholic Church.

## Summary

We return to our original question: How does the Roman Catholic Church view biblical authority? Its tripartite structure is Scripture, Tradition, and the Magisterium. Accordingly, it disavows the Protestant principle of *sola Scriptura*. Scripture is *one* authority, and it is not the *ultimate* authority, as authority is shared among the three sources. Biblical authority is part of a larger structure of authority.

Roman Catholicism agrees with Protestantism that Scripture is inspired, truthful (inerrant), and important. However, the Catholic Church's doctrine of Scripture diverges from the Protestant view at the points of Scripture's canon, sufficiency, necessity, and authority.

## REFLECTION QUESTIONS

1. Why are the inspiration and truthfulness of Scripture such important doctrines? If Scripture were not God-breathed and true, or if only parts of Scripture were God-breathed and true (while other parts were not), what difference would it make in your life and church?

2. What are the key reasons for the Catholic Church's inclusion of the Apocrypha in its Old Testament? Why did the Reformers disagree with its inclusion? Why is this decision on the canonicity of Scripture such an important matter?

---

20. Benedict XVI, *Verbum Domini*, September 30, 2010, 18, Vatican.va (italics added).

3. Why is the sufficiency of Scripture a point of divergence for the two traditions? Why is its sufficiency such an important matter?

4. Why does the necessity of Scripture separate the two traditions? Why is its necessity such an important matter?

5. Why is the authority of Scripture a matter of division for the two traditions? Where have you seen the ultimate authority of Scripture take center stage, eclipsing other authorities? Do you have concerns about the inherent instability of the Roman Catholic authority structure of Scripture, Tradition, and the Magisterium?

# What Is Tradition in the Roman Catholic Church?

Authority in the Roman Catholic Church resides in Scripture, Tradition, and the Magisterium. This question focuses on the second of these three matters.

## Definition

In terms of a definition, Tradition is the teaching of Jesus Christ that he communicated orally to his apostles, who in turn transmitted that teaching orally to their successors, the bishops. Today, this teaching is nurtured and on occasion proclaimed officially by the Magisterium. Tradition is also the instruction that the apostles learned through the urging of the Holy Spirit, instruction that they in turn communicated to their successors and that is likewise fostered by the teaching office—the pope and the bishops—of the Church.

## Oral Transmission: Tradition

This oral transmission of Tradition corresponds to one of the two modes of gospel preaching in the early church. At that time, the message of Christ was communicated orally. Peter, John, Paul, and the other apostles were the leaders in preaching the gospel, planting churches, providing instructions for all the churches, and more. They orally passed on Jesus's Sermon on the Mount and narrated his suffering, crucifixion, burial, resurrection, and ascension. All this activity they carried out personally, communicating divine revelation orally as Tradition.

## Written Transmission: Scripture

Eventually, some of this apostolic teaching and admonition was written down. At this time divine revelation was transmitted under the inspiration of the Holy Spirit. Specifically, the apostles Peter, John, Paul, and Matthew, along with a few others connected with the apostles (Mark, Luke, James, Jude), authored the twenty-seven writings in the New Testament. Under the inspiration of the Holy Spirit, Matthew wrote the Sermon of the Mount in his gospel, and Paul explained how union with Christ identifies believers with him in his suffering, death, burial, resurrection, and ascension. This written form of divine revelation eventually became the canonical New Testament.[1]

## Oral and Written Transmission: Tradition and Scripture

For the Catholic Church, as it was then, so it is now. In the early church, divine revelation was communicated orally and eventually was written down. Today, divine revelation continues to be transmitted in two modes: orally as Tradition, and in writing as Scripture. Specifically, there is one "'Sacred deposit' of the faith (the *depositum fidei*), contained in Sacred Scripture and Tradition."[2]

The two should not be confused. "Tradition transmits in its entirety the Word of God which has been entrusted to the apostles by Christ the Lord and the Holy Spirit."[3] Tradition, then, is the broader of the two modes. It contains more than Scripture while encompassing the whole of Scripture. As for this mode, "Sacred Scripture is the speech of God as it is put down in writing under the breath of the Holy Spirit."[4] Importantly, then, the Church "does not derive her certainty about all revealed truths from the holy Scriptures alone. Both Scripture and Tradition must be accepted and honored with equal sentiments of devotion and reverence."[5]

## Magisterium

Additionally, this divine revelation is closely associated with the Magisterium. At the heart of this teaching office of the Church is apostolic succession, an unbroken line of authoritative leadership from Christ to his apostles to their successors, the bishops of Rome (embodied today in Pope Francis), who continue to convey it. As the Catechism states, "This living transmission, accomplished in the Holy Spirit, is called Tradition, since it is distinct from Sacred Scripture, though closely connected to it. Through Tradition, 'the Church, in her doctrine, life and worship, perpetuates and transmits to every generation all that she herself is, all that she believes.'"[6]

---

1. See also CCC, 83: "The Tradition here in question comes from the apostles and hands on what they received from Jesus' teaching and example and what they learned from the Holy Spirit. The first generation of Christians did not yet have a written New Testament, and the New Testament itself demonstrates the process of living Tradition."
2. CCC, 84; the citation is from Vatican Council II, *Dei Verbum*, 10.
3. CCC, 81.
4. CCC, 81.
5. Vatican Council II, *Dei Verbum*, 9.
6. CCC, 78; the citation is from Vatican Council II, *Dei Verbum*, 8.

Concrete examples are, from the early church, baptismal regeneration and infant baptism and, more recently, the immaculate conception of Mary and her bodily ascension.

The concept of Tradition appears to be quite elastic. For example:

> Vital components of Tradition are therefore: a constantly re-newed study of sacred Scripture, liturgical worship, attention to what the witnesses of faith have taught through the ages, catechesis fostering growth in faith, practical love of God and neighbor, structured ecclesial ministry and the service given by the magisterium to the Word of God. What is handed on comprises "everything that serves to make the People of God live their lives in holiness and increase their faith." The Church "in her doctrine, life and worship, perpetuates and transmits to every generation all that she herself is, all that she believes."[7]

Still, the Church has some sense of a limit to what can constitute it, distinguishing between *Tradition* and *traditions*:

> Tradition is to be distinguished from the various theological, disciplinary, liturgical or devotional traditions, born in the local churches over time. These are the particular forms, adapted to different places and times, in which the great Tradition is expressed. In the light of Tradition, these traditions can be retained, modified or even abandoned under the guidance of the Church's Magisterium.[8]

### Living Voice

This transmission of divine revelation in its two modes of Scripture and Tradition, in association with the Magisterium, signifies that God continues to speak to and through the Church today: "The Father's self-communication made through his Word in the Holy Spirit, remains present and active in the Church: 'God, who spoke in the past, continues to converse with the Spouse [the Church] of his beloved Son. And the Holy Spirit, through whom the living voice of the Gospel rings out in the Church—and through her in the world—leads believers to the full truth, and makes the Word of Christ dwell in them in all its richness.'"[9]

---

7. International Theological Commission, *Theology Today: Perspectives, Principles, and Criteria*, November 29, 2011, 26, Vatican.va; the citation is from *Dei Verbum*, 8.
8. CCC, 83.
9. CCC, 79; the citation is from Vatican Council II, *Dei Verbum*, 8.

Accordingly, Scripture, Tradition, and the Magisterium are the three elements in the structure of authority that supports and continues to nourish the Roman Catholic Church. The Protestant principle of *sola Scriptura* stands against this view and raises four specific concerns with Tradition.

## Protestant Concerns with Catholic Tradition

### Poor Biblical Support

The Catholic view of Tradition has poor biblical support. The Catholic Church appeals to Jesus's words to his disciples: "I still have many things to say to you, but you cannot bear them now" (John 16:12). The Catholic interpretation focuses on the disciples' inability to grasp all that Jesus wanted to teach them. To overcome this handicap, Christ chose to supply the church that the disciples would eventually lead with a living voice—Tradition—by which he (and the Holy Spirit) would continue to instruct his people. And they, as Jesus's apostles, would be the conduit for that ongoing transmission of divine revelation.

Protestants disagree with this interpretation. The "now" of Jesus's lament refers to the salvation-historical moment in which they lived: the time prior to his death, burial, resurrection, ascension, and outpouring of the Holy Spirit to give birth to the church on the day of Pentecost. Given their situation prior to these events, the disciples were not capable of absorbing all that Jesus desired to communicate to them.

> However, on the other side of those salvation-accomplishing and church-launching events, the disciples did indeed possess the Holy Spirit, who guided them into all the truth (John 16:13) and taught them all things and brought to their remembrance all that Jesus had said to them (John 14:26). In other words, the handicap that once prevented the disciples from receiving full revelation from Jesus—and the cause of his lament—had been removed. Nothing prevented them from writing this whole divine revelation [in the New Testament]. The disciples had no need for any supplemental body of oral communication—Tradition—that they were hindered from including in their writings because of their previous ignorance.[10]

Thus, the Catholic notion of Tradition is poorly grounded in Scripture.

---

10. *RCTP*, 83.

*Late Development of Tradition*

The concept of Tradition was a late development in church history. Admittedly, the Catholic Church points to biblical passages in which the word *tradition* occurs to support its notion of Tradition:

- "Now I commend you because you remember me in everything and maintain the *traditions* even as I delivered them to you." (1 Cor. 11:2)

- "So then, brothers, stand firm and hold to the *traditions* that you were taught by us, either by our *spoken word* or by our letter." (2 Thess. 2:15)

In this regard, Protestants agree with Catholics that the *form* of the earliest transmission of apostolic instruction—the *content*, represented here by Paul's teachings—was oral. But *form* and *content* are two different matters. There is no indication that what the apostles taught in oral form was materially any different from the content that they wrote, some of which became written Scripture.

This point is confirmed by the later witness of Irenaeus, an early church leader (in the last half of the second century). He wrote about the apostles, "through whom the gospel has come down to us, which they did *at one time proclaim in public*, and, *at a later period*, by the will of God, *handed down to us in the Scriptures*, to be the ground and pillar of our faith."[11] Irenaeus underscored that the apostolic teaching on salvation—the *content*—was transmitted in two *forms*, one oral, the other written. He gives no hint of an orally communicated Tradition that contains any content other than what the apostles communicated in written Scripture. Thus, there is tradition in terms of a *form* of transmission of divine revelation, not Tradition in terms of the *content* of divine revelation.[12]

The first appearance of the kind of Tradition that the Catholic Church embraces is quite late, in the fourteenth century. Only then did claims surface about some sort of divine revelation outside of or in addition to Scripture. Several examples suffice:

---

11. Irenaeus, *Against Heresies* 3.1.1, in *ANF* 1:414 (italics added).
12. Irenaeus, *Against Heresies*, 3.preface in *ANF* 1:414. This position was confirmed much later by Thomas Aquinas (thirteenth century). He affirmed that to do theology correctly, Scripture must reign supreme over early church writings: "Theology properly uses the authority of the canonical Scriptures as an incontrovertible proof, and the authority of the doctors of the church as one that may properly be used, yet merely as probable. For our faith rests upon the revelation made to the apostles and the prophets who wrote the canonical books, and not on the revelations (if any such there are) made to other doctors." Thomas Aquinas, *Summa Theologica* pt. 1, q. 1, art. 8. Thus, midway through the Middle Ages, leading theologians emphasized Scripture and seem to have no concept of Tradition as it developed later.

- "the doctrine and traditions of the apostles . . . outside of Scripture"[13]

- "the unwritten words of the apostles and their unwritten traditions that would belong to the canon of Scripture had they been written"[14]

- "such is the dignity of the apostolic traditions which did not transmit in the Scriptures, that the same veneration and the same fervent faith is due to them as to the written ones"[15]

This concept of Tradition, appearing in the fourteenth century, is significantly different from the notion of tradition present up to that point. It signifies that the formula *Scripture plus Tradition* as two means of divine revelation is a late development within the Roman Catholic Church.

## Instability of the Multiple Authority Structure

As Question 11 noted, any multiple authority structure is inherently unstable. If there are two bosses at work, if there are two lines of granting permission in an institution, if there are two experts weighing in on a decision, conflict between the two inevitably arises. The application is that when Scripture and Tradition are not in harmony, a clash occurs. Add to this a third authority—in the Church's case, its Magisterium—and the problem multiplies significantly.

I've already used the example of the conflict between Scripture's affirmation of universal sinfulness and Tradition's affirmation of the particular sinlessness of Mary. To take another example, Scripture affirms that at death, a believer experiences the separation of her immaterial aspect (soul or spirit) and her material aspect (body). Her body is laid in a grave or cremated, while her disembodied self enters immediately into the presence of the Lord in heaven. Along with all other believers, she awaits the resurrection of her body at the return of Jesus Christ.

Roman Catholic Tradition affirms that in the case of Mary, she did not experience such separation. Her body was not sloughed off and put in a tomb. Rather, she was assumed (taken) bodily into heaven. She entered immediately into the presence of the Lord as an embodied believer. Mary, and Mary alone, exists in this embodied state in heaven (which, by the way, is not a place for embodied people). She does not await the return of her Son and will not experience the resurrection of her body like all other believers.

---

13. Gerald of Bologna, *Commentary on the Sentences*, 457, cited in *RCTP*, 88.
14. Thomas Netter Waldensis, *Doctrinale Antiquatum Fidei Catholicae Ecclesiae*, chap. 23, cited in *RCTP*, 88.
15. Thomas Netter Waldensis, *Doctrinale Antiquatum Fidei Catholicae Ecclesiae*, chap. 23, cited in *RCTP*, 88.

Thus, Scripture affirms one thing while Tradition affirms something else. This inherent instability means that Tradition trumps Scripture, overturning its teaching.

*Denial of the Sufficiency, Necessity, and Authority of Scripture*

Question 11 further noted that, at several points, the Catholic doctrine of Tradition is at odds with the Protestant doctrine of Scripture. It contradicts the sufficiency of Scripture, insisting instead that divine revelation consists of both Scripture and Tradition. Scripture is not enough for the Church to acquire truth about God and his ways, for there is other divine revelation outside of Scripture that it must know and live. Furthermore, the Catholic view denies the necessity of Scripture. Rather, it insists that should Scripture disappear, the Church could still exist on the basis of the divine revelation it has through Tradition. Moreover, the Catholic doctrine of Tradition disagrees with the Protestant principle of *sola Scriptura*, that the Bible is the ultimate authority. Rather, the Catholic view maintains that the authority structure of the Church is threefold, consisting of Scripture, Tradition, and the Magisterium.[16]

## Summary

Tradition in the Roman Catholic Church is a second means of the transmission of divine revelation. It consists of the teaching that Jesus Christ communicated orally to his disciples, who in turn communicated it to their successors, the bishops of the church. Additionally, Tradition is the instruction that the Holy Spirit communicated to the apostles. Whether from Christ or the Holy Spirit, this teaching is nurtured and proclaimed officially by the Magisterium—the teaching office of the Church. Through this one "'Sacred deposit' of the faith (the *depositum fidei*), contained in Sacred Scripture and Tradition,"[17] God continually speaks to the Church today.

The formula *Scripture plus Tradition* is a major point of division between Roman Catholics and Protestants. The latter tradition has strong concerns about the Catholic doctrine of Tradition. These are its poor biblical support, its late development, the inherent instability of the multiple authority structure, and its conflict with the Protestant doctrines of the sufficiency, necessity, and authority of Scripture.

---

16. As Leonardo De Chirico explains, "The whole Roman Catholic Church is inherently involved in Tradition. In a sense, the Church is so immersed in Tradition that it cannot possibly be corrected by the Scriptures. The Church is so inextricably a part of Tradition that the Bible cannot be above the Church. Since the Bible is part of Tradition and the Church is also part of Tradition, the Bible is submitted to the Tradition of which the Church is the present-day and living voice." Leonardo De Chirico, "Scripture and Tradition in Today's Roman Catholic Theology," *Vatican Files* 33, March 13, 2012, http://vaticanfiles.org/en/2012/03/33-scripture-and-tradition-in-todays-roman-catholic-theology.
17. CCC, 84; the citation is from Vatican Council II, *Dei Verbum*, 10.

## REFLECTION QUESTIONS

1. If you are Roman Catholic, how do you view Tradition? Clearly, you can study Scripture, either alone or in Bible studies with others. Indeed, the Catholic Church encourages you to so do. If you were to want to study Tradition, how would you go about doing so? And, as in the case of Scripture, why is there no corresponding encouragement to study Tradition?

2. If you are Protestant, do you have concerns about Tradition other than those raised in this section?

3. How does the Catholic doctrine of Tradition contradict the Protestant doctrine of the sufficiency of Scripture? Why is its sufficiency such an important matter?

4. How does the Catholic doctrine of Tradition contradict the Protestant doctrine of the necessity of Scripture? Why is its necessity such an important matter?

5. How does the Catholic doctrine of Tradition contradict the Protestant doctrine of the authority of Scripture? Why is a sole source of authoritative divine revelation—*sola Scriptura*—such an important matter?

# What Is the Catholic Magisterium, and How Does It Exercise Authority?

A uthority in the Roman Catholic Church resides in Scripture, Tradition, and the Magisterium. This question focuses on the third of these three matters.

The Magisterium is the teaching office of the Roman Catholic Church and consists of the pope together with the bishops in communion with him. This association is often called "the college of bishops." At the apex of the hierarchical Roman Catholic structure, the Magisterium bears ultimate responsibility for teaching, sanctifying, and ruling the Catholic faithful. Moreover, it possesses the necessary authority to exercise its duties.

## Grounded in Apostolicity and Apostolic Succession

The Magisterium is grounded on the Church's attribute of apostolicity and its doctrine of apostolic succession. Specifically, the Church is apostolic in that it "continues to be taught, sanctified, and guided by the apostles until Christ's return, through their successors in pastoral office: the college of bishops, 'assisted by priests, in union with the successor of Peter, the Church's supreme pastor.'"[1] When Jesus promised to build his church upon the rock with the assurance that even the gates of hell would not prevail against it (Matt. 16:13–20), he established the church's apostolicity: Peter and the other apostles would be followed by their successors, the bishops, to whom Jesus would delegate his divine authority through Peter to guarantee the unceasing progress of his church.[2]

---

1. CCC, 857; the citation is from Vatican Council II, *Ad Gentes*, 5.
2. As *Lumen Gentium* further explains of Christ's apostles: "In order that the mission assigned to them might continue after their death, they passed on to their immediate cooperators, as it were, in the form of a testament, the duty of confirming and finishing the work

This structure of apostolic succession means that "just as the office granted individually to Peter, the first among the apostles, is permanent and is to be transmitted to his successors, so also the apostles' office of nurturing the Church is permanent, and is to be exercised without interruption by the sacred order of bishops. Therefore, . . . bishops by divine institution have succeeded to the place of the apostles, as shepherds of the Church, and he who hears them, hears Christ, and he who rejects them, rejects Christ and Him who sent Christ" (Luke 10:16).[3] Accordingly, it is through the Magisterium that the living voice of the gospel continues to resound in the Church.

### Magisterium's Responsibilities regarding Scripture and Tradition

The Magisterium bears various responsibilities in relationship to divine revelation. One duty is to determine "the Church's full canon of the sacred books."[4] Thus, the Council of Trent officially proclaimed that the Old Testament not only consists of the thirty-nine writings as found in Protestant Bibles but the apocryphal writings as well.

A second duty is to proclaim the content of Tradition. Examples include the Marian dogmas. In 1854 Pope Pius IX pronounced Mary's immaculate conception in his encyclical *Ineffabilis Deus*.[5] In 1950 Pope Pius XII declared her bodily assumption in his encyclical *Munificentissimus Deus*.[6] The Magisterium may at times clarify the Church's position on an issue. An example is the fate of unbaptized infants. The Church's "traditional teaching on this topic has concentrated on the theory of *limbo*, understood as a state which includes the souls of infants who die subject to original sin and without baptism. Therefore, they neither merit the beatific vision [they do not earn the right to see God directly], nor yet are subjected to any punishment [they do not earn the final destiny of hell], because they are not guilty of any personal sin."[7] This theory has never been officially sanctioned by the Magisterium as Catholic doctrine. Because divine revelation does not explicitly affirm it, and because the Magisterium has never defined it as a dogma, it is only a theory. Should the Magisterium proclaim this idea to be doctrine, then it shall be so, because the Magisterium determines the content of Tradition.

---

begun by themselves, recommending to [exhorting] them that they attend to the whole flock in which the Holy Spirit placed them to shepherd the Church of God. They therefore appointed such men, and gave them the order that, when they should have died, other approved men would take up their ministry." Vatican Council II, *Lumen Gentium*, 20.

3. The biblical reference is Luke 10:16. Vatican Council II, *Lumen Gentium*, 20.
4. Vatican Council II, *Dei Verbum*, 8.
5. Pope Pius IX, *Ineffabilis Deus*, December 8, 1854, https://www.papalencyclicals.net/pius09/p9ineff.htm.
6. Pope Pius XII, *Munificentissimus Deus*, November 1, 1950, Vatican.va.
7. International Theological Commission, *The Hope of Salvation for Infants Who Die without Being Baptized*, January 19, 2007, opening paragraphs, Vatican.va.

A third responsibility of the Magisterium is to interpret divine revelation. "'The task of giving an authentic interpretation of the Word of God, whether in its written form or in the form of Tradition, has been entrusted to the living teaching office of the Church alone. Its authority in this matter is exercised in the name of Jesus Christ.' This means that the task of interpretation has been entrusted to the bishops in communion with the successor of Peter, the Bishop of Rome."[8] As the Magisterium provides the official, authoritative interpretation of Scripture and Tradition, "the Church constantly moves forward toward the fullness of divine truth until the words of God reach their complete fulfillment in her."[9]

Thus, the Magisterium exercises its official responsibility to provide the authoritative interpretation of divine revelation. As it does, the Church recognizes that "this teaching office is not above the word of God, but serves it, teaching only what has been handed on, listening to it devoutly, guarding it scrupulously and explaining it faithfully in accord with a divine commission and with the help of the Holy Spirit."[10] As for their personal study of Scripture, the Catholic faithful acknowledge that any and all interpretations must be carried out "under the watchful care of the sacred teaching office of the Church."[11] Ultimately, then, all interpretations are "subject finally to the judgment of the Church, which carries out the divine commission and ministry of guarding and interpreting the word of God."[12]

To summarize, divine revelation, consisting of Scripture and Tradition, together with the Magisterium, form the threefold structure of authority for the Roman Catholic Church. As the Church itself affirms, "It is clear, therefore, that sacred tradition, Sacred Scripture and the teaching authority of the Church, in accord with God's most wise design, are so linked and joined together that one cannot stand without the others, and that all together and each in its own way under the action of the one Holy Spirit contribute effectively to the salvation of souls."[13]

From a Protestant perspective, there are five specific concerns with the Magisterium.

## Protestant Concerns about the Magisterium

### Lack of Biblical Support

The first concern is with the lack of biblical support for apostolicity and apostolic succession. Certainly, Protestants join with Catholics in affirming the

---

8. CCC, 86; the citation is from Vatican Council II, *Dei Verbum*, 10.
9. Vatican Council II, *Dei Verbum*, 8.
10. Vatican Council II, *Dei Verbum*, 10.
11. Vatican Council II, *Dei Verbum*, 23.
12. Vatican Council II, *Dei Verbum*, 12.
13. Vatican Council II, *Dei Verbum*, 10.

foundational role of the apostles. Jesus discipled his twelve apostles in preparation for their leading role in founding his church. The book of Acts narrates the pioneering missionary work of Peter, John, and Paul. Together with the prophets, the apostles constitute the foundation of the church (Eph. 2:20).

So, it is not regarding apostolicity per se that Protestants disagree with Catholics. Rather, it is with the concept of apostolicity as it developed over time within the Catholic Church that disagreement exists. Matthew 16:13–20, along with other key passages of Scripture (Matt. 28:18–20; Luke 24:44–48; John 20:1–23; 2 Cor. 5:17–21), do not envision a continuation of Christ's authority, centered on Peter and delegated to the apostles and their eventual successors. Neither do these passages provide a blueprint for Christ's authority being exercised through a hierarchically structured church with a teaching office at its apex.[14] Thus, the Catholic concept of apostolicity and its structure of apostolic succession lack a biblical foundation. Therefore, the notion of the Magisterium, which is grounded on apostolicity and apostolic succession, lacks a solid base.

### The Determination of the Canon of Scripture

A second concern focuses on the claim that the Magisterium possesses the prerogative to determine the canon of Scripture. Historically, this claim is not supported by the facts. For example, the claim presupposes that the church existed prior to Scripture and thus determines its canon. The claim, however, is incorrect. The Hebrew Bible, which eventually was incorporated into Christian Scripture as its Old Testament, existed for centuries before Christ and was the Word of God upon which the church was founded. Tied to this point is the fact that the Bible of Jesus and the disciples was the Hebrew Bible, which never included the apocryphal writings.[15]

As another example, the claim that the church officially decided on the canon of the Old Testament is not supported by the earliest lists of the biblical canon. Melito of Sardis, Origen, Cyril of Jerusalem, Athanasius, and Rufinus of Aquileia[16] listed the writings of the Old Testament considered to be canonical by the early church. Their lists were similar to the Hebrew Bible canon for almost every item, and with few exceptions, they did not contain the apocryphal writings.[17]

---

14. For further discussion, see *RCTP*, 181.
15. That the Hebrew Scripture was the Bible of Jesus is seen clearly in his description of it using the traditional order of its writings (Genesis is its first book; [2] Chronicles is its last book; Matt. 23:31–35) and his preaching from it in the synagogue (the scroll that he unrolled was the Hebrew scroll of Isaiah; Luke 4:16–21).
16. Rufinus (340–410) of Aquileia, *Commentary on the Apostolic Symbol* 37. *The Apostolic Symbol* refers to the Creed of Aquileia, which was similar in many ways to the Apostles' Creed.
17. "Melito of Sardis composed the first extant list of 'the books of the old covenant' (AD 170) and it included all the books of the Hebrew Bible with the exception of Esther but

These early lists demonstrate that the early church had an Old Testament canon that did not include the Apocrypha. Indeed, the church was decidedly against their inclusion in Scripture. At the end of the fourth century, Jerome, as the translator of the Hebrew Bible and Greek New Testament into the Latin Vulgate, was poised not to include these additional books in his work. He listed them as Wisdom (of Solomon), the Book of Jesus ben Sirach (Ecclesiasticus), Judith, Tobit, and 1 and 2 Maccabees.[18]

The eventual incorporation of the Apocrypha in the canon of the Old Testament centers on the intervention of Augustine. He prevailed in persuading his friend Jerome to translate the apocryphal writings and include them in the Vulgate. Augustine's significant limitations in Hebrew (and to a lesser extent Greek), together with his (mistaken) idea that the Holy Spirit "had spoken through both the writers of the Hebrew Bible and the translators of the Septuagint,"[19] led to his costly error of pushing for the inclusion of the apocryphal writings in the Old Testament canon. Even then, only regional councils, through the influence of Augustine, promoted their inclusion in any official manner. And disagreement continued within the church as certain leaders—for example, John of Damascus, Hugh of St. Victor, John of Salisbury, and Venerable Bede—insisted that the Old Testament without the Apocrypha is canonical Scripture.[20]

---

did not contain any of the apocryphal writings. The canon of Origen (died 254) corresponded to the Hebrew canon, with the exception that he included the Letter of Jeremiah. Athanasius, whose *Thirty-ninth Easter Letter* (AD 367) contains a list of both New Testament and Old Testament books, continued this tradition of mirroring the canon of the Hebrew Bible (though he included the Letter of Jeremiah and Baruch in his Old Testament list). Additionally, Athanasius rejected 'the Wisdom of Solomon, the Wisdom of Sirach [Ecclesiasticus], and Esther, and Judith, and Tobit,' though he pointed out that these books, while 'not indeed included in the canon,' had been 'appointed by the Fathers [the early church leaders] to be read by those who newly join us, and who wish for instruction in the word of godliness.' Cyril of Jerusalem listed twenty-two books in the Old Testament, corresponding to the writings of Hebrew Scripture, and warned, 'have nothing to do with the apocryphal writings. Study earnestly these only which we read openly in the church.'" *RCTP*, 101. For further discussion, see Gregg R. Allison, *Historical Theology: An Introduction to Christian Doctrine* (Grand Rapids: Zondervan, 2011), 37–50.

18. Jerome, "Preface to the Books of Samuel and Kings" (*NPNF*[2] 6:490).
19. Augustine, *The City of God* 18:43–44 (*NPNF*[1] 2:386–87).
20. John of Damascus (676–749), *Exposition of the Orthodox Faith* 4.17; Hugh of St. Victor (1096–1141), *De Scripturis et Scriptoribus Sacris* 6; *De Sacramentis Christiane Fidei*; John of Salisbury (1120–1180), *Letter* 143 (John to Count Henry of Champagne); Venerable Bede (672–735), *The Explanation of the Apocalypse* 4:8, in which he comments on the four creatures, each having six wings: "They raise the Church on high by the perfection of their doctrine. For the number six is called perfect, because it is the first which is made complete by its several parts, in that one which is the sixth part of six, and two which are the third, and three which are the half, make up the number six. Otherwise: the six wings of the four living creatures, which are twenty-four in number, intimate as many books of the Old

The authoritative proclamation of the canon of Scripture awaited the Council of Trent (1546): "If anyone does not receive, as sacred and canonical, these books, with all their parts, as they have been read in the Catholic Church and as they are contained in the old Latin Vulgate edition, and knowingly and deliberately rejects the above mentioned traditions, let him be anathema."[21] This official recognition of the canon is very late in coming and was acclaimed in contrast with the Protestant insistence that the apocryphal writings are not canonical Scripture. Part of the Protestant case was the early church's resistance to inclusion of the Apocrypha.

### The Magisterium's Authoritative Interpretation of Scripture

The third concern is with the Magisterium's prerogative to determine the authoritative interpretation of Scripture. One specific problem this raises is when its interpretation is not supported by a correct understanding of the words, grammar, history, literary type, and context of the passage. An example is the interpretation of Jesus's words to Mary in the narrative of the wedding at Cana. When Mary brings to Jesus's attention the fact that the wine has run out, "Jesus said to her, 'O woman, what have you to do with me? My hour has not yet come'" (John 2:3–4 RSV). In his encyclical *Redemptoris Mater*, Pope John Paul II admits that "the blunt statement" to Mary "his mother sounds like a refusal" on Jesus's part. However, the pope continues with an emphasis on the "deep understanding [that] existed between Jesus and his mother" resulting in her mediation between him and human needs and desires.[22] But this interpretation is certainly flawed. Jesus's question—literally, "what to me and to you?"—is an expression that distances him from Mary and bears a note of reproach. It is a mistake to pivot from a rebuke from Jesus to an escalation of Mary's importance and cooperation with him. Poor expositions such as this example undercut the Magisterium's claim to determine the authoritative interpretation of Scripture.

### Denial of the Clarity of Scripture

A fourth concern with the Magisterium is that its ultimate responsibility to interpret the Bible clashes with the Protestant doctrine of the clarity of Scripture. Clarity is

> a property of Scripture whereby it is clear and thus comprehensible to all Christians who possess the normal acquired

---

Testament, by which the authority of the Evangelist is supported, and their truth proved." My thanks to Any Messmer for his research on these writings.

21. Council of Trent, Session 4, *Decree Concerning the Canonical Scriptures*, April 8, 1546, Papalencyclicals.net. The text has been rendered clearer.
22. John Paul II, *Redemptoris Mater*, March 25, 1987, 21.

ability to read texts or understand oral communication (when Scripture is read to them). This clarity is true regardless of their gender, age, education, language, or cultural background, though it does not mean Scripture is necessarily easy to understand. This doctrine is affirmed in the context of the church, to which God has given pastors and teachers to assist members in better understanding Scripture. Moreover, its clarity means that unbelievers can gain some cognition of Scripture in general.[23]

The Roman Catholic Church, denying the clarity of Scripture, locates its proper interpretation in the Magisterium. Protestant churches champion Scripture's clarity and, accordingly, insist that their members read and study the Bible personally and in small groups, in addition to hearing it read and exposited in their worship services.[24]

## Summary

The Roman Catholic Magisterium is the teaching office of the Church and is responsible to teach, sanctify, and rule the Catholic faithful. It consists of the pope and the college of bishops. The Magisterium determines the canon of Scripture and the content of Tradition, and provides the official, authoritative interpretation of these two modes of divine revelation. These prerogatives raise numerous concerns for Protestants, including lack of biblical support, conflict with actual historical developments, misunderstandings of Scripture, and a denial of the clarity of Scripture.

## REFLECTION QUESTIONS

1. If you are Roman Catholic, how do you view the Magisterium? To what degree would you say it is authoritative for your Catholic faith and practice?

---

23. Gregg R. Allison, *The Baker Compact Dictionary of Theological Terms* (Grand Rapids: Baker, 2016), s.v. "clarity of Scripture."
24. This situation does not necessarily lead to interpretive chaos, a "this is what the Bible means to me" madness, with any and all understandings of Scripture being equally valid. Protestant churches (should) teach their members correct principles for interpreting the Bible. And, as noted above, they champion the clarity of Scripture within the context of their churches. Pastors, elders, teachers, and other leaders help members to gain a better understanding of the Bible. No, there is no pope and no magisterial authority to determine officially the meaning of Scripture. There is, instead, individual responsibility within the context of a local church. Yes, there is disagreement and division among Protestant churches. But how is that different from the reality of widespread diversity—the hyperconservatism of Opus Dei, the progressivism of Pope Francis—within the Catholic Church?

If you disagree with its pronouncements, why do you disagree, and how do you reconcile your dissent with the Magisterium's claim to authority?

2. If you are Protestant, do you have concerns about the Magisterium other than those raised in this chapter?

3. Why is it important to understand that the church did not precede Scripture, with the corollary that the church did not determine the canon of Scripture? What does the church express when it acknowledges that it is a recipient of Scripture rather than its determiner?

4. How does the Catholic view of the Magisterium clash with the Protestant doctrine of the clarity of Scripture? Why is Scripture's clarity such an important matter?

5. As we've pointed out, there is an inherent instability with any multiple-source theory of authority. With the threefold structure of the Roman Catholic Church, which of the three poles—Scripture, Tradition, or the Magisterium—seems to possess the highest authority when they are in tension? How is this problematic?

# What Does the Catholic Church Believe about the Infallibility of the Pope?

The word *infallibility* means "not liable to error." For example, many Protestants believe one of the attributes of Scripture is infallibility. Because God cannot err, and because Scripture is the Word of God, it is not capable of error. When the Roman Catholic Church applies the term *infallibility* to the pope, it makes the claim that, when he speaks under certain conditions, his doctrinal statement is not liable to error. Rather, it is true, authoritative, and not subject to revision.

## Medieval Debates

In the Middle Ages, the Church debated whether the gift of infallibility should be applied to the church as a whole or to the pope in particular. In favor of ecclesial infallibility, the claim was made that the church "cannot err in those things that are necessary for salvation, because at the time in which it would err in these things, it would no longer be holy."[1] In favor of papal infallibility was the claim that "in the determination of the things that pertain to faith, the pope is directed by the Holy Spirit and the Holy Spirit speaks in him."[2] Then there was the mediating, complementary claim that "where the supreme pontiff with the college of the lord cardinals or with a general council are gathered together in the Lord's name and on behalf of his faith, there is Christ, who is the truth without error."[3] So who or what is infallible? The Church? The pope? The pope together with the Church? Thus, the idea of papal infallibility circulated in the Church for many centuries.

---

1. John of Ragusa, *Oration on Communion under Both Kinds*, cited in Gregg R. Allison, *Historical Theology: An Introduction to Christian Doctrine* (Grand Rapids: Zondervan, 2011), 577.
2. Guido Terrena, *Questions on the Infallible Magisterium of the Roman Pontiff*, cited in Allison, *Historical Theology*, 577.
3. Terrena, *Roman Pontiff*, cited in Allison, *Historical Theology*, 577.

## Vatican Council I and Papal Infallibility

It was not until 1870 that Vatican Council I officially pronounced the dogma, or doctrine, of papal infallibility:

> We teach and define as a divinely revealed dogma that when the Roman pontiff speaks *ex cathedra*, that is, when, in the exercise of his office as shepherd and teacher of all Christians, in virtue of his supreme apostolic authority, he defines a doctrine concerning faith or morals to be held by the whole church, he possesses, by the divine assistance promised to him in blessed Peter, that infallibility which the divine Redeemer willed his church to enjoy in defining doctrine concerning faith or morals. Therefore, such definitions of the Roman pontiff are of themselves, and not by the consent of the church, irreformable.[4]

Papal infallibility operates under four conditions. First, the pope defines a universal doctrine concerning faith or morals. Thus, infallibility pertains to issues like the fate of the wicked in hell and homosexuality but not to ones like the theory of evolution and the evils and benefits of capitalism. Importantly, an infallible pronouncement is not new revelation but a divinely assisted exposition of the faith or morals already entrusted to the Church.[5]

Second, the pope speaks *ex cathedra*, literally from (*ex*) the chair (*cathedra*) of Peter. That is, he speaks with supreme authority as the successor of Peter, the vicar of Christ, the supreme teacher of the Roman Catholic Church. Third, infallibility is an ability possessed by the pope through God's help. This assistance was willed and promised by Christ to Peter and, through him, to his successors, the popes in Rome (Matt. 16:13–20). Fourth, papal pronouncements do not and cannot require the approval of the rest of the Church. Moreover, being infallible, they cannot be altered. This makes sense, as any statement that is not liable to error cannot be corrected for error.

Vatican I supported this doctrine with both historical precedence and biblical warrant. In terms of historical precedence, the council appealed to support from the Fourth Council of Constantinople (869–870), the Second Council of Lyon (1272–1274), and the Council of Florence (1431–1449). In reality, the statements from these councils do not directly address the doctrine of infallibility. Instead, they affirm the primacy and power of the Church of Rome and of the pope as the vicar of Christ. As for biblical support, Vatican

---

4. Vatican Council I, *First Dogmatic Constitution of the Church of Christ*, Session 4, July 18, 1870, Papalencyclicals.net.

5. As the statement explained, "The Holy Spirit was promised to the successors of Peter not so that they might, by his revelation, make known some new doctrine, but that, by his assistance, they might religiously guard and faithfully expound the revelation or deposit of faith transmitted by the apostles." Vatican Council I, *First Dogmatic Constitution of the Church of Christ*.

Council I cited Jesus's commission, "You are Peter, and on this rock I will build my church" (Matt. 16:18) and Jesus's promise to that disciple, "I have prayed for you that your faith may not fail. And you, when you have turned back, strengthen your brothers" (Luke 22:32). In both cases, the doctrine of papal infallibility is a significant distance from these grounds.

In summary, the dogma of papal infallibility was officially declared at Vatican Council I. Since that time, the popes have only undertaken one *ex cathedra* pronouncement: the dogma of the bodily assumption of Mary. Pope Pius XII proclaimed it in his encyclical *Munificentissimus Deus* (November 1, 1950).[6] It is an infallible papal statement that fulfills all four conditions.

## Vatican Council II and Papal Infallibility

To Vatican I's pronouncement of papal infallibility, Vatican Council II added:

> This is the infallibility which the Roman Pontiff, the head of the college of bishops, enjoys in virtue of his office, when, as the supreme shepherd and teacher of all the faithful, who confirms his brethren in their faith, by a definitive act he proclaims a doctrine of faith or morals. And therefore his definitions, of themselves, and not from the consent of the Church, are justly styled irreformable, since they are pronounced with the assistance of the Holy Spirit, promised to him in blessed Peter, and therefore they need no approval of others, nor do they allow an appeal to any other judgment. For then the Roman Pontiff is not pronouncing judgment as a private person, but as the supreme teacher of the universal Church, in whom the charism of infallibility of the Church itself is individually present, he is expounding or defending a doctrine of Catholic faith.[7]

Several elements should be noted. First, Vatican II closely associated the pope with the college of bishops, of which he is head. This connection is important, as later in this statement the council extends this gift of infallibility to the bishops as well: "The infallibility promised to the Church resides also in the body of Bishops, when that body exercises the supreme magisterium with the successor of Peter. To these definitions the assent of the Church can never be wanting, on account of the activity of that same Holy Spirit, by which the whole flock of Christ is preserved and progresses in unity of faith."[8] An example of such papal-collegial cooperation is an ecumenical council.[9]

---

6. See Pope Pius XII, *Munificentissimus Deus*, November 1, 1950, Vatican.va.
7. Vatican Council II, *Lumen Gentium*, November 21, 1964, 25, Vatican.va.
8. Vatican Council II, *Lumen Gentium*, November 21, 1964, 25, Vatican.va.
9. This point is specifically made by CCC, 891.

Second, infallibility is identified as a gift ("charism") conferred by the Holy Spirit. Specifically, infallible papal statements "are pronounced with the assistance of the Holy Spirit, promised to him in blessed Peter." Third, the council underscores the fact that any infallible announcement comes from the pope not acting in and of himself but as the head of the Roman Catholic Church. For example, when the pope makes a spontaneous, informal remark about atheists being saved if they do good, such a comment is his private judgment and does not constitute an authoritative, infallible doctrine about salvation.[10]

What is the nature of the authority that the Church claims for infallible papal pronouncements? As for the dogma itself, Vatican Council I warned that "should anyone, which God forbid, have the temerity to reject this definition of ours: let him be *anathema*."[11] Vatican Council II specified that all infallible proclamations are binding for the Catholic faithful. Such statements "must be adhered to with the obedience of faith."[12] Both the dogma itself and all *ex cathedra* pronouncements are maximally authoritative and obligatory.

## Critiques of Papal Infallibility

The dogma of papal infallibility is susceptible to three critiques. The first is the historical fact that the bishop of Rome has not always championed sound doctrine. Two examples from the early church are Vigilius, bishop of Rome from 537 to 555, and Honorius I, bishop from 625 to 638. Being swayed by the Empress Theodora, Vigilius apparently compromised the Chalcedonian Creed. The Second Council of Constantinople (553) addressed his compromised position.[13] Honorius I held to monothelitism, affirming that the Son of God, in becoming incarnate, possessed only one will.[14] Both the Third Council of Constantinople (680–681) and Pope Leo II (682–683) condemned the bishop as a heretic.[15] Accordingly, the Church's claim that the doctrine of papal infallibility is supported by the impeccable track record of sound doctrine of all the bishops of Rome is historically inaccurate.[16] If the claim that, in fact, the popes have been

---

10. Pope Francis made this remark in his daily homily, "No One Can Kill in God's Name," in the Chapel of Domus Sanctae Marthae on May 22, 2013, Vatican.va.
11. Vatican Council I, *First Dogmatic Constitution of the Church of Christ*, 4.9, Papalencyclicals.net.
12. Vatican Council II, *Lumen Gentium*, 25. The catechism explains that "this infallibility extends as far as the deposit of divine Revelation itself." CCC, 891.
13. The development of this episode in the life of Vigilius is quite complicated, with misunderstandings of his actual view contributing to the mystery; see "The Second Council of Constantinople, AD 553," Papalencyclicals.net.
14. "Monothelitism (from Gk. *monos*, 'one'; *thelēma*, 'will') holds that the incarnate Christ has only one will, that is, a divine will. The view does not formally contradict the Chalcedonian Creed's insistence that Christ has two distinct natures. But it does reject the idea of Christ possessing two wills as leading to a division in his person." Gregg R. Allison, *The Baker Compact Dictionary of Theological Terms* (Grand Rapids: Baker, 2016), s.v. "Monothelitism."
15. This is a case of one pope condemning another pope.
16. Roman Catholic apologists offer explanations for these anomalies.

infallible is put forward as a ground for the doctrine of papal infallibility, the ground is shaky and so is the doctrine.

Second, given that all events and circumstances occur in a context, the same is certainly true of Vatican Council I's dogmatic pronouncement of papal infallibility. We rightly ask, Why, after centuries of debate and affirmation of this issue, did the Council officially declare this doctrine at that time? It certainly seems to be late in coming. Besides religious factors, many other nonreligious reasons contributed to its definitive proclamation. Earlier in the century, the whole Roman Catholic Church had been severely shaken by the demise of the French Church during the Napoleonic Empire. The Church in Italy had wrongly stood against the Italian nationalistic movement, seemingly opposing its drive toward independence. At this time, the pope refused to join the Italian confederation's effort to free the papal states, clinging tightly and futilely to his vast, centuries-old holdings instead. Indeed, concordats, or papal agreements with other national rulers, conceded a significant amount of the Church's temporal holdings. Additionally, the rise of modern ideologies such as rationalism and socialism pummeled the Church, which adopted a strong defensive position. "Accordingly, the day after Vatican Council I had proclaimed papal teaching infallible, the Franco-Prussian war broke out, and within two months, the papacy was stripped of its vast lands. . . . In other words, the onslaught of many nonreligious factors fostered the promulgation of the doctrine of papal infallibility, which was in turn a defensive reaction to them."[17] The dogma sought to establish an unshakeable ground from which the Roman Catholic Church could confront these many assaults.[18]

A third critique of papal infallibility is that, nearly a century later, it led to the dogma of the bodily assumption of Mary. This is the only implementation of the doctrine of papal infallibility since its formulation in 1870. In Questions 32 and 33, we will see that this dogma is grounded on several unbiblical views and consequently is wrong. Thus, papal infallibility, which is claimed for the papal proclamation of Mary's bodily assumption, must also be wrong.

## Summary

The doctrine of papal infallibility was officially proclaimed by Vatican Council I in 1870 and affirmed by Vatican Council II. It states that when the pope, speaking *ex cathedra* in his authoritative capacity as the supreme teacher of the Roman Catholic Church, defines a universal doctrine concerning faith or morals, he is assisted (as Christ willed and promised) by the Holy Spirit's gift of infallibility. Accordingly, his pronouncement, which does not require the approval of the rest of the Church, cannot err nor be altered or revised,

---

17. *RCTP*, 196.
18. For further discussion, see Mark E. Powell, *Papal Infallibility: A Protestant Evaluation* (Grand Rapids: Eerdmans, 2009), 2–3.

and is binding for the Catholic faithful. Vatican Council II extended infallibility to the college of bishops when, with the pope, it exercises its authoritative teaching ministry in, for example, an ecumenical council.

Three critiques of the dogma of papal infallibility are the historical inaccuracy of the claim that popes have always promoted sound doctrine, the defensive nature of the papacy at the time that Vatican Council I proclaimed the dogma, and the unbiblical nature of Pope Pius XII's infallible definition of the bodily assumption of Mary.

## REFLECTION QUESTIONS

1. If you are a Protestant, how would you respond to a Roman Catholic who argues that without an infallible teacher, Protestant churches lose their way through interpretive chaos and doctrinal disarray? For example, the many conflicting understandings of biblical passages and contradictory formulations of doctrines that lead to so many divisions among Protestants clearly demonstrate how essential it is to have an infallible pope like the Catholic Church has. How would you reply?

2. If you are a Roman Catholic, what comfort or certainty does the dogma of papal infallibility engender in you? Given that the doctrine has been invoked only once—for the pronouncement of the dogma of the bodily assumption of Mary—does it seem to be as useful or valuable as perhaps Vatican Council I envisioned?

3. How does the doctrine of papal infallibility illustrate that authority in the Roman Catholic Church is threefold, consisting of Scripture, Tradition, and the Magisterium?

4. What is the nature of the certainty that we as Christians can have in this life—not the certainty of definitions ("all bachelors are unmarried males") or the certainty of mathematical formulas ($2 + 3 = 5$), but rather, the certainty of our faith? In answering this question, consider passages such as 1 John 5:11–13 and Romans 8:16.

5. Protestants and Roman Catholics have historically embraced the doctrine of the inerrancy of Scripture. So, even without an infallible pope, we have the infallible Word of God. What kind of assurance does this truth engender in you?

# Questions about the Church

In this second section, I explore questions about why the Roman Catholic Church claims to be the only true church of Jesus Christ, what takes place during a Catholic Mass, and how a person becomes a member of the Catholic Church.

# Why Does the Catholic Church Believe It Is the Only Church of Christ?

This belief has been around for a long time. To demonstrate that it continues to be the Church's belief, we turn to Vatican Council II's affirmation of the Roman Catholic Church as the one true Church of Jesus Christ:

> This is the one Church of Christ which in the Creed is professed as one, holy, catholic and apostolic, which our Savior, after his Resurrection, commissioned Peter to shepherd [John 21:17], and him and the other apostles to extend and direct with authority [Matt. 28:18–19], which he erected for all ages as "the pillar and mainstay of the truth" [1 Tim. 3:15]. This Church constituted and organized in the world as a society, subsists in the Catholic Church, which is governed by the successor of Peter and by the bishops in communion with him.[1]

As a reaffirmation of the Church's self-identity, how did this belief develop? We begin with a short history.

## History

The early church confessed itself to be characterized by four essential attributes: the church is one, holy, catholic (universal), and apostolic. Another

---

1. Vatican Council II, *Lumen Gentium*, November 21, 1964, 8, Vatican.va.

identity marker was attached to this description: the church is the mother of all the faithful. Indeed, "our one Father, God, lives; and so does our mother, the church."[2] As mother, "the church conceives those who flee to the Word," that is, it gives birth to children.[3] As mother, she "draws the children to herself; and we seek out our mother, the church.[4] As mother, "she nurses them with holy milk," that is, she nourishes them from infancy to adulthood.[5] Moreover, the church, as mother, becomes necessary as "there is no salvation outside of the church":[6]

> The spouse of Christ cannot be adulterous; she is uncorrupted and pure. She knows one home; she guards with chaste modesty the sanctity of one couch [bed]. She keeps us for God. She appoints the sons whom she has born for the kingdom. Whoever is separated from the church and is joined to an adulteress is separated from the promises of the church; nor can he who forsakes the church of Christ attain to the rewards of Christ. He is a stranger; he is profane; he is an enemy. He can no longer have God for his Father, who has not the church for his mother. If anyone could escape who was outside the ark of Noah, then he also may escape who shall be outside the church.[7]

The one, holy, catholic, and apostolic church, as mother, is necessary for salvation.

This position is called *exclusivism* because it holds to two points: (1) salvation has been accomplished objectively by the death and resurrection of Jesus Christ, and (2) explicit knowledge of the gospel of Christ and faith in him is necessary for people to embrace salvation subjectively. Exclusivism is the opposite of *inclusivism*, which affirms the first point but denies the second point: explicit knowledge of the gospel of Christ and faith in him is *not* necessary for people to embrace salvation subjectively.

Historically, the early church invoked this exclusivist position against splinter groups—for example, the Novatians and Albigensians—who claimed to be true churches over against the false church. Church councils stood by the position. For example, the Fourth Lateran Council (1215) proclaimed, "There is but one universal Church of the faithful, outside which

---

2. Tertullian, *On Monogamy* 7, in *ANF* 4:64.
3. Methodius, *The Banquet of the Ten Virgins* 7:4–6, in *ANF* 6:336.
4. Clement of Alexandria, *The Instructor* 1.5, in *ANF* 2:214.
5. Clement of Alexandria, *The Instructor* 1.6, in *ANF* 2:220.
6. Cyprian, *Letter* 72.21, in *ANF* 5:384.
7. Cyprian, *Treatise* 1.6, "On the Unity of the Church," in *ANF* 5:423.

no one at all is saved."[8] The Council of Florence (1441) professed "that none of those existing outside the Catholic Church—not only pagans, but also Jews and heretics and schismatics—can have a share in eternal life. Rather, they will go into the 'eternal fire that was prepared for the devil and his angels' (Matt. 25:41), unless before death they are joined to her. Moreover, so important is the unity of this Church that only those remaining within this unity can profit by the sacraments of the Church unto salvation."[9] Popes repeated this position when the church was threatened politically and militarily. For example, Boniface VIII declared, "We are compelled in virtue of our faith to believe and maintain that there is only one holy catholic Church, and that one is apostolic. . . . [outside of her] there is neither salvation and nor the remission of sins."[10]

As to be expected, the Catholic Church invoked its exclusivist position against proponents of the Reformation. For example, in response to the Protestant doctrine of justification by faith alone and not by the grace conferred through the Church's sacraments, the Council of Trent warned, "If anyone says that the sacraments . . . are not necessary for salvation but are superfluous, and that without them or without the desire of them men obtain from God through faith alone the grace of justification, . . . let him be anathema."[11] Indeed, among the one hundred and fifty threats of excommunication issued by the council, many of them at least implicitly condemned Protestants for their refusal to abide by the doctrines, sacraments, laws, and practices of the Catholic Church in which salvation can alone be found.

## Support for Roman Catholic Exclusivism

The Catholic Church supports its claim by various means. One avenue of support is its understanding of its own unity and catholicity, or all-encompassing unified nature. The Church is driven by its project of furthering its oneness and universality, seeking to address, influence, and incorporate the whole of reality. On the one hand, the Church already possesses this unity and catholicity: it is the "one . . . catholic . . . Church." On the other hand, God has given the Church the responsibility of increasing its oneness and universality by bringing the whole world under its realm. Armed with the firm conviction that its mission will be accomplished, that belief takes

---

8. Fourth Lateran Council (1215) 1, https://www.papalencyclicals.net/councils/ecum12-2. htm#1.
9. Pope Eugenio IV, *Cantate Domino* (Council of Florence, 1441). Latin edition, http://www. vatican.va/content/eugenius-iv/la/documents/bulla-cantate-domino-4-febr-1442.html.
10. Pope Boniface VIII, *Unam Sanctam* (1302), https://www.papalencyclicals.net/bon08/ b8unam.htm.
11. Council of Trent, Session 7, *Decree on the Sacraments*, March 3, 1547, "On the Sacraments in General," canon 4.

over and becomes its goal, with the key to this unity and universality—the Catholic Church—at its center.[12]

A second line of support comes from one of the axioms of Catholicism, the Christ-Church interconnection. This foundational principle maintains that the Roman Catholic Church is the continuation of the incarnation of Christ, such that the Church acts as another (or a second) person of Christ. The Church, then, is the mediator—the only Church of Christ—between God and all people of the world.[13]

A third support is the concept of *totus Christus*, the Church as the mystical body of the *whole Christ*. In short, the whole Christ refers to Christ as head, in the totality of his divine and human natures, together with his body, the Church.[14] If this concept is true, it makes sense that there is only one mystical body of Christ—the Roman Catholic Church—that mediates salvation to the entire world.

Fourth, if Christ is everywhere present, and if, according to early church leader Ignatius, "where there is Christ Jesus, there is the Catholic Church," then the Catholic Church is and must be everywhere present.[15] As the *totus Christus*, the Church possesses the fullness of the means of salvation, specifically, the true faith (the Creed), the liturgy with its sacraments (especially the Eucharist), and apostolic succession resulting in a true priesthood. It is to this Church, led by Peter and the apostles and their successors (the pope and the bishops with him), that Jesus issued this command to "make disciples of all nations" (Matt. 28:19). This Great Commission is universal in scope. Thus, each particular church (or diocese)—"a community of the Christian faithful in communion of faith and sacraments with their bishop ordained in apostolic succession"—is fully catholic through its communion with the Church of Rome.[16] Outside of this Roman Catholic Church, there can be no (fullness of) salvation: "the Father willed to call the whole of humanity together into his Son's Church. The Church is the place where humanity must rediscover its unity and salvation. The Church is 'the world reconciled.'"[17]

Unity and catholicity. The Christ-Church interconnection. The *totus Christus*. The fullness of salvation because of the true faith (the Creed), the

---

12. For further discussion, see Leonardo De Chirico, *Evangelical Theological Perspectives on Post-Vatican II Roman Catholicism*, Religions and Discourse 19 (Bern: Peter Lang, 2003), 197.
13. There is a parallel between Christ and the Church, which is the ongoing incarnation of Christ. Thus, Paul's affirmation "For there is one God, and there is one mediator between God and men, the man Christ Jesus" (1 Tim. 2:5) warrants the Church's idea that it is the mediator between God and all people. For further discussion, see De Chirico, *Evangelical Theological Perspectives*, 250.
14. See Question 7.
15. CCC, 830. The citation is taken from Ignatius, *Letter to the Smyrneans* 8 (shorter version; *ANF* 1:90).
16. CCC, 833, 834.
17. CCC, 845. The citation is taken from Augustine, *Sermon* 96.7.9.

sacraments (especially the Eucharist), and apostolic succession. These elements present the case for Catholic exclusivism with its claim that the Roman Catholic Church is the only true Church of Christ.

## Vatican Council II and Inclusivism

I focus now on our context. Vatican Council II affirmed, in its *Decree on Ecumenism* (*Unitatis Redintegratio*), that Protestants are "separated brothers" because they do not enjoy "full communion with the Catholic Church" due to their lack of apostolic succession, a true priesthood (through the sacrament of holy orders), and a true Eucharist (understood as transubstantiation). Still, this decree explained that "some and even very many of the significant elements and endowments which together go to build up and give life to the Church itself, can exist outside the visible boundaries of the Catholic Church," such as Scripture, grace, Spirit-granted virtues, and more.[18] Thus, the Church does not believe that Protestant bodies are devoid of "the mystery of salvation." On the contrary, it notes that the Holy Spirit "has not refrained from using them as means of salvation which derive their efficacy from the very fullness of grace and truth entrusted to the Catholic Church."[19] But in keeping with its traditional exclusivist position, the Church underscored for Protestants that "it is through Christ's Catholic Church alone, which is the universal help towards salvation, that the fullness of the means of salvation can be obtained."[20]

At the same time, Vatican Council II stretched—some would say contradicted—its traditional position to embrace an inclusivist perspective on the salvation of Jews, Muslims, Buddhists, Hindus, animists, agnostics, and even atheists. Think of a series of concentric circles. The Roman Catholic faithful belong in the innermost circle in the sense that they experience the fullness of salvation. Protestants and Eastern Orthodox believers are in the next circle, experiencing salvation but not its fullness. The adherents of other monotheistic religions and non-Christian religions belong in the circles further out. They may be saved by following the tenets of their religions. In the outermost circles are nonreligious people who, by living according to the dictates of their conscience, may also experience salvation in some degree. Confusingly, then, the Church that traditionally claimed "there is no salvation outside the Catholic Church" now claims that even people who never encounter the gospel of Jesus Christ and embrace the Catholic Church can be saved.[21]

---

18. Vatican Council II, *Unitatis Redintegratio*, November 21, 1964, 3.
19. Vatican Council II, *Unitatis Redintegratio*, 3.
20. Vatican Council II, *Unitatis Redintegratio*, 3.
21. Vatican Council II, *Lumen Gentium*, 14–16. At the same time, Vatican Council II cautioned, "But very often, deceived by the Evil One, men have become vain in their reasonings, have exchanged the truth of God for a lie and served the world rather than the Creator (cf. Rom. 1:21 and 25). Or else, living and dying in this world without God, they

The Church raises an important question: How is the traditional affirmation "outside the Church, there is no salvation" to be understood today? The Catechism of the Catholic Church states, "Re-formulated positively, it means that all salvation comes from Christ the Head through the Church which is his Body." Furthermore, the Church is "necessary for salvation" because "Christ himself explicitly asserted the necessity of faith and Baptism, and thereby affirmed at the same time the necessity of the Church. . . . Hence they could not be saved who, knowing that the Catholic Church was founded as necessary by God through Christ, would refuse either to enter it or to remain in it."[22] It offers this clarification: "This affirmation is not aimed at those who, through no fault of their own, do not know Christ and his Church."[23] The Church believes that sincere God seekers who, "moved by grace, try in their actions to do his will as they know it through the dictates of their conscience—those too may achieve eternal salvation."[24] What God accomplishes mysteriously in these cases does not and must not detract from the Church's obligation to reach out to all people with the gospel.

In summary, Vatican Council II moved the Church from its traditional exclusivist position to embrace an inclusivist position. It seems this is another case of the Church's ability as a big-tent institution to affirm what some would consider mutually contradictory positions.

## A Protestant Assessment

Historically, Protestant churches denounced the Church's traditional exclusivist position. Against the false Church of their day, the Reformers offered two marks of a true church: the right preaching of the Word of God and the proper administration of the Lord's Supper. Where these two marks are present, "there, it is not to be doubted, a church of God exists."[25] Given that the Catholic Church was overgrown by spiritual bankruptcy, priestly immorality, simony (the buying or selling of church offices), the selling of indulgences, neglect of Scripture, a magical view of the sacraments, compromise with secular authorities, and many other deep problems, the Reformers were frustrated in their attempts to renew the Church and thus launched their own true churches.

At the same time, Protestants like John Calvin were favorable toward the early church's descriptor of the church as mother. As he promoted the

---

are exposed to ultimate despair." Vatican Council II, *Lumen Gentium*, 16. Thus, though the Catholic Church embraces a pathway to salvation for adherents of non-Christian religions, it also acknowledges that the journey they must travel is wrought with grave difficulties.

22. CCC, 846. The citation is taken from Vatican Council II, *Lumen Gentium*, 14, with biblical support given as Mark 16:16 and John 3:5.
23. CCC, 847.
24. CCC, 847. The citation is taken from Vatican Council II, *Lumen Gentium*, 16.
25. John Calvin, *Institutes of the Christian Religion*, 4.1.9 (LCC 21:1023).

necessity of the church, Calvin approved of Cyprian's maxim: "He can no longer have God for his Father, who has not the church for his mother."[26] Like human beings need their mothers, so they need the church, "into whose bosom God is pleased to gather his sons, not only that they may be nourished by her help and ministry as long as they are infants and children, but also that they may be guided by her motherly care until they mature and at last reach the goal of faith."[27] Protestants, then, should embrace the Church as their mother: "For there is no other way to enter into life unless this mother conceive us in her womb, give us birth, nourish us at her breast. . . . Our weakness does not allow us to be dismissed from her school until we have been pupils all our lives. Furthermore, away from her bosom one cannot hope for any forgiveness of sins or any salvation. . . . It is always disastrous to leave the church."[28]

Additionally, many Protestants both disagree with and are confused by Vatican Council II's move to embrace inclusivism. They object to inclusivism because its second point—explicit knowledge of the gospel of Christ and faith in him is not necessary for people to embrace salvation subjectively—has no biblical support. Even more, Scripture contradicts the idea that faith in Christ through the gospel is not needed for salvation (e.g., Rom. 10:13–17).

Moreover, the church historically has never believed it. Specifically, the Catholic Church did not begin to entertain the idea that people can be saved apart from becoming Catholic until Pope Pius IX in 1863.[29] Even then, Vatican Council I did not include the idea, which did not appear again until Pope Pius XII's 1943 encyclical *The Mystical Body of Christ*.[30] Only after a lengthy development did Vatican Council II disseminate widely the inclusivist position.[31] But the point stands: inclusivism as Catholic theology

---

26. Cyprian, *Treatise* 1.6, "On the Unity of the Church" (*ANF* 5:423).
27. Calvin, *Institutes*, 4.1.1 (LCC 21:1012).
28. Calvin, *Institutes*, 4.1.4 (LCC 21:1016).
29. Pope Pius IX, *Quanto Conficiamur Moerore*, August 10, 1863, https://www.papalencyclicals.net/pius09/p9quanto.htm. Paragraph 7 is key: "Here, too, our beloved sons and venerable brothers, it is again necessary to mention and censure a very grave error entrapping some Catholics who believe that it is possible to arrive at eternal salvation although living in error and alienated from the true faith and Catholic unity. Such belief is certainly opposed to Catholic teaching. There are, of course, those who are struggling with invincible ignorance about our most holy religion. Sincerely observing the natural law and its precepts inscribed by God on all hearts and ready to obey God, they live honest lives and are able to attain eternal life by the efficacious virtue of divine light and grace. Because God knows, searches and clearly understands the minds, hearts, thoughts, and nature of all, his supreme kindness and clemency do not permit anyone at all who is not guilty of deliberate sin to suffer eternal punishments."
30. Pope Pius XII, *Mystici Corporis Christi*, June 29, 1943, Vatican.va.
31. Sullivan notes the conciliar contributions to the topic—*Lumen Gentium*, *Nostra Aetate*, *Ad Gentes*, and *Gaudium et Spes*. Additionally, he points to several post-conciliar documents—Pope Paul VI's *Evangelii Nuntiandi* and Pope John Paul II's *Redemptor Hominis*,

of the salvation of non-Christians is a novel belief and hence a betrayal of the Church's lengthy tradition.

## Summary

The Church's traditional position affirms that "there exists a single Church of Christ, which subsists in the Catholic Church, governed by the Successor of Peter and by the bishops in communion with him."[32] This belief goes back to Cyprian and his maxims "There is no salvation outside of the church"[33] and "He can no longer have God for his Father, who has not the church for his mother."[34] The Church has supported its conviction by various means including Augustine's notion of the *totus Christus* and the Church's possession of the fullness of salvation because of its true faith (the Creed), the sacraments (especially the Eucharist), and apostolic succession.

Vatican Council II introduced a novel idea that other Christian traditions (Eastern Orthodoxy and Protestantism), other monotheistic religions (Islam and Judaism), non-Christian religions (e.g., Buddhism and Hinduism), animists, agnostics, and even atheists can be saved. Many Protestant churches have denounced this inclusivist turn, maintaining that Scripture does not support it and the Catholic Church has historically not supported it either.


## REFLECTION QUESTIONS

1. How do you assess the Catholic Church's reformulation of its traditional belief that "outside the Church, there is no salvation" to mean that "all salvation comes from Christ the Head through the Church which is his Body?"

2. Is it confusing to you that (a) the Church claims to be "necessary for salvation" because "Christ himself explicitly asserted the necessity of faith and Baptism, and thereby affirmed at the same time the necessity of the Church," yet (b) it believes that people who have never heard the gospel and do not know anything about the Catholic Church can still be saved?

3. Though there is no feminine imagery or language in Scripture for the church as mother, how might Catholic theology make the case for this

---

*Dominum et Vivificantem, Redemptoris Missio, Ecclesia in Asia*—that continued its development in Catholic theology. Francis A. Sullivan, "Vatican II on the Salvation of Other Religions," in *After Vatican II: Trajectories and Hermeneutics*, ed. James L. Heft (Grand Rapids: Eerdmans, 2012), 77–88.

32. Vatican Council II, *Lumen Gentium*, 8.
33. Cyprian, *Letter* 72.21 (*ANF* 5:384).
34. Cyprian, *Treatise* 1.6, "On the Unity of the Church" (*ANF* 5:423).

descriptor? If you are Protestant, how do you assess John Calvin's approval of this descriptor?

4. Do you believe that the Catholic Church will succeed in actualizing its mission of bringing the entire world within its realm so that complete unity and catholicity will be realized? Why or why not?

5. When the Catholic Church claims to possess the fullness of the means of salvation—specifically, the true faith (the Creed), the liturgy with its sacraments (especially the Eucharist), and apostolic succession resulting in a true priesthood—what does such a claim mean for relationships between Catholics and Protestants, Catholic involvement in ecumenical dialogues, and cooperative efforts between Catholic and Protestant churches in combating social evils such as abortion, euthanasia, sexual immorality, restrictions on free speech and freedom of religion, and similar troubles?

# What Happens during a Roman Catholic Church Mass?

If you are a Catholic, you know personally the answer to this question. If you are a Protestant and have never been to a Catholic Mass, the following is a very brief description of what takes place. This description is followed by a brief commentary on the Mass from my Protestant perspective.

As the Mass begins, the priest and several lay leaders process from the back of the sanctuary to the front, walking in the nave or central isle.[1] They carry a sizeable crucifix (Christ on the cross), a large Bible, and a censer (to burn incense).[2]

In the introduction, the priest greets the Catholic faithful, then leads them in a penitential act in which they remember their sins and plead with God for mercy (the *Kyrie Eleison*): "Lord have mercy. Christ have mercy. Lord have mercy."[3] They then praise the triune God for his majesty, singing the *Gloria* ("Glory to God in the highest," from Luke 2:14). The priest offers the collect, an opening prayer that collects the intentions of the faithful and prepares them to hear the Word of God.

---

1. For simplicity's sake I will describe a Mass in which only one priest is engaged. Other masses may be celebrated by a bishop and/or concelebrated by multiple priests, multiple bishops, and multiple bishops and priests.
2. The following is adapted from Gregg R. Allison, "The Mass They Made: What Catholics Believe about Worship," DesiringGod.org, March 17, 2018, https://www.desiringgod.org/articles/the-mass-they-made.
3. As an example: "I confess to almighty God and to you, my brothers and sisters, that I have sinned through my own fault, in my thoughts and in my words, in what I have done and in what I have failed to do; and I ask blessed Mary, ever virgin, all the angels and saints, and you, my brothers and sisters, to pray for me to the Lord, our God." The priest prays, "May almighty God have mercy on us, forgive us our sins, and bring us to everlasting life," to which the faithful reply, "Lord have mercy, Christ have mercy, Lord have mercy."

## The Liturgy of the Word

This introduction leads into the Liturgy of the Word, the first movement of the Mass.[4] It features three readings of Scripture—the Old Testament, the New Testament, and the Gospel (a selection from one of the four Gospels). Interspersed with the first two readings is the singing of a psalm. The third reading is preceded by singing "Alleluia."

Following these readings of the Word, the priest delivers a homily—a short sermon (ideally) explaining the three readings. The congregation then confesses the faith by reciting one of the creeds (the Nicene or Apostles'). The participants also pray the Prayer of the Faithful, interceding for themselves, the Church, the world, those who suffer, and their local community.

## The Liturgy of the Eucharist

The second movement of the Mass is the Liturgy of the Eucharist. It begins with the *offertory* as two lay people bring bread and wine from the back of the sanctuary to the altar. These elements will be consecrated for the sacrament of the Eucharist. Another lay person brings the financial gifts for the support of the Church and the care of the poor. While these three people are coming forward, the priest prepares the altar for the celebration of the sacrament. For example, he leads the following interchange, saying, "Pray, my brothers and sisters, that our sacrifice may be acceptable to God, the almighty Father." The congregation responds, "May the Lord accept the sacrifice at your hands, for the praise and glory of his name, for our good, and the good of all his Church."

The "heart and summit of the celebration" is called the *anaphora* (Gr. "carrying up"),[5] referring to the kneeling of the Catholic faithful as the priest carries out his offering. After giving thanks to God the Father, the priest leads the congregation in singing the *Sanctus* ("Holy, Holy, Holy"). The priest then engages in the *epiclesis* (Gr. "calling on"), that is, he calls on the Father to send down the Holy Spirit to transform the bread and wine: "Be pleased, O God, we pray, to bless, acknowledge, and approve this offering in every respect; make it spiritual and acceptable, so that it may become for us the Body and Blood of your most beloved Son, our Lord Jesus Christ."[6]

Next, in the *institution narrative*, the priest recites the words that Jesus spoke when he instituted the Eucharist at the last supper (e.g., Matt. 26:26–29).

---

4. "Liturgy" simply means a structured or ordered service of worship. Protestant worship services are also liturgical, following a specified order of events like a call to worship, singing, reading Scripture, the sermon, prayers, and more.
5. CCC, 1352.
6. Roman Missal, Eucharistic Prayer 1; International Commission on English in the Liturgy, 88. A source for this epiclesis is Paul Turner, *At the Supper of the Lamb: A Pastoral and Theological Commentary on the Mass* (Chicago: Archdiocese of Chicago Liturgy Training Publications, 2010).

These are not the priest's words, but the Eucharistic words Jesus spoke, now directed as a prayer to God the Father. To illustrate with the element of the bread, the priest prays, "On the day before he was to suffer, he took bread in his holy and venerable hands, and with eyes raised to heaven to you, O God, his almighty Father, giving you thanks, he said the blessing, broke the bread and gave it to his disciples, saying, 'Take this all of you and eat of it, for this is my body which will be given up for you.'" A similar prayer is offered with the element of the wine. By these actions of Christ and the power of the Spirit, the bread is transubstantiated, or changed, into the body of Christ, and the wine is changed into the blood of Christ.

The anaphora is followed by the *anamnesis* (Gr. "recall"), which is the Church's remembrance of Christ's death, resurrection, and second coming. Next is the *oblation* by which the Church offers to the Father the pure, holy, and spotless victim, Jesus Christ. This is not a bloody sacrifice, but an unbloody one, a sacramental re-presentation of the sacrificial Lamb of God who was slain for sinful people. Appropriately, the congregation acknowledges its unworthiness through reciting the Lord's Prayer, by which they express their need for daily bread and the forgiveness of sin. The faithful then exchange the sign of peace, symbolizing their desire for unity and love.

Next, the priest breaks the bread, as Christ himself did when he instituted the Eucharist. He puts a piece of the wafer into the chalice of wine, symbolizing the unity of the body and blood of Christ for salvation. During the breaking of the bread, the faithful proclaim the *Agnus Dei*: "Lamb of God, you take away the sins of the world: have mercy on us. Lamb of God, you take away the sins of the world: have mercy on us. Lamb of God, you take away the sins of the world: grant us peace."

As the priest elevates the host for all to see, he says, "Behold the Lamb of God, behold him who takes away the sins of the world. Blessed are those called to the supper of the Lamb." The congregation responds, praying, "Lord, I am not worthy that you should enter under my roof, but only say the word and my soul shall be healed" (based on Matt. 8:8). The faithful then stream forward to consume the consecrated bread, which is "the Body of Christ," and drink the consecrated wine, which is "the Blood of Christ." Most commonly, they take the wafer in their hands; less commonly, they receive it on their tongue. They sip a bit of wine from the chalice. After both actions, they respond with "Amen." They return to their seats and join the rest in reflective silence.

The Mass concludes with two final elements. The priest pronounces a benediction, saying, "May almighty God bless you, the Father, the Son, and the Holy Spirit." He then announces, "Go forth, the Mass is ended." In Latin, the phrase is *Ite, missa est*, with the word *missa* implying "mission." This is the reason the Roman Catholic liturgy is called the Mass.

## A Commentary on the Mass

Several comments are in order. Despite its many changes over the course of many centuries, the Mass contains or reflects many traditional, standard elements. The prayers, songs, readings, recitation of the creed, administration of the Eucharist, and more have characterized worship services from the earliest days of Christianity. An attractive aspect of the Roman Catholic Church for some Protestants is its rootedness in antiquity.

At the same time, for centuries, the Roman Catholic Church so emphasized the sacrament of the Eucharist that the Mass essentially lacked attention to Scripture. Important, then, is the momentous change that Vatican Council II introduced with its insistence that the Mass must contain two movements: the Liturgy of the Word and the Liturgy of the Eucharist.[7] While by no means minimizing the second aspect, which had nearly choked out the first aspect, Vatican II insisted: "The two parts which, in a certain sense, go to make up the Mass, namely, the Liturgy of the Word and the eucharistic liturgy, are so closely connected with each other that they form but one single act of worship. Accordingly this sacred Synod strongly urges pastors of souls that, when instructing the faithful, they insistently teach them to take their part in the entire Mass."[8] Indeed, the council underscored that the faithful are nourished by both the table of the Word and the table of Christ's Body.[9]

While Protestants may be encouraged by these high ideals of Vatican II, they should also note that the implementation of the liturgical changes still has a long way to go.

Question 21 will go into more detail about the sacrament of the Eucharist. At this point, I simply call attention to the fact that Mass, particularly its second movement, emphasizes several elements: memorial, sacrifice, offering, and presence. Positively, Protestants and Catholics agree that the sacrament or ordinance is a commemorative celebration. As Paul explains,

> For I received from the Lord what I also passed on to you: On the night when he was betrayed, the Lord Jesus took bread, and when he had given thanks, broke it, and said, "This is my body, which is for you. Do this in remembrance of me." In the same way also he took the cup, after supper, and said, "This cup is the new covenant in my blood. Do this, as often as you drink it, in remembrance of me." For as often as you eat this bread and drink the cup, you proclaim the Lord's death until he comes. (1 Cor. 11:23–26 CSB)

---

7. Vatican Council II, *Sacrosanctum Concilium*, December 4, 1963.
8. Vatican Council II, *Sacrosanctum Concilium*, 56.
9. Vatican Council II, *Sacrosanctum Concilium*, 48, 51.

The Eucharist is a memorial rite.

Additionally, many Protestants and Catholics agree that, in some sense, Jesus Christ is present as the church celebrates this sacrament or ordinance. Again, as Paul highlights, "The cup of blessing that we bless, is it not a sharing in the blood of Christ? The bread that we break, is it not a sharing in the body of Christ? Because there is one bread, we who are many are one body, since all of us share the one bread" (1 Cor. 10:16–17 CSB). As the church engages in this rite, it participates (Gr. *koinonia* = "fellowship," "communion") in Christ and his body and blood, that is, his saving benefits.[10] This sacrament or ordinance symbolizes and fosters the unity of its participants in Christ and with one another.

Negatively, Protestants balk at the Catholic idea of the Mass as a sacrifice and an offering. I note two points: First, no Protestant church accepts the doctrine of transubstantiation, which is at the heart of the Catholic insistence that the Eucharist is a re-presentation of the sacrifice of Christ. No Scripture, rightly interpreted, supports it, including Jesus's words, "This is my body. . . . This is my blood of the covenant" (Matt. 26:26, 28). Whatever the nature of Christ's presence in the Lord's Supper may be, it is not that of the crucified Christ participating in the eternality of God and thus being made present during the Liturgy of the Eucharist.

Second, as I explain elsewhere,

> evangelical theology disagrees that the elements of this sacrament are offerings given to God. The critique of this idea focuses on the wrongness of the nature-grace interdependence: the idea that nature—in this case, bread and wine—possess a capacity to convey grace, which must be tangibly communicated through nature. Accordingly, in this sacrament, the natural elements of bread and wine are capable of being offered to God so that they will be transubstantiated into an embodied grace, the body and blood of Jesus Christ himself.[11]

Question 6 critiqued this principle of the nature-grace interdependence. Because the sacrament of the Eucharist is grounded on this foundational principle, the idea of the rite being an offering is flawed.

To sum up these two negative points: yes, Scripture uses the language of offering and sacrifice for various matters. Christians are commanded to offer themselves to God (Rom. 12:1–2). They are to make "a sacrifice of praise to

---

10. For further discussion, see Gregg R. Allison, *Sojourners and Strangers: The Doctrine of the Church* (Wheaton, IL: Crossway, 2012), 395–98.

11. *RCTP*, 323.

God, that is, the fruit of lips that acknowledge his name" (Heb. 13:15). Their good works are considered to be sacrifices (Heb. 13:16). Absent from this list is the idea of the sacrament of the Eucharist being an offering of the church to God.

## A Note on Protestant Participation in the Mass

If you are a Protestant, may you participate in a Catholic Mass? Observation is one matter. When I teach my course on Roman Catholicism, I take my students to a traditional Mass and to either a Latin Mass or a charismatic Mass. These field trips are for educational purposes. Participation in a Mass is another matter. If you go to a Mass, remember that you are not permitted to participate in the sacrament of the Eucharist. The primary reason is because the Catholic Church itself does not allow you. To do so would be to express a unity with the Church that does not in reality exist, thus contradicting Scripture (1 Cor. 10:17): "Because Catholics believe that the celebration of the Eucharist is a sign of the reality of the oneness of faith, life, and worship, members of those churches with whom we are not yet fully united are ordinarily not admitted to Communion."[12] Another reason for not participating is that you don't believe in transubstantiation, so it is dangerous for you to take the bread and the wine (1 Cor. 11:29). So, if you go to a Mass, observe and learn, but don't participate.

## Summary

The Catholic Mass consists of "two great parts that form a fundamental unity . . . 'one single act of worship'": the Liturgy of the Word and the Liturgy of the Eucharist.[13] The first movement features readings of Scripture, a homily, the confession of a creed, and prayers. The second movement focuses on the preparation for, and the administration of, the sacrament of the Eucharist. In actuality, the Liturgy of the Eucharist continues to hold prominent place in many Catholic Masses.

Positively, Protestants and Catholics agree that the sacrament of the Eucharist (or ordinance of the Lord's Supper) is a commemorative celebration. Additionally, many Protestants and Catholics generally agree about

---

12. US Conference of Catholic Bishops, "Guidelines for the Reception of Communion," November 14, 1996, https://www.usccb.org/prayer-and-worship/the-mass/order-of-mass/liturgy-of-the-eucharist/guidelines-for-the-reception-of-communion. There are exceptions: "Catholic ministers may lawfully administer these same sacraments to other Christians not in full communion with the Catholic Church, who cannot approach a minister of their own community and who spontaneously ask for them, provided that they demonstrate the Catholic faith in respect of these sacraments and are properly disposed." Code of Canon Law, 844. 4. https://www.vatican.va/archive/cod-iuris-canonici/eng/documents/cic_lib4-cann834-878_en.html.
13. CCC, 1346; the citation is from *Sacrosanctum Concilium*, 56.

some type of presence of Christ during the celebration of this sacrament or ordinance. Negatively, Protestants reject the Catholic view of the Mass as a sacrifice and an offering.

## REFLECTION QUESTIONS

1. If you are a Protestant and go to a Mass, what would you like to observe and learn? Why could you not participate in the Eucharist?

2. Why are Protestant churches usually quite different from Roman Catholic buildings? Why are they usually simpler, less elaborate? Why do they have the pulpit at the center rather than an altar? Why is there no tabernacle (a sacred box that contains the remaining Eucharistic elements by which Jesus continues to be present in the sanctuary)? Stations of the cross?

3. In contrast with the Catholic Mass and its focus on the Eucharist, why do Protestant worship services feature the preaching of the Word of God?

4. If you have Catholic friends and family members, why do they go to Mass? How often? What are the takeaways for them? Have they ever attended your church? What did they think of the worship service?

5. Are you familiar with the regulative principle of worship? It states that all the elements of a church's worship service must have biblical support for including them in the liturgy. Applying this principle of worship, how does the Catholic Mass stack up?

# How Does a Person Become a Member of the Roman Catholic Church?

The process of becoming a member of the Roman Catholic Church is different in the case of infants and the case of adults and, in the second case, whether one has or has not been baptized.

## Incorporation of Infants into the Church

In the Catholic view, infants become incorporated into Christ and his Church when they are baptized. Then, years after receiving the sacrament of baptism, they become full members of the Church through the sacrament of confirmation and the sacrament of the Eucharist. Confirmation confers upon them the fullness of the Holy Spirit, who propels them as full members to be on mission for the Church. The Eucharist nourishes them with the sacramental presence of Jesus Christ and provides grace for their pilgrimage of faith. Further assistance for this journey is provided by the sacraments of penance and reconciliation for the forgiveness of their mortal sins. Should they marry, they receive grace through the sacrament of matrimony. Men enter the priesthood through the sacrament of holy orders. When they are seriously ill or at the end of their life, the Catholic faithful are helped through the sacrament of the anointing of the sick.

## Rite of Christian Initiation of Adults

Returning to the sacraments of initiation—baptism, confirmation, and the Eucharist—participation in these three rites leads to membership in the Catholic Church for anyone over seven years old. The process is called the

Rite of Christian Initiation of Adults (RCIA).[1] There are two significantly different cases, depending on whether one has or has not been baptized.

*Unbaptized "Elect"*

The first case involves an unbaptized person. After expressing her interest in becoming a Catholic, she is enrolled into the order of catechumens through the Rite of Acceptance. She begins her preparation for baptism and thus for becoming a Christian. Over the course of at least one year, she learns Catholic doctrine and practice. On the first day of Lent, with the Rite of Election, her name is written in a book along with the names of others who will receive baptism. As an "elect," she affirms her desire, which is confirmed by the Church, to become a Christian. She is more deeply prepared for this important step through a series of three rituals. On the third, fourth, and fifty Sundays of Lent, these scrutinies (including an exorcism) prompt her toward further introspection and repentance. At Masses during the third and fifth weeks of Lent, the presentations of the Apostles' Creed and the Lord's Prayer—she recites these texts along with the congregation—further prepare her for baptism.

On the Saturday evening before Easter, at the Easter Vigil (other times are permitted), she participates in a Mass that administers the three sacraments of initiation. She is baptized, confirmed, then receives the Eucharist. She is now a Christian and a member of the Catholic Church. From Easter through Pentecost (in some cases, much longer)—the period of mystagogy—she undergoes further instruction in the Catholic faith.

*Baptized "Candidate"*

The process is different in the second case of a person who has been baptized. If validly baptized already, that is, in accordance with the traditional manner of administering this initiatory rite (with water, in the name of the triune God), the person becomes a member through a different process. The Catholic Church considers her to be a Christian already. Thus, she skips the phase of the catechumenate, not mixing with those who are unbaptized and thus not yet Christians. Indeed, she is not referred to as an "elect" but as a "candidate." If her instruction in the Christian faith has been minimal or nonexistent, and/or if she has not lived in a Christian manner, she receives much of the same training were she to be a catechumen. Still, she does not engage in the series of scrutinies. If her instruction in the Christian faith has been substantive, she only needs teaching in the Catholic tradition.

In either, case, as a baptized Christian, she must first participate in the sacrament of penance and reconciliation before receiving confirmation and

---

1. US Conference of Catholic Bishops, "Christian Initiation of Adults," http://www.usccb.org/beliefs-and-teachings/who-we-teach/rite-of-christian-initiation-of-adults.

the Eucharist. Moreover, she is not received into full communion of the Catholic Church at the Easter Vigil. This avoids confusing her as a baptized Christian with the candidates for baptism. It also avoids a possible misunderstanding of, or negative reflection upon, her baptism in a non-Catholic church.[2] During her reception, the priest administers the Profession of Faith. She says, "I believe and profess all that the holy Catholic Church believes, teaches, and proclaims to be revealed by God." Next, the priest says, "Deborah, the Lord receives you into the Catholic Church. His loving kindness has led you here, so that in the unity of the Holy Spirit you may have full communion with us in the faith that you have professed in the presence of his family." She then participates in the sacraments of confirmation and of the Eucharist. Her reception into full communion with the Catholic Church occurs during the Sunday Mass in her local parish.

## Summary

At the heart of membership in the Roman Catholic Church are the sacraments of initiation: baptism, confirmation, and the Eucharist. The process of becoming a member is different in the case of infants and the case of adults. Infants become members of the Church when they are baptized. Later, through the sacraments of confirmation and the Eucharist, they become fully incorporated into the Church. Those over the age of seven become members through the Rite of Christian Initiation of Adults. The membership process is different for unbaptized people and for those who have been baptized already. The unbaptized "elect" go through a lengthy, strenuous training. The "candidates," who are baptized already (and thus cannot be rebaptized), go through a streamlined preparation. In both cases, reception into membership must be preceded by participation in the sacrament of penance. Then, in the formal rite, the sacraments of initiation are celebrated. The "elect" participate in all three. The "candidates" participate only in confirmation and the Eucharist.

## REFLECTION QUESTIONS

1. Think about the fact that the Roman Catholic Church accepts all valid baptisms, including those administered by Lutheran churches, Anglican churches, Presbyterian churches, Methodist churches, Baptist churches, and more. What does this full acceptance say about the Catholic view of the sacrament of baptism?

---

2. US Conference of Catholic Bishops, *National Statutes for the Catechumenate*, November 11, 1986, 33.

2. What are the main differences between becoming a member of the Catholic Church when one is an infant and when one is over the age of seven? Why might there be a dividing line at that age?

3. What are the main differences between becoming a member of the Catholic Church when one has never been baptized and when one has been baptized? What about when one has had little or no instruction in the Christian faith and when one has received significant instruction? What can we learn about the Roman Catholic theology of salvation and the Church from these different categories?

4. In the case of candidates for reception into full communion in the Catholic Church, why are the sacrament of penance and the Profession of Faith so important in leading up to the sacraments of confirmation and of the Eucharist? What can we learn about the Roman Catholic theology of salvation and the Church from these preparatory steps?

5. What is the practice of your church in regard to people becoming members? In what ways is it similar to the various processes in the Roman Catholic Church? In what ways is it different?

# Questions about the Seven Sacraments

In this third section, I explore questions about the nature and centrality of the sacraments, why Roman Catholics have seven sacraments and Protestants have two, and what each of the seven sacraments is and does.

# What Is a Sacrament, and Why Are the Sacraments Central to Catholicism?

It is no exaggeration to say that the sacraments are at the heart of the Roman Catholic Church. The Catholic faithful know this to be true. Even most Protestants, when they consider the Catholic Church, think in terms of its sacraments.

## Definition

The idea of a sacrament goes back to Augustine (354–430). He defined a sacrament as a visible and tangible sign of an invisible yet real grace. To illustrate, elements of nature like water, oil, bread, and wine, through consecration by the Church, become capable of receiving and communicating divine grace as baptism, confirmation, and the Eucharist. As one of the foundational principles of Roman Catholic theology, this nature-grace interdependence is at the heart of the Catholic Church.

## Sacramental Economy

The name of this central reality is the *sacramental economy*. In this case, *economy* doesn't refer to a financial system but to "the communication (or 'dispensation') of the fruits of Christ's Paschal mystery in the celebration of the Church's 'sacramental liturgy.'"[1] *Christ's Paschal mystery* is his life, ministry, and mission to save sinful human beings. The fruits of his saving work are the benefits that are made available to the Catholic faithful through the liturgy. The *liturgy* is the work of the faithful cooperating with the work of God such that Christ "continues the work of our redemption in, with, and through

---

1. CCC, 1076.

the Church."[2] The liturgy includes proclamation of the gospel, engagement in good works, prayer, catechism, and above all, the sacraments.

*Sacramental* indicates that at the center of the Church's transmission of Christ's saving benefits are the seven sacraments. They are of three types. The three sacraments of initiation are baptism, confirmation, and the Eucharist. These three sacraments together are foundational for the Catholic faithful, who "are born anew by Baptism, strengthened by the sacrament of Confirmation, and receive in the Eucharist the food of eternal life."[3] There are two sacraments of healing: penance and reconciliation, and anointing of the sick. By these two sacraments "Christ has willed that his Church continue, in the power of the Holy Spirit, his work of healing and salvation, even among her own members."[4] The two sacraments at the service of communion are holy orders and matrimony. These rites "are directed towards the salvation of others . . . [and] confer a particular mission in the Church and serve to build up the people of God."[5]

Through these rites, the grace of God is infused into the faithful, thereby transforming their character and readying them to love and engage in good works so that they can merit salvation. Thus, they manifest the key principle of the nature-grace interdependence. Moreover, as it is the Catholic Church that administers the sacraments, the sacramental economy depends on the Christ-Church interconnection for its effectiveness and validity.

## Past Tense, Present Tense

This sacramental economy has two dimensions in terms of time: a past tense and a present tense. In terms of past tense, "as Redeemer and High Priest, Jesus Christ accomplished the salvation of fallen human beings through his Paschal mystery—his passion, death, burial, resurrection, and ascension—that occurred in history and that gave birth to the sacrament of the Church."[6] In terms of present tense, "as Redeemer and High Priest, Jesus Christ continues accomplishing the salvation of fallen human beings through his Church, with particular reference to the apostles and their successors—consisting of the pope and the college of bishops—who teach, govern, and sanctify the Church through the gospel, works of charity, and above all else, the seven sacraments."[7] Thus, the work of Christ has two temporal dimensions: what Christ accomplished and what Christ is accomplishing.

---

2. CCC, 1069.
3. CCC, 1212.
4. CCC, 1421.
5. CCC, 1534.
6. *RCTP*, 230.
7. *RCTP*, 230.

## Divine Agency, Human Agency

Additionally, this sacramental economy has two dimensions in terms of agency: a divine agency and a human agency. In terms of divine agency, Christ's work accomplished salvation through his Paschal mystery. That work is complete, sufficient, once-and-for-all, and finished.[8] There is nothing to be added to the divine dimension to make up something lacking in Christ's work on the cross.[9] In terms of human agency, Christ's work of accomplishing salvation continues through the Church's liturgy. That work is ongoing, progressive, expanding, already but not yet.

## The Work of the Triune God

In more detail, the liturgy is the work of the triune God. As the source of the liturgy, God the Father works to give a blessing. God the Son works "through the sacraments he instituted to communicate his grace."[10] As noted above, his work has a dual dimension in terms of time, both a past tense and a present tense:

> His Paschal mystery is a real event that occurred in our history, but it is unique: all other historical events happen once, and then they pass away, swallowed up in the past. The Paschal mystery of Christ, by contrast, cannot remain only in the past, because by his death he destroyed death, and all that Christ is—all that he did and suffered for all men—participates in the divine eternity, and so transcends all times while being made present in them all. The event of the Cross and Resurrection *abides* and draws everything toward life.[11]

In terms of past tense, Christ was crucified once and for all. This Good Friday event took place about two thousand years ago, and by it, Christ accomplished salvation. However, uniquely, unlike all other historical events, Christ's work cannot be contained by time, as past tense. Specifically, it shares in the divine attribute of eternality or atemporality. That is, God is eternal, not temporal. He exists outside of time and is present everywhere at all times—past, present, and future. So, too, with Christ's death on the cross. It cannot be an event that is locked into the past.

Thus, in terms of present tense, Christ's work of salvation is represented every time and in every place that the Church administers the sacrament of the Eucharist. Christ is not recrucified for the 3,483,092,195th time today at

---

8. CCC, 614, 618.
9. CCC, 529, describes it as "Christ's perfect and unique oblation on the cross."
10. CCC, 1084.
11. CCC, 1085.

one particular Mass. Rather, Christ's Paschal mystery is made present when the priest consecrates the elements of nature—bread and wine—so that they become sacramentally the body and blood of Christ.

This miracle of transubstantiation has particular reference to the work of God the Holy Spirit. He is the "artisan of 'God's masterpieces,' the sacraments."[12] In regard to the liturgy, the Spirit enables the Church to remember the work of Christ. On the one hand, the liturgy "is the *memorial* of the mystery of salvation" with the Holy Spirit as "the Church's living memory."[13] On the other hand, the liturgy is more than just remembering the events of Christ's work: it "actualizes them, makes them present. The Paschal mystery of Christ is celebrated, not repeated. In the celebrations that are repeated, and in each celebration, there is an outpouring of the Holy Spirit that makes the unique mystery present."[14] Indeed, the priest engages in the "*epiclesis* ('invocation upon') [which] is the intercession in which the priest begs the Father to send the Holy Spirit, the Sanctifier, so that the offerings [the bread and wine] may become the body and blood of Christ."[15]

Thus, the liturgy is the work of the triune God.

### Concerns about the Sacramental Economy

The mere fact that Protestants know of no corresponding element in their theology and churches raises an initial concern with the Catholic notion of the sacramental economy. Upon what biblical basis is this idea built? Is the deafening silence in the Protestant ranks indicative that this is another major area in which their forebearers separated from the Roman Catholic Church?

The answer to the first question is that not only is there a dearth of biblical support for the sacramental economy, but even more, some aspects of it run counter to Scripture. As for the answer to the second question, the silence does indeed point to the sacramental economy being a major Protestant point of departure from the Catholic Church. Our focus, however, will be on a few foundational problems with the sacramental economy.

### Connection to the Christ-Church Interconnection

One of the principles at the heart of Catholicism is the Christ-Church interconnection. Specifically, the Church considers itself to be the prolongation of the incarnation of Jesus Christ. Christ became incarnate two thousand years ago. Additionally, the Church continues that historical incarnation through its sacramental economy. This principle illustrates our above discussion of two dimensions in terms of time: a past tense and a present tense. Applying

---

12. CCC, 1092.
13. CCC, 1099.
14. CCC, 1104.
15. CCC, 1105.

this framework to the person of Christ, in terms of past tense, Christ became incarnate. In terms of present tense, the Church continues the incarnation of Christ.[16] Applying this framework to the work of Christ, in terms of past tense, Christ accomplished salvation through his passion, death, burial, and resurrection two thousand years ago. In terms of present tense, Christ continues to accomplish salvation through the Church's sacramental economy. As is true for the person of Christ, so for the work of Christ.

Question 8 critiqued the principle of the Christ-Church interconnection and found it to be wanting. Because the sacramental economy is grounded on that principle, it too is found wanting.

*Hapax and Mallon*

To put it another way, we turn to Leonardo De Chirico's presentation of "two biblical [Greek] adverbs which are linked to the concept of time: *hapax* (once and for all) and *mallon* (for evermore)." Theologically, he explains, "the terms refer to two important aspects of the work of the Trinitarian God in the world. The first (*hapax*) is circumscribed by time and is definitive in regards to the completion of the work of salvation. The other (*mallon*) proceeds throughout time and develops the outworking of salvation in history. The gospel is a message that is based on what God has done (*hapax*), and on what he is doing (*mallon*)."[17]

De Chirico maintains "that Roman Catholicism performed a crucial breach of the boundary between *hapax* and *mallon* with its understanding of the Church as a prolongation of the incarnation."[18] It is this blurring of the distinction between once and for all—Christ became (*hapax*) incarnate, and forevermore the Church continues (*mallon*) the incarnation of Christ—that is wrong. Moreover, the confusion has serious repercussions for other areas of Catholic theology and practice.

One such problematic consequence of this blurring of *hapax* and *mallon* is the sacramental economy, as De Chirico explains:

> Because the Church is involved in the time of the incarnation of the Son, it is also active in his redemption which is accomplished on the cross. Both the incarnation and redemption are

---

16. This affirmation by no means denies that Christ remains incarnate even now. Indeed, from the moment of his conception through eternity future, he is God the Son incarnate. What it disputes is the Christ-Church interconnection by which the Catholic Church is the ongoing incarnation of the incarnate Son.

17. Leonardo De Chirico, "The Blurring of Time Distinctions in Roman Catholicism," Vatican Files 123, April 18, 2016,, http://vaticanfiles.org/en/2016/04/123-the-blurring-of-time-distinctions-in-roman-catholicism/#_ftn2. De Chirico credits John Stott with the idea of the two adverbs. John Stott, *Evangelical Truth: A Personal Plea for Unity* (Leicester: Inter-Varsity, 1999).

18. De Chirico, "The Blurring of Time Distinctions."

> understood as *mallon* (for evermore) instead of *hapax* (once and for all). This transition is seen most clearly in the Roman Catholic doctrine of the Eucharist. The Eucharist is based on a twofold, co-existing assumption: On the one hand there is the acceptance of the unique, historical event of the cross. On the other hand is the necessity of the re-presentation of the same sacrifice by the Church. In other words, there is both the recognition of the exclusive role of Christ in his sacrifice, and the simultaneous insistence on the role of the Church in the act of re-presenting that same sacrifice.[19]

Accordingly, in terms of past tense or *hapax*, Christ accomplished salvation through his once-and-for-all, finished work on the cross as our atoning sacrifice. In terms of present tense or *mallon*, Christ continues to accomplish salvation through the sacramental economy of the Roman Catholic Church, with particular focus on the sacrament in general and the sacrament of the Eucharist in particular.

Thus, a chief concern with the sacramental economy underscores the Christ-Church interconnection at its foundation. The result is that the salvation that Christ once-and-for-all accomplished (*hapax*, in the past) continues through the present extension (*mallon*, today) of that salvation by the Church's sacraments in general and, in particular, the Eucharist.

## Transference of Divine Prerogatives to the Church

Another concern is that the sacramental economy is a system that transfers prerogatives that solely belong to Christ, as head of his body, to the Catholic Church. And this transference is not merely a matter of delegation of authority and responsibility. On the contrary, the Catholic view is that these acts are ones that Christ allocates to human ministers that he deputizes "to act in the person of Christ."

However, Protestants understand that "the ministerial acts of Jesus Christ by the Spirit, by which he gathers, protects, and preserves the church, are, properly speaking, incommunicable [non-transferable] and non-representable. . . . Christ distributes his own benefits through his Spirit, that is, by his own hand; they are not to be thought of as some treasure turned over to the church for it to dispense."[20] These acts include his attendance with his body as it gathers to worship the triune God, his presence as his followers participate rightly in his blood and body at celebrations of the Eucharist (1 Cor. 10:16), his judgment of improper observations of the Lord's Supper (1 Cor.

---

19. De Chirico, "The Blurring of Time Distinctions."
20. John Webster, *Word and Church: Essays in Christian Dogmatics* (New York: T&T Clark, 2001), 199–200.

11:27–34), his granting of absolution when his wayward people confess their sins, his accompaniment of this disciples as they embark on mission (Matt. 28:18–20), and more. These acts, as promised in Scripture, belong to Christ and Christ alone and are wrought through the Holy Spirit, whose temple the church is (1 Cor. 3:10–15).

So as not to be misunderstood, the above position does not negate the important role of human ministers in Christ's church. Indeed, he chose twelve apostles (Matt. 10:1–4), who in turn appointed elders/bishops/pastors (Acts 14:23; 1 Tim. 3:1–7; Titus 1:5–9; 1 Peter 5:1–5), who were joined by deacons (Phil. 1:1; Acts 6:1–7). These officers constitute the human leadership of the church. As John Webster explains, "For although the acts of Christ are incommunicable, non-representable, Christ himself freely chooses to represent himself through human ministry. . . . He is not delivered into the hands of his servants, who remain entirely at his disposal. But in his lordly freedom, he elects that alongside his triumphant self-manifestation there should also be human service in the church."[21] This service through human ministers is categorically different from the sacramental economy as conceived by the Catholic Church.

## Summary

At the heart of the Roman Catholic Church are its sacraments, which are visible and tangible signs of an invisible yet real grace. The sacramental economy is the core structure by which the Church transmits the benefits of Christ's saving work to the Catholic faithful. It has both a divine dimension, what Christ did to accomplish salvation; and a human dimension, what the Church continues to do to transmit this salvation. Moreover, the sacramental economy has two dimensions in terms of time: a past tense and a present tense, or *hapax* (once and for all) and *mallon* (for evermore). It is based on the Christ-Church interconnection, with this importance for the person of Christ: his incarnation was a once-and-for-all (*hapax*) event in the past, yet the Roman Catholic Church self-identifies as the continuous (*mallon*) incarnation of Christ in the present. This has importance for the work of Christ: his work of salvation was a once-and-for-all (*hapax*) event in the past, yet the Catholic Church claims that Christ's work continues (*mallon*) through its sacramental economy in the present. What Christ's salvation accomplished (past tense) continues as he accomplishes salvation (present tense) through the Church and its sacramental economy.

Accordingly, there are two concerns. First, the sacramental system at the heart of the Roman Catholic Church is grounded on the Christ-Church interconnection. Second, the sacramental economy is based on the idea that Christ transferred prerogatives, which belong solely to him, to the Catholic Church.

---

21. Webster, *Word and Church*, 200.

## REFLECTION QUESTIONS

1. What is your assessment of the definition of "sacrament"? If you are Catholic, is this the way you view your seven sacraments? If you are Protestant, is this the way you view your two sacraments (or ordinances)?

2. How does the sacramental economy illustrate the Christ-Church interconnection? How does my critique of that principle affect the sacramental economy?

3. Why do Protestants believe it is so important to maintain the separation between Christ's accomplishment of your salvation two thousand years ago (past tense, *hapax*) and the application of Christ's salvation in your life today (present tense, *mallon*)?

4. Why do Protestants believe it is so important to distinguish between the acts of Christ that belong solely to him and cannot be transferred to the church, and those human ministries of service to which he calls his church?

5. Do you have concerns other than the ones discussed above with the Catholic sacramental economy?

# Why Do Catholics Celebrate Seven Sacraments and Protestants Only Two?

A significant distance separates the Catholic Church's understanding of its sacraments and the various Protestant churches' understanding of their sacraments or ordinances. The following discussion rehearses four issues: the proper name for these rites, the correct number of these rites, the right ground of their effectiveness and validity, and the true nature of these rites.

### Terminology: Sacraments or Ordinances?

As for their correct terminology, the word *sacrament* is used by the Catholic Church as well as by many Protestant churches. Examples include Lutheran, Anglican, Reformed, and Methodist churches. A sacrament is, according to the classical definition of Augustine, a visible and tangible sign of an invisible yet real grace. As to the nature of that grace, I withhold discussion for later. When using the term *sacrament*, both the Catholic Church and Protestant churches who adopt this terminology agree that these are means of grace given by Christ to his church and are thus to be administered faithfully.

Other churches that arose from Protestantism use the word *ordinance* for these Christian rites. Examples include Anabaptist, Baptist, and Pentecostal churches. Historically, as these churches moved away from the Catholic Church, they sought to distance themselves from the Church and its sacramental system by adopting a different name for these rites. Seeing that these rites were ordained by Christ, the name *ordinance* emerged.

Regardless of whether they refer to these rites as sacraments or ordinances, all Protestant churches administer baptism and the Lord's Supper. This point is the topic of the next discussion.

## Number of Sacraments/Ordinances

This last point is a key factor in the difference in the number of the sacraments: which rites did Christ ordain, that is, give to his church by way of command to celebrate? An additional factor goes to the very notion of a sacrament as something visible and tangible: which rites have a sign associated with them?

The Catholic Church administers seven sacraments. There are three types. The three sacraments of initiation, and their accompanying signs, are baptism with water, confirmation with oil through the laying on of hands, and the Eucharist with bread and wine. There are two sacraments of healing. Penance and reconciliation is signed by the acts of the penitent (contrition, confession, and satisfaction/penance) and by the absolution by the priest. The sign of anointing of the sick is oil. The two sacraments at the service of communion are holy orders with the laying on of hands by the bishop, and matrimony with its expression of consent on the part of the husband and wife.

Protestant churches administer only two sacraments or ordinances. At the time of the Reformation, leading Protestants like Martin Luther and John Calvin reduced the number of church rites from the seven as practiced in the Roman Catholic Church to two: baptism and the Lord's Supper. Indeed, one of the two marks of Protestant churches is the administration of these two—and only these two—sacraments or ordinances.[1]

The key reason for this reduction in number is that Christ ordained only two rites for the church to celebrate. He ordained baptism when he commissioned his missionally engaged church to baptize with water "in the name of the Father, and of the Son, and of the Holy Spirit" (Matt. 28:19). He ordained the Lord's Supper when, at his last supper with his disciples, he transformed that Passover feast into a covenant-renewing rite featuring bread and wine (Matt. 26:26–29).

For this same reason, Protestants dismissed the other five Catholic sacraments. Jesus did not ordain confirmation; indeed, it is not treated anywhere in Scripture. When Jesus called people to repentance, he directed them to a total reorientation of their life involving a definitive break from sin: "*Repent*, for the kingdom of God is at hand" (Matt. 4:17). This is the proper understanding of the Greek word *metanoeite* ("repent") as found in the Gospel. The Catholic notion of the sacrament of penance is based on the Latin Vulgate's poor translation of Jesus's command. It renders *metanoeite* ("repent") as *pœnitentiam agite*, which in English is "do [acts of] penance." However, "Jesus did not institute a sacramental action involving contrition, confession of sins to a priest, absolution, and rendering of satisfaction to make amends for harm done."[2] Thus, the Catholic sacrament of penance is not supported biblically.

---

1. The other mark is the preaching of the Word of God.
2. *RCTP*, 242.

The sacrament of anointing of the sick does have an associated sign—oil—and has a biblical basis (James 5:13–17). Certainly, Jesus healed many sick people (Matt. 4:23–24; 9:35). Indeed, one of the characteristics of his ministry—and that of his disciples as well—was healing (Matt. 10:1, 8; Acts 5:16). At the same time, Christ himself did not ordain this action as a rite of his church. Neither did he ordain holy orders. As for the sacrament of matrimony, Jesus certainly endorsed the permanent marriage of a man and woman (Matt. 19:1–9) and honored the institution by performing his first miracle at the wedding of Cana (John 2:1–10). But Christ did not ordain it; indeed, it is a creation ordinance. It has existed from the very beginning of human history (Gen. 2:18–25), and is characteristic of the majority of men and women, according to divine design (Gen. 1:26–28). But it does not exist as a church rite.

### Effectiveness/Validity of Sacraments/Ordinances

As it is the Catholic Church that administers the sacraments, the sacramental economy depends on the Christ-Church interconnection for its effectiveness and validity. Importantly, the Church insists that its sacraments are effective and valid *ex opere operato*, literally, "by the work worked." That is, when a sacrament is administered, it confers grace because a minister of the Church, acting in the person of Christ, administers the sacrament. By the fact that the sacrament is administered, it communicates divine grace.

In more detail, "celebrated worthily in faith, the sacraments confer the grace that they signify. They are efficacious because in them Christ himself is at work: it is he who baptizes, he who acts in his sacraments in order to communicate the grace that each signifies."[3] Two other examples underscore this point, but first it must be underscored that the reference to "Christ" cannot be divorced from "the Church" because of the Christ-Church interconnection. It is Christ who confirms, acting through the anointing with oil on the heads of those being confirmed through the laying on of hands of the priest who says, "Be sealed with the Gift of the Holy Spirit."[4] *Ex opere operato*, the fullness of the grace of the Spirit is conferred. It is Christ who heals, either spiritually or physically or both, through the anointing with oil on the heads of the sick or dying as the priest says, "Through this holy anointing may the Lord in his love and mercy help you with the grace of the Holy Spirit. May the Lord who frees you from sin save you and raise you up."[5] *Ex opere operato*, the grace of the Spirit for healing is infused.

Additionally, because Christ in conjunction with the Holy Spirit is the acting agent, the administration of the sacraments cannot be rendered null and void by the one who administers them. That is, the infusion of divine

---

3. CCC, 1127.
4. CCC, 1300.
5. CCC, 1513.

grace cannot fail if the sacraments are dispensed by spiritually corrupt and/ or immoral ministers. They operate "independently of the personal holiness of the minister. Nevertheless, the fruits of the sacraments also depend on the disposition of the one who receives them."[6] To illustrate, on the one hand is an elderly woman who recently participated in the sacrament of penance. When she attends Mass, giving heed to the Liturgy of the Word and the Liturgy of the Eucharist, she experiences a great benefit of grace as she partakes of the sacrament of the Eucharist. On the other hand is a drunkard who stumbles into a Mass moments after leaving a bar. He could care less about the unfolding of the liturgy. When he partakes of the sacrament of the Eucharist, his experience of grace pales in comparison with that of the woman.

In the Reformation, Protestant churches moved away from the Catholic notion of the effectiveness and validity of the sacraments in terms of *ex opere operato*. For example, John Calvin dissented from the Catholic notion that some sort of secret powers are attached to the sacraments and that they confer grace as long as their recipients do not impede it by being in mortal sin.[7] Rather, he closely tied the sacraments to the Word of God and faith. He insisted that "any man is deceived who thinks anything more is conferred upon him through the sacraments than what is offered by God's Word and received by him in true faith."[8] For Calvin, this emphasis on faith does not mean that the sacraments themselves are dependent on the receptivity of those who participate in them.[9] But as aids to help Christians in various ways, they are promises or pledges that require faith to be of benefit.[10] He further tied the effectiveness of the sacraments to the Holy Spirit, again distancing himself from the idea of *ex opere operato*: "They do not bestow any grace of themselves, but announce and tell us, and (as they are guarantees and tokens) ratify among us, those things given us by divine bounty [God's goodness]. The Holy Spirit . . . is he who brings the graces of God with him, gives a place for the sacraments among us, and makes them bear fruit."[11]

---

6. CCC, 1128.
7. John Calvin, *Institutes of the Christian Religion*, 4.14.14 (LCC 21:1289).
8. Calvin, *Institutes*, 4.14.14 (LCC 21:1290).
9. Calvin, *Institutes*, 4.14.16 (LCC 21:1291).
10. Specifically, "the sacraments have effectiveness among us in proportion as we are helped by their ministry sometime to foster, confirm, and increase the true knowledge of Christ in ourselves; at other times, to possess him more fully and enjoy his riches. But that happens when we receive in true faith what is offered there." Calvin, *Institutes*, 4.14.16 (LCC 21:1291).
11. Calvin, *Institutes*, 4.14.17 (LCC 21:1293). Another example is the statement of the Westminster Confession of Faith: "Sacraments are holy signs and seals of the covenant of grace, immediately instituted by God, to represent Christ and his benefits, and to confirm our interest in him; as also to put a visible difference between those that belong unto the Church and the rest of the world; and solemnly to engage them to the service of God in

A second example of Protestantism's rejection of *ex opere operato* is the Baptist view of the ordinances. Although Baptist confessions do not directly address the topic, they clearly stand against it.[12] This rejection is seen in four ways: They move away from calling these rites sacraments, that is, from considering them to be means by which grace is transmitted. They return to the New Testament pattern of baptizing people who hear the gospel and embrace it through repentance and faith (credobaptism). They understand the Lord's Supper to be a memorial of Christ's sacrificial death. And they emphasize that both ordinances are symbols of or testimonies to the obedience and faith of those who celebrate them. These distinctives preclude a Baptist view of the sacraments as being effective and valid *ex opere operato*.

These two examples underscore the variety of Protestant views. Still, both stand against the Roman Catholic position that the effectiveness and validity of the sacraments is *ex opere operato*.

## Nature of Sacraments/Ordinances

The Roman Catholic Church considers the seven sacraments, as being part of its sacramental economy, to be necessary for salvation because they are means by which grace is infused into the Catholic faithful. As a result of this transmission of divine favor, the character of the faithful is transformed, thereby enabling them to engage in good deeds and thus merit eternal life. Clearly, this Catholic understanding of the sacraments flows from the two principles of the nature-grace interdependence and the Christ-Church interconnection. Water, oil, bread, and wine, being elements of nature, are capable of receiving and transmitting divine grace when consecrated by the Church. The Church, which is the continuation of the incarnation of Christ, acts through its ministers in the person of Christ to consecrate the elements and thus render them sacraments of salvation.

A key divergence that emerged in the Reformation was the difference between the Catholic view of the infusion of grace and the Protestant view of imputation. The latter position centers on justification, which is the mighty act of God by which he declares sinful people "not guilty" but "righteous" instead. The first aspect of the declaration is the forgiveness of sins: God remits all sins—past, present, and future—through the atoning sacrifice of Christ. The second aspect of the declaration is the imputation of Christ's righteousness. His perfect obedience—a sinless life, full conformity to the Father's will, suffering, death, and resurrection—is credited to the account of all those forgiven of their sins. Thus, imputation rather than infusion is highlighted.

---

Christ, according to his Word" (27.1). A source for this Confession is https://www.pcaac. org/wp-content/uploads/2019/11/WCFScriptureProofs.pdf.

12. An example is the Baptist Faith and Message, 7. A source for the BFM 2000 is https://bfm. sbc.net/bfm2000/.

Accordingly, Protestants' standing before God is grounded on the work of Christ and justification. Their salvation encompasses the forgiveness of sins and perfect righteousness. Whether they embrace the sacraments as means of grace or the ordinances as symbols and testimonies, Protestants do not consider them to be necessary for salvation. This does not render them unimportant, however. But it does contrast the Protestant understanding from the Catholic view of the necessity of the sacraments for salvation. Moreover, Protestants do not adhere to the notion of salvation as a lifelong process involving the gradual and progressive transformation of their character through the sacraments. Protestants do not agree that, through this divine enablement, they are rendered capable of engaging in good deeds whereby they may merit eternal life.

Rather, by justification, they have righteous standing before God. By two other mighty acts of God—regeneration and sanctification—their nature is being transformed more and more into the image of Christ. While the sacraments contribute to this maturation process, there are many other means, especially the Word of God. They do and must engage in good works, which flow out of a heart of thanksgiving and from their new nature. Still, Protestants deny that their loving deeds achieve merit before God leading to eternal life. Salvation is not a process involving infused grace and merit. Rather, it is a position involving imputation and gift.

## Summary

The differences between the Roman Catholic view of the sacraments and Protestant views are very significant. Indeed, there are four points of divergence. One difference is over the proper terminology for these rites: are they *sacraments* or *ordinances*? Another divergence concerns the number of these rites. The Catholic Church administers seven sacraments; Protestants celebrate two. The reason for this Protestant position is that Jesus ordained only baptism and the Lord's Supper.

A third divergence focuses on the effectiveness and validity of the sacraments. According to the Catholic Church, the sacraments are effective and valid *ex opere operato*. By the fact that they are celebrated by a minister of the Church, the sacraments confer grace. Protestants deny the notion of *ex opere operato*. Their focus is instead on the association between baptism and the Lord's Supper, the Word of God, the Spirit of God, and faith that receives the benefits. A final disagreement is over the nature of these rites. The Catholic position emphasizes the infusion of grace, while the Protestant view underscores imputation.

## REFLECTION QUESTIONS

1. Why do Roman Catholics call these rites *sacraments* while some Protestants call them *sacraments* and others call them *ordinances*? What is at the heart of this difference in terminology?

2. Why does the Catholic Church have seven sacraments and Protestant churches only two? What is at the heart of this difference in number?

3. How does the Catholic Church's *ex opere operato* view of the effectiveness and validity of the sacraments contrast with the Protestant position? What is at the heart of this difference in effectiveness and validity?

4. How does the Roman Catholic emphasis on the infusion of grace contrast with the Protestant focus on the imputation of Christ's righteousness? What is at the heart of this difference in the nature of the sacraments?

5. How do the key principles of the nature-grace interdependence and the Christ-Church interconnection manifest themselves in the Catholic view of the seven sacraments that are effective and valid *ex opere operato* through the infusion of divine grace?

QUESTION 20

# What Is the Sacrament of Baptism?

The sacrament of baptism is the first of three sacraments of initiation, with confirmation and the Eucharist being the other two. These three sacraments together are foundational for the Catholic faithful, who "are born anew by Baptism, strengthened by the sacrament of Confirmation, and receive in the Eucharist the food of eternal life."[1] Through these rites, the grace of God is infused into the faithful, thereby transforming their character and readying them to love and engage in good works so that they can merit salvation. Thus, this sacrament illustrates the nature-grace interdependence and the Christ-Church interconnection. When the Church consecrates water, an element of nature, it becomes capable of receiving and transmitting divine grace.

### The First Sacrament

Baptism (Gr. *baptizein* = "to plunge" or "to immerse") is a rite common to all Christian traditions. It involves the application of water by immersion, pouring, or sprinkling using the Trinitarian formula "in the name of the Father, and of the Son, and of the Holy Spirit" (Matt. 28:19). As the initiatory rite, baptism is to be administered before the other six Catholic sacraments and before the continuing rite of the Lord's Supper in Protestant churches. For the most part, this order is true in both paedobaptist churches that baptize infants (Presbyterian, Methodist, Episcopal) and credobaptist churches that baptize those who offer a credible profession of faith (Baptist, free churches, Bible churches).

As the first sacrament, baptism is "the door which gives access to the other sacraments. Through Baptism we [the Catholic faithful] are freed from sin and reborn as sons of God; we become members of Christ, are incorporated into the Church and made sharers of her mission."[2] Specifically, infants who

---

1. CCC, 1212.
2. CCC, 1213.

are baptized are cleansed of their original sin, so they are no longer liable to condemnation due to their solidarity with Adam and his guilt. As for adults, they are cleansed of their original sin and all their actual sins up to the point of their baptism. Their liability due to Adam's guilt as well as to their own personal sins is removed. Additionally, baptism effects regeneration. Baptized infants and adults are born again, that is, their old nature is removed and they receive a new nature. Finally, they become participants in Christ and the Roman Catholic Church.

Before adults (people over the age of seven) are baptized, they must undergo a rigorous period of catechesis in which they are prepared for the sacraments of initiation, which are administered as a single ceremony.[3] They first participate in the sacrament of penance, by which they confess their mortal sins and receive absolution from a priest. Following their profession of the Catholic faith, they are baptized. The priest asks, "What do you ask of God's church?" They reply, "Faith." Next, they are confirmed and share in the Eucharist for the first time. Infants are brought to the sacrament by their parents. As these infants grow, they participate in the other two sacraments of initiation. Moreover, the Church can only administer baptism to people who have never been baptized.[4]

## Administration of Baptism

Priests, bishops, and deacons ordinarily administer this sacrament. Given the Christ-Church interconnection, the baptizer "acts in the person of Christ" such that it is Christ himself who baptizes. Moreover, in cases of emergency, anyone can baptize. The only requirement (and having been baptized is not required) is that baptism is administered with the proper intention: "The intention required is to will to do what the Church does when she baptized, and to apply the Trinitarian baptismal formula" (Matt. 28:19).[5] The prospect that even an unbaptized person may baptize underscores the importance of this sacrament and its association with salvation. The catechism states, "The Church finds the reason for this possibility in the universal saving will of God and of the necessity of Baptism for salvation."[6] There are two key points. The first has to do with God, "who desires all people to be saved and to come to the knowledge of the truth" (1 Tim. 2:4) and who is "not wishing that any should perish, but that all should reach repentance" (2 Peter 3:9). The second is that this sacrament is necessary for salvation, based on John 3:5. Clearly, then, God will make baptism available even in extreme situations so that the

---

3. Rite of Christian Initiation of Adults (RCIA). See Question 17.
4. "Every person not yet baptized and only such a person is able to be baptized." CCC, 1244.
5. CCC, 1256.
6. CCC, 1256.

non-baptized may avail themselves of this cleansing from sin and mighty work of regeneration.

## Necessity of Baptism

The Catholic Church believes that the sacrament of baptism is necessary for salvation. One reason focuses on Jesus's words to Nicodemus: "Truly, truly, I say to you, unless one is born of water and the Spirit, he cannot enter the kingdom of God" (John 3:5). From early on, the church has interpreted this saying to underscore baptism's necessity. A second reason emphasizes the Great Commission (Matt. 28:18–20), in which Jesus commands his disciples—that is, the church—to baptize. Specifically, "Baptism is necessary for salvation for those to whom the Gospel has been proclaimed and who have had the possibility of asking for this sacrament. The Church does not know of any means other than Baptism that assures entry into eternal beatitude."[7]

A final reason for the necessity of baptism brings us back to the principal effects of the sacrament. The first effect is purification from sins and removal of liability for judgment: "all sins are forgiven, original sin and all personal sins, as well as all punishment for sin."[8] With sins removed, the faithful enter the kingdom of God. The second effect is regeneration, or transformation of their nature: the baptized are born again, become new creations (2 Cor. 5:17), participate in the divine nature (2 Peter 1:4), become adopted children of God, are joined to Christ, and become temples of the Holy Spirit (1 Cor. 6:19).

Because the sacrament effects purification and regeneration, it can never be repeated: "Baptism seals the Christian with the indelible spiritual mark (*character*) of his belonging to Christ. No sin can erase this mark, even if sin prevents Baptism from bearing the fruits of salvation. Given once for all, Baptism cannot be repeated."[9] For Catholics who commit mortal sin and lose the grace of salvation, the solution is not rebaptism but the sacrament of penance. For Protestants who wish to become Roman Catholic, the process does not include rebaptism but a process for membership in which they are enrolled not as catechumens but as candidates—Christians by virtue of their baptism.[10]

## The New Testament and Baptism

The biblical pattern for the administration of baptism brings together several elements: hearing the gospel with understanding, repentance from

---

7. CCC, 1257.
8. CCC, 1263.
9. CCC, 1272.
10. Assuming it was a valid baptism, that is, administered "by immersion, pouring, or sprinkling, together with the trinitarian formula." Vatican Council II, *Ad Totam Ecclesiam*, 13(a). See Question 17.

sin, belief in Jesus Christ for salvation, the forgiveness of sin, and the gift of the Holy Spirit (Acts 2:37–47). In the narrative of Peter's proclamation of the good news on the day of Pentecost, three thousand people were baptized (Acts 2:41). Other baptism stories include the Samaritans (Acts 8:12–17), the Ethiopian eunuch (Acts 8:36, 38), Saul/Paul (Acts 9:18–19; 22:16), Cornelius and his family and friends (Acts 10:47–48; 11:15–18), Lydia and her household (Acts 16:15), the Philippian jailor and his family (Acts 16:31–33), many Corinthians (Acts 18:8), and the disciples of John the Baptist (Acts 19:1–7).

This pattern of the early church baptizing people who embraced the gospel was the application of Jesus's Great Commission. As part of making disciples throughout the nations, the church was to baptize them in the name of the triune God (Matt. 28:18–20). The church practiced credobaptism, that is, it baptized believers, associating new converts with God who is Father, Son, and Holy Spirit. The church administered this baptism by immersion, which vividly portrays these believers' identification with the death, burial, and resurrection of Jesus Christ (Rom. 6:3–5). The promise for Christians who are justified by faith is that "in Christ Jesus you are all sons of God, through faith. For as many of you as were baptized into Christ have put on Christ" (Gal. 3:26–27). Baptism by immersion also powerfully symbolizes cleansing from sin (Acts 22:16) as well as escape from divine punishment (1 Peter 3:18–22).

## Is Baptism Necessary?

The New Testament does not seem to indicate that baptism is necessary for salvation. If it were, it doesn't square with the decision of the Jerusalem Council about how Gentiles are to be saved (Acts 15). They heard the gospel and believed (v. 7). God "cleansed their hearts by faith" (v. 9). No other requirement—like circumcision—could be placed on them (v. 10). The church concluded, "We believe that we will be saved through the grace of the Lord Jesus, just as they will" (v. 11). If there were ever a time to list baptism as a necessary element for salvation, it was at this council. But it did not make this point. Nor did the apostle Paul make baptism a major aspect of his ministry. After trying to remember the Corinthian believers whom he had baptized (and there were only a handful), Paul concluded: "Christ did not send me to baptize but to preach the gospel" (1 Cor. 1:17). This truncated ministry would seem unconscionable if baptism were necessary for salvation.

The Catholic Church appeals to Jesus's words to Nicodemus (John 3:5) as support for the necessity of the sacrament; however, I believe this is based on a misinterpretation. Jesus's point that "unless one is born of water and the Spirit, he cannot enter the kingdom of God" does not prescribe two requirements for salvation, but only one. Notice his instruction:

**not**

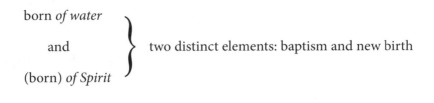

**but**

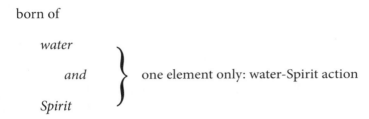

Jesus does not affirm both water baptism ("born of water") and Spirit regeneration ("born of the Spirit") as necessary. Rather, he affirms one mighty divine work ("born of") that involves cleansing from sin ("water," as symbolic of such washing) and transformation of nature ("Spirit," as the agent of regeneration). Jesus seems to challenge Nicodemus to recall Ezekiel's promise of the new covenant in association with the Holy Spirit: "I will sprinkle clean water on you, and you shall be clean from all your uncleannesses, and from all your idols I will cleanse you. And I will give you a new heart, and a new spirit I will put within you. And I will remove the heart of stone from your flesh and give you a heart of flesh. And I will put my Spirit within you and cause you to walk in my statutes and be careful to obey my rules" (Ezek. 36:25–27). Cleansing from impurity and idolatry. Transformation of character by the indwelling Spirit of God. This one mighty divine work is vividly portrayed by water baptism, but it does not mean that such baptism is necessary for salvation.

At the same time, the non-necessity of baptism does not mean that it is unimportant. By virtue of Jesus's Great Commission, the church is to baptize his disciples. In step with what it accomplishes—it associates believers with the triune God, pictures identification with Christ, symbolizes cleansing from sin, and portrays escape from divine punishment—baptism is a step of obedience incumbent upon all new Christians.

### Historical Development of Baptism

Moving beyond the New Testament, the early church practiced baptism of new believers. When the *Didache* (early second century) encouraged candidates for baptism to fast beforehand, it presupposed people old enough to understand their participation in that discipline. Moreover, it instructed that baptism should be by immersion in cold, moving water.[11] Similarly, Justin Martyr (middle second century) presented baptism as a choice following peoples' understanding of Christian teaching, repentance from sin, prayer, and fasting.[12] The early church practiced credobaptism by immersion.

An interruption in this trend first becomes apparent in the latter part of the second century. Tertullian objected to the novel practice of baptizing children. He countered: "Let them become Christians when they become able to know Christ. Why does innocent infancy rush to the forgiveness of sins?"[13] Origen was also familiar with infant baptism, claiming in the mid-third century, "The church has received a tradition from the apostles to give baptism even to little children."[14] Importantly, no trace of such an apostolic tradition exists. And Origen himself protested against the practice. Like Tertullian, he emphasized that innocent people—children who have never sinned personally—do not need forgiveness of sins.

Infant baptism did not become the official practice of the church until the fifth century. Key to its development was the association of baptism with the removal of original sin. According to Origen, "No one is clean of filth, not even if his life on earth has only been for one day. . . . Because the filth of birth is removed by the sacrament of baptism, for that reason infants, too, are baptized."[15]

> In other words, the practice of infant baptism developed as a strong link between baptism and the removal of original sin was forged. Original sin—the doctrine that Adam has transmitted his guilt and corruption to all human beings, so that everyone is born into this world guilty before God and tainted with a corrupt, sinful nature—must be dealt with, or only judgment leading to condemnation is the result. Because baptism was considered to effect the forgiveness of sin, and because infants are born with Adamic guilt and corruption (original sin), they must be baptized in order to be save.[16]

Thus, the sacrament of baptism as applied to infants was a late development in the history of the church.

11. *Didache* 7, in *ANF* 7:379.
12. Justin Martyr, *First Apology* 61, in *ANF* 1:183.
13. Tertullian, *On Baptism* 18, in *ANF* 3:678.
14. Origen, *Commentary on Romans* 5.9.3, Origen, *Commentary on the Epistle to the Romans*, trans. Thomas P. Scheck, 2 vols. in *The Fathers of the Church: A New Translation* (Washington, DC: Catholic University of America Press, 2001), 1:367.
15. Origen, *Homilies on the Gospel of Luke* 14:5; cited in *RCTP*, 277.
16. *RCTP*, 277.

Of course, many Protestant denominations adhere to paedobaptism. Indeed, there is a family resemblance between Anglican, Reformed, and Nazarene churches, for example, and the Roman Catholic Church: they all administer baptism to infants (as well as to adults). However, the theological grounding for Protestant paedobaptism and Catholic paedobaptism is completely different. Roman Catholic theology associates it with two points: the removal of original sin and regeneration. Reformed theology, to take a Protestant example, does not associate infant baptism with original sin and does not consider it to be salvific. Rather, a Presbyterian church baptizes infants because they, like their believing parents, are part of the covenant community. Like the people of Israel circumcised their infant boys as a sign of participation in the old covenant, the Presbyterian church baptizes the infant children of its believing members as a sign of participation in the new covenant. So, though the Catholic Church and the Presbyterian church baptize infants, the theological foundation and the purpose of their paedobaptism are very different.

### Baptism and Faith

When a Presbyterian girl gets older, her church expects her to embrace the gospel through a personal act of faith. Indeed, the sacrament of baptism is a sign and seal of her future salvation when she believes in Jesus Christ. This personal appropriation of salvation by faith contrasts with the Roman Catholic emphasis of the vicarious nature of faith: "It is only with the faith of the Church that each of the faithful can believe."[17] So, for infant baptism, the priest asks the godparent, "What do you ask of God's church?" The response, voiced on behalf of the infant, is "Faith." In the case of adult baptism, the same question is posed, with the same response on her part. More than personal faith, her faith is primarily the gift of faith given by the Church. In both cases, then, the Catholic Church and its sacrament of baptism are necessary for salvation. And the driving force is the Church's faith, granted to the baptized.

### Summary

The sacrament of baptism, one of three sacraments of initiation, is the first sacrament of the Roman Catholic Church. It cleanses from original sin, effects regeneration, and incorporates into Christ and his Church. Anyone who has not been baptized may participate in this sacrament. Indeed, for anyone to be saved, they must be baptized. At the heart of this sacrament is the nature-grace interdependence and the Christ-Church interconnection.

The pattern of baptism in the New Testament associates this rite with grasping the gospel, repentance, belief in Jesus Christ, forgiveness of sin, and the gift of the Holy Spirit. Additionally, the pattern is that of credobaptism by immersion. Moreover, the New Testament does not seem to support the

---

17. CCC, 1253.

Catholic view of the necessity of baptism for salvation. Such non-necessity does not render the sacrament unimportant but grounds it differently. Although the early church seems to have followed this pattern, its practice eventually gave way to paedobaptism. This change was grounded on the association of baptism with the removal of original sin. By the fifth century, infant baptism had become the official practice of the church.

At the time of the Reformation, most Protestant churches broke from the theology of infant baptism while continuing to practice it. Thus, there is a family resemblance between the Catholic Church and Protestant churches who baptize infants. The theology that grounds the two traditions, however, is very different. Credobaptism, which reappeared at this time among the Anabaptist/Baptist movement, stands against infant baptism and insists on the baptism of believers. Its emphasis on personal faith contrasts with the Roman Catholic emphasis on the gift of the Church's faith for those to be baptized.

## REFLECTION QUESTIONS

1. How does the sacrament of baptism within the Catholic Church illustrate the nature-grace interdependence and the Christ Church interconnection?

2. If you are Roman Catholic, were you baptized in the Catholic Church as an infant or as an adult? Or were you already baptized and then converted to Catholicism? How do you assess your baptism?

3. If you are part of a Protestant church that holds to paedobaptism, were you baptized as an infant or as an adult? How do you assess your baptism?

4. If you are part of a Protestant church that holds to credobaptism, what is your story leading up to your baptism? To become a member of your Protestant church, were you rebaptized? Why? If you've not been baptized, why not?

5. What are the main differences between infant baptism as practiced in the Catholic Church and infant baptism in paedobaptist Protestant churches? Though there is a family resemblance, why are these differences so important?

# QUESTION 21

# What Is the Sacrament of the Eucharist?

In many cases, when people think about the Roman Catholic Church, the initial thing that comes to mind is the Catholic faithful eating a round wafer and taking a sip of wine from a gold cup toward the end of a Mass. This sacrament, the third of the three sacraments of Christian initiation, is the Eucharist. Question 20 explored the first sacrament, baptism, which makes people Christians and introduces them into the life of God and of the Church. The second sacrament of confirmation, to be treated in Question 24, establishes the Catholic faithful in the fullness of the Holy Spirit and incorporates them as full members into the Church and its mission. This third sacrament of the Eucharist completes this initiation into the Catholic faith.

## The Sacrament and Its Names

The Eucharist is "the source and summit of the Christian life," meaning that the other six sacraments are oriented to it.[1] The "whole spiritual good of the Church, namely Christ himself," is present in the Eucharist.[2] Additionally, it is "the efficacious sign and sublime cause of that communion in the divine life and that unity of the People of God by which the Church is kept in being."[3] It has various names: (1) The *Eucharist* (Gr. *eucharistein* = to give thanks), because Jesus gave thanks to his Father at the last supper. (2) The *Lord's Supper* (1 Cor. 11:20), because at the last supper with his disciples, Jesus instituted it as a sign of the new covenant. As a supper, it also anticipates the wedding feast of the Lamb (Rev. 19:9). (3) The *Breaking of Bread*, because of Jesus's action with the unleavened loaf during the Last Supper (Matt. 26:26; 1 Cor. 11:24).

---

1. CCC, 1324. The citation is from Vatican Council II, *Lumen Gentium*, 11.
2. CCC, 1324. The citation is from Vatican Council II, *Presbyterorum Ordinis*, 5.
3. CCC, 1325.

While these names are shared with various Protestant traditions, other names unique to the Roman Catholic sacrament include *Eucharistic Assembly*, *Holy Sacrifice*, the *Most Blessed Sacrament*, and *Holy Mass*.[4]

This sacrament celebrates the "*memorial of Christ's sacrifice*, with its participants *offering* to God the Father his creational gifts of bread and wine that, "by the power of the Holy Spirit and by the words of Christ, have become the body and blood of Christ. Christ is thus really and mysteriously made *present*."[5] Given this description, I focus our discussion of the Eucharist on four themes: memorial, sacrifice, offering, and presence.

## Memorial

In the words of the catechism, "the Eucharist is the memorial of Christ's Passover," not merely in the sense of a remembrance of Christ's sacrifice but as a ceremonial commemoration of it. The Catholic faithful do not just subjectively recall his death as a memory. Rather, they objectively celebrate the memorial of Christ and his atoning work, "the making present and the sacrificial offering of his unique sacrifice."[6] Think in terms of the difference between the actual *physical structures* of the Washington Monument and the Lincoln Memorial—commemorating two American presidents—and your *memory* of having visited those buildings during a vacation to Washington, DC.

## Sacrifice

The Eucharist is a memorial, then, in terms of a re-presentation of Christ's death, which "is made present: the sacrifice of Christ offered once for all on the cross remains ever present."[7] How can this event, which occurred as a once-and-for-all atonement nearly two thousand years ago, be re-presented at a Mass today? Like God's reality of being unlimited by time, Christ's crucifixion is not timebound but is made present when a priest administers the sacrament of the Eucharist. Jesus himself affirmed of the bread, "This is my body," and he affirmed of the cup, "This cup which is poured out for you is the new covenant in my blood" (Luke 22:19–20). The catechism explains, "In the Eucharist Christ gives us the very body which he gave up for us on the cross, the very blood which he 'poured out for many for the forgiveness of sins.'"[8]

In terms of our first two themes, then, the Eucharist is "a *sacrifice* because it re-presents (makes present) the sacrifice of the cross, because it is itself a *memorial*, and because it applies its fruit."[9] To avoid a common misunderstanding, it is not the Catholic position that every time this sacrament is

---

4. CCC, 1329–32.
5. CCC, 1357 (italics original).
6. CCC, 1362.
7. CCC, 1363–64.
8. CCC, 1365. The citation is from Matthew 26:28.
9. CCC, 1366 (italics added).

celebrated, Christ is re-crucified. Rather, the once-and-for-all sacrifice on the cross is re-presented as the sacrament.

## Offering

Together with Christ's sacrifice, this sacrament includes the sacrifice of the Church as it joins in his offering: "With him, she herself is offered whole and entire. She unites herself to his intercession with the Father for all men. In the Eucharist the sacrifice of Christ becomes also the sacrifice of the members of his body."[10] This collaborative offering of the Church is seen during the Mass when lay people bring forward to the altar the created elements of bread and wine. When consecrated, these offerings become the re-presented offering of Christ on the cross. Moreover, during the Mass, the priest offers the Eucharist "in the name of the whole Church in an unbloody and sacramental manner."[11] Additionally, the sacrament is offered for the Catholic faithful so their souls may be released from purgatory and go to heaven.[12]

## Presence

While the Catholic Church acknowledges the many ways in which Christ is present with his Church, it underscores the fact that "he is present . . . most especially in the Eucharistic species"[13] of the bread and wine "by the power of his word and his Spirit."[14] His Eucharistic presence is unique in this way: "The body and blood, together with the soul and divinity, of our Lord Jesus Christ and, therefore, the whole Christ is truly, really, and substantially contained."[15] The explanation for this unique presence is transubstantiation.

## Transubstantiation

Three Latin words are visible in this term: (1) *trans*, which refers to change; (2) *substantia*, which refers to nature or essence, that which makes something what it is; and (3) *tion*, which indicates an action or a state. Trans-substantia-tion, then, refers to the action of changing something's nature, or the state of change of something's essence. With reference to the Eucharist, transubstantiation is the change that is wrought in the substance of the bread (it becomes the body of Christ) and in the substance of the wine (it becomes the blood of Christ): "it is by the conversion of the bread and wine into Christ's body and blood that Christ becomes present in this sacrament."[16]

---

10. CCC, 1368.
11. CCC, 1369. The citation is from Vatican Council II, *Presbyterorum Ordinis*, 2.4.
12. CCC, 1371.
13. CCC, 1373. The citation is from Vatican Council II, *Sacrosanctum Concilium*, 7.
14. CCC, 1358.
15. CCC, 1374 (italics removed).
16. CCC, 1375.

Catholics hold that "the Eucharistic presence of Christ begins at the moment of the consecration and endures as long as the Eucharistic species subsist."[17] That is, transubstantiation is effected when, during the Liturgy of the Eucharist, the priest engages in the epiclesis—the prayer to God the Father to send the Holy Spirit to cause the change in the bread and wine—and recites the narrative of Christ's institution of the sacrament:

> Take this [the bread], all of you, and eat of it, / for this is my Body, / which will be given up for you. . . . Take this [the cup], all of you, and drink from it, / for this is the chalice of my Blood, / the Blood of the new and eternal covenant, / which will be poured out for you and for many / for the forgiveness of sins. / Do this in memory of me.[18]

The consecrated elements, now no longer the substance of the bread and wine, remain the substance of the body and blood of Christ until the bread and wine are consumed. The change, then, is not momentary but lasting.

Additionally, "Christ is present whole and entire in each of the species and whole and entire in each of their parts."[19] That is, "Christ, the God-man, is present neither in his divine nature alone, nor in his human nature alone, but in the totality of both his divine and human natures. Additionally, in the totality of both his divine and human natures, Christ is present in the bread and in each of its grains and, in the totality of his divine and human natures, he is present in the wine and in each of its drops."[20] In terms of the administration of the sacrament, "the faithful participating in the Eucharist do not receive more or less of Christ if they take Communion in 'one kind'—that is, they receive the consecrated wafer only and not the wine—or if they take Communion in 'two kinds'—that is, they receive both the consecrated wafer and the wine. By their participation in the Eucharistic celebration, they receive all of Christ."[21]

Because the presence of Christ is continuous, lasting until the consecrated elements are consumed, the elements that remain after the completion of the Mass are placed in the tabernacle, a sacred container in the church building. The Catholic faithful are encouraged to engage in ongoing worship of Christ, who is still present. These remaining elements are also used for viaticum, that is, the administration of the sacrament to the sick and dying.

---

17. CCC, 1377.
18. Roman Missal, Eucharistic Prayer 1 (Roman Canon). 89-90. https://www.liturgyoffice.org.uk/Missal/Text/EP1-A4.pdf
19. CCC, 1377.
20. *RCTP*, 308–9.
21. *RCTP*, 309.

## Benefits of the Eucharist

The Catholic faithful who participate in this sacrament receive four benefits. First, it augments their union with Christ, which "preserves, increases, and renews the life of grace received at Baptism. This growth in Christian life needs the nourishment of Eucharistic Communion."[22] Second, the Eucharist separates the faithful from sin, by cleansing them from their past sins and preserving them from future sins. As Question 22 explains, only the sacrament of penance and reconciliation absolves the Catholic faithful from their mortal sins. The Eucharist is not designed for that purpose. However, as the sacrament for those in full communion with the Catholic Church—that is, the faithful whose mortal sins have been cancelled by the sacrament of penance and reconciliation—the Eucharist strengthens their love, "and this living charity wipes away venial sins."[23] Additionally, "by the same charity that it kindles in us, the Eucharist preserves us from future mortal sins."[24] Third, "the Eucharist makes the Church" by uniting the faithful more closely to Christ and thus to one another.[25] Fourth, the sacrament commits the Church to the poor as the Church recognizes Christ in them.[26]

Like the other six sacraments, the validity and effectiveness of the Eucharist is *ex opere operato*. When the priest celebrates the Mass, the authenticity of this sacrament does not depend on his spiritual and moral condition but solely on his administration of it. However, its fruitfulness in the lives of the Catholic faithful who participate depends on their receptivity to God's gracious activity. Indeed, the Eucharist "brings a greater or lesser benefit in proportion to their devotion."[27]

## Protestants and the Roman Catholic Sacrament

From the appearance of this sacrament, commonalities seem to unite Protestant and Catholic celebrations of it. Some names, such as the Eucharist and the Lord's Supper, are shared, as are the elements of bread and wine. Certain aspects of its administration, such as the recitation of the institution narrative and the giving of thanks, are held in common. Beneath these external family resemblances, however, significant differences are found. The very fact that the Roman Catholic Church denies its Eucharist to Protestants highlights this great divide between the two traditions.

A key difference concerns the nature of the presence of Christ in the sacrament. While Protestants disagree among themselves regarding this matter, all Protestants disagree with Catholic transubstantiation. Going back to Martin

---

22. CCC, 1392.
23. CCC, 1394 (italics removed).
24. CCC, 1396.
25. CCC, 1396.
26. CCC, 1397.
27. Pope Paul VI, *Eucharisticum Mysterium*, May 25, 1967, presented in full at https://adoremus.org/1967/05/eucharisticum-mysterium.

Luther's criticisms of this doctrine, Protestant critiques include the following. First, transubstantiation is of late origin. The Catholic Church did not officially proclaim the dogma until its Fourth Lateran Council in 1215, and Thomas Aquinas (1225–1274) did not offer its philosophical foundation until later in the thirteenth century. Second, Protestants object that transubstantiation is philosophically grounded and lacks a clear biblical basis. It was Aquinas, relying on Aristotelian philosophy, who proposed the distinction between substance and accidents as applied to the Eucharistic elements. *Substance* refers to "an essence or nature existing in itself (and not in something else)" and *accidents* refer to

> the characteristics or attributes not of its core and, thus, that can be lost without losing the thing itself. Some of these accidents can be perceived by the senses. In keeping with this distinction, Aquinas proposed the following: in the case of the Eucharistic bread and wine, though the *accidents* remain the same—the bread and wine still look like, smell like, feel like, and taste like bread and wine—the *substance* of the bread is changed into the body of Christ and the *substance* of the wine is changed into the blood of Christ. This change of substance is called *transubstantiation*.[28]

Third, Aquinas's appeal to "divine power" to explain this miracle[29]—and such a change of substance without change of accidents is completely unique to the Eucharist—was without biblical basis.

Another Protestant criticism of the Catholic sacrament focuses on the idea that the Eucharist is a re-presentation of Christ's sacrifice. Protestants do see any biblical support for this. Appeal to Jesus's words "This is my body. . . . This is my blood of the covenant" (Matt. 26:26, 28) depends on a misinterpretation of his institution of the Lord's Supper. It is not so much Jesus's words, but his actions, that explain this sacrament. The bread that is broken, not the bread itself, powerfully symbolizes the forthcoming fracturing of Christ's body on the cross. The cup of wine that is poured out, not the wine itself, powerfully symbolizes the upcoming shedding of Christ's blood on the cross. Jesus's giving of the elements themselves, together with his disciples' eating the bread and drinking the wine, powerfully symbolize the appropriate response to his saving work on the cross. Thus, "these actions-as-symbols underscore that Jesus's words cannot be taken literally."[30] The Catholic appeal to them in support of the Eucharist being a re-presentation of Christ's sacrifice is not warranted.

---

28. *RCTP*, 317–18.
29. Thomas Aquinas, *Summa Theologica* pt. 3, q. 75, art. 4. https://www.newadvent.org/summa/4075.htm.
30. *RCTP*, 320.

Protestants also critique the Catholic notion of the Eucharist being a sacrificial offering not only of Christ but of the Church as well. Certainly, Scripture employs the language of offering and sacrifice in urging believers to offer themselves to God (Rom. 12:1–2), to make "a sacrifice of praise to God, that is, the fruit of lips that confess his name" (Heb. 13:15), and to consider their good works to be sacrifices (Heb. 13:16). But Scripture never uses this language to refer to the Eucharist as the Church's sacrificial offering to God.

A final criticism focuses on the fact that the Catholic view of the Eucharist depends on the two principles of the nature-grace interdependence and the Christ-Church interconnection. We see the first principle at work in the view that the sacrament infuses divine grace—in this case, Christ himself—into the Catholic faithful through the natural elements of bread and wine. Such infused grace transforms their character so they can engage in good works and thus merit eternal life. Question 6 critiqued the nature-grace interdependence. We see the second principle operating in the practice of the Catholic faithful worshipping the remaining Eucharistic elements that are stored in the tabernacle. Christ, in the totality of his divine and human natures, remains present in the unused elements in the Church, which is the prolongation of the incarnation of Christ. Question 8 critiqued the Christ-Church interconnection.

## Summary

As "the source and summit of the Christian life," the Eucharist is the sacrament toward which the other six sacraments are oriented.[31] Indeed, the "whole spiritual good of the Church, namely Christ himself," is present in the Eucharist.[32] Focusing on four themes, the Eucharist is a memorial, sacrifice, offering, and presence. As a memorial, it is a ceremonial commemoration of Christ's crucifixion, not just a subjective remembrance of his death. As a sacrifice, the sacrament is a re-presentation of Christ's death, which "is made present: the sacrifice of Christ offered once for all on the cross remains ever present."[33] Thus, Christ is not re-sacrificed for the 3,729,500,147 time at a Mass today. Rather, his atonement of two thousand years ago is made present at the Mass. This sacrifice of Christ is joined with the sacrifices of the Church—the gifts of bread and wine—to form an offering to God. And Christ's presence in the Eucharist is unique: "The body and blood, together with the soul and divinity, of our Lord Jesus Christ and, therefore, the whole Christ is truly, really, and substantially contained."[34]

This unique presence is made possible by transubstantiation: "It is by the conversion of the bread and wine into Christ's body and blood that Christ

---

31. CCC, 1324. The citation is from Vatican Council II, *Lumen Gentium*, 11.
32. CCC, 1324. The citation is from Vatican Council II, *Presbyterorum Ordinis*, 5.
33. CCC, 1363–1364.
34. CCC, 1374 (italics removed).

becomes present in this sacrament."[35] This substantial change occurs when the elements are consecrated, and it lasts until the bread and wine are consumed. Participation in the sacrament by the Catholic faithful has four benefits: it augments their union with Christ, separates them from sin, "makes the Church" by uniting them more closely to Christ and thus to one another, and commits the Church to the poor.

This sacrament is one of the crucial points of division between the Catholic Church and Protestant churches. Nothing makes this more obvious than the fact that the Catholic Church does not permit Protestants to participate in its sacrament. This is due in part to the Protestant rejection of transubstantiation, which has several reasons. The doctrine of transubstantiation is of late origin. It is philosophically, not biblically, grounded. Specifically, the appeal to "divine power" to explain this unique miracle is without biblical basis. Similarly, the idea of the Eucharist as a re-presentation of Christ's sacrifice lacks biblical support and is based on a misunderstanding of Christ's words about the bread-body and wine-blood signs of the new covenant. So, too, the idea of the Eucharist as a collaborative offering involving Christ and the Church is without biblical basis. Finally, the sacrament is grounded on the two principles of the nature-grace interdependence and the Christ-Church interconnection, both of which are problematic.

## REFLECTION QUESTIONS

1. If you are Roman Catholic, what is your experience of participation in the Eucharist? Do you participate frequently, occasionally, annually, never? Why do you observe this rhythm?

2. If you are a Protestant, how does your church practice this sacrament? What is your experience in participating in it?

3. Why is transubstantiation essential to the Catholic view of the Eucharist, and why does Protestantism object to this doctrine?

4. Though there is a family resemblance between the Catholic sacrament of the Eucharist and the various Protestant views of the Lord's Supper, why are the underlying differences so important and still divisive for the two traditions?

5. How does the Catholic sacrament depend on and illustrate the nature-grace interdependence and the Christ-Church interconnection?

---

35. CCC, 1375.

# What Is the Sacrament of Penance and Reconciliation?

There are two sacraments of healing: penance and reconciliation, and anointing of the sick. By these two sacraments "Christ has willed that his Church continue, in the power of the Holy Spirit, his work of healing and salvation, even among her own members."[1] I will discuss anointing of the sick in Question 24 and focus on penance and reconciliation here.

## Understanding the Pairs of Sin and Forgiveness

What do the Catholic faithful do when they sin? They participate in the sacrament of penance and reconciliation to receive "pardon from God's mercy" and to be reconciled "with the Church which they have wounded by their sins."[2] In this explanation, pairs of distinct yet related matters emerge.

*First Pair: Sin against God and against the Church*

Sin is both against God and against the Church. This is the first pair. Certainly, the first failure is clear, as David expressed to God "against you, you only, have I sinned" (Ps. 51:4). All sin brings guilt before God and separates the Catholic faithful from him. At the same time, sin disrupts communion with the Church. From broken relationships to showing favoritism, and from embezzlement of parish funds to gossiping about the priest, sin is against the Catholic Church.

*Second Pair: Forgiveness and Reconciliation*

This two-sided damage due to sin demands the second pair of the means of removing sin. This sacrament has two names, as "both God's forgiveness

---

1. CCC, 1421.
2. CCC, 857. The citation is from Vatican Council II, *Lumen Gentium*, 11.2.

and reconciliation with the Church . . . are expressed and accomplished liturgically by the sacrament of Penance and Reconciliation."[3] Importantly, the Catholic Church affirms that only God has the power to forgive sin (Mark 2:5, 10). Still, Christ "gives this power to men to exercise in his name. . . . In imparting to his apostles his own power to forgive sins, the Lord also gives them the authority to reconcile sinners with the Church."[4] So God forgives the Catholic faithful for their sins against him and reconciles them with the Church that they have wounded by their sins. And through the authority that Christ designates to them, bishops and priests forgive the Catholic faithful for their sins against God and reconcile them to the Church that they have harmed by their sins.

### Third Pair: First Conversion and Second Conversion

Participation in the sacrament of penance and reconciliation is a constant practice throughout the lifetime of the Catholic faithful. Specifically, this ongoing response to Christ's invitation is called a second conversion. Thus, we have another pair: first conversion and second conversion. The first conversion is the initial response of unbelievers to the message of the gospel. Through faith in the good news and participation in the sacrament of baptism, "the first and fundamental conversion" leads to "salvation, that is, the forgiveness of sins and the gift of new life."[5] The second conversion, or "the struggle to conversion," is "an uninterrupted task for the whole Church" along "the path of penance and renewal."[6]

### Fourth Pair: Pre-baptismal Sins and Post-baptismal Sins

The importance of the sacrament of baptism for salvation has been highlighted in Question 20. Its association with the first conversion introduces another pair: pre-baptismal sins and post-baptismal sins. The sacrament of baptism cleanses an infant from her original sin and, in the case of an adult, cleanses her from her original sin as well as forgives all the sins she's committed up to her baptism. She is born again, and her pre-baptismal sins have been removed, but her first conversion "has not abolished the frailty and weakness of human nature, nor the inclination to sin."[7] Thus, she must avail herself of divine grace as she gives into temptation and sins. The sacrament of penance and reconciliation, then, is designed for the forgiveness of all her post-baptismal sins.

---

3. CCC, 1440.
4. CCC, 1441, 1444.
5. CCC, 1427.
6. CCC, 1426, 1428.
7. CCC, 1426.

*Fifth Pair: Mortal Sins and Venial Sins*

But what is sin, according to the Catholic Church? This question intro-duces another pair: mortal sins and venial sins. Roman Catholic theology explains that "sins are rightly evaluated according to their gravity."[8] Thus, generally speaking, mortal sins are more severe sins, while venial sins are less serious. The catechism states, "Mortal sin destroys charity in the heart of man by a grave violation of God's law; it turns man away from God, who is his ulti-mate end and his beatitude, by preferring an inferior good to him. Venial sin allows for charity to subsist, even though it offends and wounds it."[9]

To explain further, "*mortal sin* is a grave violation of the law of God, meeting three conditions. First, its object is a *grave matter*, as specified by the Ten Commandments; thus, it contradicts either love for God or love for neighbor, or both. Second, it is committed with *full knowledge* of 'the sinful character of the act, of its opposition to God's law.' Third, mortal sin is com-mitted with *complete consent*, involving a deliberate personal choice."[10] It re-sults in the destruction of love and the loss of grace. An example of mortal sin is premeditated murder committed with malice. If the Catholic faithful do not seek forgiveness for mortal sin through the sacrament of penance and recon-ciliation and die in this lost state, "it causes exclusion from Christ's kingdom and the eternal death of hell."[11]

Venial sin in not as serious a matter as is mortal sin. It is a violation of a less grave law, or a law is disobeyed "in a grave matter, but without full knowledge or without complete consent."[12] It results in the wounding of love and impedes progress in sanctification. Two examples of venial sin are "thoughtless chatter or immoderate laughter."[13] While venial sin does not result in the loss of grace, it does merit temporal punishment in purgatory. The Catholic faithful do not need the sacrament of penance and reconciliation for venial sin, but, with the help of grace, venial sin can be repaired through confession and repentance.

The final pair associated with this sacrament is human action and divine action. For this pairing, we turn to a discussion of the actual sacrament itself.

*Sixth Pair: Human Action and Divine Action*

The sacrament of penance and reconciliation is provided for the sinful Catholic faithful "who, since Baptism, have fallen into grave sins, and have thus lost their baptismal grace and wounded ecclesial [Church] communion."[14] It involves "two equally essential elements: on the one hand, the acts of the man

---

8. CCC, 1854.
9. CCC, 1855.
10. *RCTP*, 402 (italics original). The citation is from CCC, 1859.
11. CCC, 1861.
12. CCC, 1862.
13. CCC, 1856.
14. CCC, 1445.

who undergoes conversion . . . on the other, God's action through the intervention of the Church."[15]

On the human side, the three acts of the penitent are contrition, confession, and satisfaction or penance. The first act, *contrition*, is "sorrow of the soul and detestation [hatred] for the sin committed, together with the resolution not to sin again."[16] The second act, *confession*, is the acknowledgement of one's sin along with taking responsibility for it and being open to God and to the Church. The catechism states, "Confession to a priest is an essential part of the sacrament of Penance. 'All mortal sins of which penitents after a diligent self-examination are conscious must be recounted by them in confession.'"[17] As an example, the penitent says to the priest, "Forgive me, father, for I have sinned. It has been six months since my last confession and these are my sins: _____ (specific sins are confessed)." The priest offers counsel and the penitent makes an act of contrition, expressing deep sorrow for offending God and resolving to avoid sinning.

The third act, *satisfaction* or *penance*, involves reparation for the harm that the sins have caused to other people. "Absolution [the pronouncement of forgiveness by the priest] takes away sin, but it does not remedy all the disorders sin has caused. Raised up from sin, the sinner must still recover his full spiritual health by doing something more to make amends for the sin: he must 'make satisfaction for' or 'expiate' his sins. This satisfaction is also called 'penance.'"[18] Such acts express inner conversion and, as visible signs of it, are of three types: "*fasting, prayer*, and *almsgiving*, which express conversion in relation to oneself, to God, and to others."[19] Temporarily going without food, saying the rosary, and giving financial help to the poor are concrete examples of penance.[20]

Thus, the human element in the sacrament consists of the three acts of contrition, confession, and satisfaction or penance.

As for the divine element, the actions of God come through the intervention of the bishop or priest who administers the sacrament. By virtue of the sacrament of holy orders (discussed in Question 23), he is qualified to prompt the penitent's contrition, hear her confession, and impose the penance upon her. Following these three acts, the bishop or priest absolves her of her sin. Through the restoration of divine grace infused by this sacrament, the penitent is reunited to fellowship with God and reconciled to the Church.

15. CCC, 1448.
16. CCC, 1451.
17. CCC, 1456; the citation is from *Canons and Decrees of the Council of Trent*, 14th session (November 25, 1551), *The Most Holy Sacraments of Penance and Extreme Unction*, 5.
18. CCC, 1459.
19. CCC, 1434 (italics original).
20. "Penitential Practices for Today's Catholics," US Conference of Catholic Bishops, http://www.usccb.org/prayer-and-worship/liturgical-year/lent/penitential-practices-for-todays-catholics.cfm.

Her mortal sin, now forgiven, no longer interrupts her communion with God and the Church.

## Protestants and Penance

Whereas Protestants encourage, even insist on, confession of sin, they have little that resembles the formal Roman Catholic sacramental process outlined above. Certainly, Scripture urges constant confession: "If we confess our sins, he [God] is faithful and just to forgive us our sins and to cleanse us from all unrighteousness" (1 John 1:9). Confession entails acknowledging our sins, agreeing with God that gossip, overvaluing ourselves, and coveting another person's gifts and abilities, for instance, are wrong. It further involves acknowledging God's redemptive work, agreeing with him that through Christ's death and resurrection, our gossip, pride, and covetousness have been forgiven. Additionally, confession entails repentance, turning from our sins and purposing to avoid them in the future. Moreover, when our sin has wreaked havoc in the lives of others, we do whatever is necessary in terms of restoration and restitution. Such confession is part and parcel of Protestant maturity and growth in holiness.

With this practice of confession in place, Protestant churches do not consider penance and reconciliation to be a sacrament because Jesus did not ordain this rite for his church. The Catholic Church appeals to Jesus's words at the outset of his ministry. According to the Latin Vulgate, Jesus commanded, "*Do penance*, for the kingdom of God is at hand" (Matt. 4:17). This translation is not an accurate rendition of the Greek New Testament, according to which Jesus ordered, "*Repent*, for the kingdom of God is at hand." Textually, "Jesus never commanded his people to engage in penitential acts of fasting, praying, almsgiving, and the like as prescribed by an ecclesial rite of penance, but to make an about-face, reorient their life, change their mind and heart."[21] Penance and reconciliation is not a sacrament observed by Protestants.

A look at the pairs shows that Protestants continue their disagreement with the Catholic sacrament. In terms of its two names, penance and reconciliation, Protestants agree that God alone has the power to forgive sin (Mark 2:5, 10). Disagreement comes, however, with the Catholic insistence that Christ delegates his power to the Catholic clergy. At the heart of this wrong idea is the Christ-Church interconnection, whereby the Catholic Church is the continuation of Christ's incarnation and its clergy "act in the person of Christ the Head."[22] Question 8 critiqued this principle. By contrast, ministers of Christ proclaim the gospel as the message or word of reconciliation (2 Cor. 5:17–21). When a person responds with faith and repentance, the messengers proclaim in alignment with Scripture that her sins have been forgiven. She is

---

21. *RCTP*, 335.
22. CCC, 1563. The citation is from Vatican Council II, *Presbyterorum Ordinis*, 2.

loosed from her sins. When a person rejects or ignores the gospel, the messengers warn in accordance with Scripture that he is not forgiven but stands condemned. He is bound in his sins (Matt. 16:13–20; 18:15–20). These two sober announcements are pronouncements of *what is true*, not declarations that *make it true*.[23]

In terms of the pair of first conversion and second conversion, Protestants certainly agree that Jesus calls all people to turn from their sins and believe in Christ. This human response is rightly called conversion. As for the second, ongoing journey of breaking with sin and being renewed in the image of Christ, Protestants think the biblical term "sanctification" is to be preferred. As the process of becoming holy, "sanctification" better captures the idea of this ongoing progress.

Protestants also balk at the pair of pre-baptismal sins and post-baptismal sins. At the heart of this duality is the principle of the nature-grace interdependence. Specifically, through the infusion of grace by the means of the water of baptism, original sin (in the case of infants) and original sin and actual pre-baptismal sins (in the case of adults) are cancelled. Then, when the Catholic faithful forfeit grace by committing mortal sin, they need another infusion of grace. The sacrament of penance and reconciliation is the means to cancel all post-baptismal sins and restore the faithful to the state of grace. Question 6 critiqued this principle. It is not by an infusion of grace that pre-baptismal and post-baptismal sins are forgiven. Rather, justification is the divine declaration that sinful people are "not guilty" but "righteous" instead, and this pronouncement regards all their sins—past, present, and future.

Protestants also find problematic the Roman Catholic pairing of sins as mortal and venial. Certainly, Scripture distinguishes between intentional and unintentional sins (Num. 15:27–31) and greater and lesser sins (Ezek. 8:6, 13, 15; John 19:11). However, "this distinction focuses on the gravity of sin in terms of harmful consequences in people's lives and in terms of the loss of intimacy of people's relationship with God. It does not, however, address the issue of guilt before God. In the case of one's legal standing before God, each and every sin, no matter how serious or minor it may be, makes one guilty before God and thus incurs divine wrath (James 2:10–11; Gal. 3:10; Deut. 27:26)."[24] Thus, all sin is mortal, cutting one off from divine grace, making one guilty before God, incurring divine wrath, and requiring forgiveness. There is no distinction between mortal and venial sin in terms of the necessity of divine intervention to save.

Finally, the pair of human and divine action features both commonalities and differences between Protestants and Catholics. Some agreement comes with the human acts of contrition as feeling remorse for one's sin, confession

---

23. For further discussion, see *RCTP*, 347.
24. *RCTP*, 407.

as acknowledging one's sin, and satisfaction as making restitution in the case of harm caused to others. However, major disagreement is found in two areas. First, Protestants deny that confession must be made to a priest, who then absolves the penitent of her confessed sins. Second, the penitential act of satisfaction or penance as making amends for or expiating one's sin is both impossible and unnecessary. Penance is impossible because only Christ could render satisfaction to God; no human being can possibly do so. And penance is unnecessary because Christ did indeed render satisfaction to God (Rom. 3:23–26). No human penance—fasting, praying, almsgiving, and the like—can or need render satisfaction to God, as the Catholic Church envisions the sacrament doing.

## Summary

The sacrament of penance and reconciliation provides grace for the forgiveness of post-baptismal mortal sins committed by the Catholic faithful. It features important pairs. Sin is both against God and against the Church. To rectify this dual offense, this sacrament is named penance and reconciliation, with the former aspect dealing with sin against God and the latter aspect dealing with sin against the Church. The pair of first conversion and second conversion emphasizes that through faith in the good news and participation in the sacrament of baptism, unbelievers undergo a first conversion. This event is followed by a second conversion, which is the ongoing, lifelong struggle of turning from sin and being renewed. Baptism is also associated with another pairing. Whereas that sacrament is designed to deal with pre-baptismal sins, penance and reconciliation addresses post-baptismal sins. The pair of mortal and venial sins focuses on the gravity of sin. While the sacrament of penance and reconciliation is required to forgive mortal sin and restore the grace that was lost, it is not necessary in the case of venial sin. Finally, the sacrament itself consists of the pair of human and divine action. On the human side, the three acts of the penitent are contrition, confession, and satisfaction or penance. The actions on the divine side come through the intervention of the Catholic clergy who administers the sacrament and absolves the penitent of her confessed sins.

## REFLECTION QUESTIONS

1. How does the sacrament of penance and reconciliation illustrate the nature-grace interdependence and the Christ-Church interconnection?

2. If you are Roman Catholic, what has been your experience with this sacrament? How do you assess your contrition, confession, and penance or satisfaction?

3. If you are part of a Protestant church, how do you confess your sins? If you don't make confession to a priest, who then absolves you of your confessed sins? Does your church encourage your confession, and what does it indicate you should do when your sins hurt other people?

4. What is your evaluation of each of the pairs? Sin against God and sin against the Church. Penance and reconciliation. First conversion and second conversion. Pre-baptismal sins and post-baptismal sins. Mortal sins and venial sins. Finally, both human action and divine action of the sacrament.

5. From a Protestant perspective, why is the penitential act of satisfaction or penance as making amends for or expiating one's sin both impossible and unnecessary? If you are Roman Catholic, how do you respond to this position?

# What Is the Sacrament of Holy Orders?

As the two sacraments at the service of communion, holy orders and matrimony "are directed towards the salvation of others . . . [and] confer a particular mission in the Church and serve to build up the people of God."[1] I will discuss matrimony in Question 24 and focus on holy orders here. This sacrament consecrates priests "to feed the Church by the word and grace of God."[2]

### Apostolic Ministry, Apostolic Succession, and Holy Orders

As "one, holy, catholic, and *apostolic*," the Roman Catholic Church's apostolic ministry is grounded on the doctrine of apostolic succession and the sacrament of holy orders. The Church's hierarchical structure is headed by the Magisterium, or teaching office, that is responsible for teaching, sanctifying, and ruling the Catholic faithful. Specifically, the Church is apostolic as it "continues to be taught, sanctified, and guided by the apostles until Christ's return, through their successors in pastoral office: the college of bishops, 'assisted by priests, in union with the successor of Peter, the Church's supreme pastor.'"[3] For biblical support, the Church points to Peter's confession and Jesus's promise to build his church upon the rock (Matt. 16:13–20). The Church understands this passage to mean that Peter and the other apostles would be followed by successors, the bishops of the Catholic Church, to whom Jesus would delegate his divine authority through Peter to guarantee the unceasing progress of his church.[4] This is the doctrine of apostolic succession.

---

1. CCC, 1534.
2. CCC, 1535. The citation is from Vatican Council II, *Lumen Gentium*, 11.2.
3. CCC, 857. The citation is from Vatican Council II, *Ad Gentes*, 5.
4. As *Lumen Gentium* further explains of Christ's apostles: "In order that the mission assigned to them might continue after their death, they passed on to their immediate cooperators, as it were, in the form of a testament, the duty of confirming and finishing the work begun by themselves, recommending to [exhorting] them that they attend to the whole flock in which the Holy Spirit placed them to shepherd the Church of God. They therefore

Apostolic succession and the sacrament of holy orders are intimately and necessarily linked. Participation in the apostolic ministry of the Church is conferred through this sacrament. Its name comes from the Latin word *ordo*, or a governing structure. *Ordination*, then, means "incorporation into an *ordo*," that is, in this case, into the hierarchy of the Catholic Church.

## Three Degrees of Holy Orders: Bishop, Priest, Deacon

As this hierarchy is three-tiered, so are the degrees of holy orders. The *ordo episcoporum* is for the office of bishop. The *ordo presbyterorum* is for the office of priest. And the *ordo diaconorum* is for the office of deacon. The conferring of these orders upon bishops, priests, and deacons is not simply like an appointment to a responsibility or merely like a commissioning for a task. On the contrary, the bestowing of holy orders "goes beyond a simple election, designation, delegation, or institution by the community, for it confers a gift of the Holy Spirit that permits the exercise of a 'sacred power' (*sacra potestas*) which can come only from Christ himself through his Church."[5]

This sacramental bestowal of a sacred power means that when a priest baptizes an infant girl, Christ himself baptizes her. When a bishop anoints the sick with oil, it is Christ himself who anoints for healing. Indeed, the one ordained by means of the sacrament of holy orders "acts in the person of Christ" through the sacred power granted.[6] Such sacramentally conferred power does not protect these ordained men from weakness, error, and even sin. They remain fully human persons susceptible to the normal trials and temptations of everyday life.[7] But holy orders does guarantee that their "sin cannot impede the fruit of grace" when they administer the sacraments.[8]

As an example, let's say that moments before a priest begins to celebrate a Mass, he completes an online embezzlement of thousands of dollars from the church's investment account. When he consecrates the bread and wine and then distributes the transubstantiated elements to the Catholic faithful, they still receive the body and blood of Christ as an infusion of grace without any reduction in effect due to his sin. The validity of the sacraments is in no way dependent on the spiritual and moral state of the priest or bishop who administers them. Holy orders is the reason for this guarantee.

---

appointed such men, and gave them the order that, when they should have died, other approved men would take up their ministry." Vatican Council II, *Lumen Gentium*, 20.

5. CCC, 1538 (italics removed).
6. "It is the same priest, Christ Jesus, whose sacred person his minister truly represents. Now the minister . . . is truly made like to the high priest and possesses the authority to act in the power and place of the person of Christ himself." Pope Pius XII, *Mediator Dei*, November 20, 1947, 69, Vatican.va.
7. These ordained men leave "human traces that are not always signs of fidelity to the Gospel and consequently can harm the apostolic fruitfulness of the Church." CCC, 1550.
8. CCC, 1550.

Because of this sacrament, "it is ultimately Christ who acts and effects salvation through the ordained minister, [so] the unworthiness of the latter does not prevent Christ from acting."[9]

## Two Kinds of Priesthood: Ministerial and Common

While Protestantism emphasizes the priesthood of all believers, Roman Catholicism has two kinds of priesthood: the ministerial or hierarchical priesthood, which applies to its consecrated leaders, and the baptismal or common priesthood, which pertains to the Catholic faithful. The Catholic Church administers the sacrament of holy orders upon its ministerial or hierarchical priesthood so that it may serve the Catholic faithful, also called the baptismal or common priesthood. All the members of the Catholic Church belong to this priesthood. By virtue of being part of this baptismal or common priesthood, members participate in Christ's mission by their acts of charity, prayers, work, and more. The ministerial or hierarchical priesthood exists to serve the Catholic faithful in their ministry.

## Two Degrees of Priestly Participation (Bishops and Priests) and One Degree of Service (Deacons)

The three degrees of holy orders—for bishops, for priests, and for deacons—are of two kinds. The first kind is priestly participation, consisting of two degrees: the episcopacy is the order for bishops, and the presbyterate is for the order of priests. The second kind is the one degree of service, which is the diaconate, or the order for deacons.

Regarding the first degree of priestly participation, the episcopacy or order of bishops is bestowed on men who are already priests. This episcopal ordination is

> the fullness of the sacrament of Holy Orders. This office transmits the apostolic line, the unbroken succession of bishops that goes back to the apostle Peter at the beginning of the Church. . . . This conferring of the fullness of the sacrament "is called the high priesthood, the acme (*summa*) of the sacred ministry." Specifically, episcopal ordination confers three offices or responsibilities—teaching, ruling, and sanctifying—such that bishops "take the place of Christ himself, teacher, shepherd, and priest, and act as his representative."[10]

9. CCC, 1584.
10. *RCTP*, 360. The citations are from CCC, 1557 and 1558, reflecting Vatican Council II, *Lumen Gentium*, 21.

The effect of the sacrament is the grace of the Holy Spirit, an indelible mark (as in baptism) that can never be erased. Even in the presence of heinous sin (for example, pedophilia), the bishop retains his sacramental character even when being removed from his episcopal office and stripped of his responsibilities. The duties of a bishop include "the pastoral care of the particular Church entrusted to him, but at the same time he bears collegially with all his brothers in the episcopacy [fellow bishops] the solicitude [concern] for all the Churches."[11] He is the leader of all the parishes in his geographical area as well as part of the college of bishops that is responsible for all the parishes throughout the world.

The order of bishops is at the summit of the Church's apostolic ministry, and the presbyterate is below that level of authority and responsibility. Specifically, this order of priests is the second degree of priestly participation. The episcopate possesses the supreme degree of authority; the presbyterate possesses a subordinate degree of authority. Thus, priests are coworkers alongside of bishops in the mission of the Catholic Church, representing the bishops as they serve in teaching, ruling, and sanctifying ministries delegated to them by the bishops. Like the bishops, priests are consecrated by the sacrament of holy orders, thus receiving the grace of the Holy Spirit, which is an indelible mark. Such consecration conforms them to Christ "in such a way that they are able to act in the person of Christ the head."[12] While they teach, rule, and sanctify to a lesser degree than do the bishops, and do so in dependence on the bishops, priests nevertheless participate "in the universal dimensions of the mission that Christ entrusted to the apostles."[13]

Regarding the one degree of service, the diaconate, or the order for deacons, functions in an assisting role to the bishops and priests. The Church ordains deacons "not unto the priesthood, but unto the ministry . . . [at] a lower level of the hierarchy."[14] Diaconal duties may include baptizing, preaching the homily at the Mass, distributing the elements of the Eucharist, blessing marriages, supervising funerals, and more.[15]

## The Administration of the Sacrament

The sacrament of holy orders is administered on a Sunday in the cathedral (the church from which the bishop presides) during the Eucharistic liturgy. This solemn, elaborate celebration features consecrated oil (which symbolizes the anointing of the Holy Spirit), the laying on of hands by bishops, and the prayer of consecration. Gifts bestowed on bishops include "the book of

---

11. CCC, 1560 (italics removed).
12. CCC, 1563. The citation is from Vatican Council II, *Presbyterorum Ordinis*, 2.
13. CCC, 1565.
14. CCC, 1569. The citation is from Vatican Council II, *Lumen Gentium*, 29.
15. Whereas the early church had a flourishing diaconate, the office dropped out of use until Vatican Council II. Since then, the Church has worked to restore the permanent diaconate.

the Gospels, the ring, the miter [hat], and the crozier [staff]." Priests receive the gifts of the paten, the tray on which the Eucharistic bread is placed; and the chalice, the cup for the Eucharistic wine. Deacons are given the book of the Gospels.[16] These gifts correspond to and symbolize the ministries that are specific to bishops, priests, and deacons.

Because holy orders is conferred by bishops who act in the person of Christ, it is Christ himself who ordains men to the three degrees of this sacrament. The Catholic Church only ordains men, following the example of Christ himself in choosing twelve men as his apostles. In turn, they chose other men as their successors, and so on throughout history. As the Church is "bound by this choice made by the Lord himself . . . the ordination of women is not possible."[17] Additionally, those ordained as bishops and priests pledge themselves to remain celibate throughout their life. By contrast, deacons may be married.

### Protestant Ordination

For many Protestants, ordination is a solemn ceremony during which its pastors/priests/ministers are set apart or commissioned as the leaders, teachers, and shepherds of their church. Specifically, the ecumenical document *Baptism, Eucharist, and Ministry* defines it in this way: "Ordination denotes an action by God and the community [the church] by which the ordained are strengthened by the Spirit for their task and are upheld by the acknowledgment and prayers of the congregation."[18] Whereas there seems to be a significant degree of overlap with the Roman Catholic sacrament of holy orders, discontinuity between Protestant ordination and Catholic ordination should not be overlooked.

First, Protestant churches hold to only two sacraments, baptism and the Lord's Supper. This means that for Protestants, ordination is not a sacrament. It also means that, whereas holy orders is essential for the very existence of the Roman Catholic Church and its apostolic succession, ordination is not indispensable for Protestant churches. This point can be seen clearly by the fact that different Protestant churches define ordination and administer it in different ways. For example, Anglican churches and Methodist churches have a threefold structure (called a polity) similar to that of the Roman Catholic Church: bishops, priests/pastors/elders/presbyters, and deacons. Presbyterian churches and Baptist churches have a twofold polity: pastors/elders and deacons. This diversity underscores that, whereas leadership is important for the proper functioning and wellbeing of Protestant churches, it is not essential

---

16. CCC, 1574.
17. CCC, 1577.
18. World Council of Churches, *Baptism, Eucharist, and Ministry*, Faith and Order Paper no. 111 (Geneva: World Council of Churches, 1982), "Ministry," V.A.40. https://www.oikoumene.org/sites/default/files/Document/FO1982_111_en.pdf.

to them. This contrasts strongly with the hierarchy of the Roman Catholic Church, whose apostolic succession secured through the sacrament of holy orders is essential to the very existence of the Church.

Second, Protestant ordination is not grounded on the two axioms of the Roman Catholic Church that are at the heart of holy orders. Specifically, "the nature-grace interdependence makes a substantial contribution to the sacrament: human nature (in this case, the men consecrated by Holy Orders) possesses the capacity to mediate grace; accordingly, the ordained men act in the person of Christ the Head, as particularly evident when they administer the sacraments that convey grace on the faithful."[19] The sacrament is also closely tied to the second axiom: "the Christ-Church interconnection means that the Catholic Church is the continuation of the incarnation of Christ, who is present in his body the Church (in this case, its consecrated ministers, the priests) and acts through them to convey grace."[20] Questions 6 and 8 critiqued these two axioms. Thus, Protestant ordination is not about consecrating church leaders to become channels of grace and to act in the person of Christ.

### The Priesthood of All Believers

A characteristic of Protestantism is its emphasis on the priesthood of all believers. Scripture describes people who embrace Christ, the living stone: "You yourselves, as living stones, a spiritual house, are being built to be *a holy priesthood* to offer spiritual sacrifices acceptable to God through Jesus Christ. . . . You are a chosen race, *a royal priesthood*, a holy nation, a people for his possession, so that you may proclaim the praises of the one who called you out of darkness into his marvelous light" (1 Peter 2:5, 9 CSB, italics added). All people who trust Christ for salvation constitute a holy and royal priesthood. All Christians offer spiritual sacrifices to God and praise him for his abundant mercy that makes them his people. All believers pray for one another, hear confession of sin and offer assurance of forgiveness, love one another, evangelize together, and teach and admonish one another with the Word of God (Col. 3:16).

This Protestant priesthood of all believers does bear some similarity with the Roman Catholic idea of the baptismal or common priesthood, a descriptor of the Catholic faithful. The divide comes, however, between the Protestant ministry and the Catholic ministerial or hierarchical priesthood. At the time of the Reformation itself, Reformers like Martin Luther dissented from the Catholic division between its leaders—bishops and priests, who compose the sacred realm—and lay people—civic rulers, craftsmen, merchants, and housewives, who compose the secular realm. According to the Reformers, this centuries-old sacred-secular divide is unbiblical. All people

---

19. *RCTP*, 363.
20. *RCTP*, 364.

are image-bearers of God, and all Christians are priests to God and for one another. Certainly, there are ministers who serve in church offices, but that is a difference in divine call and pastoral vocation. It is not a difference in essence, a change in the very nature of those upon whom the sacrament of holy orders is bestowed.[21]

## Summary

Holy orders is the sacrament by which qualified men are consecrated as the Catholic Church's leaders who teach, sanctify, and rule the Catholic faithful. There are three degrees of holy orders: the *ordo episcoporum* for the office of bishop, the *ordo presbyterorum* for the office of priest, and the *ordo diaconorum* for the office of deacon. The sacrament "confers a gift of the Holy Spirit that permits the exercise of a 'sacred power' (*sacra potestas*) which can come only from Christ himself through his Church."[22] The three degrees are of two kinds. The first kind is priestly participation, consisting of two degrees: the episcopacy is the order for bishops, and the presbyterate is for the order of priests. The second kind is the one degree of service, which is the diaconate or the order for deacons. While there are some similarities between this Catholic sacrament and the varieties of Protestant ordination, the differences are quite substantial.

## REFLECTION QUESTIONS

1. How does the sacrament of holy orders illustrate the nature-grace interdependence and the Christ-Church interconnection?

2. Why are the apostolic ministry of the Roman Catholic Magisterium, apostolic succession, and holy orders linked together? Why is the belief that Catholic ministers "act in the person of Christ" so foundational to the Church and its ministry? Why is that belief so disconcerting to Protestants?

3. If you are Roman Catholic, have you ever attended a priestly ordination service in your Catholic parish or an episcopal ordination service in your diocesan cathedral? What was your experience, and how do you assess the ordination?

4. If you are Protestant, what is ordination in your church? Would you ever consider being ordained for Christian ministry? Why or why not?

---

21. For example, see Martin Luther, "To the Christian Nobility of the German Nation" (LW 44).
22. CCC, 1538 (italics removed).

5. Why is it important that the Roman Catholic Church emphasizes the baptismal or common priesthood of all Catholic faithful? What are the similarities and differences between this Catholic priesthood and the Protestant priesthood of all believers?

# What Are the Sacraments of Confirmation, Anointing the Sick, and Matrimony?

By grouping these three sacraments together for discussion, I'm not indicating that they are minor sacraments. Rather, their discussion can be briefer. Importantly, each one comes from a different category. Confirmation is a sacrament of initiation. Anointing of the sick is a sacrament of healing. Matrimony is a sacrament at the service of communion. I will keep these distinctions in mind as I rehearse the three together.

## Confirmation

As a sacrament of initiation, confirmation is closely associated with baptism and the Eucharist. "The reception of the sacrament of Confirmation is necessary for the completion of baptismal grace. For 'by the sacrament of Confirmation, [the baptized] are more perfectly bound to the Church and are enriched with a special strength of the Holy Spirit."[1] It is clear that at the heart of the sacrament is the nature-grace interdependence. When the Church consecrates oil, an element of nature, it becomes capable of receiving and transmitting divine grace. During the celebration of confirmation, the confirmands (the recipients of the sacrament) are anointed with this consecrated oil. The once-baptized and now-confirmed members of the Church have the fullness of grace and the Spirit's power. By their enriched, transformed character, the Catholic faithful may act in love and engage in good works to merit eternal life.

Participation in this sacrament is of two types. In the case of those who were baptized as infants, their confirmation takes place between the ages of

---

1. CCC, 1285. The citation is from Vatican Council II, *Lumen Gentium*, 11.

seven and sixteen. This is considered to be the age of discretion.[2] As for adults (seven years old or above), their confirmation occurs in the context of the other two sacraments of initiation. They are baptized, confirmed, and share in the Eucharist at the same time.

The celebration of confirmation is led by a bishop, who confers the Holy Spirit through this sacrament. As he extends "his hands over the whole group of confirmands," he invokes God the Father: "Send your Holy Spirit upon them."[3] The confirmands are anointed with oil on their foreheads through the laying on of hands and through the words, "Be sealed with the Gift of the Holy Spirit."[4] At the conclusion, the sign of peace symbolizes that these newly confirmed members enjoy full communion with the Church. Because it leaves an indelible mark, like baptism and holy orders, confirmation can never be repeated.

There are two primary effects of this sacrament. The first is "the full outpouring of the Holy Spirit as once granted to the apostles on the day of Pentecost." The second effect is "an increase and deepening of baptismal grace," with several aspects, in the words of the catechism:

- it roots us more deeply in the divine filiation [sonship] which makes us cry, "Abba! Father!" [Rom 8:15]
- it unites us more firmly to Christ;
- it increases the gifts of the Holy Spirit in us;
- it renders our bond with the Church more perfect;
- it gives us a special strength of the Holy Spirit to spread and defend the faith by word and action as true witnesses of Christ, to confess the name of Christ boldly, and never to be ashamed of the Cross.[5]

Again, the effects of this sacrament illustrate the quantitative aspect of grace. It is deepened, strengthened, increased, and perfected. By means of its infusion through consecrated oil, grace further transforms the character of the Catholic faithful. Once again, this is the nature-grace interdependence. The other key principle—the Christ-Church interconnection—is also on display. As the bishop presides over the sacrament, he "acts in the person of Christ" such that it is Christ himself who confirms.

---

2. CCC, 1307. The US Conference of Catholic Bishops, in accordance with canon 891 of the Code of Canon Law, established this age range (November 15, 2000).
3. CCC, 1299.
4. CCC, 1300.
5. CCC, 1303.

## Anointing of the Sick

As a sacrament of healing, anointing of the sick is the rite by which "Christ has willed that his Church continue, in the power of the Holy Spirit, his work of healing and salvation, even among her own members."[6] Specifically, this sacrament is the Church's way of commending "those who are ill to the suffering and glorified Lord, that he may raise them up and save them."[7] Many Catholics know this sacrament by the name *extreme unction*, as its almost exclusive practice prior to Vatican Council II was for those on the verge of dying. The council determined that the rite "is not a sacrament for those only who are at the point of death. Hence, as soon as anyone of the faithful begins to be in danger of death from sickness or old age, the fitting time for him to receive this sacrament has certainly arrived."[8] Clearly, then, the sacrament is repeatable, being administered in cases of serious illness and increasing frailty, as well as prior to major surgery.[9] It is not administered to those who have already died.

Whenever possible, anointing of the sick is administered in conjunction with two other sacraments: penance and the Eucharist. First, the sick person confesses her sins to the priest, who in turn grants her absolution. Following a penitential rite comes the Liturgy of the Word, to awaken faith. The priest then anoints her with consecrated oil on the forehead and hands, saying, "Through this holy anointing may the Lord in his love and mercy help you with the grace of the Holy Spirit. May the Lord who frees you from sin save you and raise you up."[10] Finally, the priest celebrates the sacrament of the Eucharist, which "should always be the last sacrament of the earthly journey, the 'viaticum' [Latin = provisions for a journey] for 'passing over' to eternal life."[11]

The effects of this sacrament are fourfold. The first grace is "strengthening, peace and courage to overcome the difficulties that go with the condition of serious illness or the frailty of old age. This grace is a gift of the Holy Spirit, who renews trust and faith in God and strengthens against the temptations of the evil one, the temptation to discouragement and anguish in the face of death." This aid "is meant to lead the sick person to healing of the soul, but also of the body if such is God's will." Additionally, and in light of James 5:15, "if he has committed sins, he will be forgiven."[12]

Second, "the sick person receives the strength and the gift of uniting himself more closely to Christ's Passion: in a certain way he is consecrated to bear fruit by configuration to the Savior's redemptive Passion. Suffering . . . acquires

---

6. CCC, 1421.
7. CCC, 1499; the citation is from Vatican Council II, *Lumen Gentium*, 11.
8. CCC, 1514; the citation is from Vatican Council II, *Sacrosanctum Concilium*, 73.
9. CCC, 1515.
10. CCC, 1513.
11. CCC, 1517.
12. CCC, 1520.

a new meaning; it becomes a participation in the saving work of Jesus."[13] A third grace concerns the Church as the anointed sick "contributes to the sanctification of the Church and to the good of all men for whom the Church suffers and offers herself through Christ to God the Father."[14]

A fourth effect is "preparation for the final journey": "The Anointing of the Sick completes our conformity to the death and resurrection of Christ, just as Baptism began it. It completes the [three] holy anointings that mark the whole Christian life: that of Baptism, which sealed the new life in us, and that of confirmation, which strengthened us for the combat of this life. This last anointing fortifies the end of our earthly life like a solid rampart for the final struggles before entering the Father's house."[15]

Once again, this sacrament is grounded on the nature-grace interdependence. The consecrated oil, an element of nature, is capable of receiving and transmitting divine grace. Moreover, the Christ-Church interconnection is at work in that the priest who administers this sacrament acts "in the person of Christ." Thus, the one who anoints is Christ himself, who continues his healing ministry through the Church. This principle is also at work in the Catholic view that the suffering of the faithful "becomes a participation in the saving work of Jesus"[16] and "contributes to the sanctification of the Church and to the good of all men."[17] Certainly, Jesus's followers are promised suffering (Phil. 1:29), called to endure suffering (1 Peter 1:6–9), follow his example of suffering (1 Peter 2:21–25), and have all they need to suffer well (2 Cor. 12:10). But this biblical teaching does not affirm that the sufferings of the faithful add to the sufferings of Christ and his church in any redemptive sense.[18]

## Matrimony

As a sacrament at the service of communion, matrimony is "directed toward the salvation of others" through consecrating spouses "for the duties and dignity of their [marital] state."[19] This marital covenant, which is between one man and one woman, "is by nature ordered toward the good of the spouses and the procreation and education of its offspring."[20] The Catholic view of marriage is very traditional, well-grounded biblically, and stands against contemporary

---

13. CCC, 1521.
14. CCC, 1522.
15. CCC, 1523.
16. CCC, 1521.
17. CCC, 1522.
18. Colossians 1:24–25, while often cited in support of the Catholic idea of the redemptive suffering of the church, does not encourage suffering as some kind of compensation for a deficiency in the sufferings of Christ. Rather, the passage focuses on the persecutions that Paul faced as he engaged in preaching the gospel among hostile people. For further discussion, see *RCTP*, 355–56.
19. CCC, 1534, 1535.
20. CCC, 1601; the citation is from the Code of Canon Law 1055.

perversions such as homosexuality and polygamy. Additionally, the Church exalts virginity, as seen in its requirement that its leaders—priests and bishops—are unmarried and its religious—monks and nuns—take a vow of celibacy.

This sacrament is administered during a Mass: "It is fitting that the spouses should seal their consent to give themselves to each other through the offering of their own lives by uniting it to the offering of Christ for his Church made present in the Eucharistic sacrifice, and by receiving the Eucharist so that, communicating [participating in] the same Body and the same Blood of Christ, they may form but 'one body' in Christ."[21] During the Mass, the man and the woman express their consent to be married—"I take you to be my wife/husband"—and thereby confer the sacrament of matrimony upon each other.[22]

There are two effects of this sacrament. First, it creates a permanent and exclusive bond between the spouses, as God himself seals the covenant. By this divine action, the marriage is rendered indissoluble and is guaranteed by God's faithfulness. Second, the sacrament confers grace that is "intended to perfect the couple's love and to strengthen their indissoluble unity."[23]

Additionally, the Church imposes two requirements on Catholic marriages. The first is indissolubility and faithfulness to the marriage. This obligation rules out polygamy and divorce (under particularly difficult situations, separation may be permitted). The second requirement is openness to fertility. That is, Catholic marriage "is ordered to the procreation and education of the offspring."[24] This obligation rules out the use of contraception (natural family planning is permitted), abortion, and infanticide (which are "abominable crimes").[25]

## Protestants and the Sacraments of Confirmation, the Anointing of the Sick, and Matrimony

Protestant churches do not consider the three rites of confirmation, anointing of the sick, and matrimony to be sacraments. At the same time, Protestants have similar practices. Confirmation has a weak biblical basis not particularly tied to oil, and Jesus Christ did not ordain it. Though they don't consider it a sacrament, many Protestant churches teach the faith and prepare their people for membership through confirmation or catechism classes. Anointing the sick, while

---

21. CCC, 1621. The biblical reference "one body" is modified from "the two shall become one flesh" (Gen. 2:24).
22. CCC, 1623. Ideally, the participants in this sacrament are a Catholic man and a Catholic woman. Two categories of exceptions exist. A "mixed marriage" is between a Catholic and a baptized non-Catholic, for example, a Protestant. A "marriage with disparity of cult" is between a Catholic and an unbaptized person, for example, a Jew. In this latter case, the Catholic Church must grant special permission for the marriage to be covenanted. In both cases, the non-Catholic spouse must agree that the children of the marriage will be baptized and educated as Catholics. CCC, 1635. Canon 1125 of the Code of Canon Law stipulates this arrangement.
23. CCC, 1641.
24. CCC, 1652; the citation is from Vatican Council II, *Gaudium et Spes*, 48.1; 50.
25. Vatican Council II, *Gaudium et Spes*, 51.

commanded to be administered by the church with oil as a sign of consecration (James 5:13–16), was not ordained by Christ.[26] While not viewing it as a sacrament, many Protestant churches, in obedience to biblical instructions (James 5:13–16), pray for the sick, anointing them with oil as a sign of consecration to the Lord and his favor. Matrimony, while certainly upheld by Jesus (Matt. 19:4–5) and honored by him (John 2:1–11), is a creation ordinance, established by God at the beginning of human history (Gen. 2:24). It lacks both a concrete sign and Jesus's ordination. Without considering it as a sacrament, Protestant churches perform marriages for their members. While often disagreeing with the Catholic proscription of contraception (though many stand against the use of abortifacients), Protestants also emphasize procreation and highly value children.

## Summary

The sacraments of confirmation, anointing of the sick, and matrimony provide grace for being fully incorporated into the Catholic Church, facing illness and death, and embarking on the journey of marriage. At the heart of each sacrament are both the nature-grace interdependence and the Christ-Church interconnection.

## REFLECTION QUESTIONS

1. How do the sacraments of confirmation, anointing of the sick, and matrimony illustrate the nature-grace interdependence?

2. How do these three sacraments illustrate the Christ-Church interconnection?

3. If you are Roman Catholic, when were you confirmed? If you are Protestant, did you participate in confirmation or catechism classes? In either case, how do you assess your experience?

4. If you are Roman Catholic, have you ever been anointed for being sick or near death? How do you assess your participation in this sacrament? If you are Protestant, does your church follow the directives of James 5:13–16 in praying for the sick and anointing them with oil? Why or why not?

5. If you are Roman Catholic and married, were you married in the Catholic Church? How do you assess your participation in the sacrament of matrimony? If you are Protestant and married, what is your church's structure for who can marry, preparation for marriage, and the wedding ceremony itself?

---

26. Moreover, Scripture never represents the presence and work of the Holy Spirit by oil.

# Questions about Salvation

In this fourth section, I explore questions about the Catholic Church's process of salvation; its doctrines of justification, regeneration, and sanctification; its view of perseverance and assurance of salvation; its perspective on good works and merit; and its doctrine of purgatory and related practices.

# What Is the Process of Salvation according to Catholic Theology?

I will place this question into the overarching narrative of the Bible, which consists of four "chapters": creation, fall, redemption, and consummation.

## Creation

The triune God created the universe and all it contains *ex nihilo* (out of nothing). At the apex of his creative work, God made human beings in his image (Gen. 1:26–28). This means that of all the creation, the human being is "the only creature on earth that God has willed for its own sake" and the only creature who is "able to know and love his creator."[1] Specifically, God created Adam and Eve as the first image-bearers (Gen. 2:7, 18–25) "in an original 'state of holiness and justice.'" The catechism goes on to say, "Original holiness means that they shared in the life of God, with no fear of suffering or death. Original righteousness means that (1) individually, Adam and Eve each experienced an inner harmony within him/herself; (2) relationally, the two together experienced harmony between themselves; and (3) environmentally, they experienced harmony with their surrounding created world."[2] Adam and Eve consisted of three elements: the spiritual faculties of a soul or reason, passions, and a body. In this original state of uprightness, their soul or reason controlled their passions and their body. The two were free from concupiscence—the inclination to sin and evil—and anything else that would be contrary to reason.

---

1. CCC, 356; the citations are from Vatican Council II, *Gaudium et Spes*, 12.3 and 24.3.
2. *RCPT*, 120; the citation is from *Canons and Decrees of the Council of Trent*, 5th session (June 17, 1546), *Decree concerning Original Sin*, introduction, 1.

## Fall

From this idyllic state, Adam and Eve fell tragically (Gen. 3:1–11), as the catechism describes: "Man, tempted by the devil, let his trust in his Creator die in his heart and, abusing his freedom, disobeyed God's command. This is what man's first sin consisted of. All subsequent sin would be disobedience to-ward God and lack of trust in his goodness. In that sin man preferred himself to God and by that very act scorned him. He chose himself over and against God, against the requirements of his creaturely status and therefore against his own good."[3] By falling, Adam and Eve forfeited "the grace of original holi-ness. They become afraid of the God of whom they have conceived a distorted image—that of a God jealous of his prerogatives."[4] They became alienated from the life of God and were plunged into fear of suffering and death.

Additionally, "the harmony in which they had found themselves, thanks to original justice, is now destroyed."[5] This loss consists of four disturbances. First, "the control of the soul's spiritual faculties over the body is shattered."[6] No longer would their soul or reason rightly function to control their pas-sions and their body. Rather, a reversal took place as their lower parts usurped the proper governing role of their soul, resulting in Adam and Eve being in-clined toward sin and evil. The second disturbance is that "the union of man and woman becomes subject to tensions, their relations henceforth marked by lust and domination."[7] What was once a relationship of love and transpar-ency became characterized by selfishness and hiding.

As for the third disturbance, "harmony with creation is broken: visible creation has become alien and hostile to man. Because of man, creation is now subject 'to its bondage to decay' [Rom 8:21]."[8] For the fallen couple, work would take on an unproductive dimension as their worksite—the cre-ation—became stingy and grudgingly yielded to their labor. "Finally, the consequence explicitly foretold for this disobedience will come true: man will 'return to the ground,' for out of it he was taken. Death makes its en-trance into human history."[9]

Even more tragically, the fall affected not only Adam and Eve but spread to all future image bearers. Following Paul's presentation in Romans 5:12–19, "the Church has always taught that the overwhelming misery which oppresses men and their inclination towards evil and death cannot be understood apart from their connection with Adam's sin and the fact that he has transmitted to us a sin with which we are all born afflicted, a sin which is the 'death of the

---

3. CCC, 397–98.
4. CCC, 399.
5. CCC, 400.
6. CCC, 400.
7. CCC, 400.
8. CCC, 400.
9. CCC, 400.

soul.'"[10] Though the transmission of this sin is shrouded in mystery, "we do know by revelation that Adam had received original holiness and justice not for himself alone, but for all human nature. By yielding to the tempter, Adam and Eve committed a personal sin, but this sin affected the human nature that they would then transmit in a fallen state. It is a sin which will be transmitted by propagation to all mankind, that is, by the transmission of a human nature deprived of original holiness and justice."[11] Importantly, this original sin, which affects all human beings from the moment of their conception, is "a sin 'contracted' and not 'committed'—a state and not an act."[12]

For Protestants holding to Reformed theology, a significant difference arises between the Catholic view of original sin and the Reformed view of it. From a Catholic perspective, original sin "is a deprivation of original holiness and justice, but human nature has not been totally corrupted: it is wounded in the natural powers proper to it, subject to ignorance, suffering and the dominion of death, and inclined to sin—an inclination to evil that is called concupiscence."[13] Specifically, the Catholic view distances itself from "the first Protestant reformers [who] taught that original sin has radically perverted man and destroyed his freedom; they identified the sin inherited by each man with the tendency to evil (concupiscence), which would be insurmountable.[14] Thus, the Catholic position denies total depravity and total inability. Sin is a serious disturbance but not a devastating disaster that encompasses even the inclination to evil.

### Redemption
The only hope for rescue out of human fallenness is redemption, including salvation accomplished and salvation applied. As for the first, the Catholic Church affirms that the triune God purposed to create and, following the fall, redeem human image bearers:

> God freely wills to communicate the glory of his blessed life. Such is the "plan of his loving kindness," conceived by the Father before the foundation of the world, in his beloved Son: "He destined us in love to be his sons" and "to be conformed to the image of his Son" through "the spirit of sonship" [Eph. 1:4–5, 9; Rom. 8:15, 29]. This plan is a "grace [that] was given to us in Christ Jesus before the ages began," stemming immediately from Trinitarian love [2 Tim. 1:9–10]. It unfolds in the work of creation, the whole history of salvation after

10. CCC, 403; the citation is from *Canons and Decrees of the Council of Trent*, 5th session (June 17, 1546), *Decree concerning Original Sin*, introduction, 2.
11. CCC, 404.
12. CCC, 404.
13. CCC, 405.
14. CCC, 406.

the fall, and the missions of the Son and the Spirit, which are continued in the mission of the Church.[15]

Accordingly, God accomplished redemption for sinful human beings.

The accomplishment of salvation has particular reference to God the Son incarnate: "Since God alone can forgive sins, it is God who, in Jesus his eternal Son made man, 'will save his people from their sins' [Matt. 1:21]." Specifically, "the name 'Jesus' signifies that the very name of God is present in the person of his Son, made man for the universal and definitive redemption from sins. It is the divine name that alone brings salvation, and henceforth all can invoke his name, for Jesus united himself to all men through his Incarnation, so that 'there is no other name under heaven given among men by which we must be saved' [Acts 4:12]."[16] Christ has accomplished salvation for all people. The divine work is complete in one sense.

In another sense, the accomplishment of salvation is continuing through the Roman Catholic Church. As it has traditionally affirmed, the Church insists that "outside the Church, there is no salvation." Additionally, the Church is "necessary for salvation" because "Christ himself explicitly asserted the necessity of faith and Baptism, and thereby affirmed at the same time the necessity of the Church."[17] Thus, if people know that God has established the Catholic Church as necessary for salvation, yet they "refuse either to enter it or to remain in it," they cannot be saved.[18]

What is the Catholic Church's specific role in the application of salvation? Remember that human beings, as divine image-bearers, are "called to beatitude but wounded by sin" and thus need salvation through the Church.[19] This process encompasses many aspects: law, grace, conversion, justification, merit, and the sacraments.

The moral law helps point people toward salvation: "it prescribes for man the ways, the rules of conduct that lead to the promised beatitude; it proscribes the ways of evil which turn him away from God and his love."[20] In addition to law, grace is needed for cleansing from sin and communicating 'the righteousness of God through faith in Jesus Christ' [Rom. 3:22] and through Baptism."[21] By means of this initial sacrament, the baptized are cleansed of original sin (and, in the case of adults, both original sin and actual sins committed up to that point), regenerated, and incorporated into Christ and his

---

15. CCC, 259.
16. CCC, 432.
17. CCC, 846. The citation is taken from Vatican Council II, *Lumen Gentium*, 14, with biblical support given as Mark 16:16 and John 3:5.
18. CCC, 846.
19. CCC, 1949.
20. CCC, 1950.
21. CCC, 1987.

Church. Next comes conversion: "The first work of the grace of the Holy Spirit is conversion, effecting justification. . . . Moved by grace, man turns toward God and away from sin, thus accepting forgiveness and righteousness from on high."[22] Conversion results in justification, which "is not only the remission of sins, but also the sanctification and renewal of the interior man."[23]

To be clear, the Church holds that "no one can merit the initial grace of forgiveness and justification."[24] Yet, once the process of the application of salvation begins, its continuation is a lifelong synergistic work of God and the Catholic faithful. The catechism states, "Justification establishes cooperation between God's grace and man's freedom. On man's part it is expressed by the assent of faith to the Word of God, which invites him to conversion, and in the cooperation of charity with the prompting of the Holy Spirit who precedes and preserves his assent."[25] This divine part of preparation and preservation intersects with the human part: "when God touches man's heart through the illumination of the Holy Spirit, man himself is not inactive while receiving that inspiration, since he could reject it; and yet, without God's grace, he cannot by his own free will move himself toward justice in God's sight."[26] Thus, following the initial, gracious work of God in forgiveness and justification, the Catholic faithful embark on a cooperative venture with God toward ultimate salvation.

The divine grace needed for complete sanctification is inextricably connected to the Church's sacraments. As just noted, baptism establishes the baptized into a state of grace. Through the other sacraments, the Catholic faithful receive new infusions of grace to continue the process of sanctification. Such grace prepares and empowers them to engage in good works and thereby merit eternal life. Good works have specific reference to almsgiving, prayers and offerings, fasting, and chastity. A merit is the recompense God owes to the Catholic faithful as a reward for their part in this divine-human cooperative process. In terms of the application of salvation, then, after the initial divine work, the process is synergistic. Indeed, "God has freely chosen to associate man with the work of his grace."[27]

## Consummation
This lifelong process of pursing salvation will come to an end either at death or at the return of Jesus Christ. Thus, the consummation has two aspects: individual and cosmic.

---

22. CCC, 1989.
23. CCC, 1989.
24. CCC, 2010.
25. CCC, 1993.
26. CCC, 1993; the citation is from *Canons and Decrees of the Council of Trent*, 6th session (January 13, 1547), *Decree on Justification*, chap. 5.
27. CCC, 2008.

In terms of individual consummation, the Catholic Church believes that each person "will be rewarded immediately at death in accordance with his works of faith."[28] Specifically, it holds to two eternal destinies and one temporal destiny. The two eternal destinies are "either entrance into the blessedness of heaven—through a purification or immediately—or immediate and everlasting damnation."[29] On the one hand, the Catholic faithful "who die in God's grace and friendship and are perfectly purified" enter immediately into heaven. On the other hand, people who freely choose to "die in mortal sin without repenting and accepting God's merciful love" enter immediately into hell.[30] This is the "state of definitive self-exclusion from communion with God and the blessed [the faithful in heaven]" to which the damned descend, "where they suffer the punishment of hell, 'eternal fire.'"[31] Thus, heaven and hell are the two possible eternal destinies.

There is also one temporal destiny. For the Catholic faithful who need an extended purification, purgatory is their fate immediately after death and before they are qualified to enter into heaven. "All who die in God's grace and friendship, but still imperfectly purified, are indeed assured of their eternal salvation; but after death they undergo purification, so as to achieve the holiness necessary to enter the joy of heaven."[32] Purgatory is "this final purification of the elect, which is entirely different from the punishment of the damned."[33]

As for cosmic consummation, the Catholic Church holds to a complex of future events: the return of Christ, the resurrection of both the righteous and unrighteous, the last judgment resulting in either eternal life or eternal damnation, and the new heavens and new earth.

## Protestant Concerns

Key concerns of Protestants include the following. The first is the Catholic Church's view of Adam and Eve's state of original justice by which their soul or reason functioned to govern their passions and their body. This view of the divine image having specifically to do with human reason is reductionistic. Moreover, the Genesis creation story gives no hint of some latent disturbance with the two that needed to be controlled by their higher part keeping in check their lower parts. Furthermore, from a Reformed Protestant perspective, the Catholic denial of total depravity and total inability exhibits a relatively weak view of sin and its devastating destructiveness.

Second, while agreeing with the Catholic view of the accomplishment of salvation by the triune God through the Son incarnate, Protestants

---

28. CCC, 1021.
29. CCC, 1022.
30. CCC, 1033.
31. CCC, 1035.
32. CCC, 1030.
33. CCC, 1031.

disagree with the centrality of the Roman Catholic Church as the only true Church through which the application of salvation comes. Additionally, most Protestant churches diverge from the Catholic Church's view of law, grace, conversion, justification, merit, and the sacraments. Finally, while broad agreement exists between the two traditions with respect to cosmic consummation, Protestants disagree with the doctrine of purgatory because the doctrine of justification renders purgatory useless. Also, Protestant churches dissent from the Catholic synergistic process for entering into eternal life.

## Summary

We have traced the Roman Catholic process of salvation according to the overarching biblical narrative of creation, fall, redemption, and consummation. While God created Adam and Eve in an upright state, they fell into sin, harming not only themselves but plunging all future humanity into a nightmare of sin and evil. The triune God purposed to rescue his fallen image bearers, and this rescue scheme involves both salvation accomplished and salvation applied. The Catholic Church figures significantly in both of these aspects. The final chapter of this story—consummation—consists of both an individual element (death and the afterlife) and a cosmic element featuring Christ's return and the events associated with his second coming.

## REFLECTION QUESTIONS

1. What is your assessment of the Roman Catholic perspective on creation?

2. What is your assessment of the Roman Catholic perspective on the fall?

3. What is your assessment of the Roman Catholic perspective on redemption?

4. What is your assessment of the Roman Catholic perspective on the consummation?

5. What is your assessment of the necessity of the Roman Catholic Church for the various aspects of redemption and consummation?

# What Is the Catholic View of Justification?

In accordance with the Council of Trent, the Roman Catholic Church defines justification[1] as "not only the remission of sins, but also the sanctification and renewal of the interior man."[2] Accordingly, the Catholic view of justification links the forgiveness of sins, progression in righteous character and deeds, and regeneration. Written as it was by the Council of Trent to distinguish the Catholic theology of justification from that of Protestant theology, it was a clear point of division between the two traditions. After five hundred years, it remains one of the most important dividing points between Catholicism and Protestantism. The specific elements of the Catholic view that differ from the Protestant perspective are justification as inward transformation, the appropriation of justification, the cooperation between God and people in the process of justification, the operation of the sacraments to effect justification, and meriting eternal life.

## Justification as Inward Transformation

As its definition of justification notes, the Catholic view highlights the transformative nature of justification. This inner renewal starts with conversion: "The first work of the grace of the Holy Spirit is conversion, effecting justification."[3] This conversion consists of a double turning: "Moved by grace, man turns toward God and away from sin, thus accepting forgiveness and

---

1. The following is adapted from Gregg R. Allison, "A Justified Divide," *Primer*, no. 4 (2017): 32–45. Used by permission.
2. Council of Trent, Session 6, *Decree on Justification*, January 13, 1547, chap. 7. See the discussion in CCC, 1989.
3. CCC, 1989. Cf. 1990: "Justification follows upon God's merciful initiative of offering forgiveness."

righteousness from on high."[4] Thus, while not only involving remission of sins, the Catholic view of justification includes forgiveness as one aspect. Additionally, for Protestants who wrongly think that Catholicism is all about works and weak on grace, Catholic theology emphasizes the initiating role of grace for justification: "no one can merit the initial grace of forgiveness and justification."[5] While some Protestants call this divine favor *prevenient* (Lat. *pre* = before; *venire* = go) *grace*, Catholics call it *preparatory grace*. Such divine favor "goes before" fallen human beings and readies them for conversion.[6]

This divine preparatory work must find a corresponding human response. Not by coercion but prompted by grace, sinful human beings offer the "free response" of conversion. They indeed repent from sin and turn toward God.[7] This conversion results in their justification, which "is at the same time *the acceptance of God's righteousness* through faith in Jesus Christ." This righteousness is defined as "the rectitude of divine love," the goodness of God himself.[8] Unlike the Protestant view of righteousness as the perfect obedience of Christ that is imputed to people, the Catholic perspective of righteousness focuses on the infusion of grace. Specifically, justification conforms people "to the righteousness of God, who makes us inwardly just by the power of his mercy."[9] Here, the transformative nature of justification becomes clear. Justification inwardly changes sinful people. It renews their nature such that they begin to become actually righteous. They will manifest this transformation by loving God and loving other people.

## The Appropriation of Justification: Faith and Baptism

There is a distinction between the *accomplishment* of justification and the *appropriation* of justification. The Roman Catholic Church and Protestant churches agree that Jesus Christ—through his sinless life of obedience, passion, death, burial, resurrection, and ascension—accomplished justification. As Paul affirms, "all have sinned and fall short of the glory of God, and are justified by his grace as a gift, through *the redemption that is in Christ Jesus*, whom God put forward as *a propitiation by his blood*, to be received by faith" (Rom. 3:23–25). It was Christ's bloody sacrifice—his propitiation that atoned for sin—that assuaged the divine wrath against sinful human beings. It is this act of redemption that is the ground of our justification. Both traditions affirm this truth.

While this agreement about the accomplishment of justification stands, its appropriation—the way that justification is received—differs. For Catholicism,

---

4. CCC, 1989.
5. CCC, 2010.
6. CCC, 2001.
7. CCC, 2002.
8. CCC, 1991. Italics original.
9. CCC, 1992.

sinful people appropriate justification through faith and the sacrament of baptism: "Justification is conferred in Baptism, the sacrament of faith."[10] This sacrament effects cleansing from original sin (and, in the case of adults, personal sins prior to baptism), regeneration, and incorporation into Christ and his Church. Forgiveness of sin and regeneration are elements of the Catholic view of justification, so its tie to the sacrament makes sense. However, Protestantism strongly disagrees with this view. Indeed, its material principle—the major doctrinal point of Protestantism—emphasizes *sola fidei*—justification is by *faith alone*. Not faith plus works. Not faith plus baptism. Not faith plus anything else. Catholicism and Protestantism diverge significantly over the way of receiving justification—that is, how it is appropriated.

### Justification by Cooperation

Another major point of divergence between Protestantism and Catholicism is the issue of who is engaged in justification. Two technical terms, when explained, help distinguish two views. *Monergism* (Gr. *mono* = one, *ergon* = work) refers to only one source who works salvation. From this perspective, it is God and God alone who justifies people. *Synergism* (Gr. *syn* = with, ergon = *work*) refers to two or more sources who work with one another for salvation. From this perspective, it is God and people who collaborate in justification. Protestantism holds to monergism; Catholicism holds to synergism.

The Catholic view of justification emphasizes a cooperative work between God and the Catholic faithful. In terms of the divine aspect, the originating and sustaining work of the grace of the Spirit—called illumination and inspiration—stimulates and advances the faithful's response. This human aspect of cooperation "is expressed by the assent of faith to the Word of God, which invites him to conversion, and in the cooperation of charity with the prompting of the Holy Spirit who precedes and preserves his assent."[11] The Spirit initiates and calls people to conversion, that is, turning to God and away from sin. They respond by assenting to the divine Word. This conversion effects their justification. Moreover, the Spirit conserves their response of faith and prompts them to act in love. Clearly, then, justification engages both God and people. It is synergistic, a divine-human cooperation.

As the Council of Trent explained: "When God touches man's heart through the illumination of the Holy Spirit, man himself is not inactive while receiving that inspiration, since he could reject it; and yet, without God's grace, he cannot by his own free will move himself toward justice in God's sight."[12] As the initiator, the Holy Spirit acts graciously and, in response,

---

10. CCC, 1992.
11. CCC, 1993.
12. Council of Trent, Session 6, *Decree on Justification*, March 3, 1547, chap. 5. See the discussion in CCC, 1993.

people touched by this grace freely cooperate with it. Because of their sin-fulness, they could never make the first move toward God. Even more, they could resist God's grace. Still, cooperating with grace, they turn from sin and turn to God by giving the assent of faith. Accordingly, their nature is inwardly transformed so they begin to become righteousness. By an ongoing cooperative effort, they lovingly work to love God and others. Thus, we have justification (including but not limited to forgiveness of sins), regeneration (becoming righteous people), and sanctification (an ongoing transformation into greater and greater righteousness).

## The Operation of the Sacraments to Effect Justification

The principle of the nature-grace interdependence means that divine grace is intimately associated with the Church's sacraments. So, when the Church affirms that "justification comes from the grace of God,"[13] that grace must be understood as linked to the sacraments. Grace for justification is ini-tiated by the sacrament of baptism, but grace itself "is the gratuitous gift that God makes to us of his own life, infused by the Holy Spirit into our soul to heal it of sin and to sanctify it."[14] After baptism, the other sacraments con-tinue to meditate grace for justification. Specifically, confirmation completes baptismal grace. This sacrament binds those who have been baptized more closely to the Church and grants them the special strength of the Spirit. The sacrament of penance provides grace for the Catholic faithful who have com-mitted mortal sin. By this sacrament they are absolved of their sin and once again experience justifying grace. The grace of the sacrament of the Eucharist augments their union with Christ, discourages them from sinning, and more. Thus, the grace of justification is closely linked to the reception of grace through the Church's sacraments.

This sacramental grace is infused into the Catholic faithful. It transforms their nature, and this transformation is a process that continues throughout their entire lifetime. Grace operates by "giving birth to the inner man," effects "the sanctification of his whole being," and makes him "inwardly just."[15] This Catholic notion of infused grace for ongoing inward renewal differs com-pletely from the Protestant idea of a once-and-for-all imputed righteousness.

## Meriting Eternal Life

Through their cooperation with divine grace, the Catholic faithful are en-abled to earn merits and thus to gain eternal salvation. A merit is the recom-pense God owes to the faithful as a reward for their part in this divine-human

---

13. CCC, 1996.
14. CCC, 1999.
15. CCC, 1995, 1992.

cooperative process.[16] God initiates the process by providing grace. People freely respond to this divine initiative. Through this divine-human cooperation, the Catholic faithful engage in good deeds so as to merit eternal life. To avoid misunderstanding, Catholicism emphasizes that "the merit of good works is to be attributed in the first place to the grace of God, then to the faithful."[17] As already noted, human merit is not involved at the beginning of salvation; God alone initiates grace for salvation: "no one can merit the initial grace of forgiveness and justification, at the beginning of conversion."[18] Rather, human merit results from the process of justification. Moved by the Holy Spirit and love, the Catholic faithful cooperate with divine grace and thus merit for themselves and for others "the graces needed for [their] sanctification, for the increase of grace and charity, and for the attainment of eternal life."[19]

In summary, the Catholic view of justification includes the forgiveness of sins, regeneration, sanctification, a synergy of divine-human cooperation, divine grace infused through the sacraments, and the earning of merits for the attainment of eternal life.

### The Protestant View of Justification

As the doctrine of justification is the material principle of Protestantism, we rightly expect the Protestant view to be very different from the Catholic doctrine. The divergence centers on the nature of justification. According to Protestantism, it is a legal declaration by which God pronounces a person "not guilty" but "righteous" instead. This divine declaration establishes a new reality, with two aspects. First, a sinful person, declared to be "not guilty," is forgiven of all her sins. Second, declared to be "righteous" instead, she stands before God as having fulfilled all the requirements of the law. It is not the case that she herself has fulfilled them. Rather, she has fulfilled the divine requirements because the righteousness of Christ, who perfectly fulfilled them, has been credited to her account.

The Protestant view closely follows the biblical affirmations about justification. For example, Scripture contrasts "justification" with "condemnation" in legal contexts (e.g., Deut. 25:1; Prov. 17:15; Rom. 5:16, 18). Condemnation is the divine judgment on the wicked. Justification is the opposite verdict for those rendered righteous. Remarkably (because it is all by divine grace), God "justifies the ungodly" (Rom. 4:5). He does not forgive and declare righteous good people who are trying hard to earn his love, who are working

---

16. Catholic theology notes that this rescue scheme did not have to be this way, but God himself designed justification to be synergistic: "God has freely chosen to associate man with the work of his grace." CCC, 2008.
17. CCC, 2008.
18. CCC, 2010.
19. CCC, 2010.

cooperatively with his grace to merit eternal life. The opposite is true: God "justifies the ungodly."

Paul especially emphasizes justification as a legal declaration. Picking up David's language (Ps. 32:1–2), Paul underscores the two aspects of justification. He notes the blessing for those "whose sin the Lord will never count against them": forgiven of their sins, they are "not guilty." Paul also affirms that "God credits righteousness apart from works": on the basis of Christ's righteousness, they are "righteous" instead (Rom. 4:6–8).

Specifically, the first aspect of justification is the forgiveness of sins. The ground is the substitutionary death of Christ on the cross (Rom. 3:25; 5:9). Christ has atoned for all their sins—past, present, and future—and God declares them "not guilty." Indeed, "therefore there is now no condemnation for those who are in Christ Jesus" (Rom. 8:1). The second aspect of justification is the imputation of righteousness. God reckons people righteous, not because they actually are righteous in themselves or through their good works meriting righteousness for them, but because he credits the righteousness of his Son to them. Abram is the quintessential example of such imputation. God had promised that Abram would become the father of a great nation (Gen. 12:1–3). But he was childless. As Abram was about to trust that his servant Eliezer would become the fulfillment of the divine promise, God intervened. "He took him outside and said, 'Look up at the sky and count the stars—if indeed you can count them.' Then he said to him, 'So shall your offspring be.' Abram believed the Lord, and he credited it to him as righteousness" (Gen. 15:5–6 CSB). As he believed the divine promise, ungodly Abram was declared righteous before God. And so it is for us Christians. Like Abram, we who are ungodly are pronounced righteous on the basis of Christ's righteousness credited to us (Rom. 4:22–25).

## Summary

The Roman Catholic and Protestant doctrines of justification differ significantly in five aspects. First, the Catholic doctrine emphasizes inward transformation. This view, which fuses forgiveness, sanctification, and regeneration, does not reflect the biblical affirmations about justification as a divine, legal declaration.

Second, the Catholic view holds that the appropriation of justification is faith and baptism. Specifically, it maintains that justification is conferred in the sacrament of baptism, which is the sacrament of faith. Protestant theology insists that justification is appropriated by faith alone.

Third, Catholic theology affirms that justification is a joint venture between God and people. This is synergism. God initiates the process by calling people to conversion. They respond by assenting to the Word of God. This conversion effects their justification. Additionally, God preserves their response of faith and prompts them to act in love. Justification is a cooperative, divine-human effort. By contrast, Protestant theology affirms that justification is monergistic. It is God alone who justifies the ungodly (Rom. 4:5), who cannot contribute anything to their justification. God alone declares the unrighteous "not guilty" but "righteous" instead.

Fourth, the Catholic principle of the nature-grace interdependence manifests itself in linking the operation of the sacraments to grace for justification. Divine grace is transmitted through the sacraments to the Catholic faithful, who receive an infusion of grace by which their nature is transformed. Indeed, sacramental grace is necessary for this process of justification. This view of grace differs significantly between Catholicism and Protestantism.

Fifth, the Catholic approach to justification as a synergistic cooperation between God and people provides—indeed, requires—that the Catholic faithful lovingly engage in grace-aided good works so as to merit eternal life. By contrast, the Protestant approach to justification has no room, nor need, for merit. God's declaration of "not guilty" but "righteous" instead means that eternal life is based not on this gracious divine act plus human effort (even effort nourished and advanced by divine grace), but on God's declaration alone received by faith alone.

## REFLECTION QUESTIONS

1. What is your assessment of the wide divide between the Catholic doctrine of justification and inward transformation and the Protestant doctrine of justification as a legal declaration involving the forgiveness of sins and the imputation of Christ's righteousness?

2. What is your assessment of the difference between the Catholic view of the appropriation of justification—faith and the sacrament of baptism—and the Protestant view of faith alone?

3. What is your assessment of the divergence between the Catholic synergistic position emphasizing the divine-human cooperation in the process of justification and the Protestant monergistic position of justification by grace alone?

4. What is your assessment of the Catholic link of justification with the sacraments as a manifestation of the principle of the nature-grace interdependence?

5. What is your assessment of the disagreement of the Catholic insistence on merits for the attainment of eternal life and the Protestant denial of any possibility for such meritorious good works?

# Did Catholicism and Protestantism Come to Agreement about Justification?

To give an idea of the gravity of this question, we must appreciate the importance of the historical divide over this doctrine. According to Martin Luther, "If the doctrine of justification is lost, the whole of Christian doctrine is lost."[1] John Calvin called justification "the main hinge on which religion turns" and exhorted the church "to devote the greatest attention and care to it."[2] As the material principle of Protestantism, justification by grace alone received by faith alone in Christ alone was the central doctrine of the Reformation and one of the key points of division between Protestants and Catholics. No wonder that the document on which I will focus in answering this question underscores the following: "Opposing interpretations and applications of the biblical message of justification were in the sixteenth century a principal cause of the division of the Western church and led as well to doctrinal condemnations. A common understanding of justification is therefore fundamental and indispensable to overcoming that division."[3]

## The Joint Declaration on the Doctrine of Justification

On October 31, 1999, in Augsburg, Germany, the Roman Catholic Church and the Lutheran World Federation signed the Joint Declaration on the Doctrine of Justification (abbreviated JDDJ). The declaration intended to

---

1. Martin Luther, *Lectures on Galatians: Chapters 1–4* (LW 26:9).
2. John Calvin, *Institutes of the Christian Religion* 3.11.1 (LCC 20:726).
3. Joint Declaration on the Doctrine of Justification, 13. http://www.christianunity. va/content/unitacristiani/en/dialoghi/sezione-occidentale/luterani/dialogo/docu-menti-di-dialogo/1999-dichiarazione-congiunta-sulla-dottrina-della-giustificazion/ en.html.

show that the two traditions "are now able to articulate a common under-standing of our justification by God's grace through faith in Christ" (JDDJ, 5). Indeed, the two groups asserted that JDDJ "does encompass a consensus on basic truths of the doctrine of justification and shows that the remaining differences in its explication are no longer the occasion for doctrinal con-demnations" (JDDJ, 5).[4] Though not the only joint agreement between the Roman Catholic Church and various Protestant churches,[5] JDDJ represents a concerted effort to find consensus on this doctrine. This chapter's question, then, uses this declaration as a well-recognized attempt to show that Roman Catholicism and Protestantism have come to an agreement on justification.[6] Does it, indeed, demonstrate that such agreement exists?[7]

---

4. See also JDDJ, 13: "In light of this consensus, the corresponding doctrinal condemnations of the sixteenth century do not apply to today's partner." By this last phrase, JDDJ refers to the Roman Catholic Church and the Lutheran churches who "partner" in signing the declaration.

5. For example, the Anglican-Roman Catholic International Commission (ARCIC II) produced a joint statement entitled "Salvation and the Church" (September 4, 1986). Furthermore, the World Methodist Council adopted the JDDJ (July 18, 2006), as did the World Communion of Reformed Churches (July 5, 2017).

6. For clarification, not even the official response of the Roman Catholic Church to JDDJ endorsed it as a consensus. It cautioned instead that the Church "cannot yet speak of a con-sensus such as would eliminate every difference between Catholics and Lutherans in the understanding of justification." Congregation for the Doctrine of the Faith and Pontifical Council for Promoting Christian Unity, "Response of the Catholic Church to the Joint Declaration of the Catholic Church and the Lutheran World Federation on the Doctrine of Justification," http://www.christianunity.va/content/unitacristiani/en/dialoghi/sezione-occidentale/luterani/dialogo/documenti-di-dialogo/1999-dichiarazione-congiunta-sulla-dottrina-della-giustificazion/en1.html. Moreover, the response warned that "some of these differences concern aspects of substance and are therefore not at all mutually compatible." "Response," Clarifications, 5. https://www.vatican.va/roman_curia/pontifical_councils/chrstuni/documents/rc_pc_chrstuni_doc_01081998_off-answer-catholic_en.html.

7. The Lutheran Church—Missouri Synod (LCMS, which is not a member of the Lutheran World Commission) certainly does not think that such an agreement exists. For a brief history of its dissent, see Samuel H. Nafzger, "A Missouri Synod Perspective," *Concordia Journal* 27, no. 3 (July 2001): 178–95. In 1999, the Commission on Theology of the LCMS evaluated the alleged agreement. It concluded: "JDDJ does not settle the major disagree-ment between Lutheran theology and Roman Catholic theology on justification. Lutherans teach that justification is essentially a declaration of 'not guilty' and 'righteous' pronounced by God on a sinner because of Christ and His work. Roman Catholics teach that justifi-cation involves an internal process in which a believer is transformed and 'made' more and more righteous. The nonsettlement of this issue forms the chief defect of JDDJ." "The Joint Declaration on the Doctrine of Justification in Confessional Lutheran Perspective" (1999), 10. https://files.lcms.org/wl/?id=TvD30QiItKQEEAQPi4Xpgdf8FztpEbuE More pointedly, Paul T. McCain called the JDDJ "a fraud . . . a sell-out by revisionist Lutherans to Rome." Paul T. McCain, "A Betrayal of the Gospel: The Joint Declaration on the Doctrine of Justification," *First Things*, March 12, 2010, https://www.firstthings.com/blogs/firstthoughts/2010/03/a-betrayal-of-the-gospel-the-joint-declaration-on-the-doctrine-of-justification.

## Definition of Justification

JDDJ offers this definition:

> Justification is the forgiveness of sins (cf. *Rom* 3:23–25; *Acts* 13:39; *Lk* 18:14), liberation from the dominating power of sin and death (*Rom* 5:12–21) and from the curse of the law (*Gal* 3:10–14). It is acceptance into communion with God: already now, but then fully in God's coming kingdom (*Rom* 5:1f). It unites with Christ and with his death and resurrection (*Rom* 6:5). It occurs in the reception of the Holy Spirit in baptism and incorporation into the one body (*Rom* 8:1f, 9f; *I Cor* 12:12f). All this is from God alone, for Christ's sake, by grace, through faith in "the gospel of God's Son" (*Rom* 1:1–3). (JDDJ, 11)

This definition leans toward the Roman Catholic view of justification. Certainly, it is the forgiveness of sins. Even the Protestant doctrine has this as its first element of justification. But JDDJ defines it as more. Justification involves a progressive renewal in terms of freedom from the ruling power of sin, death, and the law. It is appropriated through reception of the Spirit. This idea seems to privilege the Catholic emphasis on justification as including regeneration and sanctification. Furthermore, justification is received in the sacrament of baptism. While this sacramental link is indeed a feature of both Roman Catholicism and Lutheranism, it is foreign to many other Protestant denominations. Importantly, this definition makes no mention of the imputation of Christ's righteousness as the second element as affirmed by the Protestant definition of justification.

## The Common Understanding of Justification

The next major section sets forth the two traditions' common understanding of justification. One point addresses justification and the Trinity:

> In faith we together hold the conviction that justification is the work of the triune God. The Father sent his Son into the world to save sinners. The foundation and presupposition of justification is the incarnation, death, and resurrection of Christ. Justification thus means that Christ himself is our righteousness, in which we share through the Holy Spirit in accord with the will of the Father. Together we confess: By grace alone, in faith in Christ's saving work and not because of any merit on our part, we are accepted by God and receive the Holy Spirit, who renews our hearts while equipping and calling us to good works. (JDDJ, 15)

The affirmation that justification is work of the triune God is completely noncontroversial. The controversy lies with the last phrase that associates justification with renewal of the Holy Spirit and engagement in good works. If by this phrase JDDJ means that, in addition to justification, other mighty acts of the triune God in saving people are regeneration and sanctification, expressed in good works, then all Protestants would agree with it. More likely, however, the phrase expresses the Catholic conviction that justification is "not only the forgiveness of sins, but also sanctification and the renewal of the inner person,"[8] by which people are enabled to engage in good works and thereby merit eternal life.

A second point of common understanding is the accomplishment and appropriation of justification: "All people are called by God to salvation in Christ. Through Christ alone are we justified, when we receive this salvation in faith. Faith is itself God's gift through the Holy Spirit who works through word and sacrament in the community of believers and who, at the same time, leads believers into that renewal of life which God will bring to completion in eternal life" (JDDJ, 16). Certainly, all Protestants and Roman Catholics agree that the accomplishment of justification is the finished work of Jesus Christ alone. Moreover, there is full accord on the appropriation of justification by faith. Importantly, there is no mention of the Protestant insistence on faith *alone*. Furthermore, the last phrase seems to associate justification with ongoing renovation of life through the Holy Spirit, a renewal process that lasts one's entire lifetime. Again, this point leans toward the Roman Catholic view of justification.

A third point focuses on God's mercy in justification: "We also share the conviction that the message of justification . . . tells us that as sinners, our new life is solely due to the forgiving and renewing mercy that God imparts as a gift and we receive in faith, and never can merit in any way" (JDDJ, 17). Again, we see justification—which is certainly due to the mercy of God in Christ—is not only the forgiveness of sins but also the renewal of life. Still, JDDJ highlights the fact that divine mercy rules out human merit. But Catholic theology already maintains that human merit is not involved only at the beginning of salvation. Divine mercy alone initiates it: "no one can merit the initial grace of forgiveness and justification, at the beginning of conversion."[9] However, the Catholic view of justification does indeed insist on the necessary role of human cooperation with divine mercy for the attainment of eternal life through the merits of good works. So, JDDJ seems skewed in the direction of the Catholic position.

---

8. CCC, 1989; the citation is from *Canons and Decrees of the Council of Trent*, 6th session (January 13, 1547), *Decree on Justification*, chap. 7.
9. CCC, 2010.

### Explanations of the Common Understanding of Justification

The final major section of JDDJ addresses seven explanations, each of which has three elements. For each topic there is a statement of common understanding ("we confess together"), followed by the unique Lutheran perspective on that topic and concluding with the unique Catholic perspective on that topic. Each topic will be discussed in turn.

*Human Powerlessness and Sin in Relation to Justification*

The first explanation is human powerlessness and sin in relation to justification:

> We confess together that all persons depend completely on the saving grace of God for their salvation. The freedom they possess in relation to persons and the things of this world is no freedom in relation to salvation, for as sinners they stand under God's judgment and are incapable of turning by themselves to God to seek deliverance, of meriting their justification before God, or of attaining salvation by their own abilities. Justification takes place solely by God's grace. (JDDJ, 19)

This statement captures several important points about the depravity of sin and the resulting human inability to seek salvation apart from divine grace.

The particular Lutheran perspective maintains the emphasis on the impossibility of any human contribution to justification. The particular Catholic perspective, however, tries to retain a role for human cooperation, specifying that such contribution is "itself an effect of grace, not as an action arising from innate human abilities" (JDDJ, 20). But this is indisputable, even from a Protestant perspective. The issue for the doctrine of justification is not (1) do people cooperate with divine grace according to their innate human abilities? or (2) do people cooperate with divine grace, and that cooperation itself is prompted by grace? Rather, the issue is (1) do people not cooperate with divine grace at all? or (2) do people cooperate with divine grace, and that cooperation itself is prompted by grace? Protestantism as monergistic affirms the first, while Catholicism as synergistic affirms the second. The division between the two is still very real and significant.

*Justification as Forgiveness of Sins and Making Righteous*

Topic two is justification as forgiveness of sins and making one righteous:

> We confess together that God forgives sin by grace and at the same time frees human beings from sin's enslaving power and imparts the gift of new life in Christ. When persons

> come by faith to share in Christ, God no longer imputes to
> them their sin and through the Holy Spirit effects in them
> an active love. These two aspects of God's gracious action
> are not to be separated, for persons are by faith united with
> Christ, who in his person is our righteousness (1 Cor 1:30):
> both the forgiveness of sin and the saving presence of God
> himself. (JDDJ, 22)

This statement leans heavily in the Catholic direction, restating the Catholic definition of sin as forgiveness, new birth, and renewal. Moreover, while the statement notes the imputation of sin to Christ (the aspect of forgiveness), it makes no mention of the imputation of Christ's righteousness to the justified.

The particular Lutheran perspective does emphasize this latter imputation and distinguishes justification as one mighty act of God from union with Christ and renewal as other mighty divine acts. The particular Catholic perspective repeats the connectedness of forgiveness with new birth and acting in love. Again, two different ideas of the nature of justification are still at play.

## Justification by Faith and through Grace

The third explanation is justification by faith and through grace:

> We confess together that sinners are justified by faith in the
> saving action of God in Christ. By the action of the Holy
> Spirit in baptism, they are granted the gift of salvation, which
> lays the basis for the whole Christian life. They place their
> trust in God's gracious promise by justifying faith, which in-
> cludes hope in God and love for him. Such a faith is active in
> love and thus the Christian cannot and should not remain
> without works. But whatever in the justified precedes or fol-
> lows the free gift of faith is neither the basis of justification
> nor merits it. (JDDJ, 25)

This statement gets to the heart of two Protestant *solas*: faith alone and grace alone. Importantly, JDDJ does not affirm faith alone. Moreover, even the faith for justification that is affirmed is part of the three virtues—faith, hope, and love—that give preference to the Catholic view of justification as a lifelong process involving love and good works.

In the particular Lutheran "doctrine of 'justification by faith alone,' a distinction but not a separation is made between justification itself and the renewal of one's way of life that necessarily follows from justification and without which faith does not exist" (JDDJ, 26). Indeed, Protestantism has always emphasized justification and sanctification together while avoiding collapsing the two as the Catholic notion does. The particular Catholic perspective underscores faith, but not faith alone, focusing mostly on justifying grace as involving both forgiveness and renewal. Accordingly, the Protestant doctrine of justification by faith *alone* and the Catholic doctrine of justification by faith remain at odds.

### The Justified as Sinner

For its fourth topic, JDDJ addresses the justified as sinner. It focuses on the ongoing sin that plagues those who are justified. The particular Lutheran perspective understands "this condition of the Christian as being 'at the same time righteous and sinner.' Believers are totally righteous, in that God forgives their sins through Word and Sacrament and grants the righteousness of Christ which they appropriate in faith. . . . Looking at themselves through the law, however, they recognize that they remain also totally sinners. Sin still lives in them. . . . This contradiction to God is as such truly sin." In short, "justified persons are also sinners and their opposition to God is truly sin." Still, because of justification, their "sin no longer brings damnation and eternal death" (JDDJ, 29).

The particular Catholic perspective holds that

> the grace of Jesus Christ imparted in baptism takes away all that is sin "in the proper sense" and that is "worthy of damnation." . . . There does, however, remain in the person an inclination (concupiscence) which comes from sin and presses toward sin. . . . Catholics do not see this inclination as sin in an authentic sense . . . [and] they underscore that this inclination in contradiction to God does not merit the punishment of eternal death and does not separate the justified person from God. But [in the case of mortal sin] they must receive pardon and peace in the Sacrament of Reconciliation. (JDDJ, 30)

A wide gap continues to separate the two traditions. Protestants consider all sin to be mortal sin in that it leads to the condemnation of death. However, justification means that such "sin no longer brings damnation and eternal death" (JDDJ, 29). Catholics distinguish between venial sin (for example, concupiscence) and mortal sin. Venial sin does not lead to condemnation and does not require sacramental intervention. Mortal sin results in the loss of justifying grace, leads to condemnation, and requires absolution through the sacrament of penance. These points continue to divide the two traditions.

### Law and Gospel

The fifth explanation is law and gospel. The particular Lutheran perspective insists that "the distinction and right ordering of law and gospel is essential for the understanding of justification" (JDDJ, 32). The particular Catholic perspective does not adhere to this distinction. The point is not a major one.

*Assurance of Salvation*

Topic six is assurance of salvation: "We confess together that the faithful can rely on the mercy and promises of God. In spite of their own weakness and the manifold threats to their faith, on the strength of Christ's death and resurrection they can build on the effective promise of God's grace in Word and Sacrament and so be sure of this grace" (JDDJ, 34). Assurance of salvation can be defined as "the subjective confidence that is the privilege of all genuine believers that they will remain Christians throughout their life. This doctrine is dependent on the doctrine of perseverance, which is God's mighty act to preserve true Christians by his power through their ongoing faith, until their salvation is complete (1 Pet. 1:5)."[10]

The particular Lutheran perspective underscores that the Reformers emphasized this doctrine. Indeed, it was a major point of division with Catholic theology. Protestants affirmed that by "trust in God's promise they are assured of their salvation, but are never secure looking at themselves" (JDDJ, 35). The particular Catholic perspective echoes the futility of seeking assurance of salvation by looking at "one's own experience" and one's own "weaknesses and shortcomings" (JDDJ, 36). However, even when the Catholic perspective emphasizes "the objective reality of Christ's promises" and "trust in Christ's forgiving word alone," it does not embrace assurance of salvation. At best it affirms that "recognizing his own failures, however, the believer may yet be certain that God intends his salvation" (JDDJ, 36). But trusting in God's intent to save and possessing the assurance of one's salvation are two very different matters. On this point there is still disagreement.

*The Good Works of the Justified*

The seventh and final explanation is the good works of the justified: "We confess together that good works—a Christian life lived in faith, hope and love—follow justification and are its fruits. . . . This consequence of justification is also for them an obligation they must fulfill" (JDDJ, 37). The particular Lutheran perspective distinguishes between two matters. First is the preservation of grace for those who stand completely righteous before God through justification. Second is growth of grace in terms of bringing forth good works "as the fruits and signs of justification and not as one's own 'merits'" (JDDJ, 39). From the particular Catholic perspective, "good works, made possible by grace and the working of the Holy Spirit, contribute to growth in grace,

---

10. Gregg R. Allison, *The Baker Compact Dictionary of Theological Terms* (Grand Rapids: Baker, 2016), s.v. "assurance of salvation."

so that the righteousness that comes from God is preserved and communion with Christ is deepened" (JDDJ, 38). What is not answered is this question: (1) does the lifelong engagement in good works belong to the essential nature of justification? or (2) is it the fruit of the divine declaration of justification? Catholicism affirms the first. Protestantism affirms the second. This point continues to be a significant difference.

Having defined justification, expressed the common understanding between the two traditions on this doctrine, and explained seven key elements of that common understanding, JDDJ claims to show that "a consensus in basic truths of the doctrine of justification exists between Lutherans and Catholics" (JDDJ, 40). Upon closer look, JDDJ does not actually support this claim. Catholics and Protestants still remain at odds over this doctrine.

### Summary

The Joint Declaration on the Doctrine of Justification defines justification, expresses the common understanding between the World Lutheran Federation and the Roman Catholic Church on this doctrine, and explains seven key elements of that common understanding. While it claims to show that Roman Catholicism and Protestantism have come to an agreement on justification, it does not demonstrate that such agreement exists.

## REFLECTION QUESTIONS

1. What is your overall assessment of JDDJ? Does it achieve the consensus on justification that it claims?

2. What is your specific assessment of the JDDJ's definition of justification? Does it lean in a more Catholic direction? A more Protestant direction? Does it express a synthesis of these two traditions?

3. Which of the two positions do you affirm: (1) people do not cooperate with divine grace at all for justification; or (2) people cooperate with divine grace for justification and that cooperation itself is prompted by grace? Why?

4. With Protestantism, do you affirm assurance of salvation or, with Catholicism, do you deny it?

5. Which of the two positions do you affirm: (1) the lifelong engagement in good works belongs to the essential nature of justification; or (2) the lifelong engagement with good works is the fruit of the divine declaration of justification? Why?

# What Is the Catholic View of Regeneration and Sanctification?

The Roman Catholic Church holds that justification "is not only the forgiveness of sins, but also sanctification and the renewal of the inner person."[1] The last two aspects of this definition—sanctification and inward renewal, or regeneration—are the focus of this question.

### Regeneration

Regeneration is, in one sense, a first sanctification. Inextricably tied to baptism, regeneration comes about by the infusion of grace through the sacrament. This grace cleanses infants of their original sin (or, in the case of adults, their original sin and actual sins), causes them to be born again, and joins them to Christ and his Church. They now have a new nature, one that is characterized by holiness and justice. In one sense, regeneration is a return to the original state of Adam and Eve, who were characterized by righteousness. God dwells in them as they are in the state of sanctifying grace.

The Catholic Church supports this close association of regeneration with baptism by Jesus's exhortation that "unless one is born of water and the Spirit, he cannot enter the kingdom of God" (John 3:5). According to the Catholic interpretation, "born of water" refers to the sacrament of baptism, while "[born] of the Spirit" refers to the divine regenerating work. But on closer inspection, Jesus does not affirm two elements—a sacramental aspect and a Spirit action— but only one water-Spirit action. Being born again is a divine work that involves cleansing from sin (washing symbolized by water) and inward transformation (by the Holy Spirit as the agent of regeneration). Jesus refers to Ezekiel's promise of cleansing and inward renewal through the Spirit as part of the future new

---

1. CCC, 1989; the citation is from *Canons and Decrees of the Council of Trent*, 6th session (January 13, 1547), *Decree on Justification*, chap. 7.

covenant (Ezek. 36:25–27). Water baptism brilliantly pictures this mighty divine act of regeneration, but the Roman Catholic insistence on baptismal regeneration is based on a misunderstanding of Jesus's exhortation.[2]

Part and parcel of this cleansing of original sin (and actual sins, in the case of adults) and new birth is, according to Catholic theology, incorporation into Christ and thus into the Church. Through union with God, the Catholic faithful begin their lifelong journey toward ultimate salvation. This pilgrimage is the process of sanctification.

## Sanctification

The sacrament of baptism establishes the baptized into a state of grace. Through the sacramental economy of the Church, the Catholic faithful continue to receive new infusions of grace for the increase of sanctification. This process lasts their entire life as they grow into the likeness of Christ, experience the reality of the indwelling Trinity, and become holy through the Holy Spirit.

When this lifelong process continues properly all the way to the end of their life, the Catholic faithful "die in God's grace and friendship and are perfectly purified."[3] Having been completely sanctified in their lifetime, they enter immediately into heaven. In the majority of cases, however, their entrance into heaven is delayed and comes about through an additional process of purification in purgatory. "All who die in God's grace and friendship, but still imperfectly purified, are indeed assured of their eternal salvation; but after death they undergo purification, so as to achieve the holiness necessary to enter the joy of heaven."[4] Not having been completely sanctified in their lifetime, the Catholic faithful must undergo a final purification of purgatory. When that process is done and they are fully sanctified, they enter into heaven.

## A Protestant View of Regeneration and Sanctification

According to Protestant thought, regeneration is "the mighty work of God by which unbelievers are given a new nature, being born again. Regeneration is particularly ascribed to the Holy Spirit (John 3:3–8) working through the gospel (James 1:18; 1 Peter 1:23–25). It is both (1) the removal of one's old, sinful nature, and (2) the imparting of a new nature that is responsive to God. Unlike conversion, which is the human response to the gospel, regeneration is completely a divine work, to which human beings contribute nothing."[5] While some Protestants associate it with baptism, there is still a significant difference from the Catholic view of baptismal regeneration.

---

2. For further discussion, see Question 20.
3. CCC, 1023.
4. CCC, 1030.
5. Gregg R. Allison, *The Baker Compact Dictionary of Theological Terms* (Grand Rapids: Baker, 2016), s.v. "regeneration."

Sanctification, according to Protestants, is "the cooperative work of God and Christians (Phil. 2:12–13) by which ongoing transformation into greater Christ-likeness occurs. Such maturing transpires particularly through the Holy Spirit (2 Cor. 3:18; Gal. 5:16–23) and the Word of God (John 17:17)."[6] While most Protestants include the sacraments or ordinances as essential means of grace, they break with the Roman Catholic view of infused grace that enables Christians to engage in good deeds by which they can merit eternal life. Sanctification, according to Protestantism, is not oriented to achieving ultimate salvation but will conclude with it.

This difference is due to the basic Catholic-Protestant disagreement about the doctrine of justification. The Catholic position conflates justification and sanctification. The Protestant perspective distinguishes them. This divergence means that justification-sanctification is a lifelong endeavor for the Catholic faithful. But for Protestants, justification establishes their eternal standing before God—they are declared "not guilty" but "righteous" instead—while sanctification is the natural outworking of justification in terms of progress in Christlikeness. Importantly, justification is solely a work of God. As a monergistic work, it involves no human effort or cooperation. By contrast, "sanctification is synergistic. God operates in ways that are proper to his divine agency (e.g., convicting of sin, empowering by the Spirit, willing and working to accomplish his good pleasure) and Christians work in ways that are proper to their human agency (e.g., reading Scripture, praying, mortifying sin, yielding to the Spirit)."[7] To emphasize once again, this collaborative operation is not about a divine provision of grace that supports human effort for the meriting of eternal life.

Another major difference between the two traditions is that the Catholic Church believes that the faithful can fail to cooperate with sacramental grace, turn from their lifelong journey of sanctification, and lose their salvation. While some Protestants agree with this view, others hold to perseverance in sanctification. Genuine Christians "are being guarded by God's power through faith for a salvation that is ready to be revealed in the last time" (1 Peter 1:5 CSB). Thus, despite the many trials and tribulations they will face during their lifetime, they will continue by God's gracious protection to make progress in their sanctification until their death or the return of Christ.

## Summary

The Catholic Church closely associates justification with regeneration and sanctification. Regeneration takes place through the sacrament of baptism and initiates people into a life of infused grace. Sanctification is the lifelong progress that follows. It depends on new infusions of sacramental grace

6. Allison, *Baker Compact Dictionary of Theological Terms*, s.v. "sanctification."
7. Allison, *Baker Compact Dictionary of Theological Terms*, s.v. "sanctification."

by which the Catholic faithful are enabled to engage in good works to merit eternal life. Protestantism rejects this confusion of justification, regeneration, and sanctification. Additionally, in many cases, it disagrees with baptismal regeneration. Moreover, its understanding of the nature of regeneration and sanctification is quite different from the Catholic view of them.

## REFLECTION QUESTIONS

1. Review: How are the Roman Catholic and Protestant definitions of justification different, and why is this divergence so important?

2. What is your assessment of the Catholic view of regeneration? How does the Protestant perspective differ from it? Why is this difference important?

3. What is your assessment of the Catholic view of sanctification? How does the Protestant perspective differ from it? Why is this difference important?

4. What is your interpretation of Jesus's exhortation, "unless one is born of water and the Spirit, he cannot enter the kingdom of God" (John 3:5)?

5. Do you believe that God's work of sanctification in your life will surely be brought to completion such that you can never fall away from the faith and lose your salvation? Or do you believe that your lifelong journey of sanctification can so deteriorate that you can lose your salvation?

# What Is the Catholic View of Perseverance and Assurance of Salvation?

Because the Catholic Church considers grace to be resistible and faith to be a virtue that can be lost, it denies the Reformed Protestant doctrines of the perseverance of the saints and the assurance of salvation.[1]

## Definitions

I begin with definitions of two doctrines. *Perseverance of the saints* is

> the mighty act of God to preserve Christians by his power through their ongoing faith, until their salvation is complete (1 Pet. 1:5). It does not apply to everyone who professes faith, but is promised to genuine believers. These Christians, though they may fall temporarily into sin, will certainly persist in engaging in good works and exercising faith. Indeed, the saving faith of genuine Christians includes perseverance as an essential element. Moreover, because perseverance is a continuing work of God, these believers may enjoy the assurance of salvation.[2]

To expand briefly, perseverance is a divine work: God himself undertakes to preserve his people in the salvation that he has accomplished for them. At

---

1. In its rejection of these two doctrines, Catholic theology is aligned with Arminian Protestant theology.
2. Gregg R. Allison, *The Baker Compact Dictionary of Theological Terms* (Grand Rapids: Baker, 2016), s.v. "perseverance."

the same time, this divine operation is connected to their human response of faith, as they trust the Lord today, tomorrow, next week, next year, and so on. One day that journey of faith will come to an end as they step into eternity and experience the fullness of their salvation.

*Assurance of salvation* is "the subjective confidence that is the privilege of all genuine believers that they will remain Christians throughout their life. This doctrine is dependent on the doctrine of perseverance. . . . Such assurance is experienced by means of Christ's sacrificial death (Heb. 10:19–20), through the inner testimony of the Holy Spirit (Rom. 8:16), and by the confidence that comes through faith in the promises of Scripture (1 John 5:11–13)."[3] To expand a bit, for Christians to be assured of their salvation, they must depend on the work of the triune God and trust in the promises of the Word of God. God the Father has elected, called, adopted, and justified his people, and he is faithfully and powerfully protecting them for ultimate salvation (1 Cor. 1:9; Gal. 4:4–7; Eph. 1:4, 5). God the Son pledges to hold tightly to his disciples, never lose them, and grant them eternal life (John 6:37–40; 10:27–30). And he unceasingly prays for their salvation (John 17:24; Heb. 7:23–25). Additionally, God the Spirit has regenerated (John 3:3–8) and sealed (Eph. 1:13–14; 4:30) them. He bears witness that they are children of God (Rom. 8:16) even as he transforms them into the image of Christ (2 Cor. 3:18; Gal. 5:16–25).

As Christians depend on the work of the triune God, they also must trust the promises of the Word of God, which assure them of salvation: "And this is the testimony, that God gave us eternal life, and this life is in his Son. Whoever has the Son has life; whoever does not have the Son of God does not have life. I write these things to you who believe in the name of the Son of God, *that you may know that you have eternal life*" (1 John 5:11–13, emphasis added). For those who believe in Christ and his work of salvation, they may be assured of eternal life as they trust in the promises of the Word of God.

## Roman Catholic Denial of Perseverance and Assurance[4]

The Church maintains that the Catholic faithful, though assisted throughout their life by divine grace, can resist that grace, lose their faith, and forfeit their salvation.[5] As the Council of Trent expressed, "For even as no devout person should doubt the mercy of God, the merit of Christ, and the virtue and effectiveness of the sacraments, even so each person, when he regards himself and his own weakness and unsoundness, may have fear and worry about his own grace. Indeed, no one can know with the certainty

---

3. Allison, *Baker Compact Dictionary of Theological Terms*, s.v. "assurance."
4. Some of this material is adapted from Gregg R. Allison, "A Justified Divide," *Primer*, no. 4 (2017): 32–45. Used with permission.
5. CCC, 1993.

of unerring faith that he has obtained the grace of God."[6] The Council further warned about a rash presumption concerning the gift of persevering in salvation: "Let no person promise himself anything as certain with an absolute certainty, though all people should place and rest their most firm hope in God's help. For as God . . . has begun a good work, so he will he perfect it [Phil. 1:6], working in them to will and to accomplish [his good pleasure; Phil. 2:13]." Trent accompanied this exhortation with a warning: "Nevertheless, let those who think that they stand take heed lest they fall [1 Cor. 10:12] and, with fear and trembling, work out their salvation [Phil. 2:12] in good works, in attentiveness, in almsgiving, in prayers and offerings, in fasting and chastity. . . . They ought to fear for the battle that still remains with the flesh, the world, and the devil, against which they cannot be victorious unless they fight with God's grace."[7] While the particular target of this warning was the Catholic faithful, it also served to condemn Protestants who held to the perseverance of the saints and assurance of salvation: "If anyone says that he has, with an absolute and infallible certainty, the great gift of perseverance unto the end, let him be anathema."[8]

The Catholic position is based on several points. One point of support depends on the Catholic distinction between mortal and venial sins. Specifically, mortal sin results in the loss of grace and demands a fresh infusion of it through the sacrament of penance and reconciliation.[9] Should the Catholic faithful die without being absolved of their mortal sin(s), their soul goes immediately to hell. With this ever-present specter of committing mortal sin and not availing themselves of the sacrament haunting them, the Catholic faithful cannot embrace perseverance and assurance of salvation.

A second support for the Catholic position is its view of human free will. Everyone agrees that freedom is the ability to decide and act without coercion. People who are forced to decide and act in a certain way are not free. Within this framework, two opposing positions exist.

One view is called libertarian freedom. No causal factors, such as God's eternal purpose and his gift of grace, can decisively incline a person's will in one direction or another.[10] For example, though God may desire for Beth to become a Christian, though he may work in powerful ways to extend his grace to her, though Christians may pray for Beth's salvation, no single factor,

---

6. The citation is from *Canons and Decrees of the Council of Trent*, 6th session (January 13, 1547), *Decree on Justification*, chap. 9, "Against the Vain Confidence of Heretics."

7. The citation is from *Canons and Decrees of the Council of Trent*, *Decree on Justification*, chap. 13, "On the Gift of Perseverance."

8. The citation is from *Canons and Decrees of the Council of Trent*, 6th session (January 13, 1547), *Decree on Justification*, "On Justification," canon 16.

9. CCC, 1446. For further discussion, see Question 22.

10. Still, this is not randomness. People decide and act for reasons, even if those reasons are not clear to those people themselves and to others observing their decisions and actions.

nor any combination of factors, can definitively prompt Beth to embrace the gospel and be saved. She may use her libertarian free will to become a Christian. Alternatively, she may use her libertarian freedom to reject the good news and thus not become a Christian.

The other view is call compatibilistic freedom. There are causal factors, such as God's eternal purpose and his gift of grace, that can decisively incline a person's will in one direction or another.[11] For example, from eternity, God chose Monica to become a Christian. As she turned seventeen, God worked in powerful ways to extend his grace to her, and her friends prayed for Monica's salvation. These causal (but not coercive) conditions definitively prompted Monica to embrace the gospel and be saved.

I've used illustrations of these two positions as they play out at the beginning of salvation. In the case of Beth, she used her libertarian free will to embrace or reject the gospel. For the sake of illustration, let's say Beth chose to become a Christian. In the case of Monica, she used her compatibilistic freedom to embrace the gospel. So we have two women who are Christians.

Let's extend these illustrations to the continuation of salvation for these two women. In Beth's case, just as she used her freedom to embrace the gospel, she could—weeks, months, or even years after living for Christ—decide to resist God's grace, choose to abandon her faith, and thus lose her salvation. Her libertarian free will permits her to become a Christian but also to stop being a Christian. And there are no causal conditions—the sanctifying work of the Holy Spirit, support from her church—that can either individually or collectively decisively incline Beth's will to continue living as a Christian.

In Monica's case, she embraced the gospel through the interplay of causal conditions—God's eternal purpose and his gift of grace—that decisively inclined her will to do so. These and other causal conditions—the sanctifying work of the Holy Spirit, support from her church—continue to operate so that she perseveres as a Christian and lives joyfully with assurance of her salvation.

Thus, we have one woman—Beth—who embraced the gospel and became a Christian but later lost her faith and forfeited her salvation. The other woman—Monica—embraced the good news and became a Christian and remained so throughout her entire life. In her case, perseverance and assurance are true.

Clearly, the Catholic Church holds to the first kind of free will—libertarian freedom—as illustrated by Beth. The Catholic faithful, though assisted throughout their life by divine grace, can resist that grace, lose their faith, and forfeit their salvation.[12] By contrast, Reformed Protestantism holds to

---

11. Still, this is not coercion. People decide and act in accordance with their own nature and will.

12. "Faith is an entirely free gift that God makes to man. We can lose this priceless gift, as St. Paul indicated to St. Timothy: 'Wage the good warfare, holding faith and a good conscience. By rejecting conscience, certain persons have made shipwreck of their faith.' [1 Tim. 1:18–19] To live, grow, and persevere in the faith until the end, we must nourish

the second kind of free will—compatibilistic freedom—as exemplified by Monica. Reformed Protestants, protected throughout their life by the power of God operating through their faith, believe that they will persevere to the end and all the while joyfully experience the assurance of their salvation.

A third support for the Catholic position is its view of justification. Combining forgiveness, sanctification, and regeneration, this view emphasizes inward transformation through divine grace, which is infused through the sacraments. God initiates and continues the process by providing grace. The Catholic faithful freely respond to this divine initiative. Should they stop responding and relying on divine grace, they commit mortal sin, lose their faith, and forfeit salvation. Thus, this view denies that the Catholic faithful can be sure of their salvation.

On a Reformed Protestant understanding, justification goes hand in hand with perseverance of the saints and assurance of salvation. As a divine declaration, justification renders sinful people "not guilty" but "righteous" instead. Being in Christ, Christians will persevere in him. God plans on keeping his covenant with his people who, as part of that covenant, "by God's power are being guarded through faith for a salvation ready to be revealed in the last time" (1 Peter 1:5). Furthermore, because of God's preserving work on their behalf, his people enjoy the assurance of salvation.

## Summary

The Catholic Church and Reformed Protestant churches disagree on the two important doctrines of the perseverance of the saints and the assurance of salvation. The Catholic position considers grace to be resistible and faith to be a virtue that can be lost. Thus, the Catholic faithful may forfeit the salvation they once enjoyed. Living under this dark shadow, they deny assurance of salvation.

The Catholic view is based on several points. One is that mortal sin results in the loss of grace, which can only be recovered by the sacrament of penance and reconciliation. Should the Catholic faithful commit mortal sin and not avail themselves of grace through this sacrament, they will go to hell. A second support is the Catholic view of human freedom. Possessing libertarian free will, the Catholic faithful may resist the grace of God, lose their faith, and forfeit their salvation. And there are no causal factors, including divine intervention and provision of grace, that can decisively stop such a drift away from God. A third point is the Catholic view of justification. As a divine-human cooperative process, if the Catholic faithful do not continue to collaborate and progress in holiness, they will not persevere. By contrast,

---

it with the word of God; we must beg the Lord to increase our faith; it must be 'working through charity,' abounding in hope, and rooted in the faith of the Church." CCC, 162.

the Protestant doctrine of justification coheres well with Reformed Protestant views of the perseverance of the saints and assurance of salvation.

## REFLECTION QUESTIONS

1. If you are Roman Catholic, how do you respond to the Church's denial of perseverance and assurance of salvation?

2. If you are a Protestant, why is perseverance of the saints so dear to you? How has your assurance of salvation brought comfort to you in difficult times?

3. One charge that is often voiced against these two doctrines is that they lead to spiritual indifference and moral laxity. After all, if Christians are assured of their salvation, what will keep them from presuming on God's grace and what will motivate them to continue making progress in holiness? How do your respond to this accusation?

4. What is your view of human freedom, and why do you hold it?

5. What is your assessment of the Council of Trent's warnings to the Catholic faithful about perseverance and assurance and its condemnation of Protestants who hold those doctrines?

QUESTION 30

# What Is the Catholic View of the Role of Good Works and Merit?

While both Roman Catholics and Protestants alike insist on the importance of good works for Christians, they disagree about the role they serve in salvation. Moreover, the Catholic emphasis on merit does not find a counterpart in Protestantism.

## Biblical Affirmations about Good Works

Catholics and Protestants agree about the importance of good works because Scripture emphasizes that Christians are to, and will indeed, engage in them. As Jesus instructed his disciples, "let your light shine before others, so that they may see your good works and give glory to your Father who is in heaven" (Matt. 5:16). Several times in his letter to Titus, Paul insists that believers are to be "model[s] of good works" (2:7), "zealous for good works" (2:14), and devoted to good works (3:8, 14). For this reason, both Protestants and Catholics urge their members to engage earnestly and increasingly in good works.

## The Timing and Contribution of Good Works in Relationship to Justification

Not only does Scripture emphasize good works as befitting of Christians. It also indicates the relationship of good works to justification. Paul is clear on this matter: "we hold that one is justified by faith apart from works of the law" (Rom. 3:28). Paul turns to the example of Abraham, who was justified by faith and not by works: ·

> What then shall we say was gained by Abraham, our forefather according to the flesh? For if Abraham was justified by works, he has something to boast about, but not before God.

235

For what does the Scripture say? "Abraham believed God, and it was counted to him as righteousness." Now to the one who works, his wages are not counted as a gift but as his due. And to the one who does not work but believes in him who justifies the ungodly, his faith is counted as righteousness. (Rom. 4:1–5)

Again, Paul drives this point home: "For by grace you have been saved through faith. And this is not your own doing; it is the gift of God, not a result of works, so that no one may boast" (Eph. 2:8–9). Once he's emphasized that good works do not contribute to justification, Paul underscores the proper role for them: "we are his workmanship, created in Christ Jesus for good works, which God prepared beforehand, that we should walk in them" (Eph. 2:10). Not before, as contributing to justification, but afterward, as flowing from salvation—this is Paul's doctrine of good works.

## Good Works according to Roman Catholicism

Strike up a conversation with a typical Protestant about what Catholics believe about good works, and the usual response is, "Catholics think they have to do good works to get into heaven." As common as that answer may be, it's untrue in one sense yet true in another sense. Catholicism is not soft on grace and strong on works at the outset of salvation. Rather, it highlights the necessity of grace to initiate justification: "No one can merit the initial grace of forgiveness and justification."[1] This *preparatory grace*, which does not include good works, readies sinful people for conversion leading to justification.[2] Of course, the sacrament of baptism is critical to salvation. Specifically, justification is appropriated by both faith—supplied by the Catholic Church—and the sacrament—administered by the Church. Through this infusion of sacramental grace, the new Catholic faithful are cleansed from original sin (and, in the case of adults, actual sin), regenerated (born again), and incorporated into Christ and his Church.

As transformed people, the faithful are positioned to cooperate with divine grace infused through baptism and the other sacraments. Thus, they are strengthened to exhibit love and engage in good works. Moreover, these good works, which are essential to salvation, are meritorious. Merit is our next topic.

## Good Works and Merit according to Catholicism

Enabled by grace infused through the sacraments, the Catholic faithful engage in good works and thus merit eternal life. The catechism states, "Moved by the Holy Spirit, we can merit for ourselves and for others the graces needed

---

1. CCC, 2010.
2. CCC, 2001.

for sanctification, for the increase of grace and charity, and for the attainment of eternal life."[3] To Protestant ears, this notion is strange and seems to hint of human achievement, leading to boasting in salvation attained through effort. The Catholic Church dispels such a misunderstanding, insisting instead that "the merit of man before God in the Christian life arises from the fact that God has freely chosen to associate man with the work of his grace. The fatherly action of God is first on his own initiative, and then follows man's free acting through his collaboration, so that the merit of good works is to be attributed in the first place to the grace of God, then to the faithful."[4] Synergism is at the heart of the Catholic view of salvation. God, by his initiative, prepares people through grace and, once they have received it, continues to strengthen and equip his people with grace. The Catholic faithful, then, responding to God's initiative and transformed by infused grace, cooperate with it, engage in good works, and thus do their part to merit eternal life. God rewards his people's good works and considers them as meritorious for salvation.

## Good Works and Merit according to Protestantism[5]

Protestantism considers human effort toward the meriting of eternal life to be superfluous. The Protestant view of justification leaves no room nor need for merit. As God declares the ungodly "not guilty" but "righteous" instead, their eternal life is based not on this gracious act of God plus their own effort (even effort prompted and steadied by divine grace), but on God's declaration alone received by faith alone. They are reckoned completely righteous because God has imputed the perfect righteousness of Christ to them by faith. What could they possibly add to this salvation? Nothing at all. How could they possibly merit eternal life? They cannot.

At the core of this difference is the contrast between the Catholic view of the infusion of grace and the Protestant view of God's gracious imputation of Christ's righteousness. The Catholic Church's perspective considers grace to be infused through its sacraments, resulting in a transformation of the Catholic faithful's nature and positioning them to do good works for the meriting of eternal life. By contrast, Protestant churches understand the divine act of justification not in terms of the infusion of grace but as the imputation of Christ's righteousness. In addition to declaring sinful people "not guilty," God also pronounces them "righteous" instead. This divine declaration is not made on the basis of their own righteous character transformed by infused grace. Rather, it is pronounced on the basis of God's accrediting to their account the perfect righteousness of his Son. God justifies the ungodly who have faith in Jesus Christ.

---

3. CCC, 2010.
4. CCC, 2008.
5. The following is adapted from Gregg R. Allison, "A Justified Divide," *Primer*, no. 4 (2017): 32–45. Used by permission.

And what of good works? Out of thankfulness for their standing before God through justification, and as the fruit of their new nature through regeneration and sanctification, Christians engage in good works, which God himself will richly reward—grace upon grace! Such rewards, however, have nothing to do with merit as Catholic theology understands that idea. God alone has accomplished salvation for sinful people through Christ's sacrificial death and resurrection. They have been declared completely righteous through the divine act of justification. They cannot contribute to their salvation nor increase their justification. So they engage in good works out of a heart of thankfulness for divine grace.

Catholics and Protestants alike may point out that they know people who claim to have experienced this salvation but do not engage in good works. In fact, these people may live very un-Christian-like lives while still claiming to be redeemed and bound for eternal life. Four points help make sense of this commonplace experience.

First, our intuitive sense of the wrongness of the above scenario is correct. God's people in Christ have always been characterized by good works, so when people claim to be Christians and don't live a life of good works, it is proper for us to think something is amiss.[6]

Second, the Protestant perspective does not apply to those who merely profess faith in Christ. Rather, it applies to genuine Christians. As John underscores, "By this we may know that we are in him [Christ]: whoever says he abides in him ought to walk in the same way in which he walked" (1 John 2:5–6). By definition, genuine Christians engage in good works as the fruit of their justification. Those who merely profess to know Christ but do not live like he lived are false Christians.

A third point reflects James's exposition of faith and works:

> Do you want to be shown, you foolish person, that faith apart from works is useless? Was not Abraham our father justified by works when he offered up his son Isaac on the altar? You see that faith was active along with his works, and faith was completed by his works; and the Scripture was fulfilled that says, "Abraham believed God, and it was counted to him as righteousness"—and he was called a friend of God. You see that a person is justified by works and not by faith alone. (James 2:20–24)

---

6. Of course, our intuition is not inerrant. There may be an explanation for a lack of good works that is not that people are not genuine Christians. For example, a jarring experience such as a loss of a job or loved one, a traumatic event, or a state of depression may account for a period of stagnation.

Is James contradicting Paul when it comes to the relationship of justification, faith, and good works? Certainly not! According to Paul (Rom. 4:1–12), Abraham was justified by faith apart from good works. That is, the patriarch was declared not guilty but righteous instead as he believed the promise of God by faith alone. This pronouncement took place on Mount Hebron when God "brought him outside and said, 'Look toward heaven, and number the stars, if you are able to number them.' Then he said to him, 'So shall your offspring be.' And he believed the LORD, and he counted it to him as righteousness" (Gen. 15:5–6). Abraham did not engage in works to prompt God's pronouncement nor to prod God into being favorable toward him. Abraham did not rely on circumcision; that covenant sign followed his justification. Abraham did not do the works of the law; the law was given centuries after his justification. He did not engage in good works; indeed, just before believing God's promise of Isaac, Abraham was trusting in Eliezer to be the fulfillment of the promise (Gen. 15:2–4). On the contrary, Abraham was justified by faith without any good works.

According to James (2:20–24), Abraham was justified by works and not by faith alone as he exhibited his righteous status before God and others. There are two issues: First, James contrasts *bogus* faith—mere assent, like the demonic acknowledgement that God is one (2:19)—with *saving* faith. That Abraham had saving faith is clear because he obeyed God by offering to sacrifice Isaac on Mount Moriah (Gen. 22). Additionally, this saving faith goes all the way back to when Abraham first believed on Mount Hebron, when "the Scripture was fulfilled that says, 'Abraham believed God, and it was counted to him as righteousness'—and he was called a friend of God" (James 2:23). At that moment—years before God called upon him to sacrifice Isaac—Abraham expressed saving faith, which was then later demonstrated through that offering of his son.

This leads to the second issue: James's use of "justification" is not the Pauline idea of "declared not guilty but righteous instead." It could not be. James himself underscores that Abraham had already received that verdict decades before God called upon him to sacrifice Isaac. Rather, James's idea of "justification" has the sense of a vivid demonstration. In this sense, Abraham's saving faith by which he was justified—declared not guilty but righteous instead—was exhibited for God and others to see through Abraham's obedience in offering his son on Mount Moriah. So Scripture was fulfilled: "The word *fulfilled* does not mean that Abraham's works made the Scripture true . . . but that Abraham's works brought the declaration in Hebron to its appointed end. The declaration was meant to be displayed so that God's word would be vindicated. God declared Abraham's faith as righteousness, and Abraham's action, particularly his test with Isaac, affirmed the truth of Scripture."[7]

---

7. Brian Vickers, *Justification by Grace through Faith: Finding Freedom from Legalism, Lawlessness, Pride, and Despair*, Explorations in Biblical Theology, ed. Robert A. Peterson (Phillipsburg, NJ: P&R, 2013), 153.

To sum up, Abraham was justified by faith alone in a declarative sense on Mount Hebron as he believed God's promise of an offspring. And Abraham was justified by faith and works as that declarative justification was vividly demonstrated on Mount Moriah as he offered to sacrifice his son in obedience to God's command. Paul's affirmation and James's affirmation, while appearing on the surface to clash, do not contradict one another. Rather, the two emphasize that those whom God justifies will indeed engage in good works.

But how can we be confident that the justified will indeed do good works? As I write elsewhere, quoting Brian Vickers, "'God plans on keeping his word with a particular kind of people—those who follow him in obedience' through engaging in good works. The declaration stands firm and is unconditional. Its reality does not depend on the good works in its recipients, but its reality is 'concurrent, or parallel, with obedience.' Simply put, saving faith that justifies results in good works, but it is not contingent on those works."[8] As Paul instructs the justified, "work out your own salvation with fear and trembling, for it is God who works in you, both to will and to work for his good pleasure" (Phil. 2:12–13). Such human activity is not for the purpose of gaining merit leading to eternal life. Rather, it is the fruit of divine activity prompting the willing, and the engaging in good works, that are pleasing to God and beneficial to others.

## Summary

Both the Roman Catholic Church and all Protestant churches instruct and prepare their members to engage conscientiously and bountifully in good works. From a biblical perspective, it is not by good works but by faith alone that the ungodly are declared not guilty but righteous instead by God. Good works, then, do not come before salvation as contributing to it, but come afterward, as flowing from salvation.

The two traditions, however, put these pieces together quite differently. According to the synergistic framework of Catholicism, God and the Catholic faithful cooperate in the progress of the latter group's salvation. As the faithful receive grace and do their part to merit eternal life, God rewards their good works and considers them as meritorious for salvation. From the monergistic framework of Protestantism, justification is the divine pronouncement of a "not guilty" verdict as well as the declaration that the ungodly are now righteous instead. Good works do not and cannot contribute to their salvation because they already possess the imputed, perfect righteousness of Christ. Good works do not and cannot be meritorious because there is no human activity to be joined to the divine activity of justification. Still, good works flow from the thankful hearts of the justified and are the necessary demonstration of saving

---

8. *RCTP*, 441–42. The citation is from Vickers, *Justification by Grace through Faith*, 152

faith. The righteous will indeed live lives of good works as commanded by Scripture and guaranteed by God himself in covenant relationship with them.

## REFLECTION QUESTIONS

1. In line with both the Roman Catholic Church and Protestant churches, do you believe that good works can in no way precede and contribute to justification but can only follow as the fruit of justification?

2. If you are Roman Catholic, how do you respond to the Church's perspective on good works that are enabled by sacramental grace and that are oriented toward meriting eternal life?

3. If you are a Protestant, how do you respond to the common criticism that your view permits people to live very un-Christian-like lives while they still claim to be redeemed and bound for eternal life?

4. Do you agree that there is no conflict between Paul's account of justification by faith alone as being declared not guilty but righteous instead, and James's account of justification by both faith and works as being the vivid demonstration of God's prior declaration? How does Abraham illustrate both Paul's perspective and James's perspective?

5. With Roman Catholicism, do you hold to synergistic salvation or, with Protestantism, do you hold to monergistic salvation? Why?

# What Is the Role of Purgatory in the Catholic View of Salvation?

When Protestants consider the major differences between them and Roman Catholics, one that surfaces almost immediately is purgatory. Protestants wonder, Is purgatory a halfway station between heaven and hell? Do Catholics earn indulgences to get out of purgatory? Are the fires of purgatory as hot as the ones in hell? I focus this chapter's question on the Roman Catholic view of purgatory in relationship to its view of salvation.

## Two Eternal Destinies, One Temporal Destiny

The Catholic Church acknowledges that each and every person "will be rewarded immediately at death in accordance with his works of faith."[1] In terms of the divine judgment, the two eternal destinies are "either entrance into the blessedness of heaven—through a purification or immediately—or immediate and everlasting damnation."[2] The Catholic faithful "who die in God's grace and friendship and are perfectly purified" enter immediately into heaven. In that state they "see the divine essence with an intuitive vision, and even face to face, without the mediation of any creature."[3] Seeing God through this beatific vision brings them ultimate fulfillment and supreme happiness. This is the first of the two possible eternal destinies.

People who freely choose to "die in mortal sin without repenting and accepting God's merciful love" enter immediately into hell.[4] This is the "state of definitive self-exclusion from communion with God and the blessed [the faithful in heaven]" to which the damned descend, "where they suffer the

---

1. CCC, 1021.
2. CCC, 1022.
3. CCC, 1023.
4. CCC, 1033.

punishment of hell, 'eternal fire.'"[5] This is the second of the two possible eternal destinies.

Let's go back to the first destiny that noted that entrance into heaven comes about in two ways: "through a purification or immediately." We have focused on the latter, immediate entrance into heaven. The other way is "through a purification." This process of purification is the temporal destiny known as purgatory. It is not an eternal state; only heaven and hell are. Rather, it is a temporal state, for the souls of all those who are in purgatory will eventually go to heaven, the first of the eternal destinies. They will not go to hell, the second of the eternal destinies.

## Purgatory as Extended Purification

Specifically, purgatory is for the Catholic faithful for whom an extended purification is needed. "All who die in God's grace and friendship, but still imperfectly purified, are indeed assured of their eternal salvation; but after death they undergo purification, so as to achieve the holiness necessary to enter the joy of heaven."[6] Purgatory is "this final purification of the elect, which is entirely different from the punishment of the damned."[7]

Primary support for purgatory comes from the noncanonical book of 2 Maccabees and from two New Testament passages.

## The Apocrypha and Purgatory

Though Protestants do not consider 2 Maccabees to be canonical Scripture, Catholics do. This writing includes the narrative of Jewish military forces, led by Judas Maccabeus, following a battle with a pagan army (2 Macc. 12:38–46). During the fighting, some Jewish soldiers were killed. Per Jewish funeral custom, their bodies needed burial. "Judas rallied his army and went to the city of Adullam. As the seventh day was approaching, they purified themselves according to custom and kept the sabbath there. On the following day, since the task had now become urgent, Judas and his companions went to gather up the bodies of the fallen and bury them with their kindred in their ancestral tombs" (vv. 38–39 NABRE) Much to their surprise, this collection of the bodies revealed a secret: "But under the tunic of each of the dead they found amulets sacred to the idols of Jamnia, which the law forbids the Jews to wear. So it was clear to all that this was why these men had fallen. They all therefore praised the ways of the Lord, the just judge who brings to light the things that are hidden" (vv. 40–41 NABRE). The secret was that these fallen soldiers were idolaters, and as such they had paid the ultimate price: death.

Judas and his men acted decisively in this situation:

---

5. CCC, 1035.
6. CCC, 1030.
7. CCC, 1031.

Turning to supplication, *they prayed that the sinful deed [idol-atry] might be fully blotted out.* The noble Judas exhorted the people to keep themselves free from sin, for they had seen with their own eyes what had happened because of the sin of those who had fallen. He then *took up a collection* among all his soldiers, amounting to two thousand silver drachmas, which he sent to Jerusalem *to provide for an expiatory sacri-fice.* In doing this he acted in a very excellent and noble way, inasmuch as he had the resurrection in mind; for if he were not expecting the fallen to rise again, it would have been su-perfluous and foolish to *pray for the dead.* But if he did this with a view to the splendid reward that awaits those who had gone to rest in godliness, it was a holy and pious thought. Thus *he made atonement for the dead that they might be ab-solved from their sin.* (vv. 42–46 NABRE, italics added)

Prayer for the forgiveness of these dead soldiers' sins. A collection so that an atoning sacrifice for their idolatry may be offered. Hope that by atonement for sin and absolution, the dead men might be holy and thus participate in the resurrection. These elements are the ground of the Catholic doctrine of pur-gatory. Practically speaking, "the Church encourages various practices done on behalf of the dead and in their honor: praying, offering Eucharistic sacri-fices, almsgiving, purchasing or earning indulgences, and engaging in works of penance."[8] For example, the saints in heaven and the Catholic faithful on earth may intercede for souls in purgatory, "that they may be loosed from their sins" and thus go to heaven, their eternal destiny.[9]

Protestants dismiss this support because 2 Maccabees is not part of Scripture. They also question how a narrative such as this can be authoritative for church doctrine. That is, how does an incident like this become normative for today? Some Protestants observe that idolatry, the sin of these soldiers, is a mortal sin. Assuming these men died having committed mortal sin and without absolution, how does this align with the Catholic view that mortal sin leads not to purgatory but to hell?

### Saved through Fire

The first New Testament passage to which the Catholic Church turns in support of purgatory is 1 Corinthians 3:10–15:

According to the grace of God given to me, like a skilled master builder I laid a foundation, and someone else is

---

8. *RCTP*, 214.
9. CCC, 958; citation from Vatican Council II, *Lumen Gentium*, 50.

building upon it. Let each one take care how he builds upon it. For no one can lay a foundation other than that which is laid, which is Jesus Christ. Now if anyone builds on the foundation with gold, silver, precious stones, wood, hay, straw—each one's work will become manifest, for the Day will disclose it, because it will be revealed by fire, and the fire will test what sort of work each one has done. If the work that anyone has built on the foundation survives, he will receive a reward. If anyone's work is burned up, he will suffer loss, though he himself will be saved, but only as through fire.

The Catholic interpretation of this passage focuses on the fire through which some people will be saved. It is identified with the torment and misery the souls in purgatory experience as the dross of their sin is purged away.

Protestants view this passage differently. Paul's point about fire is not that it is used to purify people of their sinful taint but for testing their works. The passage is directed to church members, especially to leaders. Through their works—preaching, discipling, shepherding, leading—they build the church. Paul exhorts these leaders to be careful with their building process. They are to engage in their ministries with faith, obedience, holiness, wisdom, and watchfulness. They are to avoid worldliness, arrogance, platform building, and prideful displays. At the judgment seat of Christ, their works will be tested by fire and evaluated. If they were careful in their building, they will receive a reward. If they were carnal in their building, they themselves will be saved but their works will be burned. Thus, this passage is not seen as support for the Catholic doctrine of purgatory.

## Forgiven in the Age to Come

The second New Testament passage is from the gospel of Matthew. The narrative is Jesus's exorcism and healing of a demon-oppressed, blind, and mute man. According to the onlooking Pharisees, "It is only by Beelzebul, the prince of demons, that this man casts out demons" (Matt. 12:24). But Jesus sternly warns them about their irrational, slanderous pronouncement. He concludes: "Therefore I tell you, every sin and blasphemy will be forgiven people, but the blasphemy against the Spirit will not be forgiven. And whoever speaks a word against the Son of Man will be forgiven, but whoever speaks against the Holy Spirit will not be forgiven, either in this age or in the age to come" (Matt. 12:31–32).

The Catholic understanding of this passage focuses on the last expression. There is (at least) one sin—blasphemy against the Spirit—that cannot be forgiven "either in this age or in the age to come." Doesn't this phrase imply that there other (less grievous) sins that, if they go unforgiven in this life, may be forgiven "in the age to come," that is, after death, in purgatory? The

Catholic interpretation agrees with this implication. People may commit sins that, though they are not pardoned while these people live, may be pardoned through the purification these people will experience in purgatory.

Protestants object "to this implication as being far removed from Jesus's point, which is to emphasize the heinousness of one particular sin against the Holy Spirit: it is unpardonable now and in eternity. The fact that forgiveness of such blasphemy is *impossible* even after death does not make forgiveness of other sins *possible* even after death, in purgatory."[10] Accordingly, the Catholic doctrine of purgatory is not seen to be supported by this passage.

Chris Castaldo offers a helpful framework to consider. The pervasiveness and perversity of sin prompts two questions, both of which he asks from a Catholic perspective. The first question concerning sanctification is, "How are imperfect people able to enter the presence of the holy God?" The second question concerning satisfaction is, "How are venial sins punished when sinful people fail to do penance in this life?" The Catholic Church answers "purgatory" to both questions:

> The logic of purgatory is specifically concerned with these two issues: making believers actually holy and making satis-faction for unconfessed sins. Catholics believe that it is not enough to have simply been forgiven in the past or to have had righteousness imputed (as Protestants believe). Because entrance into God's holy presence requires the complete sanctification and satisfaction of all sins, cleansing and pun-ishment in purgatory are both essential.[11]

The Protestant doctrine of justification—that God declares sinful people completely forgiven of all their sins and imputes the perfect righteousness of Christ to them—renders the Catholic doctrine of purgatory superfluous.

### Summary

According to the Catholic Church, there are two eternal destinies and one temporal destiny. The two eternal destinies are heaven and hell. The one temporal destiny is purgatory. The catechism states, "All who die in God's grace and friendship, but still imperfectly purified, are indeed assured of their eternal salvation; but after death they undergo purification, so as to achieve the holiness necessary to enter the joy of heaven."[12] This temporary state of purification from the taint of sin is purgatory.

---

10. *RCTP*, 219.
11. Gregg Allison and Chris Castaldo, *The Unfinished Reformation: What Unites and Divides Catholics and Protestants after 500 Years* (Grand Rapids: Zondervan, 2016), 137.
12. CCC, 1030.

Catholic theology grounds this doctrine on one apocryphal passage and two New Testament passages. Second Maccabees 12:38–46 is seen as support for the Catholic practices of praying for the dead, offering Eucharistic sacrifices on their behalf, using indulgences, and more. First Corinthians 3:12–15 is interpreted to refer to the fires of purgatory by which the souls of the Catholic faithful are purged from the taint of sin. Matthew 12:31–32 is understood to imply that some sins, if not forgiven in this life, may be forgiven after death, in purgatory. Protestants do not believe apocryphal books are authoritative or that the 2 Maccabees story should be considered normative, and they believe the two New Testament passages are misinterpreted and misused. Thus, Protestants disagree with this Catholic doctrine because they believe it lacks biblical support. Moreover, they consider it to clash with their doctrine of justification.

## REFLECTION QUESTIONS

1. If you are Catholic, how do you view purgatory? Are you involved in any practices—for example, praying and earning indulgences—on behalf of the souls in purgatory?

2. If you are Protestant, how does the mighty act of justification do away with the need for a post-death cleansing from sins and a rendering of satisfaction for them?

3. Looking at 2 Maccabees 12:38–46, how does this passage (from a Catholic perspective) support this doctrine, and how does it (from a Protestant perspective) not support it?

4. Looking at 1 Corinthians 3:10–15, how does this passage (from a Catholic perspective) support this doctrine, and how does it (from a Protestant perspective) not support it?

5. Looking at Matthew 12:31–32, how does this passage (from a Catholic perspective) support this doctrine, and how does it (from a Protestant perspective) not support it?

# Questions about Mary and the Saints

In this fifth section, I explore questions about the Catholic Church's biblical theology of Mary, its doctrines of Mary's immaculate conception and bodily assumption, its view of Marian titles, and its role for the saints.

# How Does Catholicism Understand the Biblical Teaching about Mary?

Pope John Paul II wrote an encyclical about the Catholic Church's doctrine of Mary. Entitled *Redemptoris Mater* (*The Mother of the Redeemer*), it sets forth a biblical theology of Mary.[1] The following outline highlights its main points in relation to Catholic beliefs about her. Each point includes a brief critique from the Protestant perspective.

### Mary's Predestination

Mary's predestination to her role as the mother of Jesus is foreshadowed in Genesis 3:15:

> I will put enmity between you and the woman,
> and between your offspring and her offspring;
> he shall bruise your head,
> and you shall bruise his heel.

God's curse upon the serpent/Satan is a prophecy of the Messiah, who will come through a woman to rescue God's people. Thus, from the very beginning of the Bible, Mary's role is set forth as crucial to the plan of salvation—a plan that God predestined from all eternity.

Additionally, Isaiah predicted the virgin birth: "Behold, the virgin shall conceive and bear a son, and shall call his name Immanuel" (Isa. 7:14). Matthew's gospel quotes this prophecy and applies it to Mary and her son, Jesus: "When his mother Mary had been betrothed to Joseph, before they

---

1. John Paul II, *Redemptoris Mater*, March 25, 1987, Vatican.va, (abbreviated *RM*). Papal encyclicals are named according to Latin words in the opening lines of their official Latin version.

came together she was found to be with child from the Holy Spirit. . . . All this took place to fulfill what the Lord had spoken by the prophet" (Matt. 1:18, 22). Together, Isaiah's prophecy and Matthew's note of fulfillment highlight Mary's role in the eternal plan of salvation.

With reference to Galatians 4:4–5, *Redemptoris Mater* comments, "In this way the Old Testament prepares that 'fullness of time' when God 'sent forth his Son, born of a woman . . . so that we might receive adoption as sons.'"[2] Thus, two thousand years ago, when a virgin girl became pregnant with a son through the Holy Spirit, she entered into God's purpose for her—a plan that had been established from eternity past.

Many people agree about Mary's predestined role in the incarnation yet maintain that this is not unusual. For example, Paul speaks of Christians being "predestined according to the purpose of him [God] who works all things according to the counsel of his will" (Eph. 1:11). Certainly, the incarnation—and Mary's distinctive role in it—was a completely unique event and essential for the divine accomplishment of salvation. Still, it forms part of God's sovereign will for all things that occur in this world. Moreover, Protestants affirm the virginal conception of Jesus through the Holy Spirit.

## Mary's Preparation

On God's part, he had predestined that Mary would play this essential role in salvation. On Mary's part, she would need to cooperate willingly with this eternal plan. Being free to say yes to it (option 1) or no to it (option 2), Mary needed to be prepared to choose option 1 and not option 2.[3] Imagine the chaos that would have resulted if she had chosen option 2! But if she chose option 1, Mary's obedience as the second Eve would reverse the curse that followed from the disobedience of the first Eve.

As *Redemptoris Mater* affirms, "The Father of mercies willed that the Incarnation should be preceded by assent on the part of the predestined mother, so that just as a woman had a share in the coming of death, so also should a woman contribute to the coming of life."[4] Question 33 treats Mary's immaculate conception—from the moment of her conception, she was graciously protected from original sin—that prepared her to say yes to God's role for her.

There is no biblical support for the parallelism between the first Eve, who disobeyed and plunged humanity into misery, and the second Eve, Mary, who obeyed and thus contributed to the reverse of the curse.[5] Additionally, Protestants dissent from the doctrine of the immaculate conception of Mary. She was indeed

---

2. *RM* 7, citing Vatican Council II, *Lumen Gentium*, 55.
3. This position is called libertarian free will, explained further in Question 29.
4. Vatican Council II, *Lumen Gentium*, 56.
5. There is biblical support for a parallelism between the first Adam, who disobeyed and plunged humanity into misery, and the second Adam, Jesus Christ, who obeyed and thus reversed the curse: Romans 5:12–21.

the woman whom God chose to conceive the Son of God in her womb, but it was not due to any preparation—especially sinlessness—on her part.

## Mary's Cooperation

Mary was made aware of this divinely designed plan through an angelic visitation (Luke 1:26–38). Gabriel greeted her, "Hail, full of grace, the Lord is with you!" (v. 28).[6] According to *Redemptoris Mater*'s interpretation, the angel does not call Mary by her proper earthly name but by this new name ("full of grace") "as if it were her real name."[7] Specifically, "full of grace" refers to "the election of Mary as Mother of the Son of God" as well as to "the supernatural munificence [lavish gift] from which Mary benefits by being chosen to be the Mother of Christ."[8]

Mary responded to Gabriel, "Behold, I am the servant of the Lord; let it be to me according to your word" (v. 38). According to the encyclical's understanding, the expression "Let it be to me according to your word" was Mary's fiat, or authoritative command. Uttered in faith without reserve and with total devotion, it "was decisive on the human level for the accomplishment" of the eternal, divine plan. Mary cooperated and, as far as it depended on her collaboration, the incarnation became a reality.[9]

As a critique, "full of grace" is not a new name for Mary. Rather, it is a commendation of God's undeserved favor, which is extended to Mary apart from any preparation or status on her part.[10] Earlier in the narrative of the annunciation, the angel had said, "Do not be afraid, Mary, for you have found favor [grace] with God" (Luke 1:30). There is nothing about Mary that prepares her for, or merits, the reception of such grace; rather, she found God's favor. Moreover, "full of grace" is open to a misunderstanding that grace is a

---

6. *RM*, 8. This discussion will cite the translation of Scripture used in *Redemptoris Mater*.
7. *RM*, 8.
8. *RM*, 9.
9. *RM*, 13.
10. As Beverly Gaventa notes, "Luke identifies Mary with the leanest of descriptions, especially when considered against the role about to be handed to her. He introduces her by means of a report that Gabriel is sent by God to Nazareth in Galilee to 'a virgin engaged to a man by the name of Joseph, from the house of David, and the name of the virgin is Mary' (Luke 1:26–27). By stunning contrast with his introduction of Elizabeth and Zechariah, Luke says not a word about Mary's righteousness, her faithfulness to the Law, or her family of origin (see 1:5–25). Nothing in the introduction of Mary qualifies her for this role apart from God's own favor dispensed to her. . . . As Joel Green has put it, Mary 'is not introduced in any way that would recommend her to us as particularly noteworthy or deserving of honor. In light of the care with which other characters are introduced and portrayed as women and men of status in Luke 1–2, this is remarkable.'" Beverly Gaventa, "Nothing Will Be Impossible with God," in *Mary: Mother of God*, eds. Carl E. Braaten and Robert W. Jenson (Grand Rapids: Eerdmans, 2004), 24–25. Her quotation is from Joel Green, "The Social Status of Mary in Luke, 1:5–2:52: A Plea for Methodological Integration," *Biblica* 73 (1992): 457–71 (quotation on 465).

substance infused (to a supreme degree) into Mary such that she is unique in her cooperation with the divine plan.[11]

Additionally, it is not true that Mary's response to Gabriel is a fiat, or authoritative decree. Rather, "Let it be done to me according to your word" expresses Mary's wish or desire as a servant of the Lord to submit to his will. This obedience has special reference to his will as it was communicated to her by Gabriel's final words: "Nothing will be impossible with God." Acknowledging such impossibility with faith, Mary yields to the Lord: let what seems impossible with human beings happen to me as God makes it possible. This cannot be "decisive on the human level" for the fulfillment of the divine plan because what is to take place within Mary's womb is impossible with her. Her decision adds nothing to the supernatural and gracious work of God.

At the same time, Mary's faith brings great blessing both to her and to all humanity. She is rightly called "blessed" (Luke 1:48), because of God's mighty work in and through her on behalf of all people to accomplish his promise of salvation (Luke 1:46–55). Additionally, Mary is a stellar model of the obedience of faith. But she believed "that there would be a fulfillment of what was spoken to her from the Lord" (Luke 1:45). She believed that God himself would fulfill his promised word. So, too, should we.

## Mary and Jesus

*Redemptoris Mater* discusses several key passages that treat the Mary-Jesus relationship. In the first, an unknown woman cries out to Jesus: "'Blessed is the womb that bore you and the breasts a which you nursed!' Jesus replied, 'Blessed rather are those who hear the word of God and keep it!'" (Luke 11:27–28). A second passage presents an actual encounter between Jesus and his family: "Then his mother and his brothers came to him, but they could not reach him because of the crowd. And he was told, 'Your mother and your brothers are standing outside, desiring to see you.' But he answered them, 'My mother and my brothers are those who hear the word of God and do it'" (Luke 8:19–21).

According to *Redemptoris Mater*, Jesus diverts attention from motherhood as only a natural or family bond to motherhood as supremely a spiritual bond between those who are attentive to God's word. In the narratives themselves, the tone of the words seems to indicate that Jesus is distancing himself from his mother. Despite this appearance, the encyclical insists that Jesus is

---

11. As one Catholic theology explains, "Mary is more thoroughly redeemed than we are, and has the greater cause for gratitude to God in Christ." Aidan Nichols, *Epiphany: A Theological Introduction to Catholicism*, 2nd ed. (n.p.: Ex Fontibus, 2016), 388. Earlier questions have presented the distinction between infusion of grace and imputation. The extent or quantity of redemption makes sense within the Catholic system and its view of the infusion of grace. But it makes no sense within the Protestant system and its view of justification as the divine declaration of "not guilty"—forgiven of *all sins*—but "righteous" instead through the imputation of the *whole righteousness* of Christ to believers.

referring to Mary in a very special way: "Thus we can say that the blessing proclaimed by Jesus is not in opposition, despite appearances, to the blessing uttered by the unknown woman but rather coincides with the blessing in the person of this Virgin Mother."[12]

But Protestants disagree with this interpretation of the first narrative. The second word of Jesus's response to the unknown woman is key: "Blessed *rather* are those who hear the word of God and keep it!" (Luke 11:28). *Rather* (or *on the contrary*) is a strong contrast often used to correct an error. *Redemptoris Mater* seems to adhere to the principle that Mary was the first to hear the word and obey it, and that she always continued to obey it. With this assumption, it misunderstands the force of the contrasting word *rather*. It indicates that Mary did *not* grasp Jesus's significance and therefore was *not* in obedience. He does distance himself from her. Indeed, Jesus elevates discipleship based on obedience to Scripture over common natural connections—including the familial tie of motherhood. If Mary (or any other person, for that matter) is to be blessed, it is because she (or that other person) gives heed to the word of God.[13]

In the second story, Jesus distances himself even more strongly from familial ties. In Mark's account, two earlier narratives lead up to this encounter. In the first (Mark 3:20–21), Jesus's family stunningly considers him to be insane and want to take him away from his followers.[14] In the second (Mark 3:22–30), Jesus's opponents imagine that he is demon-possessed. These two narratives lead to the story on which *Redemptoris Mater* comments: Jesus's family cannot get to him because of the crowd. Given this context, a question is raised: For what reason did Jesus's mother and brothers desire to see him? They think he is crazy. Others think he is demonically influenced. To read this final narrative as expressive of a sincere wish to be with Jesus for the right reasons is mistaken. Indeed, Jesus's reply—"My mother and my brothers are those who hear the word of God and do it"—highlights the strong contrast between his misguided family according to the flesh and his true family of obedient disciples.[15]

---

12. *RM*, 20.
13. For further discussion, see Joel Green, "Blessed Is She Who Believed," in *Blessed One: Protestant Perspectives on Mary*, eds. Beverly Roberts Gaventa and Cynthia L. Rigby (Philadelphia: Westminster John Knox, 2002), 12–13.
14. As one Catholic theologian explains, "We need not suppose that Mary agreed with the opinion of the family council, but she evidently agreed with their purpose. When she comes with his brethren, he lets her wait outside the door and go home without achieving anything (Mark 3:31–35). In the Marian tradition of the Church, this is her training for the Cross." Nichols, *Epiphany*, 399.
15. For further discussion, see Elizabeth Johnson, "Who Is My Mother?" in *Blessed One: Protestant Perspectives on Mary*, 34–36.

Protestants believe *Redemptoris Mater's* interpretation of these stories about the Mary-Jesus relationship is mistaken. They are not about her blessing but highlight her misunderstanding of her son.

## Mary's Motherly Mediation

A similar tension is felt in the story of the wedding at Cana (John 2:1–11): "When the wine gave out, the mother of Jesus said to him, 'They have no wine.' And Jesus said to her, 'O woman, what have you to do with me? My hour has not yet come.' His mother said to the servants, 'Do whatever he tells you'" (vv. 3–5 RSV). *Redemptoris Mater* underscores how Mary significantly contributes to the first miraculous sign of Jesus, through a deep understanding that existed between him and her. "Even though Jesus' reply to his mother sounds like a refusal (especially if we consider the blunt statement 'My hour has not yet come' rather than the question), Mary nevertheless turns to the servants and says to them: 'Do whatever he tells you' (John 2:5)."[16] Then Jesus performs a miracle.

The encyclical now escalates its theology of Mary. It emphasizes that this event manifests "Mary's solicitude for human beings." Her statement ("They have no wine") "has a symbolic value" in that her "coming to the aid of human needs means . . . bringing those needs within the radius of Christ's mission and salvific power."[17] But there is more, as the encyclical continues:

> There is mediation: Mary places herself between her Son and mankind in the reality of their wants, needs and sufferings. She puts herself "in the middle," that is to say she acts as a mediatrix not as an outsider, but in her position as mother. She knows that as such she can point out to her son the needs of mankind, and in fact, she "has the right" to do so. Her mediation is thus in the nature of intercession: Mary "intercedes" for mankind. The Mother of Christ presents herself as the spokeswoman of her Son's will, pointing out those things which must be done so that the salvific power of the Messiah may be manifested.[18]

Thus, between Jesus and the fallen human race stands Mary, the motherly mediatrix. She intercedes for them. She calls her Son's attention to their needs. She helps direct them to her Son's saving work.

A critique of this interpretation focuses on Jesus's reply to Mary: "O woman, what have you to do with me? My hour has not yet come." "Woman"

---

16. *RM*, 21.
17. *RM*, 21.
18. *RM*, 21.

is not a term of endearment, though it is courteous. The question he poses to her—literally, "what to me and to you?"—is an expression that distances the two parties and bears a note of reproach. Mary's action is particularly improper because, as Jesus explains, his hour—the time of his death and subsequent resurrection—has not yet come. Jesus has been sent to accomplish the Father's will and not his own or that of someone else, including that of his mother.

In response to her Son's critique, Mary leaves the matter in his hands: "Do whatever he tells you." And Jesus performs a miracle, with this result: Jesus's glory is manifested (v. 11). Protestants believe *Redemptoris Mater*'s escalation of the importance of Mary is wrong. It is the glory of Jesus—not that of Mary—that is revealed. Certainly, the idea of her as a mediatrix is far from the text. Indeed, if her mediating action is seen as due to Mary being not an outsider but Jesus's mother, it completely misses the whole point of the rebuke. Mary has no claim on her Son. "What is there between you and me in this matter?" Answer: "Nothing whatsoever!" And Mary's response, "Do whatever he tells you to do," does not present Mary as the spokesperson for her Son's will. Rather, she resigns herself to the fact that she does not exercise a privileged control over her Son.

### Mary's Motherly, Suffering Sacrifice

This central role of Mary is most clearly seen at the crucifixion of her Son:[19] "Standing by the cross of Jesus were his mother [and other women]. . . . When Jesus saw his mother and the disciple whom he loved [John] standing nearby, he said to his mother, 'Woman, behold your son!' Then he said to the disciple, 'Behold, your mother!' And from that hour the disciple took her to his own home" (John 19:25–27).

*Redemptoris Mater* underscores two points. The first is Jesus's action in directing John toward Mary in a new, motherly manner. The encyclical interprets the figure of John as each and every human being, as well as the model of all true disciples in the church: "The Mother of Christ, who stands at the very center of this mystery [the Son's redemptive work] . . . is given as mother to every single individual and all mankind. The man at the foot of the cross

---

19. *Redemptoris Mater* notes that Mary's suffering is foreshadowed elsewhere in Scripture. The Old Testament foretold the intense spiritual struggle between Satan and Mary (Gen. 3:15). Simeon prophesied her path of suffering, saying to Mary about her Son, "Behold, this child is appointed for the fall and rising of many in Israel, and for a sign that is opposed (and a sword will pierce through your own soul also), so that thoughts from many hearts may be revealed" (Luke 2:34–35). According to the encyclical, Simeon reveals to Mary that "she will have to live her obedience of faith in suffering, at the side of the suffering Savior" (*RM*, 16). Furthermore, the apocalyptic sign of a woman in danger from a great red dragon, who threatened to devour her newborn son (Rev. 12:1–6), is, according to the encyclical, confirmation of Mary's central role in the battle between the evil of sin and Jesus (*RM*, 11).

is John . . . but it is not he alone."[20] Mary is mother of both the entire human race and the church.

The second point is the horrific yet salvific ordeal that Mary experiences at Jesus's crucifixion: "by 'suffering deeply with her only begotten Son and joining herself with her maternal spirit to his sacrifice,' Mary lovingly consented 'to the immolation [sacrifice] of the victim to whom she had given birth.'"[21] In so doing, Mary continued in her perfect submission to the eternal divine plan. "How great, how heroic then is the obedience of faith shown by Mary in the face of God's 'unsearchable judgments!' How completely she 'abandons herself to God' without reserve, 'offering the full assent of the intellect and the will.'" Still more: "Through faith the Mother shares in the death of her Son, in his redeeming death."[22] Mary plays a central role in the saving death of her Son for the redemption of the world.

A critique underscores the problem with both points of interpretation. First, *Redemptoris Mater* emphasizes that John comes under the care of Mary. But the text also notes that John took Mary into his home. As one of his final acts before dying, Jesus simply and lovingly displayed his concern for his mother by giving her into the care of his beloved disciple. Jesus does not symbolically establish his mother as the mother of all humanity and Mother of the Church.

Second, Jesus's love for Mary is particularly timely as she faces his horrendous and tragic crucifixion. Importantly, it was *his suffering*—not that of Mary—that the text underscores. It was *his "hour"*—the time of Jesus's death. It was *his crucifixion* that meant "all was now finished" in fulfillment of Scripture (John 19:28). It was *his cry*—"It is finished"—that meant his sacrifice was once and for all (John 19:30). The narrative is all about Jesus. It is not about Mary, even though we can extrapolate and empathize with her horrific suffering. But it was Jesus who manifests "heroic . . . obedience of faith." It was Jesus who "abandons [him]self to God without reserve." It was Jesus who offered "the full assent of the intellect and the will" to the divine plan of salvation.[23] This was true of Jesus, not of Mary.

## Mary as Mother of the Church

In the final narrative about Mary, the book of Acts recounts Mary's presence in the upper room at Pentecost (Acts 1:12–14). Luke names the eleven apostles—the Twelve minus Judas Iscariot—who were gathered, then adds: "All these with one accord were devoting themselves to prayer, together with the women and Mary the mother of Jesus, and his brothers" (v. 14). *Redemptoris*

---

20. *RM*, 23.
21. *RM*, 18, citing Vatican Council II, *Dei Verbum*, 5.
22. *RM*, 18, citing Vatican Council II, *Lumen Gentium*, 58.
23. *RM*, 18.

*Mater* explains: "We see Mary powerfully imploring the gift of the Spirit, who had already overshadowed her in the Annunciation."[24] As Mary gave birth to the incarnate Son, so she gave birth to the church.[25] Accordingly, she is both mother of Jesus and Mother of the Church. Indeed, though not chosen as one of the twelve apostles, Mary received a type of apostolic mission.[26]

Protestants believe this interpretation is incorrect. Luke's list of the eleven apostles serves a certain purpose, but there is no mention or even an implication of a type of apostleship for Mary. Rather, she along with Jesus's brothers are mentioned among those joining the apostles in prayer. We learn from this that Mary, his mother, continues to be one of Jesus's followers.[27] Beyond this point, Luke will not allow us to imagine more of a role for Mary.

Though the biblical account ends with this last mention of Mary, the Catholic Church embraces the doctrine of her bodily assumption. Question 33 addresses this doctrine that at her death, Mary's body was immediately taken up into heaven.

### Summary

Three areas of agreement between Roman Catholics and Protestants arise from this interaction with Pope John Paul II's encyclical *Redemptoris Mater*: The first is the virginal conception of Jesus. Second, there is great blessing both to Mary and to all humanity that she believed Gabriel's words announcing that she would become the mother of Jesus. Mary is rightly called "blessed" (Luke 1:48). Third, Mary is a stellar model of the obedience of faith. Still, the object of her faith, not Mary herself, is key. She believed that God himself would fulfill his promised word. This is a model to be imitated.

Despite these areas of agreement, there are many points of Protestant disagreement with this Roman Catholic biblical theology of Mary. Seven areas of disagreement follow: First, the emphasis on Mary's predestination to her role as the mother of Jesus may predominate and thereby minimize God's sovereign plan for all that transpires in this world. Second, Mary's preparation for her role through the immaculate conception (see Question 33) is without biblical support. So too is the alleged parallelism between Eve and her disobedience and Mary—the second Eve—and her obedience without biblical support. Third, Mary's cooperation with the divine plan has a tendency to overlook God's unmerited favor in her life. And it exaggerates her role by elevating her obedience of faith to a level of decisiveness: without her believing response to the divine plan, it would have failed.

---

24. *RM*, 24, citing Vatican Council II, *Lumen Gentium*, 59.
25. *RM*, 24.
26. *RM*, 26.
27. This point was left in doubt in Luke's Gospel (8:19–21 and 11:27–28). We learn also that Jesus's brothers, though they had not believed in him during his life (John 7:5), became his disciples following his death and resurrection.

Fourth, while the Catholic biblical theology of Mary interprets texts that narrate her interaction with Jesus in a positive way, Protestant interpretations note not her blessing but her misunderstanding of her son and his mission. Fifth, Mary's motherly mediation—her intercession for others, her intervention between Jesus and others—is seen by Protestants to be grounded on a misunderstanding of biblical passages. Sixth, this misinterpretation is particularly keen and tragic when it comes to the Catholic view of her motherly suffering and sacrifice. As much as the Catholic position insists that the central role that it ascribes to her in Jesus's saving death does not detract from his redemptive work, many people are perplexed and unconvinced. This elevation of her is seen, seventh, in the Catholic view of Mary as Mother of the Church. Again, without biblical support, it exalts Mary to an undeserved role in the work and application of salvation.

## REFLECTION QUESTIONS

1. In what ways do Hebrews 2:14–18 and 4:14–16 call into question the Roman Catholic biblical theology of Mary?

2. Do you ever engage in conversation with a Catholic friend or family member about their beliefs about Mary? After reading this chapter, in what ways might you alter your approach to those conversations?

3. Have you ever found yourself intentionally avoiding appreciation for Mary out of concern that to do so might detract from Jesus and his work? Looking at the three areas of agreement between Roman Catholics and Protestants on Mary, how might you appropriately marvel at the virginal conception of Jesus, bless Mary, and imitate her example?

4. Does it seem to you that the Catholic biblical theology of Mary emphasizes her ideal faith, perfect obedience, steadfast understanding, and flawless suffering and sacrifice—could we say "perfection"? If so, does Mary actually serve as a model for us who are wavering in faith, inconsistently obedient, bumbling in our understanding, and complaining sufferers—certainly imperfect in all ways?

5. Does it seem to you that the Catholic biblical theology of Mary presents a human being as capable of receiving and transmitting the grace of God rather than as one who is unworthy of divine grace except by direct intervention on his part? Does Mary become an example of the nature-grace interdependence? How would you critique this view?

# What Are the Immaculate Conception and Bodily Assumption of Mary?

Authority in the Roman Catholic Church has three interconnected elements: Scripture, Tradition, and the Magisterium. Question 32 looked at Scripture, addressing a Catholic biblical theology of Mary. This chapter's question adds two important elements in the Church's Tradition about Mary, doctrines proclaimed by the Magisterium to be authoritatively true and binding on all Catholics. It also explains the titles of Mary and their implications for the Catholic Church. Each point includes a brief critique.

## The Immaculate Conception

As Question 32 explained, Mary had to be well prepared to say yes to the angel's announcement and so participate in the eternal divine plan for her. To become the mother of the Savior, Mary "was enriched by God with gifts appropriate to such a role."[1] Indeed, at the moment of the annunciation, Gabriel saluted her as "full of grace" (Luke 1:28). Through the centuries the Catholic Church has become ever more aware that Mary, "full of grace" through God, was redeemed from the moment of her conception.

This is what the doctrine of the immaculate conception confesses, as Pope Pius IX proclaimed in 1854:

> The most Blessed Virgin Mary was, from the first moment of her conception, by a singular grace and privilege of almighty God and by virtue of the merits of Jesus Christ, Savior of the human race, preserved immune from all stain of original sin.[2]

---

1. Vatican Council II, *Lumen Gentium*, 56.
2. Pope Pius IX, *Ineffabilis Deus*, December 8, 1854, https://www.papalencyclicals.net/pius09/p9ineff.htm.

Just to be clear, this papal proclamation has nothing to do with the conception of Jesus Christ. Rather, it decrees that at the conception of Mary, the one who would become the mother of Jesus Christ did not inherit the devastating taint of original sin, which includes guilt before God and a fallen human nature. Therefore, she was well prepared to be a worthy vessel for the incarnation of the Son.

At the same time, Vatican Council II affirmed that the "splendor of an entirely unique holiness" by which Mary is "enriched from the first instant of her conception" comes wholly from Christ. Indeed, she is "redeemed, in a more exalted fashion, by reason of the merits of her Son."[3] Protestants wonder how it is appropriate to speak of Mary as being redeemed when, according to the immaculate conception, she was preserved from original sin. If such were true, she did not stand in need of redemption.

It appears that some equivocation is involved with the word "redemption." For all other human beings, due to the ruinous stain of original sin, redemption is—indeed, must be—*salvation out of sin*. In the case of Mary, however, because her immaculate conception preserved her from original sin, redemption was—indeed, could only be—*protection from sin*. In the case of all other human beings, redemption involves the removal of their guilt and the transformation of their corrupt nature. In the case of Mary, redemption involved the prevention of her inheritance of guilt and the protection from her receiving a corrupt nature.[4]

But Protestants object to more. The immaculate conception is not part of a biblical theology of Mary, as no Scripture supports it. Rather, the doctrine is Tradition, a papal proclamation that becomes, by its proclamation, authoritative divine revelation. Protestants reject Catholic Tradition as divine revelation alongside of Scripture.

Additionally, it is with this doctrine that the clash of Scripture and Tradition becomes evident. According to Scripture, all human beings without exception are sinful (e.g., 1 Kings 8:46; Eccl. 7:20; Rom. 3:10–18, 23; 1 John 1:8–10). According to Catholic Tradition, however, one human being was conceived without sin and, as we will see, lived her entire life without sin. Regarding this tension between Scripture and Tradition, the Magisterium elevates the latter over the former and affirms that Mary was immaculately conceived. As the evangelical participants in Evangelicals and Catholics Together offered, "The doctrine of the Immaculate Conception is incongruent with

---

3. Vatican Council II, *Lumen Gentium*, 56, 53.
4. Catholic theologian Aidan Nichols, appealing to Dun Scotus, refers to this as *"praere-demptio*—Mary's redemption by anticipation which made feasible the historical coming of humankind's Redeemer." Nichols explains that Mary's "redemption was not so much deliverance as preservation." Aidan Nichols, *Epiphany: A Theological Introduction to Catholicism*, 2nd ed. (n.p.: *Ex Fontibus*, 2016), 385, 387.

Sacred Scripture because it exempts Mary from original sin and declares that she is thus saved by Jesus in a unique manner."[5]

## Mary's Sinlessness and Perpetual Virginity

Flowing from this doctrine, Catholicism embraces Mary's sinlessness: "By the grace of God Mary remained free of every personal sin her whole life long."[6] She exemplified this sinlessness in her response to Gabriel's announcement: "Let it be to me according to your word" (Luke 1:38). As in the case of Mary's immaculate conception, the Church's belief in her sinlessness is supported by Tradition but contradicts Scripture. Therefore, Protestants reject the belief.

Further evidence of Mary's total and uninterrupted holiness is her perpetual virginity. The Church celebrates Mary as *Aeiparthenos*, the "Ever-virgin."[7] Certainly, Scripture supports the truth that Mary was a virgin when she conceived Jesus. The narrative in Matthew's gospel (1:18–25) begins with an affirmation of her virginity: "When his mother Mary had been betrothed to Joseph, before they came together she was found to be with child from the Holy Spirit" (v. 18). It concludes with the assurance that Joseph "knew her not until she had given birth to a son" (v. 25). Moreover, Catholic Mariology believes that even in the act of giving birth, Mary remained a virgin. In fact, Christ's birth "did not diminish his mother's virginal integrity but sanctified it."[8] Even more, "The deepening of faith in the virginal motherhood led the Church to confess Mary's real and perpetual virginity."[9]

There are three objections. The first appeals to the lack of biblical evidence for any kind of miraculous event that preserved Mary's virginity as she was went through childbirth. Instead, Luke's gospel presents it as normal in every way: "And she gave birth to her firstborn son and wrapped him in swaddling cloths and laid him in a manger" (Luke 2:7). The second objection focuses on Matthew's statement that Joseph "knew her not until she had given birth to a son" (Matt. 1:25). The word "until" indicates that Mary's state of virginity concluded sometime after Jesus's birth; she did indeed engage in sexual intercourse with her husband, Joseph.[10] The third objection ties into

---

5. Evangelicals and Catholics Together, "Do Whatever He Tells You: The Blessed Virgin Mary in Christian Faith and Life," November 2009, in the section entitled "An Evangelical Word to Catholics," 3, https://www.firstthings.com/article/2009/11/do-whatever-he-tells-you-the-blessed-virgin-mary-in-christian-faith-and-life.

6. CCC, 493.

7. Vatican Council II, *Lumen Gentium*, 52.

8. Vatican Council II, *Lumen Gentium*, 57.

9. CCC, 499.

10. As I explain elsewhere, "It is true that 'until' can connote an ongoing state of things that continues past the specified time, which is indicated for its particular importance rather than as an end point. For example, if I exclaim, 'I will be a Chicago Cubs fan until they win a second World Series!' I am not indicating that as soon as the Cubs win another championship, I will

the second: sexual intercourse between Joseph and Mary resulted in brothers and sisters of Jesus.[11] Thus, Jesus, as Mary's firstborn son (2:7), had siblings. Dissenting from this position, "The [Catholic] Church has always understood these passages as not referring to other children of the Virgin Mary. In fact, James and Joseph, 'brothers of Jesus,' are the sons of another Mary, a disciple of Christ, whom St. Matthew significantly calls 'the other Mary' [Matt. 13:55; 28:1; cf. Matt. 27:56]. They are close relations of Jesus, according to an Old Testament expression [Gen. 13:8; 14:16; 29:15; etc.]."[12] But this interpretation misidentifies these people; they are, instead, Jesus's siblings. Thus, the perpetual virginity of Mary lacks a biblical basis.[13]

## The Bodily Assumption

The doctrine of the bodily assumption of Mary, proclaimed by Pope Pius XII, affirms the following in relationship to the end of her life:

> Finally the Immaculate Virgin, preserved free from all stain of original sin, when the course of her earthly life was

---

cease to be a fan. But in its twenty-five occurrences in the Gospel of Matthew, this sense of 'until' is not found, making it highly unlikely that it is Matthew's sense in 1:24–25." *RCTP*, 141n830. This point stands even when the use of "until" in the last sentence of the gospel is considered: "And behold, I am with you always, *until* the end of the age" (28:20). The objection that "Jesus will be with the apostles even after this present age comes to an end" misses the point. The time arc of this gospel is from Abraham (1:2) to the close of human history on this earth as we know it, associated with Jesus's victorious return (13:39, 24:3; chap. 25). It is his Great Commission, given to his apostles, that is the marching orders of the church for that age. Thus, the "you" in "I am with *you* always" cannot refer only to the original apostles; it must refer to the church from its inception to its conclusion, at Jesus's return. From that point—the end of the age—onward, nothing is known; the gospel reveals nothing about it. Accordingly, the claim that Jesus will be with the apostles after that point lacks support. This objection is raised in Trent Horn, *The Case for Catholicism: Answers to Classic and Contemporary Protestant Objections* (San Francisco: Ignatius, 2017), 312.

11. Matt. 12:46 (par. Mark 3:31–35; Luke 8:19); 13:55–56 (par. Mark 6:3); Acts 1:14; 1 Cor. 9:5; Gal. 1:19.

12. CCC, 500.

13. Historically, church leaders like Jerome supported the perpetual virginity of Mary. Arguments include the following: (1) The supposition that Joseph was never the actual husband of Mary; thus, never being married, Mary never had sexual intercourse with Joseph (or with any other man, for that matter). (2) The so-called "brothers and sisters" of Jesus were actually his cousins, not siblings. (3) The state of virginity is higher than the state of marriage; thus, for Mary to be in the highest state in keeping with her motherhood of the incarnate Son, she would be in a perpetual state of virginity. Jerome, *Of the Perpetual Virginity of the Blessed Mary against Helvidius*, in *Saint Jerome, Dogmatic and Polemical Works*, trans. John N. Hritzu, Fathers of the Church 53 (Washington, DC: Catholic University Press of America, 1965), 3–44. Whereas some of the early Reformers (appear to have) embraced this doctrine, the tide eventually turned against it such that most Protestants today deny Mary's perpetual virginity because it lacks solid biblical support.

> finished, was taken up body and soul into heavenly glory, and exalted by the Lord as Queen over all things, so that she might be the more fully conformed to her Son, the Lord of lords and conqueror of sin and death.[14]

This doctrine flows from the belief in Mary's immaculate conception and sinlessness. She was preserved from original sin at her conception and lived a life of thoroughgoing holiness. Thus, there was no need for Mary to suffer the usual penalty assessed to sinful human beings: the separation of their body, which is laid in a tomb or grave, from their soul, which enters into the presence of the Lord. Rather, in the integrity of body and soul, Mary was assumed into heaven.[15] And, there, alongside her son, Mary reigns according to various titles (discussed below).

Additionally, "the Assumption of the Blessed Virgin is a singular participation in her Son's Resurrection and an anticipation of the resurrection of other Christians."[16] It means that she is the only Christ-follower in heaven who is embodied, a hope to which all Christians look forward when Christ returns.

Again, Protestants disagree with this doctrine. As with the immaculate conception, the bodily assumption is not part of a biblical theology of Mary, as no Scripture supports it. Rather, the doctrine is Tradition, and of recent vintage (1950, though the Church insists that it has acknowledged it for many centuries). Moreover, it runs into difficulty with the biblical insistence that Christ-followers, following their death, are disembodied in heaven (2 Cor. 5:1–9).[17] The contrast between this truth of Scripture and the belief of Catholic Tradition that Mary is embodied in heaven is quite evident.

## Mary's Titles

In light of its biblical theology of Mary and its Tradition-based doctrines of her immaculate conception, sinlessness, perpetual virginity, and bodily assumption, the Roman Catholic Church invokes Mary "under the titles of Advocate, Helper, Benefactress, and Mediatrix."[18]

---

14. Pope Pius XII, *Munificentissimus Deus*, November 1, 1950, Vatican.va.
15. "There was no sin to obstruct her union with him [God] from the very start of her life. . . . Similarly, at the end of her life there were to be no obstacles to prevent the perfect fulfillment of her redemption: not even the need of the material world for reordering, for harmonizing with the final end of humanity." Nichols, *Epiphany*, 403.
16. CCC, 966.
17. The intermediate state—the period between our death and Christ's return, which will be associated with our bodily resurrection—is one of both blessing (in the presence of Christ) and loss (the absence of our body).
18. CCC, 969.

*Advocate*, a term from the lawcourts, is a promoter who pleads a case on behalf of another. Mary's advocacy has particular reference to her prayers. As Pope Pius VII proclaimed, "While the prayers of those in heaven have, it is true, some claim on God's watchful eye, Mary's prayers place their assurance in a mother's right. For that reason, when she approaches her Divine Son's throne, as Advocate she begs, as Handmaid she prays, but as Mother she commands."[19] *Helper* apparently applies to Mary as a fierce and victorious warrior battling alongside of her Church against its many enemies. As *Benefactress* she confers gifts and benefits upon her Church. As *Mediatrix*, Mary is the one through whom God the Son became incarnate as Jesus Christ. Moreover, she stands between Jesus and the fallen human race interceding for people, calling her Son's attention to their needs, and directing them to her Son's saving work.

Accordingly, the Catholic faithful pray for Mary's motherly mediation on their behalf. The quintessential prayer is the "Hail Mary":

> Hail Mary, full of grace,
> the Lord is with thee.
> Blessed art thou among women,
> and blessed is the fruit of thy womb, Jesus.
> Holy Mary, mother of God,
> pray for us sinners now,
> and at the hour of our death.

Pope Pius XII's proclamation of Mary's bodily assumption also referred to her as "Queen over all things." This title stems from Mary's relationship to her Son, who is the King (Matt. 2:2; 27:11; Col. 1:13; 1 Tim. 1:17).[20] It also picks up on the apocalyptic imagery of a woman in heaven on whose head is "a crown of twelve stars" (Rev. 12:1). In her role as queen, Mary is invoked by the Catholic faithful. An example is the prayer *Regina Caeli* (Queen of Heaven), recited during the Easter season, which begins: "Queen of Heaven, rejoice, alleluia, for He whom you did merit to bear, alleluia, has risen, as he said, alleluia. Pray for us to God, alleluia."

These Marian titles—Advocate, Helper, Benefactress, Mediatrix, Queen— are consistent with her person and role as the mother of all humanity and Mother of the Church. Still, their exalted tenor creates problems. Acknowledging this potential confusion, the Church insists, "In the words of the apostle [Paul] there is but one mediator: 'for there is but one God and one mediator of God and men, the man Christ Jesus, who gave himself a redemption for all' (1 Tim.

---

19. Pope Pius VII, *Tanto Studio*, February 19, 1805 in *Our Lady* (Boston: St. Paul Editions, 1961), 42.
20. Appeal is made to the Old Testament monarchy in which the king, while having many wives, had only one mother, who was referred to as the queen (e.g., 2 Kings 24:12).

2:5–6). But Mary's function as mother of men in no way obscures or diminishes this unique mediation of Christ, but rather shows its power."[21]

Protestants wonder: If everything that was necessary for the salvation of fallen humanity was accomplished by God the Son incarnate, why then the Catholic insistence on Mary as Advocate, Helper, Benefactress, Mediatrix, and Queen? Indeed, Protestants believe that "through the Son of God's immaculate conception, sinlessness, perfect obedience of faith, passion, death, burial, resurrection, ascension, sending of the Holy Spirit to give birth to the church, baptism of Christians with the Spirit to incorporate them into his body, and union with them, Jesus Christ has accomplished salvation completely. Nothing more is or can be added to that which he did to perfectly save fallen human beings."[22] It is in this truth that Protestants rest.

There is one more title of Mary with which both Roman Catholics and Protestants agree. The early church acknowledged Mary to be *Theotokos*, literally, "the one who bears [the one who is] God,"[23] or, more briefly, "the Mother of God."[24] As originally formulated, *Theotokos* indicates that the one to whom Mary gave birth is fully God. It is a statement about the identity of the Son incarnate: he is God, not some exalted man, not some half-god. On this confession of the Son's deity, Catholics and Protestants concur. However, Protestants deny *Theotokos* as an affirmation of some type of exalted status for Mary. This idea is a common misperception at odds with its historical meaning.[25]

## Summary

The Roman Catholic Church believes in the immaculate conception, sinlessness, perpetual virginity, and bodily assumption of Mary. Additionally, it refers to her with various titles. One area of agreement between Catholics and Protestants is the reference to Mary as *Theotokos*. In all other areas, there is disagreement. The overarching critique is that these beliefs about Mary are grounded not in Scripture but in Tradition as proclaimed by the Magisterium. As these Catholic beliefs do not have biblical support, Protestants believe they are not true and do not carry authority. Each may also be critiqued specifically.

Mary's immaculate conception contradicts Scripture, which insists that all human beings bear the guilt of Adam and are characterized by a corrupt nature (Rom. 5:12–21). Additionally, the belief refers to Mary's redemption in a way that uses "redemption" in an unusual sense: not salvation out of sin but protection from sin. Her sinlessness contradicts Scripture, which rehearses over and over and over again the truth that "all have sinned and fall short

---

21. Vatican Council II, *Lumen Gentium*, 60.
22. *RCTP*, 204–5.
23. Jaroslav Pelikan, *Mary through the Centuries* (Cambridge: Yale University Press, 1998), 55.
24. *Theotokos* is a word that combines two Greek words, *theos* (God) and *tokos* (childbirth).
25. For further discussion, see *RCTP*, 133, 135.

of the glory of God" (Rom. 3:23). Furthermore, a strong biblical case can be made for Mary engaging in sexual intercourse with Joseph after Jesus's birth, with the result that he was not her only son, but her firstborn son: Jesus had brothers and sisters. Thus, Scripture overturns the belief in Mary's perpetual virginity. The doctrine of the bodily assumption of Mary is overturned because it relies on the doctrine of her sinlessness, which is unbiblical. Moreover, her (alleged) embodiment in heaven wreaks havoc with the nature of the intermediate state: it is a place of disembodiment.

Mary's titles—Advocate, Helper, Benefactress, Mediatrix, and Queen—are problematic for two reasons. Some take prerogatives that apply exclusively to God and use them of Mary. For example, Scripture addresses both the incarnate Son and the Holy Spirit as Advocate and Helper, and it uses Mediator in reference to the Son. The others are either poorly defined (Benefactress) or without any biblical support (Queen). For these reasons, Protestants balk at referring to Mary by these exalted titles.

## REFLECTION QUESTIONS

1. How do the doctrines of the immaculate conception, sinlessness, perpetual virginity, and bodily assumption of Mary illustrate the Roman Catholic authority structure composed of Scripture, Tradition, and the Magisterium? By contrast, what is the nature of Protestant church authority?

2. Does it seem to you that Catholic belief in Mary's immaculate conception, sinlessness, perpetual virginity, and bodily assumption emphasize her perfection? If so, does Mary actually serve as a model for us who are born with and suffer from original sin, who continuously and reprehensibly sin, who (if married) engage in sexual intercourse with our spouses, and who (at death) decay in our grave or become ashes when cremated—imperfect from start to finish?

3. In what ways do Hebrews 2:14–18 and 4:14–16 call into question the Roman Catholic titles of Mary as Advocate, Helper, Benefactress, Mediatrix, and Queen?

4. How is the Catholic insistence on Mary's redemption confusing, given the normal understanding of that word as referring to salvation from sin, not protection from sin?

5. Do you ever engage in conversation with a Catholic friend or family member about Mary and hear them refer to her with these titles? After reading this chapter, in what ways might you alter your approach to those conversations?

# Who Are the Saints, and What Is Their Role?

The Roman Catholic notion of the saints and their role is associated with three other matters: the holiness of the Church, the communion of saints, and the treasury of the saints.

## The Holiness of the Church

The Church's attribute of holiness refers primarily to its position of being set apart for God. It is consecrated for his purposes. It also refers to its progress in holiness, which is necessary because, regrettably, the Church is not perfectly pure in reality. Indeed, in many ways and at many times, the Church is identifiable as holy only with great difficulty. Accordingly, the Church must continually pursue greater and greater purity.

According to Catholicism, there are exceptions to this dismal picture. One exception (discussed in Questions 32 and 33) is Mary. As the sinless Mother of God, she lived a life of perfect holiness. Other exceptions are the saints. These faithful Catholics "practiced heroic virtue and lived in fidelity to God's grace."[1] Through divine assistance especially by means of the sacraments, they were enabled to live in love and engage in good works, thereby meriting eternal life. Like all those in heaven, the saints enjoy the beatific vision, that is, they see God face-to-face. Examples of the many thousands of saints include Augustine, Francis of Assisi, Thomas Aquinas, Catherine of Siena, Teresa of Avila, the apostles Peter and Paul, Elizabeth and Joseph, Mother Teresa of Calcutta, and (most recently) John Paul II. Additionally, by canonizing[2]—solemnly proclaiming—these faithful as saints, "the Church

---

1. CCC, 828.
2. According to the US Conference of Catholic Bishops, "In official Church procedures there are three steps to sainthood: a candidate becomes 'Venerable,' then 'Blessed' and then

recognizes the power of the Spirit of holiness within her and sustains the hope of believers by proposing the saints to them as models and intercessors."[3]

Being models, the saints exemplify what the obedience of faith, carrying the cross, suffering, and a life of love look like concretely. As the Catholic faithful pattern themselves after the saints, the Church experiences renewal and increased ministry. In particular, "the saints have always been the source and origin of renewal in the most difficult moments in the Church's history." Moreover, the holiness demonstrated in their lives "is the hidden source and infallible measure of her apostolic activity and missionary zeal."[4]

In regard to the intercession of the saints, "being more closely united to Christ, those who dwell in heaven fix the whole Church more firmly in holiness. . . . They do not cease to intercede with the Father for us, as they proffer the merits which they acquired on earth through the one mediator between God and men, Christ Jesus. . . . So by their fraternal concern is our weakness greatly helped."[5] The saints in heaven pray for the Catholic faithful on earth and for the souls in purgatory.

## The Communion of Saints

This interchange between these various realms of existence—heaven, earth, and purgatory—is an aspect of the communion of saints.[6] The catechism states, "Since all the faithful form one body, the good of each is communicated to the others."[7] This transference of goods among the Catholic faithful comes through Christ, the head of the Church, especially through the sacraments. Moreover, "as this Church is governed by one and the same Spirit, all the goods she has received necessarily become a common fund."[8] Specifically, the exchangeable goods in this shared treasury are "holy persons" and "holy things."[9]

As for the exchange of holy persons,

---

'Saint.' Venerable is the title given to a deceased person recognized formally by the pope as having lived a heroically virtuous life or offered their life [i.e., martyrdom]. To be beatified and recognized as a Blessed, one miracle acquired through the candidate's intercession is required in addition to recognition of heroic virtue or offering of life. Canonization requires a second miracle after beatification. The pope may waive these requirements. A miracle is not required prior to a martyr's beatification, but one is required before canonization." US Conference of Catholic Bishops, "Saints," http://www.usccb.org/about/public-affairs/backgrounders/saints-backgrounder.cfm.

3. CCC, 828; the citation is from Vatican Council II, *Lumen Gentium*, 40.
4. John Paul II, *Christifideles Laici*, December 30, 1988, 16.3, 17.3.
5. Vatican Council II, *Lumen Gentium*, 49.
6. The expression comes from the Apostles' Creed. After the confession of the church as "one, holy, catholic, and apostolic," the creed confesses, "the communion of saints."
7. CCC, 947.
8. CCC, 947.
9. CCC, 948.

The communion of the saints means that the fellowship of the members of these "churches" [the heavenly church, the earthly church, and the purgatorial church] is uninterrupted so that an exchange of spiritual goods takes place. Such exchange is seen in intercession: the faithful in the heavenly church unceasingly pray for the faithful in the earthly and purgatorial churches. Regarding this latter intercession, prayers for the dead are offered "that they may be loosed from their sins" and thus be transferred to the heavenly church. The exchange is further seen in the experience of closer communion with Christ through communion with the saints in heaven.[10]

Thus, there is a parallel: just as we enjoy fellowship with other believers on earth, they bring us closer to Christ, and they pray for us, so also we enjoy fellowship with the saints in heaven, they bring us closer to Christ, and they pray for us.[11]

### The Treasury of the Saints

The exchange of holy things "includes communion in the faith, the sacraments, charisms (gifts), possessions (in every sense of that word), and charity."[12] Moreover, "the holiness of one profits others. . . . Thus recourse to the communion of saints lets the contrite sinner be more promptly and efficaciously purified in the punishment for sin."[13] For example, the saints, who have excelled in holiness and acquired merits beyond what they need, may help the souls of the faithful in purgatory to progress more quickly and effectively toward purification and transferal from purgatory to heaven.

These spiritual goods, then, compose the treasury of the saints: the infinite merits of Christ, "the prayers and good works of the Blessed Virgin Mary," and "the prayers and good works of all the saints."[14] To benefit from the treasury, the Catholic faithful on earth obtain indulgences on behalf of themselves and for specific people in purgatory. Then, the Church "intervenes in favor of [these] individual Christians and opens for them the treasury of the merits of Christ and the saints to obtain from the Father of mercies the remission of the temporal punishments due for their sins."[15] In this way, the holiness of Church in its saints, the communion of saints, and the treasury

---

10. *RCTP*, 189. The citation is from Vatican Council II, *Lumen Gentium*, 50, which derives the expression from 2 Maccabees 12:45.
11. Vatican Council II, *Lumen Gentium*, 50.
12. *RCTP*, 189.
13. CCC, 1475.
14. CCC, 1476–77.
15. CCC, 1478.

of the saints effect an exchange of spiritual goods. This provision of merits needed for the remission of sin's temporal punishment is used to benefit the Catholic Church in its earthly, heavenly, and purgatorial aspects.

## Concerns

Protestants raise several concerns about the Catholic perspectives on the holiness of saints (which is tied to the idea of salvation as a progressive movement), the communion of saints, and the treasury of the saints. As most Protestants are quite unfamiliar with these three elements of Roman Catholicism, the wide divergence between the Catholic Church and Protestant churches is deeply felt.

### The Attribute of Holiness

First of all, Protestants agree that the attribute of holiness pertains to the standing of the church before God. In this sense, all Christians are "sanctified in Christ Jesus, called to be saints together with all those who in every place call upon the name of our Lord Jesus Christ" (1 Cor. 1:2). Positionally, the church is holy. Position and reality, however, are two different matters, and reality is that complete holiness during this earthly life is never actualized. It is not that the church lacks all the necessary resources for full obedience and total faithfulness. Indeed, God's "power has granted to us all things that pertain to life and godliness, through the knowledge of him who called us to his own glory and excellence, by which he has granted to us his precious and very great promises, so that through them you may become partakers of the divine nature, having escaped from the corruption that is in the world because of sinful desire" (2 Peter 1:3–4). In terms of the divine provision for salvation, there is no lack.

Rather, the failure to progress consistently and to attain to complete holiness in this life falls squarely on the shoulders of Christians. Still beset by the ravaging effects of their sinful nature (even though "sinner" is not their primary identity), all believers continue to yield to temptation and thus sin. No wonder Scripture underscores, "If we say we have no sin, we deceive ourselves, and the truth is not in us. If we confess our sins, he is faithful and just to forgive us our sins and to cleanse us from all unrighteousness" (1 John 1:8–9). In terms of the human persistence in salvation, there is failure.

The conclusion is that the Catholic Church wrongly claims that certain of its faithful members have "practiced heroic virtue and lived in fidelity to God's grace" so as to become saints.[16] Either this view contradicts Scripture, or it understands holiness in an unusual way, or both.

---

16. CCC, 828. The same assessment holds true for the Protestant theology, following John Wesley, of Christian perfection. For example, John Wesley defined this state as "the loving [of] God with all our heart, mind, soul and strength. This implies that no wrong temper, none contrary to love, remains in the soul and that all the thoughts, words and actions are

*Salvation as a Progressive Movement*

A second concern focuses on the Catholic doctrine of salvation as a progressive movement that, through the infusion of grace through the sacraments, transforms the faithful's nature so they can merit eternal life. If that transformation is adequate in their lifetime—if they have "done what is in them to do" in terms of cooperation with divine grace—they enter heaven. If that transformation falls short such that they require further purification, they experience that remaining renovation in purgatory.

The Protestant doctrine of justification stands against this view. It insists that by God's declaration, sinful people are proclaimed "not guilty" but "righteous" instead. Indeed, they are pronounced completely holy, not on the basis of their own acquired righteousness (even if moved and increased by divine grace) but because the perfect righteousness of Jesus Christ is imputed to their account. Accordingly, through the gospel, sinful people are saints by divine decree, or they are not saints but lost instead. There is no such thing as sufficient progress toward meriting eternal life.

*The Communion of Saints*

The communion of the saints is the third concern. There is a lack of biblical support for the notion of an interchange between the earthly church and the heavenly church (not to mention the purgatorial church). Scripture never treats a supposed connection between believers in heaven and believers on earth. It never indicates that the former "saints" are praying for their earthly brothers and sisters. Thus, any affirmation of such activity is conjecture, which is dangerous. It is also extraneous, as Scripture highlights the intercessory work of God the Son and God the Holy Spirit on behalf of the earthly church (Rom. 8:26–27, 34). As the evangelical representatives to Evangelicals and Catholics Together urged:

> Whether Mary and other departed believers with the Lord in glory can hear and answer words addressed to them from this life, the Bible does not say. Evangelicals believe that through the finished work of Christ on the cross, and by the power of the Spirit who intercedes for us, we may come directly and "boldly to the throne of grace" (Heb. 4:16). Although the Church triumphant [the heavenly church] and the Church militant [the earthly church] join together in common worship by means of the one Spirit (Rev. 5:6–14), there is no mention of prayers to

governed by pure love." John Wesley, *Thoughts on Christian Perfection*, q. 6, ans. 4, in *John Wesley*, ed. Albert C. Outler (New York: Oxford University Press, 1964), 287. For further discussion, see Gregg R. Allison, *Historical Theology: An Introduction to Christian Doctrine* (Grand Rapids: Zondervan, 2011), 537–38.

Mary or the saints in the witness of the New Testament and the first two hundred years of the Church.[17]

Without biblical support, and with no attestation in the early church, the communion of saints is a speculative idea at best.[18]

### The Treasury of the Saints

The fourth concern is the notion of the treasury of the saints with its three aspects: (1) the accumulation of merits by Mary and the saints; (2) the exchange of those spiritual goods through obtaining indulgences; and (3) the application of those goods to the faithful in the earthly church and the purgatorial church. These three ideas lack biblical support. Additionally, Protestants wonder, "If Christ's merits are indeed infinite, as Catholic theology maintains, then what possible benefit could be superadded . . . by the deeds and prayers of Mary and the saints?"[19] Moreover, if the salvation of sinful people is fully accomplished by Jesus Christ and is fully applied to them through the divine declaration of justification, then no exchange of merits on the part of the saints for the benefit of others is needed.

## Summary

Catholics hold saints to be those faithful Catholics who have "practiced heroic virtue and lived in fidelity to God's grace."[20] Through divine assistance, especially by means of the sacraments, they were enabled to live in love and engage in good works, thereby meriting eternal life. When they are canonized by the Catholic Church, they are offered as models of holiness and as intercessors. Thus, their sainthood has particular reference to the holiness of the Church and its progress in salvation.

The saints and their role in Catholic theology and practice must also be understood in the light of the communion of saints. This communion features an interchange of spiritual goods between the Catholic faithful who exist in three "churches": the heavenly church, the church on earth, and the purgatorial church. These goods are of two types: holy people and holy things. The interchange of holy people means that the saints in heaven constantly pray for the faithful on earth and in purgatory.

---

17. Evangelicals and Catholic Together, "Do Whatever He Tells You: The Blessed Virgin Mary in Christian Faith and Life," November 2009, in the section entitled "An Evangelical Word to Catholics," 4, https://www.firstthings.com/article/2009/11/do-whatever-he-tells-you-the-blessed-virgin-mary-in-christian-faith-and-life.
18. This point is not to deny that the Apostles' Creed affirmed "the communion of saints," but it did not do so in the Roman Catholic sense of praying to believers in heaven.
19. *RCTP*, 349.
20. *CCC*, 828.

The interchange of holy things is at the heart of the treasury of the saints. This treasury is composed of the infinite merits of Christ along with the prayers and good works of Mary and of the saints. The saints in heaven pray for the Catholic faithful on earth and in purgatory. On behalf of themselves and of the souls in purgatory, the faithful on earth may obtain indulgences, the remission of the temporal punishments due for sins. These benefits are stored in the treasury of the saints and disbursed by the Catholic Church.

Various concerns are voiced by Protestants in relation to the Catholic views of the holiness of the saints, the communion of saints, and the treasury of the saints. Of particular note is the lack of biblical support for the three ideas. They also contradict the Protestant doctrine of justification.

## REFLECTION QUESTIONS

1. How do the holiness of the saints (and its tie to progress in salvation), the communion of saints, and the treasury of the saints contribute to the Roman Catholic view of the saints and their role?

2. How do these three topics relate to the Protestant emphasis on justification by God's grace alone through faith alone in Christ alone?

3. How do you respond to this parallel: "Just like I ask my friends Brad and Beth to pray for me, so I ask St. Bartholomew and St. Bernadette to pray for me"?

4. If you are Catholic, have you ever obtained an indulgence for yourself or for someone else? How do you assess that experience?

5. If you are Protestant, how do you assess the practice of obtaining indulgences for oneself or for the souls of the faithful in purgatory?

# PART 3

# Contemporary and Personal Questions

# Questions about the State of the Roman Catholic Church Today

In this section, I explore questions about major challenges that the Catholic Church faces today, and the contributions of its last three popes.

# What Are the Major Challenges Facing the Catholic Church Today?

Major challenges are nothing new to us individually or as educational institutions, businesses, government agencies, and nations. It should come as no surprise, then, that the Roman Catholic Church—as well as Eastern Orthodox churches and Protestant churches—finds itself facing many major challenges today. The specific problems treated in this question are the sexual abuse scandal, the scandal of clerical homosexuality, the ambiguity of Pope Francis, and the crisis of priestly vocations and the reluctance of priests to accept episcopal nomination.

## Sexual Abuse Scandal

For several decades, former and current Catholics have come forward reporting how they were sexually abused by clergy. This abuse runs the gamut from fondling genitals to sexual intercourse with girls/women and homosexual acts with boys/men. The majority of cases involved boys. The age of abuse began as young as two years old and included adults. The number of victims abused by any one priest was scores. The number of abusive acts against any one victim went as high as hundreds of times. The duration of the abuse could have extended for many years. The abuse took place in cars, offices, first communion parties, schools, seminaries, and confessionals.

In addition to the sexual abuse itself, the Catholic hierarchy acted negligently by failing to deal promptly and decisively with its own members who were accused of abuse. In many cases, bishops transferred accused priests from one parish to another without reporting the abuse to the police. At times, Church officials paid large sums of money to buy the victims' silence. The failure to expose the abuse contributed to its continuation in the Church. The abuse and its cover-up have led to thousands of lawsuits charging criminal behavior and seeking billions of dollars in recompense for the survivors.

Additionally, priests have been expelled from the priesthood, bishops have resigned from their offices, and dioceses have filed for bankruptcy to settle lawsuits in federal court and seek bankruptcy protection.

In a high-profile case, on January 11, 2019, the Church decreed that Cardinal Theodore McCarrick was guilty of "solicitation in the Sacrament of Confession, and sins against the Sixth Commandment with minors and with adults, with the aggravating factor of the abuse of power."[1] On February 15, 2019, Pope Francis defrocked McCarrick, expelling him from the ministry. On May 7, 2019, the pope issued a *motu proprio* (a personal edict) setting forth steps for the Church to follow in reporting and investigating charges of sexual abuse by clergy.[2]

In a controversial publication, Pope Emeritus Benedict XVI offered a cogent analysis of the situation titled "The Church and the Scandal of Sexual Abuse" (April 11, 2019). He set the problem in its wider societal context: the sexual revolution of the 1960s, sex education for young people, sexual freedom without any norms of constraint, the acceptance of pedophilia, the disappearance of absolute morality and moral standards, and the questioning of a unique Catholic moral theology based on natural theology and Scripture. Benedict detailed the effect of this societal degradation on the formation of priests and the lives of priests, noting the existence of homosexual clubs in seminaries, the rise of pedophilia, and the growing difficulty in bringing formal charges against those accused of pedophilia. His straightforward proposal for how to move ahead was love: "It is the real counterforce against evil. The power of evil arises from our refusal to love God. He who entrusts himself to the love of God is redeemed. Our being not redeemed is a consequence of our inability to love God. Learning to love God is therefore the path of human redemption." Benedict concluded his analysis by bemoaning the loss of the Eucharist and of the mystery of the Church, which has come to be regarded as little more than a political reality.[3]

## Scandal of Clerical Homosexuality

Despite their vow of chastity and pledge to abstain from sexual intercourse for their entire life, a growing number of Catholic clergy engage in homosexual activity, creating another sexual scandal in the Church.

---

1. *Congresso* for the Congregation for the Doctrine of the Faith, "Communication of the Congregation for the Doctrine of the Faith," January 11, 2019, https://press.vatican.va/content/salastampa/it/bollettino/pubblico/2019/02/16/0133/00272.html#en.
2. Pope Francis, "*Vos Estis Lux Mundi*," May 7, 2019, http://www.vatican.va/content/francesco/en/motu_proprio/documents/papa-francesco-motu-proprio-20190507_vos-estis-lux-mundi.html.
3. Pope Emeritus Benedict XVI, "The Church and the Scandal of Sexual Abuse," *Catholic News Agency*, April 10, 2019, https://www.catholicnewsagency.com/news/full-text-of-benedict-xvi-the-church-and-the-scandal-of-sexual-abuse-59639.

Going back sixty years or more, concern about homosexuality among the clergy was minimum.[4] Accordingly, homosexuality received the briefest of treatment in *Religiosorum Institutio*, a 1961 training manual for ordination to the priesthood: "Advantage [Access] to religious vows and ordination should be barred to those who are afflicted with evil tendencies to homosexuality or pederasty, since for them the common life and the priestly ministry would constitute serious dangers."[5] Sadly, a lack of enforcement of this rule fostered a seminarian culture favorable to homosexuality. Based on the experiences and reports of seminary faculty and reports of observers, ethnographers, and journalists, "homosexual men entered the seminaries in noticeable numbers from the late 1970s through the 1980s" leading to "a situation that included much more open expression of homosexual identity, or what is called 'homosexual lifestyle.'"[6]

Decades later, the Church spelled out a bit more explicitly what consideration should be given to the ordination of men who actively engage in homosexuality or who have homosexual tendencies. In its "Instruction Concerning the Criteria for the Discernment of Vocations with regard to Persons with Homosexual Tendencies in View of their Admission to the Seminary and to Holy Orders," the Congregation for Catholic Education underscored that its directives reflect—indeed, must reflect—the traditional teaching of the Catholic Church on homosexuality. Following the Catechism of the Catholic Church, this instructional document distinguished between homosexual *acts* and homosexual *tendencies*:

> Regarding *acts*, it teaches that Sacred Scripture presents them as grave sins. The Tradition has constantly considered them as intrinsically immoral and contrary to the natural law. Consequently, under no circumstance can they be approved. Deep-seated homosexual *tendencies*, which are found in a number of men and women, are also objectively disordered and, for those same people, often constitute a trial. Such persons must be accepted with respect and sensitivity. . . . In

---

4. As one report noted, "A review of the narratives of men who were seminarians in the 1950s and of published histories of the seminaries themselves does not reveal any record of noticeable or widespread sexual activity by seminarians." John Jay College Research Team, "The Causes and Contexts of Sexual Abuse of Minors by Catholic Priests in the United States, 1950–2010," May 2011, 38. For a summary of the report, including the above citation, see https://www.catholicleague.org/politics-color-john-jay-study.

5. Sacred Congregation for Religious, "*Religiosorum Institutio*: Instruction on the Careful Selection and Training of Candidates for the States of Perfection and Sacred Orders," *Adoremus*, February 2, 1961, 30.4 https://adoremus.org/1961/02/02/religiosorum-institutio/#anchorri29.

6. John Jay College Research Team, "Causes and Contexts of Sexual Abuse," 38.

> the light of such teaching . . . it [is] necessary to state clearly that the Church, while profoundly respecting the persons in question, cannot admit to the seminary or to holy orders those who practice homosexuality, present deep-seated homosexual tendencies, or support the so-called "gay culture."[7]

Thus, the Church reiterated its historical position on homosexuality and continued to bar—at least formally—practicing homosexuals from its priestly ranks.

Despite this official position, a percentage of Catholic clergy struggle with homosexual tendencies or engage actively in homosexual activity. Accurate statistics of the extent of this problem are difficult to come by. Estimates range from thirty to fifty percent of the clergy are homosexual.[8] Apparently, Pope Francis has confirmed the existence of a "gay lobby" in the Vatican.[9]

Grabbing the headlines are three famous cases. Father Robert Carter was a priest who helped to start the National Gay Task Force (now called the National Gay and Lesbian Task Force). Father Bernárd J. Lynch was an Irish priest who was the first to enter into a civil partnership with a man. Bishop Juan Carlos Maccarone resigned his position when a video of him having sex with his chauffeur went public.

## Pope Francis's Ambiguity and the Example of Divorced and Remarried Participation in the Eucharist

In his apostolic exhortation *Amoris Laetitia* (*The Joy of Love*; March 19, 2016), Pope Francis seemed to speak ambiguously on several important doctrinal and practical areas, perhaps to the point of contradicting Scripture and Tradition, including recent papal pronouncements. An example of his ambiguity regards possible access to the sacrament of the Eucharist by divorced and remarried Catholics under certain circumstances.

In response to *Amoris Laetitia*, four former cardinals made public five questions, or *dubia*, for the pope to answer so as to clarify certain ambiguities in his exhortation.[10] These five questions are (1) "Has [it] now become

---

7. Congregation for Christian Education, "Instruction Concerning the Criteria for the Discernment of Vocations with regard to Persons with Homosexual Tendencies in View of Their Admission to the Seminary and to Holy Orders," November 4, 2005, 2, Vatican.va.

8. The percentage of homosexually oriented priests is estimated to be higher than it is in the general population. Similarly, the incidence of AIDS-related illness is higher among the clergy than it is among the population at large.

9. "Pope Francis 'Confirms Vatican Gay Lobby and Corruption,'" BBC News, June 12, 2013, https://www.bbc.com/news/world-europe-22869399.

10. Cardinal Walter Brandmüller, Cardinal Raymond Burke, Cardinal Carlo Caffarra, and Cardinal Joachim Meisner, "Seeking Clarity: A Plea to Untie the Knots in *Amoris Laetitia*," *Aleteia*, November 14, 2016, https://aleteia.org/2016/11/14/full-text-seeking-clarity-a-plea-to-untie-the-knots-in-amoris-laetitia.

possible to grant absolution in the sacrament of penance and thus to admit to holy Communion a person who, while bound by a valid marital bond, lives together with a different person as husband and wife?" That is, may "divorced persons who are in a new union and who continue to live as husband and wife" participate in the sacrament of the Eucharist? As the cardinals' explanation of their question put it, "It would seem that admitting to Communion those of the faithful who are separated or divorced from their rightful spouse and who have entered a new union in which they live with someone else as if they were husband and wife would mean for the Church to *teach by her practice*" something inconsistent with the Church's traditional positions on "marriage, human sexuality, and the nature of the sacraments."

(2) Are there "absolute moral norms that prohibit intrinsically evil acts and that are binding without exceptions?" This question sought clarification for Francis's seeming dismissal of "the existence of so-called intrinsically evil acts." The cardinals affirmed traditional Catholic teaching "that there are acts that are always evil, which are forbidden by moral norms that bind without exception ('moral absolutes'). These moral absolutes are always negative, that is, they tell us what we should *not* do. 'Do not kill.' 'Do not commit adultery.' Only negative norms can bind without exception." The second *dubia* wondered if Pope Francis affirmed this traditional Catholic position.

(3) "Is it still possible to affirm that a person who habitually lives in contradiction to a commandment of God's law, as for instance the one that prohibits adultery (Matthew 19:3–9), finds him or herself in an objective situation of grave habitual sin?" With their third *dubia*, the cardinals directly questioned the pope's affirmation in *Amoris Laetitia,* 301: "The Church possesses a solid body of reflection concerning mitigating factors and situations. . . . Hence it can no longer simply be said that all those in any 'irregular' situation are living in a state of mortal sin and are deprived of sanctifying grace." For the cardinals, the pope's position seemed to contradict the Church's Code of Canon Law (canon 915)[11] and its statement that people—with particular application to the Catholic faithful "who are divorced and civilly remarried"—who "obstinately persist in manifest grave sin are not to be admitted to holy Communion."

(4) To the pope's affirmation of the existence of certain "circumstances which mitigate moral responsibility," the cardinals' wondered if certain "circumstances or intentions can [ever] transform an act intrinsically evil by virtue of its object into an act 'subjectively' good or defensible as a choice"? Think of homicide or homosexuality as examples. The cardinals wondered: "Do these acts, which the Church's Tradition has called bad in themselves and grave sins, continue to be destructive and harmful for anyone committing them in whatever subjective state of moral responsibility he may be? Or could these acts, depending on a person's subjective state and depending on the

---

11. http://www.vatican.va/archive/cod-iuris-canonici/eng/documents/cic_lib4-cann879-958_en.html.

circumstances and intentions, cease to be injurious and become commendable or at least excusable?" Obviously, the cardinals held the first position and questioned whether the pope embraced the second position.

(5) The fifth question asked: Is it still possible to affirm traditional Church teaching that "excludes a creative interpretation of the role of conscience and that emphasizes that conscience can never be authorized to legitimate exceptions to absolute moral norms that prohibit intrinsically evil acts by virtue of their object?" This *dubia* raised the specter of attempts "made to legitimize so-called 'pastoral' solutions contrary to the teaching of the magisterium, and to justify a 'creative' hermeneutic according to which the moral conscience is in no way obliged, in every case, by a particular negative precept." Turning to the example of adultery, the cardinals traced out the implications of the pope's apparent position:

> In this perspective, it will never be enough for moral conscience to know "this is adultery," or "this is murder," in order to know that this is something one cannot and must not do. Rather, one would also need to look at the circumstances or the intentions to know if this act could not, after all, be excusable or even obligatory. . . . For these theories, conscience could indeed rightfully decide that, in a given case, God's will for me consists in an act by which I transgress one of his commandments. "Do not commit adultery" is seen as just a general norm. In the here and now, and given my good intentions, committing adultery is what God really requires of me. Under these terms, cases of virtuous adultery, lawful murder and obligatory perjury are at least conceivable.

Was this the position and its implications that the pope was championing?

This almost unprecedented public questioning of a pope illustrates a major challenge facing the Church today: the ambiguity of Pope Francis in his apparent relaxing of traditional doctrines and practices for the purpose of creating a more inclusive, tolerant, welcoming face for the Catholic Church.

## Crisis of Priestly Vocations and Episcopal Acceptance

The common perception is that the Catholic Church is in crisis due to a catastrophic plunge in the number of men entering the priesthood and thus the number of priests worldwide. Statistics show otherwise. In 1970 there were about 420,000 priests in the world. That number decreased only slightly to about 414,500 in 2017. However, the problem lies in the fact that, given the increase in the number of Roman Catholics worldwide, the relatively stable number of priests means the ratio of the Catholic faithful to priests has risen significantly, from about 2,000 lay people per priest to more than 3,000 lay people per priest. Geographically, the crisis is most pronounced in the West, where decreasing numbers of priestly vocations and priests are most acutely felt. By contrast, in Poland and in many countries in Africa, numbers are stable or even increasing. Two key reasons for this diversity are that the progressive parishes in the West find it difficult to encourage young men toward priestly vocations, and the sexual abuse scandal has soured many with regard to serving such a morally corrupt Church. By contrast, the traditional Catholic areas continue to foster the call to priestly service.

Added to this declining situation is the growing reluctance of qualified priests to accept the invitation to become bishops. Estimates vary from 30 percent to 50 percent of priests nominated by the pope to the episcopal office decline his invitation. Reasons for refusal include involvement in sexual abuse that would come under closer scrutiny in the more public venue of the episcopate, fear of having to deal with the ongoing accusations of priestly sexual abuse and the accompanying lawsuits and financial payments, reluctance toward managing the crisis of declining number of parishes and schools, and an unwillingness to play the political game required of officeholders.[12]

## Summary

I focused on four major challenges to the Roman Catholic Church today. The sexual abuse scandal has ruined the lives of thousands of boys, girls, men, and women. It has soured many of the Catholic faithful on the Church and resulted in hundreds of lawsuits and payments of billions of dollars for damages caused. The scandal of clerical homosexuality means that a significant number of seminarians and clergy, despite their vows of celibacy and the Church's traditional condemnation of homosexuality, engage in homosexual activity and live a gay lifestyle. The ambiguity of Pope Francis toward some traditional Catholic doctrines and practices is illustrated by his apostolic exhortation *Amoris Laetitia* and the five *dubia* addressed to him by four former cardinals. The final major challenge is the number of priestly vocations and priests worldwide in relation to the growing number of Catholic faithful. The difficulty is compounded by the reluctance of priests to accept papal invitations to become bishops.

## REFLECTION QUESTIONS

1. How familiar are you with the sexual abuse scandal? Have you seen the movie *Spotlight*, a portrayal of the scandal? Do you think the Church is

---

12. For further discussion, see Father Raymond de Souza, "Why Ever More Priests Are Declining to Become Bishops," *Catholic Herald*, September 26, 2019, https://catholich-erald.co.uk/why-ever-more-priests-are-declining-to-become-bishops.

doing enough to help the survivors, to hold its clergy accountable, to ensure the proper reporting of accusations, and to stop the cover-up?

2. How do you react to the pope's admission that a "gay lobby" exists within the Vatican? Whatever your view might be of homosexuality, how do you reconcile the Church's formal and traditional stance of classifying homosexual activity as a mortal sin with its ordination of practicing homosexuals?

3. What is your assessment of the five *dubia* in response to Pope Francis's *Amoris Laetitia*? Do you think that the pope is being ambiguous?

4. Do you know of anyone studying to be a priest? What are some of the key issues he faces in making the decision to enter the priesthood? How would the major challenges addressed in this question pose problems for men considering the priesthood? What do you think of the reasons for the reluctance of priests to accept the papal nomination to the office of bishop?

5. If you are not Roman Catholic, what major challenges does your church face today? Why? What do you think are some important ways of addressing those challenges?

# What Contributions Have the Last Three Popes Made to the Church?

## Pope John Paul II

John Paul II (1920–2005) was one of the most influential of all popes, due in no small part to the length of his papacy: more than twenty-seven years (1978–2005), the second longest papacy in history. His election on October 16, 1978, as the first non-Italian pope in more than 450 years was particularly noteworthy. John Paul's papacy was very productive as he made 104 papal trips in 129 countries. During many of these visits he delivered scores of public messages that were heard by millions of people worldwide.

As a participant at Vatican Council II, his work on *The Pastoral Constitution on the Church in the Modern World* (*Gaudium et Spes*; December 7, 1965) was decisive for the Catholic Church going forward, and he oversaw many of the practical applications of the Council's *aggiornamento* (updating). For example, he convened the first full meeting of the College of Cardinals (1979) in more than four hundred years. He heard confessions in St. Peter's Basilica, promoted a new edition of the Code of Canon Law (1983), and initiated World Youth Days (1987). In 1986, his commissioning of twelve cardinals, led by Cardinal Joseph Ratzinger (the future Pope Benedict XVI), to prepare a new catechism led to the eventual publication of the Catechism of the Catholic Church (1992).[1] His leadership in ecumenical activities included meeting with Jewish and Muslim leaders, hosting the first World Day

---

1. He declared the catechism to be "a statement of the Church's faith and of catholic doctrine, attested to or illumined by sacred Scripture, the apostolic Tradition, and the Church's Magisterium," consequently "a sure norm for teaching the faith and thus a valid and legitimate instrument for ecclesial communion." John Paul II, "On the Publication of the Catechism of the Catholic Church," 3, October 11, 1992, in the CCC.

of Prayer for Peace in Assisi, Italy (October 27, 1986), with more than one hundred fifty religious leaders, and contributing to the thawing of hostilities between Catholics and Protestants. In keeping further with *The Pastoral Constitution on the Church in the Modern World*, John Paul II extended the Church's influence well beyond its own borders as he played a leading role in the collapse of communism in his homeland of Poland and the other Soviet-bloc counties in Eastern Europe. He was a tireless advocate of human rights, human freedom, and democracy.

While John Paul II was well known for shaping the Catholic Church as a major voice in the contemporary world, he was also a proponent of many traditional aspects of the Church as seen in several of his encyclicals. In *The Gospel of Life* (*Evangelium Vitae*; March 25, 1995), the pope presented the clash between the world's advocacy of a culture of death and the Church's promotion of a culture of life. He affirmed the Church's traditional teaching on personal and sexual ethics, voicing its opposition to abortion, euthanasia, contraception, premarital sex, homosexuality, and capital punishment. Two months later he offered *That They May Be One* (*Ut Unum Sint*; May 25, 1995), expressing the Church's irrevocable commitment to ecumenism. Following Vatican II's *Decree on Ecumenism* (*Unitatis Redintegratio*; November 21, 1964), the pope emphasized the necessity of dialogue with Eastern Orthodox churches and Protestant ecclesial communities for the sake of the fulfillment of Jesus's prayer for unity (John 17).[2]

John Paul II's well-known Marian devotion found expression in *Mother of the Redeemed* (*Redemptoris Mater*; March 25, 1987 [see Question 32]). This biblical theology of Mary affirmed the Church's traditional doctrines of her immaculate conception, perpetual virginity, sinlessness, suffering at the cross, and bodily assumption, together with her traditional titles of Advocate, Benefactress, Helper, and Co-Mediatrix and her traditional role as Mother of the Church and of all people. John Paul II's dedication to the Virgin Mary was well known. It featured devotion to Our Lady of Czestochowa in Poland. Upon asked if he would accept his election to the papacy, he responded positively while pledging

---

2. Importantly, the pope rightly noted, "It is already possible to identify the areas in need of fuller study before a true consensus of faith can be achieved: 1) the relationship between Sacred Scripture, as the highest authority in matters of faith, and Sacred Tradition, as indispensable to the interpretation of the Word of God; 2) the Eucharist, as the Sacrament of the Body and Blood of Christ, an offering of praise to the Father, the sacrificial memorial and Real Presence of Christ and the sanctifying outpouring of the Holy Spirit; 3) Ordination, as a Sacrament, to the threefold ministry of the episcopate, presbyterate and diaconate; 4) the Magisterium of the Church, entrusted to the pope and the bishops in communion with him, understood as a responsibility and an authority exercised in the name of Christ for teaching and safeguarding the faith; 5) the Virgin Mary, as Mother of God and Icon of the Church, the spiritual Mother who intercedes for Christ's disciples and for all humanity." John Paul II, *Ut Unum Sint*, May 25, 1995, 79.

to abandon himself "to the Mother of Christ and the Church."[3] Additionally, his papal motto was *totus tuus* ("wholly yours," with reference to Mary), and his papal coat of arms had the letter *M* below the cross, symbolizing Mary's position at the foot of Jesus's cross. When he was shot May 13, 1981, John Paul invoked the Blessed Mother and later attributed his miraculous survival to her intervention. On the first anniversary of his narrow escape, he dedicated the whole world to the Immaculate Heart of Mary.

In *The Splendor of Truth* (*Veritatis Splendor*; August 6, 1993), the pope decried the contemporary evils of moral relativism, affirmed the objectivity of morality and truth, and underscored the moral authority of the Church's Magisterium. His encyclical *Faith and Reason* (*Fides et Ratio*; September 14, 1998) affirmed the traditional Catholic view that faith presupposes reason and that reason is not contrary to faith. Though not an encyclical, John Paul II's letter "On Preserving Priestly Ordination to Men Alone" (*Ordinatio Sacerdotalis*; May 22, 1994) reaffirmed the Church's traditional rejection of the ordination of women to the priesthood and echoed its traditional opposition to clerical marriage.

Pope John Paul II died on April 2, 2005, and was canonized as a saint (together with Pope John XXIII) on April 27, 2014.

## Pope Benedict XVI

Benedict XVI (b. 1927) is Pope Emeritus of the Catholic Church, having stepped down from the papacy in 2013. By this unprecedented resignation, Benedict created the phenomenon in which there are two popes, with Francis being the active pope and Benedict being retired. Closely tied to John Paul II, as Cardinal Joseph Ratzinger, he was appointed Prefect of the Congregation for the Doctrine of the Faith and Dean of the College of Cardinals. When John Paul II chose him to lead a commission of twelve cardinals to write a new catechism, Cardinal Ratzinger and his team produced the Catechism of the Catholic Church (1992). As the visible fruit of the *aggiornamento* of Vatican Council II, it sets forth the doctrine and practice of the Church at the turn of the third millennium. It affirmed many traditional Catholic positions such as Mariology, justification, purgatory, the sacramental economy, and the relationship of Scripture, Tradition, and the Magisterium. The catechism also updated many issues such as the two movements of the Mass, an inclusivist view of salvation, and the necessity of ecumenical dialogue.[4]

With regard to ecumenism, Cardinal Ratzinger offered clarification of the status of Eastern Orthodoxy and Protestantism in his declaration *On the Unicity and Salvific Universality of Jesus Christ and the Church* (*Dominus*

---

3. George Weigel: *Witness to Hope: The Biography of John Paul II*, 1920–2005 (New York: HarperCollins, 1999), 254.

4. See Question 4 for a discussion of Vatican Council II.

*Iesus*; August 6, 2000). As a statement about the Church's universal mission, it decried religious pluralism and its accompanying denial of the uniqueness of the revelation of Jesus Christ and the salvation accomplished by his crucifixion and resurrection. Moreover, it lamented the marginalization of the Catholic Church as Christ's chosen instrument to announce and extend salvation to the world. Accordingly, Cardinal Ratzinger concluded, "Just as there is one Christ, so there exists a single body of Christ, a single Bride of Christ: a single Catholic and apostolic Church."[5] This is the traditional self-understanding of the Roman Catholic Church.

Benedict drew two implications of his view: Eastern Orthodox bodies are true churches in close communion with the Roman Catholic Church. However, Protestant gatherings are not churches but "ecclesial communities" whose participation in salvation derives its "efficacy from the very fullness of grace and truth entrusted to the Catholic Church."[6]

As a theologian, Benedict XVI was noted for several themes throughout his papacy. Like his predecessor, Benedict championed a close relationship between faith and reason: "Faith presupposes reason and perfects it, and reason, enlightened by faith, finds the strength to rise to knowledge of God and spiritual realities."[7] While embracing science, he decried the dominion of naturalistic science and its attempt to eliminate God and supernatural realities. While acknowledging the approach of higher criticism, he bemoaned the strictures it places on biblical interpretation and instead called for a hermeneutic of faith "which does not do dogmatic violence to the Bible, but precisely allows the solitary possibility for the Bible to be itself."[8] He also championed the theological virtues of faith, hope, and love as seen in his papal encyclicals: *God Is Love* (*Deus Caritas Est*; January 25, 2006), *Saved by Hope* (*Spe Salvi*; November 30, 2007), and *Love in Truth* (*Caritas in Veritate*; July 7, 2009). Benedict left a fourth encyclical, *The Light of Faith* (*Lumen Fidei*) unfinished at the time of his resignation. Pope Francis later completed and published it (June 29, 2013).

## Pope Francis

Francis (b. 1936) is the current pope (2013–). As the first non-European pope and the first Jesuit priest to hold this office, he is well known for his humility and shunning of many of the trappings traditionally associated with the papacy. His tenure as pope has been marked by controversy.

---

5. Cardinal Joseph Ratzinger, *Dominus Iesus*, August 6, 2000, 16.
6. Ratzinger, *Dominus Iesus*, 17.
7. Benedict XVI, Angelus Address, St. Peter's Square, January 28, 2007. See especially his Regensburg address: "Faith, Reason and the University: Memories and Reflections," September 12, 2006.
8. Benedict XVI, "Biblical Interpretation in Crisis," *First Things*, April 26, 2008, https://www.firstthings.com/web-exclusives/2008/04/biblical-interpretation-in-crisis.

If his predecessor Benedict XVI can be characterized by the "Roman" element, Francis epitomizes the "Catholic" element:

> It is as if Francis stresses the genius of the "catholicity" of Vatican II (i.e., openness, renewal, inclusion, accommodation), whereas the old Ratzinger sees problematic outcomes that have plagued the Church. The tension between the "catholic" and the "roman" elements of the Roman Catholic Church is now embodied in the dialectic between the two Popes. Francis tends to the "catholic" Pope in line with the elasticity of Vatican II whereas Benedict looks like more of the "roman" Pope calling his Church to its doctrinal identity shaped around its sacramental system.[9]

Francis's more open stance can be seen especially in some of the controversial positions for which he has become famous. Several examples follow.

In his apostolic exhortation *The Joy of the Gospel* (*Evangelii Gaudium*; November 24, 2013), Francis called for an overhaul of the Church's evangelization: "Pastoral ministry in a missionary key seeks to abandon the complacent attitude that says: 'We have always done it this way.' I invite everyone to be bold and creative in this task of rethinking the goals, structures, style and methods of evangelization in their respective communities. . . . I prefer a Church which is bruised, hurting and dirty because it has been out on the streets, rather than a Church which is unhealthy from being confined and from clinging to its own security."[10] Addressing several scientific and environmental issues, Francis affirmed the compatibility of the Bible's story of creation and an evolutionary theory of the universe's origin.[11] In his encyclical *Praise Be to You* (*Laudato Si'*; May 24, 2015), Francis lamented the threat of global warming and championed a new approach to the ecological treatment of the earth. Many of the Catholic faithful wondered about the pope's deep concern over this matter when there are so many other pressing issues that need to be addressed.

---

9. Leonardo De Chirico, "Are There Two Popes of the Roman Catholic Church?," *Vatican Files* 161, April 19, 2019, http://vaticanfiles.org/en/2019/04/vf161.
10. Pope Francis, *Evangelii Gaudium*, November 24, 2013, 33, 49.
11. "The beginning of the world was not a work of chaos that owes its origin to another, but derives directly from a supreme Principle who creates out of love. The Big Bang theory, which is proposed today as the origin of the world, does not contradict the intervention of a divine creator but depends on it. Evolution in nature does not conflict with the notion of Creation, because evolution presupposes the creation of beings who evolve." Pope Francis, "Address of His Holiness Pope Francis on the Occasion of the Inauguration of the Bust in Honor of Pope Benedict XVI," October 27, 2014.

Turning to spiritual and moral controversies, Francis caused consternation among the faithful when he affirmed that even atheists can be forgiven. In a response to a series of questions in the Italian newspaper *La Repubblica*, the pope offered, "You ask me if the God of the Christians forgives those who don't believe and who don't seek the faith. I start by saying—and this is the fundamental thing—that God's mercy has no limits if you go to him with a sincere and contrite heart. The issue for those who do not believe in God is to obey their conscience."[12] Similarly, when asked by a distressed young boy if his deceased atheist father was in heaven, Francis replied, "God has the heart of a father, your father was a good man, he is in heaven with him, be sure. God has a father's heart and, would God ever abandon a non-believing father who baptizes his children? God was certainly proud of your father, because it is easier to be a believer and have your children baptized than to be a non-believer and have your children baptized. Pray for your father, talk to your father. That is the answer."[13] In a fictitious dialogue as part of his homily in St. Peter's Square (May 21, 2013), the pope again mentioned the fate of atheists: "The Lord has redeemed all of us, all of us, with the blood of Christ: all of us, not just Catholics. Everyone! 'Father, the atheists?' Even the atheists. Everyone! . . . We must meet one another doing good. 'But I don't believe, Father, I am an atheist!' But do good: we will meet one another there."[14]

Further worry arose in reaction to Francis's declaration for the Year of Mercy (2016) that priests have the authority to forgive the sin of "procuring abortion." This phrase covers those who perform an abortion, women who obtain an abortion, and anyone else who assists in the tragic process. Furthermore, the pope extended this priestly authority to forgive "the sin of procured abortion" after the conclusion of the Holy Year.[15] Francis clarified his position: "I wish to restate as firmly as I can that abortion is a grave sin, since it puts an end to an innocent life. In the same way, however, I can and must state that there is no sin that God's mercy cannot reach and wipe away when it finds

---

12. Pope Francis, response to the editor, *La Repubblica*, September 11, 2013, https://www.re-pubblica.it/cultura/2013/09/11/news/the_pope_s_letter-66336961.

13. "A Child Cries for the Death of His Father. The Pope, 'He Was a Good Man, He Is with God,'" *La Stampa: Vatican Insider*, April 16, 2018, https://www.lastampa.it/vatican-insider/en/2018/04/16/news/a-child-cries-for-the-death-of-his-father-the-pope-he-was-a-good-man-he-is-with-god-1.34005494.

14. Pope Francis, "Homily" at Domus Santa Marta, May 22, 2013. https://www.npr.org/sections/parallels/2013/05/29/187009384/Pope-Francis-Even-Atheists-Can-Be-Redeemed.

15. "Lest any obstacle arise between the request for reconciliation and God's forgiveness, I henceforth grant to all priests, in virtue of their ministry, the faculty to absolve those who have committed the sin of procured abortion. The provision I had made in this regard, limited to the duration of the Extraordinary Holy Year, is hereby extended, notwithstanding anything to the contrary." Pope Francis, "Letter of the Holy Father Francis to the President of the Pontifical Council for the Promotion of the New Evangelization as the Extraordinary Jubilee of Mercy Approaches," September 1, 2015, Vatican.va.

a repentant heart seeking to be reconciled with the Father."[16] Accordingly, an act that had historically been considered one of the gravest sins and punishable by excommunication (a penalty that could be lifted only by a bishop) can now be forgiven by a priest.

## Summary

The three most recent popes—John Paul II, Benedict XVI, and Francis— have each exerted significant influence on the Roman Catholic Church. Each of their distinctive contributions has also affected the other two traditions of Christendom—Eastern Orthodoxy and Protestantism—as well as the world at large.

## REFLECTION QUESTIONS

1. How do you assess the papacy of Pope John Paul II?

2. How do you assess the papacy of Pope Benedict XVI?

3. How do you assess the papacy of Pope Francis?

4. What does it mean that Benedict XVI illustrates the "Roman" aspect and Francis illustrates the "Catholic" aspect of the Roman Catholic Church?

5. Whom do you think might become the next pope? What would you like to see him emphasize during his papacy?

---

16. Francis, "Letter of the Holy Father Francis."

# Personal Questions about Roman Catholic Friends and Family Members

In this final section, I explore questions about why Protestants leave their church and join the Catholic Church, the rationale for some Catholic practices, misconceptions that Catholics have of Protestants, and practical counsel for how Protestants can love their Catholic friends and family members.

QUESTION 37

# Why Are Some Leaving Protestant Churches and Joining Catholic Churches?

During my university days, I was deeply involved in Campus Crusade for Christ (now Cru). Critical to my spiritual development was Steve, the campus director of Campus Crusade, who discipled me and a number of other students. One of these was my close friend, Dave. He was a strong believer, a solid leader in Campus Crusade, and deeply committed to evangelism and mission. To say the least, it shocked me when after many years of his evangelical identity, he converted to Roman Catholicism. You probably know of similar stories.

What motivates our friends to leave their Protestant churches and join the Catholic Church? For what reasons do they make this move? Scot McKnight offers an illuminating answer that focuses on the search for transcendence as a framework for understanding why evangelicals become Roman Catholic (he refers to such converts as ERCs):

> A desire for transcendence is a crisis about the limitations of the human condition and a desire to go beyond the human experience. This occurs, for the ERC, in four manifestations. First, the ERC wants to transcend the human limits of knowledge to find certainty; second, the ERC wants to transcend the human limits of temporality to find connection to the entire history of the Church; third, the ERC wants

to transcend the human limits of division among churches to find unity and universality in the faith and Church; and fourth, the ERC wants to transcend the human limits of interpretive diversity to find an interpretive authority. These four desires—certainty, history, unity, and authority—are the four manifestations of the ERC's crisis of transcendence.[1]

Following his discussion of these four manifestations, I will present each in turn.

## The Desire for Certainty

Especially in these days of postmodern denial of absolute truth, the chicness of doubt, and the uncertainty of living in a world that is seemingly out of control, the desire for certainty makes sense. Protestants who convert to Catholicism believe that what their churches could not offer them, the Catholic Church can and does: absolute truth, precision as to the canon of Scripture, the sure interpretation of the Bible, the unadulterated gospel, papal infallibility, a rock-solid foundation for the Church (pun intended; Matt. 16:13–20), assurance of doctrinal fidelity, a firmness of faith, and the fullness of salvation. Whereas their Protestant identity and experience was often (negatively) storm-tossed and confusing, or (positively) possible or even probable, it did not provide them with the certainty for which they were seeking. Thus, they become Roman Catholic.

## The Desire for History

In our contemporary context of temporariness, unmooring, and impermanence, the desire for history, specifically to be connected to the Church that spans two thousand years, is understandable. Protestantism, especially in its evangelical form, is often known for its idiosyncrasies, particularly its disregard of, even contempt for, historical precedence and tradition. The naive motto "no creed but the Bible!" and the nearsighted notion that "my church is a true New Testament church" have created the impression that many Protestant churches exist in a cul-de-sac off by themselves, intentionally isolated and ignorant of what has gone before them. This idea is reinforced by the impression they often give that the fathers of the early church (e.g., Augustine), the great theologians of the Middle Ages (e.g., Thomas Aquinas), and even the eminent Reformers (e.g., Martin Luther) are not worth consulting for their biblical interpretations and theological formulation. Indeed, Protestants may be discouraged from reading these important sources, out of

---

1. Scot McKnight, "From Wheaton to Rome: Why Evangelicals Become Roman Catholic," *Journal of the Evangelical Theological Society* 45, no. 3 (September 2002): 451–72 (460).

fear of what John Henry Newman claimed, "To be deep in history is to cease to be Protestant."[2]

Protestants who grow weary of this impression of being unmoored and who become concerned about this ahistorical mindset may drift toward the Catholic Church and feel that they've finally "come home." The Church's historical consciousness contrasts with the temporality of evangelicalism. It provides Protestants who become Catholic with a sense of connectedness to the past.

### The Desire for Unity

An urban legend introduces us to our third discussion about the desire for unity. In an apparent attempt to embarrass Protestants by emphasizing the disunity that exists among them, some Catholic apologists allege that there are 33,000 Protestant denominations.[3] To add insult to injury, some like to count each independent Bible church and nondenominational church as its own separate entity. This results in a number well over 50,000, perhaps approaching 100,000. The point is then scored by asking the devastating question (based on John 17:11, 21–22): How does such rampant divisiveness square with Jesus's prayer that all his disciples be one?

Putting aside this urban legend, the fact remains that there are numerous Protestant denominations. Consequently, some Protestants tire of the constant (and seemingly flippant) division among their churches. They turn to the Roman Catholic Church for a sense of unity and universality. After all, it self-identifies as the one true Church (see Question 15).[4] After all, the Church is united in its common confession of the faith (the Creed). It is unified in its common liturgy. No matter where in the world one attends Mass, the worship service is largely the same in content and form. It is structurally organized according to apostolic succession and a defined hierarchy. Protestants who desire unity and want to belong to the one church that offers hope for the eventual unity of all churches convert to the Roman Catholic Church.[5]

---

2. John Henry Newman, introduction to *An Essay on the Development of Christian Doctrine* (London: Longmans, Green, 1845), part 5.

3. To support this figure, proponents often cite resources like the *World Christian Encyclopedia*, appealing to its first edition (1982) and second edition (2001) for numbers. Updated statistics are needed. Still, the biggest challenge to an accurate determination is the definition of "denomination." For example, does the Church of Christ, divided into churches that use noninstrumental music and churches that use instrumental music, count as one "denomination" or two "denominations"? And what do Catholic apologists do with sources that list 242 "denominations" for the Roman Catholic Church instead of the 1 "denomination" that it claims for itself?

4. Vatican Council II, *Lumen Gentium*, November 21, 1964, 8.

5. The Catholic Church acknowledges that "many elements of sanctification and of truth are found outside of its visible structure. These elements, as gifts belonging to the Church of Christ, are forces impelling toward catholic unity." With its orientation to the salvation of

## The Desire for Authority

Finally, the contemporary cultural rejection of and widespread challenge to all types of authority—traditional, parental, institutional, governmental, biblical, and church-based authority—fosters in some the desire for authority. This has special reference to the wish to overcome the many diverse interpretations of the Bible. Protestants may be accustomed to small group Bible studies in which the question "what does this verse mean to you?" abounds. As they listen in horror to the many opinions that participants voice—each of which is accompanied by the affirmation "That is *so* good!" no matter how far removed from the actual biblical text—they weary of the hopeless subjectivism afoot in the group. In their churches they may be greeted by an opening line of the sermon: "We all know the Bible is hard to understand, and our passage for this morning proves this point." Even when they hear expositions of Scripture that are articulated by shouting and punctuated by fist-pumping, they wonder if all the fuss serves merely to cover up an uncertain interpretation of the passage. Leaving Protestantism behind, they look to the Magisterium of the Church to provide the official and authoritative interpretation of Scripture (and Tradition).[6]

To summarize: our friends leave their Protestant churches and convert to the Catholic Church in search of transcendence, manifested as four desires: certainty, history, unity, and authority.

## A Protestant Response

How might Protestants respond to the movement of their friends toward the Roman Catholic Church? Applying the question personally, we must attend to our own development as Christians and become part of robust churches. We ground our *certainty*, both individually and church-wise, in the triune God and his self-revelation in Scripture. God the Father has elected us, united us with his Son, poured out the Holy Spirit upon us, justified us, and adopted us into his family.

---

the whole world, the Church envisions its mission as eventually uniting all churches—indeed, all humanity—within itself. Vatican Council II, *Lumen Gentium*, 8.

6. Two other reasons for this movement from Protestantism to Roman Catholicism deserve brief mention. One reason is the far-too-common attachment of Protestant churches to political agendas. The gospel becomes saddled to a particular political party or platform, an attachment that seems to compromise the good news and exclude people who hold a different point of view. Another reason is the experience of worship. Protestants accustomed to superficial worship services focused on entertainment and individual satisfaction find in the Roman Catholic Mass a robust worship with ancient ties and a corporate, even global, focus. Additionally, the sacramental system provides concrete experiences of grace. One example is the sacrament of penance. A priest voices the absolution of sins. This external pronouncement stands in contrast with the person confessing sin assuring herself of forgiveness. Another example is the sacrament of the Eucharist. Grace is infused as the Catholic faithful physically consume the consecrated bread and wine.

God the Son is our atoning sacrifice who has paid the penalty for our sins by becoming our substitute and dying on the cross to accomplish our salvation. His work of propitiation appeased the divine wrath. His work of expiation removed our liability to suffer death and condemnation. His work of redemption purchased our freedom from sin through the ransom he paid. His work of reconciliation removed our alienation from God and restored us to fellowship with him. His work of intercession assures us that we are saved to the uttermost. His pledges underscore the fact that nothing can wrest us from the divine hand and separate us from the divine love.

God the Holy Spirit has convicted us of sin, regenerated us, sealed us, granted us assurance of salvation, and is transforming us into the image of Christ. The Word of God testifies, as the apostle John writes, "that God gave us eternal life, and this life is in his Son. Whoever has the Son has life; whoever does not have the Son of God does not have life. I write these things to you who believe in the name of the Son of God, that you may know that you have eternal life" (1 John 5:11–13). The fruit that arises from these mighty acts of God expresses itself as love for God, love for others, a self-sacrificial lifestyle, thanksgiving, missional engagement, and much more.

The mighty acts of God and the promises of his Word are our certainty, both personally and corporately.

If necessary, we awake from our *ahistorical slumber* by acknowledging that the one true church of Jesus Christ did not begin when Martin Luther nailed his Ninety-Five Theses on the door of the Wittenburg church or when First Baptist Church—whether that be in London in the seventeenth century or Louisville in the nineteenth century—was incorporated. We read the early church fathers and the great theologians of the Middle Ages, always with an eye on the touchstone of all correct biblical interpretation and theological formulation: Scripture. We reject the common misunderstanding that *sola Scriptura* means that as Protestants we can't consult any authority other than the Bible. Rather, we affirm the early church creeds— Nicene-Constantinopolitan, Apostles', Athanasian, Chalcedonian—and the early church councils—Nicea, Constantinople, Ephesus, and Chalcedon. We stand against the early church heresies as condemned by Scripture and these creeds and councils: Adoptionism, Arianism, Apollinarianism, Nestorianism, Eutychianism, and more. In this way, we reject Newman's claim that "to be deep in history is to cease to be Protestant."[7]

As Protestants, we embrace the two principles—the ultimate authority of Scripture and justification as divine declaration—and the five *solas* of Protestantism: *sola Scriptura, solus Christus, sola fidei, sola gratia*, and *soli Deo Gloria*. If we are evangelicals, we stand against both fundamentalism

---

7. John Henry Newman, introduction to *An Essay on the Development of Christian Doctrine* (London: Longmans, Green, 1845), part 5.

and liberalism and champion conversionism, biblicism, crucicentrism, and activism.[8] As members of particular Protestant traditions, we adhere to and defend our denominational statements of faith, from the Thirty-Nine Articles to the Westminster Confession of Faith, from the Augsburg Confession to the Baptist Faith and Message. The history of the church and its tradition, always chastened by Scripture, is our guide, not in a magisterial sense, but serving our theology and practice ministerially.

In terms of the desire for *unity*, we first offer a caution, then a clarification. The caution poses this question: Is true unity possible when the Roman Catholic Church continues to insist that it alone is the one, holy, catholic, and apostolic Church? Does its ongoing claim that the only true church "subsists in the Catholic Church" actually promote unity among Christians and all non-Catholic churches? Does Pope Benedict's clarification that Protestant assemblies aren't churches but "ecclesial communities" foster unity?[9]

The clarification focuses on a common Catholic misunderstanding of the Protestant view of unity. It is not, as some suspect, the oneness of some spiritual entity, an invisible church. Rather, in addition to the four classical identity markers that it assumes—oneness, holiness, catholicity, and apostolicity—Protestantism defines unity in terms of the two marks of the true church. The Lutheran Augsburg Confession affirms, "The church is the congregation of the saints in which the gospel is rightly taught and the sacraments rightly administered. And unto the true unity of the church, it is sufficient to agree concerning the doctrine of the gospel and the administration of the sacraments."[10] Similarly, John Calvin and the Reformed Church states, "Whenever we see the Word of God purely preached and heard, and the sacraments administered according to Christ's institution, there, it is not to be doubted, a church of God exists."[11] Accordingly, the unity of the church centers on the preaching of the gospel and the celebration of baptism and the Lord's Supper. The gospel preached and celebrated by the sacraments is the sufficient basis for unity among Protestant churches.

As should be clear from the above discussion, the *authority* that is proposed by Protestants is the triune God through his self-revelation in Scripture. As the sovereign King and Lord, as the Creator and Sustainer of all that exists,

---

8. The four characteristics of evangelicalism were articulated by David W. Bebbington, *Evangelicalism in Modern Britain: A History from the 1730s to the 1930s* (London: Unwin Hyman, 1989).

9. Cardinal Joseph Ratzinger, *Dominus Iesus*, August 6, 200, 17. See also Benedict XVI, "Responses to Some Questions regarding Certain Aspects of the Doctrine of the Church," July 10, 2007, Vatican.va. The internal reference and citation are from John Paul II, *Ut Unum Sint*, 11.3 and Vatican Council II, *Lumen Gentium*, 8.

10. Augsburg Confession, 7.1–2. https://bookofconcord.org/augsburg-confession.

11. John Calvin, *Institutes of the Christian Religion*, ed. John T. McNeill, trans. Ford Lewis Battles (Philadelphia: Westminster, 1960), 4.1.9 (LCC 21:1023).

as the Redeemer and Sanctifier of his people, God himself is the ultimate authority. He expresses his authoritative rulership through Scripture. In it he states, commands, promises, warns, exhorts, rebukes, corrects, and equips his people. His Word to them is God-breathed, truthful (inerrant), sufficient, necessary, clear, and authoritative. The Protestant principle of *sola Scriptura* stands over against the Catholic formula of Scripture plus Tradition plus the Magisterium. Question 11 underscores the inherent instability of this multiple-source theory of authority. It does not and cannot function.

But what of the interpretive chaos into which Protestantism has allegedly thrown us? When accused of fostering a spirit of protest leading to interpretive chaos and church division, Protestants do not have to shoulder the burden of the charge. As Kevin Vanhoozer underscores, "the accidental truths of European history ought never become the proof of necessary truths of Protestant theology." Yes, the Reformation resulted in Lutheranism, Zwinglianism, Calvinism, Anglicanism, Anabaptist/Baptist movements, and more. "Yet," Vanhoozer continues, "things could and should have proceeded otherwise, and sometimes did."[12] There is nothing in the principle of *sola Scriptura* that necessarily leads to interpretive chaos and anarchy rather than authority.

Importantly, the ultimate arbiter of Scripture is not the individual reader or interpreter. Rather, because of its divine authorship, Scripture itself is its own self-interpreting, ultimate authority. Protestants should understand and apply it with reliance on the illumination of the Holy Spirit. They should read it with a proper theological framework. They should follow proven interpretive principles—for example, sensitivity to the literary genre, attention to authorial intent, consideration of the whole canon of Scripture[13]—as they seek to understand and enact it. They should engage in Bible study in the context of their local church, to whom have been given "pastor-teachers" (Eph. 4:11; 1 Tim. 5:17) to guide them in their understanding. By following the inspired Word of the triune God, the church receives a sure and authoritative message.

## Summary

Our friends leave their Protestant churches and join the Roman Catholic Church as they seek for transcendence, manifested in four desires—certainty, history, unity, and authority. Instead of Protestant doubt and insecurity, they find certainty in the absolute truth and sure foundation of the Catholic Church. In place of the temporariness, impermanence, and ahistorical nature of Protestantism, our friends find a connection to the past and feel like they've "come home" when they join the Catholic Church. Tired of the constant (and

---

12. Kevin J. Vanhoozer, *Biblical Authority after Babel: Retrieving the Solas in the Spirit of Mere Protestant Christianity* (Grand Rapids: Brazos, 2016), ix.
13. These principles come from Vatican Council II, *Dei Verbum*, November 18, 1965, 12. They are basic interpretive principles with which all Protestants agree.

seemingly flippant) divisions within Protestantism, they cling to the unity and universality of the Catholic Church. Instead of interpretive chaos and theological opinions, our friends embrace the authority of the Catholic Church.

These reasons for leaving their Protestant churches and converting to Roman Catholicism call for a response: The mighty acts of God are our certainty, both personally and corporately. The history of the church and its tradition is indeed a fine guide. But it must always be chastened by Scripture and never be allowed to exercise magisterial authority over Scripture. As for unity, I offer both a caution and a clarification. The caution is that joining the Catholic Church and adhering to its claim to be the only true church of Jesus Christ will do nothing to foster unity among non-Catholic churches. In terms of a clarification, the gospel preached and celebrated by the sacraments is the sufficient basis for unity among Protestant churches. Finally, the authority by which Protestants live is that of the triune God who reveals himself by his authoritative Word.

## REFLECTION QUESTIONS

1. What is the difference between the Protestant and Catholic ideas of certainty?

2. What is the difference between the Protestant and Catholic ideas of history?

3. What is the difference between the Protestant and Catholic ideas of unity?

4. What is the difference between the Protestant and Catholic ideas of authority?

5. How might you engage and share these ideas with your Protestant friends who are considering a move to join the Roman Catholic Church?

# What Is the Rationale behind Some of the Practices of My Catholic Friends?

Though many Catholic practices prompt questions by Protestants, I focus on five: indulgences, abstaining from meat on Friday, wearing/displaying a crucifix, making the sign of the cross, and praying the rosary.

## Indulgences

Occasionally Protestants will hear the word *indulgence* mentioned. The usual reaction is a scoffing comment something like, "The Catholic Church doesn't still sell indulgences, does it?" Actually, indulgences continue to be an important part of the Catholic way of salvation. As a recent example, the Church celebrated 2016 as the Year of Mercy.[1] This special Jubilee Year featured the granting of indulgences for the purpose of removing the temporal punishment for the sins of the Catholic faithful. Specifically, "an indulgence is a remission before God of the temporal punishment due to sins whose guilt has already been forgiven, which the faithful Christian who is duly disposed gains under certain prescribed conditions through the action of the Church which, as the minister of redemption, dispenses and applies with authority the treasury of the satisfactions of Christ and the saints."[2]

For this Year of Mercy, the Church offered a global means of obtaining indulgences:

---

1. For further discussion, see Chris Castaldo and Gregg Allison, "The Pope Offers Mercy—Protestants Won't Be Indulged," *The Gospel Coalition*, September 13, 2016, https://www.thegospelcoalition.org/article/the-pope-offers-mercy-protestants-wont-be-indulged; and Gregg R. Allison, "A Justified Divide," *Primer*, no. 4 (2017): 32–45. Used by permission.
2. CCC, 1471.

It opened a Holy Door of Mercy in every Catholic cathedral (for example, St. Peter's Basilica in Rome) and at major pilgrimage sites (for example, the Sanctuary of Lourdes in France) throughout the world. And whereas there are two types of indulgences—providing either a partial or a plenary (complete) remission of all temporal punishment due to sin—the Church established the type of indulgence that would be obtained by passing through a Holy Door to be a plenary indulgence.[3]

Protestants shake their head and wonder in disbelief. By simply walking through a designated door of a cathedral, do Catholics imagine that they can obtain mercy from God?

First of all, it wasn't quite that simple. The Catholic faithful had to satisfy four conditions: "(1) pray (the Creed, the Our Father, the Hail Mary, the Gloria . . .) and for the intentions [prayer requests] of the Holy Father; (2) within fifteen days, approach the sacrament of Penance, confessing one's sins, and participate in the Mass, taking Holy Communion; (3) have the inner attitude of actual and affective separation from every sin, not only grave and mortal, but also slight and venial; (4) engage in a work of mercy, whether corporeal or spiritual."[4] By satisfying these conditions, the Catholic faithful were in a state of grace by which they walked through a Holy Door. Their reward was a full indulgence for themselves by which they obtained immediate access into heaven should they have died in that state. Alternatively, they may have undertaken this pilgrimage on behalf of a deceased loved one whose soul was in purgatory. Because of the plenary indulgence, that soul was transferred immediately into heaven.

Second, there is a rationale for indulgences. As Question 34 explained, the Catholic doctrine of the communion and treasury of the saints grounds this practice. The Catholic faithful on earth may benefit from this treasury by obtaining indulgences for themselves or for souls in purgatory. Then, the Church "intervenes in favor of [these] individual Christians and opens for them the treasury of the merits of Christ and the saints to obtain from the Father of mercies the remission of the temporal punishments due for their sins."[5]

Accordingly, the Year of Mercy, with its opening of a Holy Door of Mercy in cathedrals throughout the world, is an example of the Catholic Church's ongoing use of indulgences. Protestant churches dissent from this practice because its support, rather than being biblical, is built on the communion and treasury

---

3. Castaldo and Allison, "Pope Offers Mercy."
4. These were the instructions found at the entrance to the Holy Door of the Basilica della Madonna di San Luca, Bologna, Italy. My translation.
5. CCC, 1478.

of the saints, which lacks biblical warrant. Additionally, the doctrine of purgatory has no biblical basis and contradicts the Protestant doctrine of justification.

## Not Eating Meat on Fridays

A second Catholic practice about which Protestants wonder is not eating meat on Fridays. First, because Protestants know few Catholics who actually abstain, Protestants wonder if this practice is still binding on Catholics. Second, Protestants question the rationale for it.

According to the Code of Canon Law, "In order for all [Catholics] to be united among themselves by some common observance of penance, penitential days are prescribed on which the Christian faithful devote themselves in a special way to prayer, perform works of piety and charity, and deny themselves by fulfilling their own obligations more faithfully and especially by observing fast and abstinence."[6] Fasting from all food and abstaining from meat constitute acts of penance. The Code stipulates a penitential rhythm: "The penitential days and times in the universal Church are every Friday of the whole year and the season of Lent," including Ash Wednesday and Good Friday.[7] So, yes, the Catholic faithful are still bound to abstain from eating meat on Fridays.

As for the rationale for this practice, Scripture presents the people of God engaging in concrete acts of repentance such as fasting. For example, when Daniel became aware of the future destruction of Jerusalem, he reacted: "Then I turned my face to the Lord God, seeking him by prayer and pleas for mercy with fasting and sackcloth and ashes . . . [and confessing] 'we have sinned and done wrong and acted wickedly and rebelled, turning aside from your commandments and rules'" (Dan. 9:3, 5). Jesus instructed his followers to fast (Matt. 6:16–18). Moreover, the early church held weekly fasts. According to the *Didache* (mid-second century): "Let not your fasts be with the hypocrites, for they fast on Mondays and Thursdays, but you fast on Wednesdays and Fridays."[8]

Accordingly, the Catholic Church insists on fasting, which is a practice grounded in Scripture. Protestant churches do not object to the call to fasting, even if that call goes beyond an appeal to individuals and becomes a plea for their churches to fast corporately. Rather, Protestant complaints are twofold. First, the binding nature of the Catholic rule—going beyond Scripture and being backed by the Code of Canon Law—contradicts the sufficiency of Scripture. Second, the establishment of abstinence from meat on Fridays as a penitential

---

6. Code of Canon Law (1983), canon 1249. http://www.vatican.va/archive/cod-iuris-canonici/eng/documents/cic_lib4-cann1244-1253_en.html.
7. Code of Canon Law (1983), canon 1250. Specifically, "Abstinence from meat . . . is to be observed on all Fridays, unless a solemnity [a feast day such as the Assumption of the Blessed Virgin on August 15 and the Immaculate Conception on December 8] should fall on a Friday. Abstinence and fasting are to be observed on Ash Wednesday and Good Friday." Canon 1251.
8. *Didache* 8.1, in *ANF* 7:379.

act goes beyond the biblical association of fasting with repentance and locates it within the sacramental economy of the Catholic Church. Abstinence becomes an act of a Catholic penitent that functions as a means to make satisfaction for or expiate her sins. Question 22 critiques this notion of rendering satisfaction for sins as compromising the sufficiency of the death of Christ.

## The Crucifix

The Catholic habit of wearing a crucifix—or displaying it prominently during a Mass or in a church building—is a third practice about which Protestants wonder. A crucifix is an image of a cross upon which a dying Jesus hangs. The question is not one of proper fashion, the correctness of the Catholic procession, or the propriety of church art and decoration. Rather, it is why Catholics use a symbol for Christ's death when he is now resurrected and no longer on the cross.

The display of a crucifix during the Mass is a requirement of the Catholic Church.[9] The sign serves as a reminder of Jesus's death by crucifixion to accomplish the salvation of sinful people. Every aspect of the Mass leads up to its high point—the sacrament of the Eucharist—which re-presents Christ's redemptive work. It is fitting, therefore, for the Catholic faithful to have a constant reminder of their Savior's death throughout the liturgy. Moreover, as they leave the Mass and live their daily lives, they are continuously reminded of their salvation by the crucifix that they are wearing.

To the Protestant argument that Jesus died once and for all, then was resurrected—with the implication that any cross that is worn or displayed in church should not have Christ hanging on it—Catholics have a ready reply: of course they believe in the resurrection! However, the crucifix is appropriate as a reminder of that which preceded Christ's rising from the dead: his atoning sacrifice for our sins. Moreover, a crucifix serves as a clarion call to follow Christ's instructions about self-denial by carrying our cross (Matt. 16:24) and to imitate him by suffering like he did (1 Peter 2:21–25; 4:12–13). First comes humiliation; then comes exaltation.

Protestants still counter: the Catholic use of a crucifix results in a well-known emphasis on suffering, penance as a satisfaction for sin, the re-presentation of Christ in the Liturgy of the Eucharist, and human cooperation (even though aided by grace) in salvation. The Catholic view of salvation as a lifelong process precludes any sense of certainty that the Catholic faithful have done enough to merit eternal life. And does not an empty cross, with its symbolism that Christ is risen, better focus attention on Christ's completed salvation? A cross without the body of the crucified Christ better symbolizes this redemption.

---

9. "On the altar or close to it, there is to be a cross adorned with a figure of Christ crucified." *The General Instruction of the Roman Missal*, 117. https://www.usccb.org/prayer-and-worship/the-mass/general-instruction-of-the-roman-missal/girm-chapter-4.

## The Sign of the Cross

A fourth practice prompting Protestant questioning is the sign of the cross. This symbol (with accompanying words spoken or said to oneself) is made in the name of the triune God (Matt. 28:19) by a sequential touching of four bodily locations with one's right hand. The first is one's forehead, "in the name of the Father." The second is the middle of one's chest, "and of the Son." The third is one's left shoulder, "and of the Holy." The fourth is one's right shoulder, "Spirit." Put differently, "in the name of the Father" (touch one's forehead), "and of the Son" (touch the middle of one's chest), "and of the Holy" (touch one's left shoulder), "Spirit" (touch one's right shoulder).

The Church encourages the Catholic faithful to regularly engage in this symbolic act: "The Christian begins his day, his prayers, and his activities with the Sign of the Cross: 'in the name of the Father and of the Son and of the Holy Spirit. Amen.' The baptized person dedicates the day to the glory of God and calls on the Savior's grace which lets him act in the Spirit as a child of the Father. The sign of the cross strengthens us in temptations and difficulties."[10] This common, repeated practice marks the Catholic faithful as genuine believers, voices their profession of the mystery of the Trinity, reminds them of Christ's saving work on the cross, and supports them in their daily struggles.

The rationale is twofold. Although he made no mention of the sign of the cross in giving his Great Commission to the church, Jesus certainly indicated that baptism is into the name of the triune God (Matt. 28:19). And it is this God—the Father, the Son, and the Holy Spirit—whom Christians worship. Thus, there is a strong biblical and theological basis for acknowledging God the Trinity.

Furthermore, the early church practiced the sign of the cross. In the second century, Tertullian noted the widespread use of this practice: "At every forward step and movement, at every going in and out, when we put on our clothes and shoes, when we bathe, when we sit at table, when we light the lamps, on couch, on seat, in all the ordinary actions of daily life, we trace upon the forehead the sign."[11] In the fourth century, Cyril of Jerusalem urged, "Let us not then be ashamed to confess the crucified. Be the cross our seal made with boldness by our fingers on our brow, and on everything; over the bread we eat, and the cups we drink; in our comings in, and goings out; before our sleep, when we lie down and when we rise up; when we are in the way, and when we are still."[12] Other early church leaders who mention this practice include Basil the Great, John Chrysostom, and Athanasius.

---

10. CCC, 2157.
11. Tertullian, *De Corona* 3, in *ANF* 3:165.
12. Cyril of Jerusalem, *Catechetical Lectures* 13.36, in *NPNF*[2] 7:92. For Cyril, the sign of the cross had two effects: to mark out the faithful believers and prompt them to honor Christ, and to cause fear among the devils.

Among the Reformers, Martin Luther approved of the sign of the cross. In his *Small Catechism*, he addressed the morning blessing: "In the morning, as soon as you get out of bed, you are to make the sign of the holy cross and say: 'God the Father, Son, and Holy Spirit watch over me. Amen.'"[13] Today, some Lutherans continue this practice while others do not. By contrast John Calvin, who was strongly against all images and Catholic rituals, denounced the practice, even calling it a superstitious rite.[14] Overall, because the practice clashes with the regulative principle of worship—any elements of Christian worship must have a biblical basis for them—the majority of Protestants do not make the sign of the cross.

## Praying the Rosary

The fifth and final Catholic practice that prompts Protestants to wonder is praying the rosary. To demystify this practice, we note first that the string—or chaplet—of beads is a counting device. It consists of five sets each containing ten beads, with one set separated from the next set by a larger bead. Each set of ten beads is called a decade. The two ends of the chaplet are linked together by another small string containing a crucifix, two large beads, and three small beads. There is nothing magical about this counting device.

The Catholic faithful use a rosary for an exercise of prayer. They recite certain prayers and count them using the beads. In its most common expression, the rosary centers on prayers to the Virgin Mary. The term "rosary" itself indicates this devotion. The Latin word refers to a garland of roses, and the rose is traditionally a symbol for Mary. Indeed, as they move along the chaplet, the Catholic faithful recite one "Hail Mary" for each bead:

> Hail Mary, full of grace,
> the Lord is with thee.
> Blessed art thou among women,
> and blessed is the fruit of thy womb, Jesus.
> Holy Mary, mother of God,
> pray for us sinners now,
> and at the hour of our death.

One pass through the string is 150 "Hail Marys." Often, the faithful do three turns around the chaplet, meaning that they say 450 prayers to Mary.[15]

---

13. Martin Luther, *Small Catechism*, "Morning Blessing," https://bookofconcord.org/small-catechism/appendix-i.

14. John Calvin, *Institutes of the Christian Religion*, 4.17.28 (LCC 21:1397).

15. Praying the rosary actually starts with the short string—with a crucifix, two large beads, and three small beads—that links the two ends of the chaplet together. The Catholic faithful make the sign of the cross and recite the Apostles' Creed. They repeat the Lord's Prayer ("Our Father"), say three "Hail Marys," then say the "Gloria" ("Glory be to the Father,

To the Protestant objection that the rosary is unbiblical, Catholics may try to demonstrate its biblical basis. For example, they point to the opening line as repeating the angel Gabriel's greeting to Mary: "Hail Mary full of Grace, the Lord is with thee," based on Luke 1:28. Protestants find this appeal problematic, not because it is indeed a quote from Scripture, but because of the Catholic misinterpretation of the angel's word: they do not single her out as the immaculately conceived, sinless, grace-infused second Eve well prepared to become the mother of God.[16] As another example, Catholics note that the second line—"Blessed are thou amongst women and blessed is the fruit of thy womb Jesus"—is a close citation of Elizabeth's words when she met her cousin Mary (see Luke 1:42). Again, the Protestant response is not a quibble about a biblical citation, but its misunderstanding: Elizabeth is not acknowledging a peculiar state of blessedness for Mary (a status by which Mary is accorded hyperdulia, that is, super veneration).

Beyond these concerns, the third line with its invocation of prayers to Mary links this act of devotion with the Catholic communion of saints and the treasury of the saints. Question 34 critiques this position.

## Summary

While many Catholic practices and their rationale prompt questions from Protestants, I have focused on five: indulgences, abstaining from meat on Friday, wearing/displaying a crucifix, making the sign of the cross, and praying the rosary.

Indulgences are still a vital part of the Catholic Church, as they remove the temporal punishment for the sins of the Catholic faithful. The rationale is the communion of saints and the treasury of the saints. Protestant concerns with indulgences include the lack of biblical basis and the practice's contradiction of the Protestant doctrine of justification.

The Catholic faithful are still bound to abstain from eating meat on Fridays. The rationale includes the biblical association of fasting with repentance. Moreover, fasting was very common in the early church and has been a constant practice. While not objecting to fasting itself, Protestants hold that the Catholic rules about the practice go beyond Scripture, violating its sufficiency. An additional concern is that fasting is located within the sacramental economy of the Catholic Church. Abstinence from meat on Friday is a

---

and to the Son, and to the Holy Spirit . . ."). Moving to the first ten beads on the chaplet, they pray ten "Hail Marys." This first segment concludes with another recitation of the Lord's Prayer and the "Gloria." And so it goes through the rest of the first run through the sequence of beads, followed by two more turns through the chaplet. The faithful conclude the exercise with two closing prayers: "Hail Holy Queen" and "Final Prayer." For further discussion, see "How to Pray the Rosary" by the Rosary Center and Confraternity, https://www.rosarycenter.org/homepage-2/rosary/how-to-pray-the-rosary.

16. See Questions 32 and 33.

penitential act for the purpose of making satisfaction for or expiating the sins of the Catholic faithful. Such satisfaction and sacrifice is not possible, nor is it needed, given Christ's completed work of salvation.

Wearing or displaying a crucifix raises the question of why the Catholic Church focuses on the cross of Christ rather than on his resurrection. Making the sign of the cross raises the question of why this practice—even if popular very early on in the church's history and a widespread practice still today—should exist if there is no biblical warrant for it. Praying the rosary is a spiritual exercise directed primarily to the Virgin Mary. Prayer, not the chaplet, or string of beads for counting purposes, is the focus. Protestants do not engage in this practice because it involves the invocation of Mary and is tied to the communion of saints and the treasury of the saints, both of which they deny.

## REFLECTION QUESTIONS

1. What is at the heart of the difference between the Catholic use of indulgences and the Protestant rejection of this practice?

2. In what way does abstaining from meat on Friday contribute to the overall Catholic view of salvation? Why do Protestants reject this practice?

3. What difference does it make if Christ hangs from the cross, as he does with a crucifix, or if he is absent from the cross?

4. Why do Catholics make the sign of the cross while most Protestants don't?

5. If you are Catholic, do you pray the rosary, and why? If you are Protestant, what concerns does this devotional practice raise?

# What Are Some Common Misconceptions That Catholics Have of Protestants?

Historically, Roman Catholics have harbored plenty of misconceptions of Protestants. To be fair, the same can be said of Protestants toward Catholics. This question focuses on Catholic misconceptions of Protestants, particularly, misunderstandings of the five *solas* (specifically, *sola Scriptura, sola gratia, sola fidei*), individualistic conscience, and interpretive chaos.

### The Five *Solas*

Many Catholics misunderstand the five *solas* of Protestantism. For example, *sola Scriptura* as the Bible alone is misunderstood to mean that Protestants have no other authority than Scripture and denounce any kind of tradition outside of it.

This is not the case. The early Reformers, while decrying the Roman Catholic view of divine revelation as consisting of Scripture plus Tradition, did not toss out fifteen hundred years of accumulated tradition. For example, the Lutheran Formula of Concord emphasized the ultimate authority of Scripture: "We believe, confess, and teach that the only rule and norm, according to which all dogmas and all doctors ought to be esteemed and judged, is no other whatever than the prophets and apostolic writings both of the Old Testament and of the New Testament. . . . But other writings, whether of the [early church] fathers or of the moderns . . . are in no way to be equaled to the Holy Scriptures but are all to be esteemed inferior to them." Still, the formula maintained a role for tradition, specifically the Apostles' Creed, the Nicene Creed, and the Athanasian Creed: "We publicly profess that we embrace them, and reject all heresies and all dogmas that have ever been brought into the church of God contrary to their decisions."[1]

Thus, *sola Scriptura* does not mean what many Catholics think it means. Certainly, it rejects the Scripture plus Tradition (capital T) position of the Catholic Church. But it embraces a Scripture plus tradition (small t) framework: Scripture has ultimate authority, and where tradition chastened by Scripture articulates sound doctrine, Protestant churches consider that tradition to enjoy presumptive authority.[2]

As another example, many Catholics misunderstand *sola gratia* and *sola fidei* to mean that Protestants have no role for good works. The misconception is that because good works do not and cannot contribute to salvation, which is by *grace alone*, they must play no role for those who are saved by *faith alone*.

This misunderstanding goes back to Martin Luther himself. In *The Freedom of a Christian* (1520), Luther emphasized: "If works are sought after as a means to righteousness . . . and are done under the false impression that through them one is justified, they are made necessary [for salvation] and freedom and faith are destroyed; and this addition to them makes them no longer good but truly damnable works."[3] This position is the classical Protestant doctrine that the divine work of salvation is accomplished by *grace alone*. Moreover, God's mighty act of justification is received by *faith alone* without any mixture of good works in an attempt to merit salvation. At the same time, Luther insisted that those who are saved, as freed for obedient service to others, must engage in good works: "This is a truly Christian life. Here faith is truly active through love [Gal. 5:6], that is, it finds expression in works of the freest service, cheerfully, and lovingly done, with which a person willingly serves another without hope of reward."[4] As Luther concluded, "We do not reject good works; on the contrary, we cherish and teach them as much as possible."[5] Indeed, Luther restored dignity and honor to common good works, opposing the Catholic Church's concept of them as spiritual deeds like "praying in church, fasting, and almsgiving."[6]

---

1. Formula of Concord, "Of the Compendious Rule and Norm," epitome 1, in Philip Schaff, *Creeds of Christendom*, 3 vols. (New York: Harper, 1877–1905), 3:95.
2. For this idea of presumptive authority, see Gregg R. Allison, "The *Corpus Theologicum* of the Church and Presumptive Authority," in *Revisioning, Renewing, and Rediscovering the Triune Center: Essays in Honor of Stanley J. Grenz*, eds. Derek Tidball, Brian Harris, and Jason S. Sexton (Eugene, OR: Wipf & Stock, 2014). As an example, see my development of the doctrine of the Holy Spirit that incorporates historical formulations from the Cappadocian Fathers, Augustine, Thomas Aquinas, John Calvin, and others. Gregg R. Allison and Andreas J. Köstenberger, *The Holy Spirit: Theology for the People of God* (Nashville: B&H Academic, 2020), part 2, "Systematic Theology."
3. Martin Luther, *The Freedom of a Christian*, 51 (LW 31:363).
4. Luther, *Freedom of a Christian*, 55 (LW 31:365).
5. Luther, *Freedom of a Christian*, 51 (LW 31:363).
6. Martin Luther, *Treatise on Good Works*, 2 (LW 44:24).

Thus, while Protestants deny any role for good works in cooperating with divine grace to merit salvation, they insist on good works following salvation. These good works are done without any consideration of merit and reward, and they flow from a renewed heart full of thanksgiving.[7]

### Protestant Individualistic Conscience

Another misconception is the matter of individualistic conscience. Some Catholics think that, at the heart of Protestantism, is the elevation of one's personal conscience to the point of extreme authority. Each person is an individual, is duty bound to follow the judgment of their own conscience, and is accountable to nothing and to no one else. This elevation of conscience manifests itself in various ways. Two examples suffice: the fracturing of Christendom into Roman Catholicism and Protestantism, with the latter expressing itself in Lutheranism, Calvinism, Anglicanism, and Anabaptist/ Baptist movements[8]; and the continuation of such divisions for the last five hundred years as individualistically driven churches split into thousands of Protestant denominations.

At the time of the Reformation, this misunderstanding centered on the Protestant rejection of the Roman Catholic Church and papal authority. It certainly appeared to be correct, given Martin Luther's refusal to recant his position as he was directed to do by the Catholic authorities at the Diet of Worms in 1521: "Unless I am convinced by the testimony of the Scriptures or by clear reason (for I do not trust either in the pope or in councils alone, since it is well known that they have often erred and contradicted themselves), I am bound by the Scriptures I have quoted and my *conscience* is captive to the Word of God. I cannot and I will not recant anything, since it is neither safe nor right to go against *conscience*. May God help me. Amen."[9]

Certainly, Luther and the other Reformers rejected the hierarchical, papally ruled Catholic Church of their day. However, their intent was not to overturn the church and overthrow its rightful authority. Yes, Luther insisted on following his conscience, but his conscience was tethered to Scripture. It, and it alone (*sola Scriptura*), was his ultimate authority. Indeed, Scripture was

---

7. Some of the Catholic misunderstanding of the Protestant view of good works may be due to the motto of some Protestants: "once saved, always saved." Certainly, this expression has some truth to it: genuine believers will indeed persevere, and nothing can interfere with their ultimate salvation. However, it is easily abused when applied to professing Christians who, by their lack of good works and their unchristian lifestyle, clearly manifest that they are not saved. Thus, this so-called Catholic "misunderstanding," based on the motto "once saved, always saved," is actually on target.

8. It should be noted that centuries before the Reformation occurred, the church had split decisively into the (Western) Roman Catholic Church and the (Eastern) Orthodox Church.

9. Martin Luther, "Reply to the Diet of Worms," April 18, 1521 (LW 32:112–13).

superior to the papacy and church councils. But it was also superior to his conscience, which formed him into the Reformer that he was.

Moreover, the Reformers were not revolutionaries seeking to dispense with the Church and depose its authority. Rather, they were convinced that they had to reform its current manifestation—the spiritually bankrupt, morally compromised Roman Catholic Church—for the sake of *the* catholic church. Theirs was a reformation, not a revolution. This was certainly Luther's approach when he posted his *Ninety-Five Theses* on October 17, 1517. With this call for reform, Luther indeed prompted a reaction on the part of the Catholic Church. But it was Pope Leo X, on June 15, 1520, who excommunicated Luther with the papal bull *Exurge Domine*: "Arise, O Lord, and judge your own cause. Remember your reproaches to those who are filled with foolishness all through the day. Listen to our prayers, for foxes have arisen seeking to destroy the vineyard whose winepress you alone have trod."[10] It was the Catholic Church that tossed out Luther. So much for trying to reform it from the inside.

### Protestant Interpretive Chaos

As a final misconception, many Catholics point to the interpretive chaos that exists among Protestant churches. For example, Martin Luther literally understood Jesus's words "This [bread] *is* my body" and developed an approach to the Lord's Supper known as sacramental union (or, more commonly among non-Lutherans, consubstantiation). Huldrych Zwingli interpreted Jesus's words figuratively, as "This [bread] *symbolizes* my body." As a consequence, he developed the memorial view of the Lord's Supper. The same passage. Two different Reformers. Two different interpretations. Two different practices of the Lord's Supper. Two different Protestant traditions. Conclusion: Protestant interpretive chaos leads to divisions in the church.

This misunderstanding may also be fueled by experiences that Catholics have at small group Bible studies in which their evangelical friends participate. They may be horrified—rightly so!—when the group leader asks, "So what does this verse mean to you?" and accepts all answers as equally valid. Such experiences or reports promote this Catholic misunderstanding of Protestant interpretive chaos.

Many of these Catholics maintain that such chaos could be quelled if Protestants would only submit themselves to the Church's authority. If Protestants would accept the Magisterium's correct, official understanding of Jesus's words—and embrace it as grounds for transubstantiation—these divisions would be overcome. This movement back to Rome is indeed the goal of the Catholic Church, not only for all Protestants but for the entire world as well.

---

10. Pope Leo X, *Exurge Domine*, June 15, 1520, Papalencyclicals.net. For further discussion, see Chris Castaldo, "Did Luther Really Split the Church?," *The Gospel Coalition*, October 20, 2016, https://www.thegospelcoalition.org/article/did-luther-really-split-the-church.

As discussed earlier, while acknowledging the disconcerting variety of biblical interpretations, Protestants refuse to shoulder all the blame. Additionally, they seriously doubt that submission to the Magisterium will dispel the chaos, especially in light of their perception of its numerous misinterpretations of Scripture. Interpretive chaos is not resolved when the official, authoritative understanding of Scripture is contested. As also noted above, Protestants reject the idea that the final arbiter of Scripture is the individual reader or interpreter. Rather, the biblical text is the touchstone against which all interpretations are to be assessed. Validity in interpretation can be achieved.[11]

Historically, Protestants have relied on Scripture to be its own interpreter. The principle "Scripture interprets Scripture" arises from its inspiration: while written by scores of human authors, it has one divine author and one authorial intent. The principle also arises from Scripture's truthfulness or inerrancy: Scripture does not and cannot contradict itself. Accordingly, the clearer parts of Scripture are to be used to interpret the more obscure parts of Scripture. Importantly, all these points were expressed by the leaders of the early church as they sought to provide help for interpreting the Bible.[12] A related principle is reading passages of Scripture in light of the context of the entire Bible, with some Protestants giving special consideration to Paul's letter to the Romans.

Protestants follow other sound principles of biblical interpretation. First and foremost is reliance upon the illumination of the Holy Spirit to guide those seeking to understand it. The one who inspired Scripture also illumines its meaning. Dissenting from the traditional Catholic position that Scripture has a fourfold meaning, the Reformers insisted instead on seeking its "literal" meaning, that is, its "grammatical, historical meaning."[13] This has particular reference to Scripture's focus on Christ: it is to be interpreted christologically. Additionally, interpreters are to pay close attention to the literary style of the passage studied, that is, its genre as narrative, prophecy, poetry, letter, wisdom, and the like. Reading Scripture within the proper theological framework is another important principle for correct interpretation.[14]

Submitted to the illumination of the Holy Spirit, and adhering to these principles, Protestants engage in the interpretation of Scripture. As part of their tradition, they approach the Bible with an expectation that they will understand it. This persuasion arises from the Protestant doctrine of the clarity

11. For further discussion, see E. D. Hirsch, *Validity in Interpretation* (New Haven, CT: Yale University Press, 1967).
12. For the historical development of the church's interpretation of Scripture, see Gregg R. Allison, *Historical Theology: An Introduction to Christian Doctrine* (Grand Rapids: Zondervan, 2011), chap. 8.
13. Martin Luther, *Answers to the Hyperchristian, Hyperspiritual, Hyperlearned Book by Goat Emser in Leipzig* (LW 39:181).
14. Interestingly, Vatican Council II listed many of these principles in its discussion of how to properly interpret Scripture. Vatican Council II, *Dei Verbum*, 12.

of Scripture. Part of that doctrine includes an affirmation that Protestants are to interpret Scripture within the context of their church, to whom have been given "pastor-teachers" (Eph. 4:11; 1 Tim. 5:17) to guide them in their understanding.

## Summary

Roman Catholics have many misunderstandings of Protestantism. Selecting a few for our consideration, they are the five *solas* (particularly *sola Scriptura, sola gratia, sola fidei*), the Protestant individualistic conscience, and Protestant interpretive chaos.

Many Catholics misunderstand the principle of *sola Scriptura* to mean that Protestants recognize no authority other than Scripture and denounce any kind of tradition outside of it. This is simply not true. Protestants do not dismiss wisdom from the past in terms of biblically chastened tradition. Additionally, Catholics misunderstand *sola gratia* and *sola fidei* to mean that Protestants see no role for good works. Again, this is not the case. Protestants deny any role for works prior to salvation, as it is accomplished by God's grace alone and appropriated by faith alone, without any addition of good works. However, those justified on the basis of divine grace by faith lovingly and thankfully engage in good works as the fruit of their salvation.

Some Catholics allege that at the heart of Protestantism is the elevation of one's personal conscience to the point of extreme authority. This emphasis on the individualistic conscience accounts for the early Protestant divisions and explains the thousands of Protestant denominations throughout the world today. This misunderstanding is often based on Luther's appeal to conscience and overlooks the historical fact that he and the other Reformers did not set out to destroy the church but to reform it.

As for Protestant interpretive chaos, Catholic critics point out an evident problem. However, the solution is not to come under the authority of the Magisterium, as it clearly has misinterpreted Scripture. Rather, relying on the illumination of the Spirit and following standard principles of interpretation, Protestants (may) engage rightly in biblical interpretation.

## REFLECTION QUESTIONS

1. What do Protestants mean by *sola Scriptura*? How do Catholics misunderstand this principle?

2. What do Protestants mean by *sola gratia* and *sola fidei*? How do Catholics misunderstand these two *solas*?

3. Why did Martin Luther insist that he must follow his conscience rather than recant of his views when ordered to do so by the Catholic authorities? How do Catholics misunderstand his appeal?

4. Do you agree that Protestants are not the only ones to blame for interpretive chaos? How do Catholics contribute to this confusion?

5. When you interpret the Bible, do you rely on the Spirit's illumination and follow the well-established principles of interpretation?

# How Can I Talk with My Catholic Loved Ones about the Gospel?

B efore we get into a discussion of how to talk about the gospel, we need to consider the kind of gospel-centered people we need to be.[1]

## Called to Love

It is of great importance that we cultivate strong, loving relationships with our Catholic friends and family members. Some Protestants who have left the Catholic Church are filled with bitterness toward it. They vent that anger against their loved ones who have not yet embraced the gospel but continue in the Church. Though I understand this resentment, expressing it will probably destroy the relationship with their loved ones and preclude any opportunity to discuss the gospel with them. More importantly still, as gospel-centered people, we are called to love all people. This is true if they are close family members or more distant relatives. God has uniquely placed us within their sphere of kinship so that we bear a particular responsibility toward them. This is also true if they are our enemies, for example, former dear friends who have belittled and rebuked us for leaving/not being part of the Catholic Church or for being Protestant. In every case, we are called to love them.

Concretely, we may express our love as prayer for them and on their behalf. What are their needs and burdens? Let's pray for them and for those matters. What needs to take place for them to move closer to the gospel? Let's pray that God will bring other gospel-centered people into their life.[2]

---

1. For further discussion, see Chris Castaldo, *Holy Ground: Walking with Jesus as a Former Catholic* (Grand Rapids: Zondervan, 2009), and Chris Castaldo, *Talking with Catholics about the Gospel* (Grand Rapids: Zondervan, 2015).
2. We may need to acknowledge that Christians other than us may be the ones that God uses to bring them to faith in Christ. Sometimes the closeness of relationship or kinship functions as a deterrent to meaningful gospel conversations.

Additionally, we may care for them concretely. Do they need help with their studies, switching apartments, financial struggles, ethical quandaries, relational difficulties? Let's offer concrete help. Importantly, as we express love and care for them, we should avoid viewing them as projects for salvation. Such a crass, instrumentalist perspective dehumanizes them and trivializes the gospel. They are instead friends, loved ones, family members—divine image-bearers. Let's love them as prodigal sons and daughters whom God the Father longs to bring back home through the good news of Christ.

It may be that our Catholic friends and family members become embittered against us, even to the point of cutting off the friendship or disowning us. Indeed, it may seem that the more we try to love them, the more they push us away. If this is the case, we may need to think of some other ways to love and care for them. But we should never stop loving them. And we should never write them off as lost causes. Their attitude and posture toward us, while even hurtful today, may change over the course of time. Indeed, I will venture to say that when the going gets rough for them—when their financial struggles become overwhelming, when their relational difficulties plunge them into crisis—the people whom they will seek out will be us because they know that we love and care for them.

We are called to love our Catholic friends and family members with the love of God.

Being the right kind of people—gospel-centered people—how do we talk with them about the gospel?

### Reading Group of the Gospel

One way that I've used many times to talk about the gospel with Catholic friends and neighbors is reading the Bible with them. We gather at my home or at their home with six to ten people for a reading group of the gospel. Our text for the study is the gospel reading for the Mass the upcoming Sunday. (The Catholic Church publishes a liturgical calendar that indicates an Old Testament reading, a New Testament reading, and a reading from one of the four Gospels for its daily Masses.[3] Our reading group simply consults this calendar to know the gospel text for our gathering.) We use a very simple Bible study method: Read the text twice. Pray for God to help us understand what we've read. Study the text by following these three steps: observation, interpretation, application. End with prayer.

As an example, meeting on Tuesday evening, we pull out our calendar, turn to the upcoming Sunday, note the reading of the gospel for that Sunday Mass. That text becomes our passage for discussion.[4] Let's say it is Luke

---

3. See Committee on Divine Worship, "Liturgical Calendar for the Dioceses of the United States of America, 2021" (Washington, DC: US Conference of Catholic Bishops, 2019), https://www.usccb.org/resources/2021cal.pdf.

4. The following example is adapted from Gregg Allison, "Reading Groups of the Gospel," Secret Church.

19:1–10, the story of Zacchaeus's encounter with Jesus. We read the passage out loud and then pause for a time of silent reflection. We read the passage a second time, followed again by a pause. I pray that God would help us understand this remarkable story and apply it to our lives. Then we study the text by means of the three steps of observation, interpretation, and application.

Here's an abbreviated example of how our reading group of the gospel might unfold. The questions are examples that I as the leader pose to the participants, and the notes (in parentheses) indicate the direction in which I want to steer the discussion.

Observation:

- Who are the characters in this story, and what do they say and do? (Make sure the participants carefully observe how the text presents the characters.)
- Do you understand what a tax collector was in those days? (Help the group see that as a tax collector, Zacchaeus was viewed very negatively by the culture.)
- Why did Jesus tell Zacchaeus to come down? (Focus on Jesus's emphasis that he *must* stay at Zacchaeus's house.)
- After Zacchaeus hurried down from the tree and received Jesus joyfully, why wasn't the crowd as happy as Zacchaeus? (Make sure the participants grasp how sinful Zacchaeus was, and how upset the crowd was because of Jesus being the guest of a "sinner.")
- What does Zacchaeus do after he receives Jesus? (Help the group see how serious Zacchaeus was about Jesus and how different a person he was after encountering Jesus.)
- According to Jesus, "salvation" came to Zacchaeus, so what is salvation? (Be sure to clear up any possible misconceptions that salvation is about cleaning up your life so you can meet Jesus, and do so by focusing on the flow of this story: *first* Zacchaeus meets Jesus, *then* the change comes.)

Interpretation:

- What are we to learn from the character Zacchaeus? (Focus on the radical change of life that comes as a result of him receiving Jesus.)
- What are we to learn from the character Jesus? (Make sure the participants understand Jesus's radical mission to seek out the terrible sinner Zacchaeus.)
- What are we to learn from the character "the crowd"? (Help the group see that following Jesus may set off an angry reaction by others.)
- Where in this narrative do we find the "big idea" or "take away" of the story? (Guide the participants to articulating in their own words the "big idea" of verse 10.)

- In this story, how do we see Jesus coming to seek and to save the lost? (Make sure the group grasps the initiative of Jesus to seek out Zacchaeus and the salvation that follows from Zacchaeus's joyful reception of Jesus.)

Application:

- Is Jesus coming to seek and to save you? (Depending on their readiness to be open and share with the group, prompt each person to express the way[s] in which Jesus is working in their life.)
- What does God want you to do or believe or be in response to this narrative? (Emphasize that each of us must respond personally to what God is saying in this story.)

Prayer:

- Would anyone like to pray? (It may take weeks or even months before anyone in the group feels comfortable or even capable of praying, and when someone does, expect a very simple prayer like "God help me to be like Zacchaeus.")
- If no one offers to pray, I as the leader do. "Jesus, thank you for coming to seek and to save us, because we are lost without you. Amen." (The prayer needs to be clear, simple, brief, to the point, and related to the "big idea" of the gospel reading.)

This abbreviated example of how our conversation might unfold gives you a glimpse into the dynamics of a reading group of the gospel. A couple of points to underscore: First, the focus is on who Jesus is and what he does, because the group members might be largely ignorant of him. Second, the discussion centers on the text of Scripture through a simple Bible study method of reading the text, observation, interpretation, application, and prayer. Third, if the participants go to their Catholic Church that upcoming Sunday, they've already immersed themselves in the gospel reading for that Mass. Fourth, if they come to our reading group the next Tuesday evening and say something like "Well, my priest said X about this text, but you said Y about this text," the proper response is "but you've read and studied the text, so what does the Bible say?" There's no need to get into a fight about the priest's authority versus your authority. What matters is the authority of the Bible: hat did we learn about Jesus from the Bible?

Fifth, if they raise a concern like "I've always been told that the Bible is very hard to understand, so we need to be cautious reading it," the proper response is, "But we read and study the Bible together, and we don't find it too difficult to understand, do we?" What matters is the clarity of Scripture. God intends for us to understand the Bible, and we are indeed able to understand it. We promote this approach to Scripture by actually reading it and figuring out what it means. Sixth, it will probably take months before group members will begin to grasp who Jesus is and what he has done for them. Don't get discouraged by the lack of apparent progress at the start. And don't rush the process. You want to make sure the participants understand essential matters about Jesus so that the gospel becomes clear for them. It's nonsensical and wrong to push them to trust Jesus by accepting the gospel if they don't yet know whom Jesus is and what he has done for their salvation.

### The Gospel as Our Only Hope

Let's be reminded that the one and only hope of Roman Catholics—and Protestants, and Muslims, and Hindus, and agnostics, and atheists, and anyone else—is the gospel of Jesus Christ. This is the primary reason for my encouragement to involve our Catholic friends and family members in a reading group of the gospel or some other form of Bible discussion. To reverse Paul's action steps, missional engagement consists of being sent to preach, preaching the good news, hearing the message, believing the gospel, and calling on the Lord (Rom. 10:14–16). At the conclusion of these stages is this affirmation: "So faith comes from hearing, and hearing through the word of Christ" (Rom. 10:17). Whatever situation our Catholic neighbors and loved ones find themselves in—daily Mass attenders, occasional participants in the sacraments, Christmas and Easter Catholics, disenfranchised Catholics, agnostics, atheists, followers of another religion—the only way for them to come to faith in the Savior is through embracing the gospel. In conjunction with the Holy Spirit, the gospel ignites faith, convicts of sin, exposes the futility of religious practices, softens hardened hearts, and brings about the new birth.

Most Catholics, like the majority of people today, need a significant exposure to the person and work of Christ on their behalf. Going through a truncated presentation of the gospel, prompting our Catholic friends to pray with us to receive Christ (who wouldn't want to do that?), rushing them through a commitment when it's clear that they don't understand the gospel—we need to avoid these wrong ways to true saving faith. Indeed, when sharing the gospel with Catholics, the final question I ask them before encouraging them to turn to Christ is, "Have you ceased to rely on all your own efforts to earn God's love and forgiveness?" My question highlights that doing good works, going to Mass, trusting in our baptism and participation in the other sacraments, and more, still expresses reliance on our self-righteousness and our good works to prepare us for salvation.

It may be that our Catholic friend responds to the question with something like, "I'm trying to attend Mass more regularly" or "I'm definitely working hard to be a better person." What do we do in that case? Her answer indicates that she continues to be committed to adding something to faith in Christ alone. Accordingly, she is not yet ready to embrace the gospel. It may be that our Catholic cousin responds with something like, "Yes, I get it that I can't do anything to make God love me." What do we do in that case? His answer indicates that he has indeed understood the proper means of receiving God's gracious salvation is by faith alone. We take the next step of encouraging him to trust Christ for salvation. Clarification as to the proper way to appropriate salvation is key. And central to our concern is the simple formula "faith + _____" (fill in the blank: going to Mass, doing good works, depending on our baptism, relying on the infusion of sacramental grace, praying the rosary, and more) cancels faith and renders salvation null and void.

## Summary

How can my Roman Catholic loved ones and I talk about the gospel? We love and care for our Catholic friends and neighbors. We engage our Catholic family members in a reading group of the gospel or some other form of Bible study. We trust God's promise that "faith comes from hearing, and hearing through the word of Christ" (Rom. 10:17). And we seek to clarify that it is faith alone and not "faith + _____."

## REFLECTION QUESTIONS

1. Do you find it hard to love and care for your Catholic friends and family members? Why is that? What are some particular obstacles in the way? What can you do to overcome them?

2. Can you see yourself inviting your Catholic friends and neighbors to be in a reading group of the gospel with you? If you don't feel confident in being able to lead it, do you have a friend from your church who could?

3. Why is it important to engage our Catholic loved ones in a Bible study that continues for a significant period of time?

4. Why it is important to ask Catholics the question, "Have you ceased to rely on all your own efforts to earn God's love and forgiveness?" What does a negative answer—or a response that indicates that they have not ceased to do so—indicate? What does a positive answer indicate?

5. Do you agree that the formula "faith + _____" (fill in the blank: going to Mass, doing good works, depending on our baptism, relying on the in-fusion of sacramental grace, praying the rosary, and more) cancels faith and renders salvation null and void? Why or why not?

# Select Bibliography

Allison, Gregg R. *Roman Catholic Theology and Practice: An Evangelical Assessment*. Wheaton, IL: Crossway, 2014.

Allison, Gregg and Chris Castaldo. *The Unfinished Reformation: What Unites and Divides Catholics and Protestants after 500 Years*. Grand Rapids: Zondervan, 2016.

Castaldo, Chris. *Holy Ground: Walking with Jesus as a Former Catholic*. Grand Rapids: Zondervan, 2009.

Castaldo, Chris. *Talking with Catholics about the Gospel*. Grand Rapids: Zondervan, 2015.

De Chirico, Leonardo. *Evangelical Theological Perspectives on Post-Vatican II Roman Catholicism*. Religions and Discourse 19. Bern: Peter Lang, 2003.

De Chirico, Leonardo. "Vatican Files: Evangelical Theological Perspectives on Roman Catholicism." Vaticanfiles.org.

Plummer, Robert L. *Journeys of Faith: Evangelicalism, Eastern Orthodoxy, Catholicism, and Anglicanism*. Grand Rapids: Zondervan, 2012.

# Scripture Index

# 40 QUESTIONS SERIES